The British left and Zionism

Manchester University Press

The British left and Zionism

History of a divorce

Paul Kelemen

Manchester University Press
Manchester and New York
distributed in the United States exclusively by Palgrave Macmillan

Copyright © Paul Kelemen 2012

The right of Paul Kelemen to be identified as the author of this work has been asserted by him in accordance with the Copyright, Designs and Patents Act 1988.

Published by Manchester University Press
Oxford Road, Manchester M13 9NR, UK
and Room 400, 175 Fifth Avenue, New York, NY 10010, USA
www.manchesteruniversitypress.co.uk

Distributed exclusively in the USA by
Palgrave Macmillan, 175 Fifth Avenue, New York,
NY 10010, USA

Distributed exclusively in Canada by
UBC Press, University of British Columbia, 2029 West Mall,
Vancouver, BC, Canada V6T 1Z2

British Library Cataloguing-in-Publication Data
A catalogue record for this book is available from the British Library

Library of Congress Cataloging-in-Publication Data applied for

ISBN 978 0 7190 8812 4 hardback
ISBN 978 0 7190 8813 1 paperback

First published 2012

The publisher has no responsibility for the persistance or accuracy of URLs for any external or third-party internet websites referred to in this book, and does not guarantee that any content on such websites is, or will remain, accurate or appropriate.

Typeset
by Helen Skelton, Brighton, UK
Printed in Great Britain
by TJ International Ltd, Padstow

Contents

Acknowledgements		page vii
Abbreviations		ix
	Introduction	1
1	The Labour Party and the Zionist project	11
2	Zionism and Anglo-Jewry	44
3	British communists and Palestine	86
4	Post-war social democracy and Israel	111
5	The new left and the Palestinians	150
6	A new anti-semitism?	185
	Conclusion	203
	Bibliography	208
	Index	219

Acknowledgements

I am indebted to the knowledge and help of several archivists particularly in relation to the documentation at the Labour Party Archive, in Manchester, and to none more so than to Stephen Bird, whose premature retirement represents a great loss to researchers of British labour history. I have benefited from the moral support and intellectual contribution of many friends in Sheffield and Manchester. In the last phase of writing up I was fortunate to have Sheila Rowbotham cast a critical eye over the manuscript. Her comments led to many improvements as did the suggestions of the MUP referees.

An earlier version of Chapter 3 was published as 'British Communists and the Palestine Conflict, 1929–1948', *Holy Land Studies*, 5:2 (2006), 131–153.

Abbreviations

AAM	Anti-Apartheid Movement
AEUW	Amalgamated Union of Engineering Workers
BNP	British National Party
BUF	British Union of Fascists
CGT	Confédération Générale du Travail
CLP	Constituency Labour Party
CND	Campaign for Nuclear Disarmament
CBF	Central British Fund for German Jewry
CST	Community Security Trust
CPGB	Communist Party of Great Britain
DPs	Displaced Persons
EETPU	Electrical, Electronic Telecommunication and Plumbing Union
EUMC	European Monitoring Centre on Racism and Xenophobia
EZF	English Zionist Federation
FJYS	Federation of Jewish Youth Societies
FWZ	Federation of Women Zionists
GLC	Greater London Council
ILP	Independent Labour Party
IMG	International Marxist Group
JNF	Jewish National Fund
JPA	Joint Palestine Appeal
JPC	Jewish People's Council
JSHS	Jewish Society for Human Suffering
LFI	Labour Friends of Israel
LMEC	Labour Middle East Council
MCF	Movement for Colonial Freedom
MPS	Metropolitan Police Service
NALGO	National Association of Local Government Officers
NEC	National Executive Committee

NJC	National Jewish Committee
NUPE	National Union of Public Employees
PAWS	Palestinian Arab Workers' Society
PCP	Palestine Communist Party
PDFLP	Popular Democratic Front for the Liberation of Palestine
PFLP	Popular Front for the Liberation of Palestine
PLL	Palestine Labour League
PLO	Palestine Liberation Organisation
PLP	Parliamentary Labour Party
PSC	Palestine Solidarity Campaign
Sogat 82	Society of Graphical and Allied Trades 1982
SWP	Socialist Workers' Party
TAC	Trades Advisory Council
TASS	Technical, Administrative and Supervisory Section
TUC	Trades Union Congress
TUFI	Trade Union Friends of Israel
TUFP	Trade Union Friends of Palestine
TGWU	Transport and General Workers Union
UCU	University and College Union
UDC	Union of Democratic Control
UNRRA	United Nations Relief and Rehabilitation Administration
UNRWA	United Nations Relief and Works Agency
WZO	World Zionist Organisation

Introduction

In the immediate post-war years, the left no less than the right envisioned consolidating the new world order on the basis of ethnically homogenous nation states. Convinced that this was the most viable model for nation-building and with the belief that the colonial world was there to be reshaped, what could have been more compelling for the victorious powers than to deal with survivors of the Holocaust by acceding to the Zionist movement's demand that a nation state be set up in Palestine for the Jewish survivors of Nazism?

Israel was always destined, however, to fall short of serving as a symbolic atonement for European civilisation's responsibility for the Holocaust. Not merely was it borne through the expulsion of the Palestinians but the Zionist project's ethno-nationalism carried a strand of the ideological legacy that the state's existence was meant to refute. Arendt noted this in a brief aside in her report on the Israeli state's trial of Eichmann, in 1961. The trial of this Nazi functionary, responsible for organising the transportation of half a million Hungarian Jews to be exterminated, was intended by Ben-Gurion as 'a solemn act of historical vindication' for Israel's existence.[1] There was, wrote Arendt, who was reporting the trial for *The New Yorker*, 'something breathtaking in the naiveté with which the prosecution denounced the infamous Nuremberg Laws of 1935, which had prohibited intermarriage and sexual intercourse between Jews and Germans. The better informed among the correspondents were well aware of the irony, but they did not mention it in their reports.' The 'irony' Arendt referred to was that according to the rabbinical law governing the personal status of Israel's Jewish citizens 'no Jew can marry a non-Jew; marriages concluded abroad are recognised but children of mixed marriages are legally bastards …'.[2] If, in 1961, this aspect of ethnic exclusiveness was accepted by what was considered to be the 'international community', as the defensive response of a persecuted people, the same indulgence would be less willingly accorded later to a Jewish state that has the strongest armed forces in the Middle East, has close ties to the US and pursues, through military and administrative means, policies aimed at denying a national existence to another ethnic group. The disillusionment with Israel has been most pronounced on the left but, in retrospect, it is the left's previous and longstanding commitment to the Zionist project that stands out. Moreover, the left had helped to popularise the Zionist cause, which turned public support for Israel into a factor that successive British governments have had to take into account. A Foreign Office report in 1970 explained that a pro-Arab policy 'would be hard or impossible to adopt: (a) because of British public and political commitment to Israel as an ideal and the political force of the support for Israel in the country; (b) because of the pressure which the US government undoubtedly exert on HMG to keep us in line ...'.[3] There were several ideological strands which drew the left to Israel.

British Labour Party leaders who came to the fore in the aftermath of Second World War were generally of the view that Jewish nation-building in its Labour Zionist variant would deliver socialism in Israel and development to the Middle East. Neither of these objectives was to be realised and, by the 1980s, the Israeli Labour movement was itself in decline. Israel's military occupation of the West Bank and Gaza and neo-liberal economic reforms of the state-led sector have fragmented its social base and have encouraged the rise of a messianic nationalism and a drift to the right.[4] Against this backdrop the British left's earlier sympathy for the Zionist project yielded to an increasingly critical attitude to Israel and a commitment to Palestinian statehood. The following chapters recount how socialists of various hues viewing developments in the Palestine conflict chose their allegiance. The left's period of alliance with the Zionist movement was accomplished mainly through the intervention of Poale Zion (Workers of Zion), a party linked to the Zionist labour organisations in Palestine. The relationship that Poale Zion established with the British Labour Party proved crucial in defining the left's pre-Second World War perception of Zionist settlement activity and state-building in Palestine. It forms the theme of Chapter 1. The Zionist movement's influence in the Jewish community, which gave it a certain leverage in its relations with the Labour Party, is explored in Chapter 2. Chapter 3 discusses the British Communist Party's anti-Zionism and its abandonment of that position in the crucial period that led to the setting up of the state of Israel and resulted in the destruction of Palestinian society. Chapter 4 traces the Labour Party's policy from the immediate aftermath of Israel's establishment until the 1970s. The subject of Chapter 5 is the conjunction between the rise of the new left, a radical movement mainly of youth that strongly identified with anti-colonial struggles, and the emergence of a unified, Palestinian nationalist movement. I have not pursued the discussion into the New Labour period, which began in 1994 with Tony Blair's election to the leadership of the Labour Party, partly because it would have prolonged a research that has taken already far too long but also for the intellectually more justifiable reason that, by the late 1980s, the political basis on which the left had come to oppose Israeli policies and to support Palestinian self-determination was firmly set. There have been, of course, several important developments in the Palestine conflict after that date, but they did not alter the perspective from which the left assessed the conflict or the possible solutions that it envisaged to bring the conflict to an end. Thus Chapter 6, instead of extending the historical discussion, takes up the argument that runs directly counter to the interpretation advanced in this book. It examines the claim that much of the left's opposition to Israel since 1967 has been driven by a new form of anti-semitism. The earlier chapters will have demonstrated, I hope, that other factors provide a more compelling explanation; the purpose of the final chapter is to show how these risk being occluded by the allegation of left-wing anti-semitism.

The remainder of this introductory chapter introduces the main political actors which interpreted the Zionist project for the left. Here, as in the other chapters, that interpretation is examined in the light of current historical knowledge, though attentive to what was knowable at the time and to aspects that are still bitterly contested. With these provisos in mind, a history of the left's thinking on this issue that goes beyond its own claims, requires that histories normally confined to separate compartments, those of the left and of the Middle East, speak to each other.

In the Zionist movement's lobbying activities in Britain, after the First World War, there developed a division of labour between Chaim Weizmann and the Labour Zionists. Weizmann was the head of the 'general Zionists', who envisaged a future Jewish state on the liberal capitalist model. He appealed for support largely on the grounds that a Jewish state could render invaluable service to the Empire. The British, he wrote in 1924, 'have come to realise that they have very little to lean on for the protection of the jugular vein of the British Empire, except a Palestine peacefully developed and economically and politically stable. They begin to realise that such a Palestine can only be brought into effect if Jewish enterprise is allowed free course in that country …'.[5] While Weizmann concentrated on getting a hearing from the British government, officials and journalists, the Labour or left wing of the Zionist movement, made up of trade unions, agricultural co-operatives and competing socialist parties in Palestine, and represented in Europe and the US by Poale Zion parties, addressed the international labour movement. By the beginning of the First World War, the World Union of Poale Zion had emerged as the international umbrella organisation for Poale Zion parties and was recognised by the World Zionist Organisation (WZO) as a separate federation. Its political bureau opened in London, in 1920, and many leading Labour Zionists from Palestine came to assist its propaganda work. Between 1932 and 1938 the main political work abroad was carried out by the British Poale Zion party.[6]

Poale Zion's ideological roots lay in the attempt to combine Marxism and Zionism which, between 1898 and 1907, inspired the formation of a number of Socialist Zionist groups among the Jewish socialist circles in the Russian Empire, Austro-Hungary, Palestine, England and the USA. The WZO's funds collected from Jewish communities around the world, but mostly from the Jewish bourgeoisie, were directed into capital investment in Palestine while Poale Zion, along with other socialist Zionist parties, recruited and organised workers for the task of establishing a viable economy for the settlers. They formed, as Michael Shalev has expressed, 'a marriage of convenience between a settlement movement without settlers and a workers' movement without work',[7] enabling the Labour Zionist movement to become, by the early 1930s, the dominant political force in the Jewish community in Palestine (the *Yishuv*).

Labour Zionism's nation-building ambition was predicated on Jewish labour organisations in Palestine controlling the economy and facilitating the absorption of Jewish immigrants and it was the basis on which they appealed for the backing of labour movements abroad. Poale Zion in Britain, which affiliated to the Labour Party in 1920, focused on lobbying Labour leaders. It made representations to policy-making bodies and came to be routinely consulted by the Labour Party's advisory committee dealing with policy matters related to imperial affairs. From the 1920s, Poale Zion, found significant support in the Labour Party.

By this time London had emerged as an important focus of diplomatic and propaganda activities for Arabs as well as Zionists, though the two sides were to be very unevenly matched in terms of their support in Britain. A Palestine Information Centre was launched in 1921 by a handful of colonial old-hands for the purpose of putting across the Arab case but it was not until 1936 that, with the support of the Mufti of Jerusalem, an Arab-led propaganda centre was opened 'to carry out what was deemed to be its most important work, the efficient distribution of literature and the provision of statements to both press and public'.[8] After the Second World War, with Arab League funding, an office was opened in London to publicise the Arab nationalist cause. It published pamphlets and approached public figures with a special interest in the Middle East.

The Zionist movement, which it sought to rival, was able to develop a much wider support base despite representing until the Second World War a small, minority tendency in the Anglo-Jewish community. Between 1880 and 1921 Britain's Jewish population grew from 60,000 to about 317,000 as a result of immigration and the new entrants' high birth rate. Over the following three decades, the influx of refugees from fascism in the 1930s and natural growth increased the community's number to about 450,000.[9] The membership of the English Zionist Federation was boosted by the Balfour Declaration. With the perception in the Jewish community that Zionism had the British government's backing, the Federation's membership 'rose dramatically from about 4000 in 1917 to over 30,000 in 1921; the number of affiliated societies from 61 to 234; and the sums contributed to various funds from just over 500 pounds in 1916 to just over 120,000 pounds in 1918'.[10] The leader of the English Zionist Federation from 1917 to 1924 was Chaim Weizmann, the future first president of Israel, who came to Britain from Russia. He gathered around himself in Manchester, where he resided, a small group of 'insiders', recruits from the new Jewish middle class. They were successful individuals in business or in the professions who by virtue of their social status were able to develop extensive contacts in the power structure of British society. Of the three main political parties, the Labour Party gave the most wholehearted endorsement to Zionism. Although there were influential Liberals, such as C.P. Scott, the *Manchester Guardian*'s editor, and David Lloyd George, who were committed Zionists, the Liberal Party, in any case a diminishing force in the interwar years, did not have a policy on Palestine prior to 1948. The Conservative Party also had strong advocates for Zionism, most notably Balfour, Churchill and Amery, but its official policy was 'quasi-neutral as between Jew and Arab'.[11]

Labour Zionist emissaries from Palestine gained ready access to the Labour Party's colonial experts and, at various times, prominent Labour figures, among them, Ramsay MacDonald, Josiah Wedgwood, Herbert Morrison, Arthur Creech Jones, Richard Crossman and Harold Wilson, visited the Labour Zionist movement in Palestine and took a special interest in its progress.

Of Britain's overseas territories in the 1930s and 1940s, India alone exceeded Palestine in press coverage and the time devoted to it by Parliament. Ireland's prominence in imperial affairs had receded by the late 1920s as the turmoil over partition subsided. Although Palestine did not have India's economic importance, it was valued as a strategic asset in the defence of Britain's trade routes to south Asia and the Far East and recognised as a place of special significance for three major religions of the world. British officials of the Mandatory administration dealing with the conflicting demands of the Arab and Jewish communities were conscious of the potential international reverberation of their decisions particularly in the US and in Muslim countries. They were inclined to see the Zionists as more troublesome, endlessly petitioning with new demands and calling the administration to account on the basis of the Mandate and the Balfour Declaration. If the Zionist movement's demand in Palestine was turned down at the first port of call its representatives were likely to raise the matter at a higher level, if necessary all the way up the chain of command to ministers in London. With anti-semitism endemic among colonial officials, as among all sections of British society, they often expressed their resentment at attempts to outmanoeuvre them in racist terms. Yet, if this was an overtly hostile form of racism by comparison with the apparently more benign, paternalistic version directed at the Arabs, British rule nonetheless maintained the political and economic framework that favoured Jewish nation-building at the expense of Arab interests.

In the 1930s, contemporaneously with Poale Zion's growing success in establishing close ties with the Labour Party, the India League led by Krishna Menon, campaigning for the Indian nationalist movement, was also appealing to the British labour movement for support. His efforts met with less success. The India League sought to win backing for the Congress Party's demand that India be granted self-rule. There was considerable sympathy for this in Labour Party ranks, but the leadership saw it as an objective to be attained only in the distant future and through gradual constitutional reform. It was, on the one hand, mistrustful of the Congress Party's middle-class leadership and lack of commitment to social reform and, on the other, disapproving of its use of mass civil disobedience campaigns rather than electoral politics to capture legislative power. On behalf of the India League, Menon travelled tirelessly around the country, addressing public meetings to recruit activists and to encourage the setting up of local branches. In 1931, he reported twenty-three branches and a membership of 270, but there appears to have been little growth thereafter. In 1943 the League had thirteen branches of which only seven sent reports to head office on their work over the previous twelve months. Most branches had brief flourishes of activity and then fell dormant.[12] Menon therefore turned for support to the Independent Labour Parties, Labour parties and co-operative guilds and, as the decade wore on, to the Communist Party. 'Since campaigners for India lacked the authority and resources to have sufficient supporters of their own they needed to tie themselves to campaigns or parties that could ... Theosophists, socialists, communists, feminists, Christians and pacifists each served this purpose at times. Each cause had, for its own reasons, certain affinities with the Indian freedom struggle, but each had other priorities too ....'[13]

The Indian community in Britain was not sufficiently numerous or well resourced to sustain an effective campaign. Menon's approach to its small middle class, made up of students and professionals, yielded meagre results. An Indian working class was beginning to form, during the war, in the docks of East London and in the war-related industries in the Midlands, but it numbered only around 3,000 and was still in the early stages of developing its own community organisations.[14] Reflecting the League's tenuous support, securing funds for its office and publications was a constant struggle. The Special Branch, which closely monitored its activities, reported that the League's turnover, in 1941, was £722 and had increased, in 1942, as a result of contributions from 'wealthy sympathisers' to £1,092 (the equivalent of about £22,000 in 2011).[15]

The Poale Zion party in Britain disposed of considerably larger human and financial resources. Although it was a small organisation with only around 500 members for most of the pre-Second World War period, it had its own affiliated organisations and worked alongside, though not without tensions, the much larger, English Zionist Federation (EZF). It functioned as the communication channel between the Zionist labour movement and the Labour Party. The two labour organisations' brand of social democracy had much in common and there developed between them, through frequent contact, a sense of comradeship. In 1946, following the British army's arrest of 2,000 Jerusalem-based officials of various Zionist organisations, including the executive of the Jewish Agency, Michael Foot pleaded: 'the people who are accused by the Government of instituting violence against law and order are men we know well, men who have come to our Socialist conferences, and who are colleagues of ours.'[16]

On the history of the Labour Party's relationship with the Zionist movement,

Joseph Gorny's *The British Labour Movement and Zionism, 1917–1948*, published in 1983, remains the most comprehensive study. Gorny highlights the 'special and unique bond' that developed between the two organisations. This was founded he claims on 'sympathy on the part of the British and faith on the part of the Jews' and not on socialist principles. He does not, however, disavow the influence of socialism altogether and attributes the Labour Party's attitude to Zionism, to its 'socialist humanistic tradition' and a 'belief in the advantage of establishing a socialist society in Palestine'.[17] There are, as we shall see, good reasons to doubt that the British Labour Party's outlook on Palestine and Zionism can be explained in this way but Gorny's other premise, that Labour Zionism was building a socialist society, has been demonstrated by a substantial body of historical work to be fundamentally flawed. The social organisation of the Jewish community in Palestine was determined not by the professed socialist ideology of its leaders but by the economic obstacles that Zionist colonisation had to confront in seeking to absorb Jewish immigrant labour in the face of competition from Palestinian labour.[18]

In the alliance that the Zionist movement forged among different social groups it was the organisations of its labour wing, through the trade union movement and the *kibbutzim*, which became the key instruments in developing a separate Jewish economy. Labour Zionism successfully harnessed collectivist forms of organisation to nation-building by privileging ethnic over class solidarity. It was in the tradition of the 'blood and soil', biological nationalism which from the middle of the nineteenth century, argues the Israeli historian Zeev Sternhell, was characteristic of ethnic movements in Eastern and Central Europe, from where most of the Labour Zionist leaders originated.[19] In Palestine, the Labour Zionist movement, in order to ensure that Jewish immigrant labourers were prioritised over indigenous labour, adopted the strategies of 'conquest of land' and 'conquest of labour'. The 'conquest of land' took the form of the Zionist movement purchasing land and turning it over to exclusively Jewish agriculture labour mainly through the *kibbutzim* and other forms of co-operatives. These colonies of rural settlement were often strategically placed and served the dual function of absorbing Jewish immigrants into productive work and establishing armed outposts. The *kibbutzim*'s collectivist ethos, which drew on socialist idealism while implementing the ethnic exclusion of Arabs, enhanced their military capacity, leading the number of *kibbutz* to be increased in periods when there was an upsurge in Palestinian opposition.[20] The 'conquest of labour' in the private sector was pursued by the Zionist trade union organisation, the Histadrut, using its organisational strength to pressure Jewish employers to hire only Jewish workers. In the public sector, controlled by the British authorities, the Zionist movement could not hope to exclude Arab labour but sought to increase the proportion of Jewish workers by the Histadrut's commercial arm, Solel Boneh, acting as a subcontractor for some of the work.[21] It was these efforts at Jewish economic separatism that required the WZO's financial backing, in order to purchase land, subsidise the Histadrut and invest in infrastructure. Private capital invested more, between 70 and 84 per cent, particularly in the urban sector, but it did not have the level of political organisation and therefore influence of the Labour Zionist movement.[22]

The WZO leadership acted as the executive of the Zionist movement and was answerable to its Congress. The delegates to it were elected by affiliated Zionist organisations around the world, whose principal function was to raise funds from the Jewish communities they represented to finance the settlement project in Palestine. At the second Zionist Congress in 1898, the founder and first president of the WZO, Theodor Herzl, in response to opposition from Jews to the Zionist project, declared: 'I place among our future aims the conquest of communities.' He explained: 'The authorities of the communities, the means of which they dispose, and the officials must not be employed to work against the National Idea.'[23] This then was the third 'conquest' that was integral to Zionist politics and to its success in establishing a state.

Until the rise of fascism in Europe in the 1930s, the Zionist movement remained politically marginal in Jewish communities including in Eastern Europe, where the majority of world's Jewish population lived until the Second World War. In the face of economic hardship and anti-semitism which at times took the form of pogroms, most Jews when it was possible left for destinations in the West. 'In the ten years considered decisive for the creation of Zionist settlement in Palestine, for example, that is, the years 1905–1914, over one million Jews immigrated from Eastern Europe to the United States, whereas less than thirty thousand immigrated to Palestine.'[24] Although in this period relatively few Jews could be persuaded to make *aliya* (settle in Palestine) and only a small minority was persuaded of the Zionist case, a much larger number responded to WZO appeals to help fund those who wanted to make their home in Palestine. Keren Hayesod (the Foundation Fund), which was established by the Zionist Congress in 1920, to finance the economic infrastructure of the *Yishuv* collected during its first ten years of existence £3.8 million. Over the same period, the Jewish National Fund which purchased land in Palestine exclusively for Jewish settlement collected an additional £170,000.[25] In the period 1920–1945, a total of £14.5 million (the equivalent in 2011 would be roughly twenty-five times this sum) was collected by the Foundation Fund, of which just over half came from US Jewry and 6.3 per cent from Anglo-Jewry.[26]

Philanthropic activity in the Jewish community, which vastly expanded in response to the flight of Jews from Nazi persecution, played an important role in the 'conquest' of Jewish communities that Herzl hoped for. But later, the sociological transformation of the Anglo-Jewish community, its embourgeoisement, also facilitated this process. Zionism's post-war ascendancy among Anglo-Jewry which accompanied the Jewish population's post-war migration to suburbia did not however weaken British Labour's resolve to gain Jewish voters' support. Although by the 1950s Poale Zion played a minor role in mobilising Jewish voters, it acted as the main intermediary between the British and Israeli Labour parties. Their close connection did not determine the British Labour Party's Middle East policy, whether in or out of power, but it gave that connection an ideological legitimacy and emotional charge among the party membership. The policy itself accorded with Britain's strategic interests in the Middle East, which after the Second World War and still more after the 1956 Suez War were seen by Whitehall to require an alliance with the United States and with conservative Arab states. Israel's defence concerns were convergent and it became a key regional ally to counter the Soviet influence and nationalist movements. The Labour Party was therefore supportive of Israel both in the name of Britain's imperial policy and for its social democratic values. On these grounds it could command the sympathy of both wings of the party and act as the principal vector for popularising more widely an image of Israel as the beacon of progress in the Middle East.

Notes

1. I. Zertal, *Israel's Holocaust and the Politics of Nationhood* (Cambridge: Cambridge University Press, 2005), p. 108.
2. H. Arendt, *Eichmann in Jerusalem* (London: Faber & Faber, 1963), p. 5.
3. Quoted in M.Curtis, *Unpeople* (London: Vintage, 2004), p. 155.
4. A. Hanieh, 'From State-led Growth to Globlization: The Evolution of Israeli Capitalism', *Journal of Palestine Studies*, 32:4 (2003), 5–21.
5. C. Weizmann, *Letters and Papers* (New Brunswick, NJ: Transaction Books, 1977), v. 12, p. 219.
6. P. Gourney, 'Sixty Years of Poalei Zion', *Zionist Year Book 1966–1967*, p. 354.
7. M. Shalev, 'Jewish Organised Labour and the Palestinians: A Study of State/Society Relations in Israel', in B. Kimmerling (ed.), *The Israeli State and Society, Boundaries and Frontiers* (New York: State University of New York, 1979), p. 95.
8. R. Miller, 'The Other Side of the Coin: Arab Propaganda and the Battle Against Zionism in London, 1937–48', in E. Karsh (ed.), *Israel's Transition from Community to State* (London: Frank Cass, 1999), p. 202.
9. H. Neustatter, 'Demographic and Other Statistical Aspects of Anglo-Jewry', in M. Freedman (ed.), *A Minority in Britain* (London: Vallentine, Mitchell & Co., 1955), p. 77.
10. S. Cohen, *English Zionists and British Jews* (Princeton, NJ: Princeton University Press, 1982), p. 282.
11. H. Defries, *Conservative Party and Attitudes to Jews, 1900–1950* (London: Frank Cass, 2001), p. 193.
12. Nehru Memorial Library, Box 7 File 1b, India League, Secretary's Report, n.d. circa beginning 1932 and Box 2 File 5/9, Menon Papers, Minutes of Secretariat, 4 April 1943.
13. N. Owen, *The British Left and India, Metropolitan Anti-Imperialism* (Oxford: Oxford University Press, 2007), pp. 195–200.
14. R. Visram, *Asians in Britain, 400 Years of History* (London: Pluto Press, 2002), p. 268.
15. British Library, India Office Papers, LP & J/12/454, New Scotland Yard Report, No. 233, 25 November 1942.
16. Commons, *Hansard*, 1 July 1946, v. 424, c. 1898.

17 J. Gorny, *The British Labour Movement and Zionism, 1917–1948* (London: Frank Cass, 1983), p. xii and p. 233.
18 G. Shafir, *Land, Labour and the Origins of the Israeli-Palestinian Conflict, 1882–1914* (Berkeley: University of California Press, 1989); Michael Shalev, *Labour and the Political Economy of Israel* (Oxford: Oxford University Press, 1992); Z. Lockman, *Comrades and Enemies* (Berkeley: University of California Press, 1996).
19 Z. Sternhell, *The Founding Myths of Israel* (Princeton, NJ: Princeton University Press, 1997), p.10.
20 B. Kimmerling, *Zionism and Territory: the Socio-Territorial Dimension of Zionist Politics* (Berkeley: University of California Press, 1983), p. 86.
21 D. Bernstein, *Constructing Boundaries: Jewish and Arab Workers in Mandatory Palestine* (Albany: State University of New York, 2000), p. 164.
22 B. Kimmerling, *Zionism and Economy* (Cambridge: Shenkman Publishing Company, 1983), p. 28.
23 *Jewish Chronicle* (2 September 1898).
24 Kimmerling, *Zionism and Economy*, p. 32.
25 Levenberg Papers, British Library of Political and Economic Science, S.Levenberg, 'Trends in British Zionism, An Historical Survey', n.d. circa 1960, Box 'Zionism, Levenberg Papers. The Levenberg Papers are archived in 41 boxes of which only the contents of first three are filed and listed. The other boxes contain material grouped into very broad categories such as 'Articles', 'Correspondence', etc.
26 *Zionist Year Book 1960*, pp. 321–322.

1 The Labour Party and the Zionist project

In the last two decades of the nineteenth century, it was common among socialists, anarchists and radicals of all sorts to give voice to anti-semitic sentiments by identifying the harshest forms of capitalist exploitation at home and abroad with Jewish financiers and industrialists. In Britain, there was a surge of anti-semitism in 1899–1900 during the Boer War, anti-semitic attacks against 'rich Jews' persisted for some years in sections of the socialist press[1] and isolated outbursts of such prejudices also continued to occur in the labour movement, but anti-capitalism and anti-semitism were increasingly viewed by socialists as incompatible. The Russian pogroms and the Dreyfus affair had underlined the association of anti-semitism with autocracy and reactionary politics and most Labour leaders distanced themselves from the anti-alien agitation, which led to the passing of the 1905 Aliens Act. Labour politicians had opposed it with humanitarian arguments but the influence of Marxism among socialists also ran counter to anti-semitism by attributing the comportment of capitalists to their position in the dynamics of class relations instead of their ethnic origins.

Left-wing and radical groups associated with working-class politics whatever their attitude to anti-semitism showed little interest in the early Zionist movement yet, in August 1917, two and half months before the Balfour Declaration committed Britain to support the setting up of a 'Jewish home' in Palestine, the Labour Party took the first step to adopting a near identical policy in its *War Aims Memorandum*. The document drafted by a subcommittee of the party's executive included the proposal that Palestine should be set free from Turkish rule 'in order that this country may form a Free State under international guarantee, to which such of the Jewish people as desire to do so may return and work out their own salvation'.[2] The *Manchester Guardian* reported that once the draft was completed 'the Executive had no time to go into it at all'.[3] For the Zionist movement, which represented at this time the aspiration of a small minority of Jews, the document's commitment to a 'Jewish home' in Palestine would prove a useful asset. The Labour Party was still in its formative period but it had already become the major force in British left-wing politics and from the 1922 general election came to eclipse the Liberal Party as the main electoral rival to the Conservatives. Its membership was formed mainly by its affiliated organisations: the majority from trade unions and some from socialist groups of which the most influential, until its disaffiliation in 1932, was the Independent Labour Party (ILP). From 1918, local Labour parties were also open to individual membership. Combining the individual membership with those of the affiliated organisations, the Labour Party had about 3 million members in 1918, 5 million in 1947 and 6.5 million for most of the 1960s and 1970s. But the individual membership of local parties is a more accurate gauge of the number of party activists and this was about 215,000 in 1928, the first year that figures were separately compiled for this category, which doubled by 1937 and peaked at just over a million in 1952. Thereafter, with minor fluctuations, membership declined to 348,000 in 1980 and to 311,000 in 1990.[4]

The *War Aims Memorandum* embraced the dominant view among Labour leaders that the war should be pursued till victory but drew on the ideas of groups that had been critical though not outrightly opposed to the war. Thus some of the points derived from the League of Nations Society and the Fabians, which campaigned for the war to be settled on terms that would secure a 'permanent peace' and the setting up of a supranational authority and international laws to regulate the future conduct of state to state relations. From the Union of Democratic Control (UDC), a group highly critical of the war, the document took the more radical demands that there be no annexation of territory without taking into account the wishes of the people affected by it and for the future conduct of relations between states to be subject to the control of popularly elected legislatures.

The *Memorandum*, as A.J.P. Taylor has remarked, proved to be remarkably successful.[5] It was adopted in December 1917 by the Labour Party at a specially convened conference and, the following year, with only minor modifications by the labour and socialist parties of the Allied states. It also put pressure on the Lloyd George led coalition government to define the Allies' war aims. Yet, on one of its central principles, on the right of nations to self-determination, the *Memorandum* appeared to equivocate. A writer in a UDC publication complained that Labour politicians upheld the principle of self-determination only where it concerned Christians. 'Self determination for Poland? Yes; for Palestine? No.'[6]

The Balfour Declaration was also given a mixed reception on the left. *Labour Leader* and *Forward* publications linked to the ILP made no reference to it. The Labour Party's *The Herald* expressed support, briefly commenting that 'it is hard for any people to retain its individuality and develop itself to the full without a local and visible home somewhere in the world' and the *New Statesman*, which had close links with the Fabians, welcomed 'a Zionist restoration' as a way of making Palestine 'once more prosperous and populous, with a population attached to the British Empire'.[7] By contrast, the British Socialist Party, which would be one of the groups to form the Communist Party in 1920, condemned the Zionist plan as 'a veiled attempt at the annexation of Palestine, and also a means to enlist the assistance of the Jews the world over for the Imperial ends of Great Britain and its Allies'.[8]

The immediate impetus behind the Labour Party's statement on Palestine in the Memorandum was the wave of enthusiasm in left-wing circles for the American president, Woodrow Wilson's adoption of national self-determination as a guiding principle for the post-war world order. In March 1917, Beatrice Webb had commented on Wilson's declaration: 'Self-government for each self-conscious community combined with International Law for the world, based not on relative power but on public right, becomes the watchword of the Allies – whether they like it or not?'[9] Wilson, who was soon to launch the US into the war, sought morally to rearm the Allies and counter the Bolshevik's call for the belligerent countries' war-weary working classes to bring an immediate end to the war and topple their governments. But whereas Lenin saw in national self-determination a way to undermine imperialism and therefore insisted on its applicability to the colonial world, Wilson understood it in a much more restricted sense. Although he did not 'exclude non-European peoples from the right to self-determination as a matter of principle … he envisioned them achieving it through an evolutionary process under the benevolent tutelage of a "civilized" power that would prepare them for self-government'.[10] Opinion in Labour circles wavered, uncertainly, between the Bolshevik and Wilsonian positions.

The February revolution in Russia and the subsequent propaganda by the Bolsheviks on the basis of no annexation, no indemnities and the right of peoples to self-determination not only stimulated left-wing activity in Britain in favour of peace but also 'helped to bring the trade unionists over to views hitherto monopolized by the socialist societies'.[11] Mayer points to 'Petrograd's indelible imprint'[12] on Arthur Henderson's draft of Labour's peace terms which had stated: 'We accept the principle of self-determination … for all people and believe that this can be secured for Egypt and India by a rapid extension of self-governing institutions on Dominion lines'.[13] This did not imply dismantling the Empire but it accepted the Egyptian and Indian nationalist movements' demand of the time. The *War Aims Memorandum* was less specific on these two countries but for the African colonies and for the peoples of the Turkish Empire, it looked forward to an end of the imperial system by declaring that since their peoples were not ready to settle their own destinies, the present colonies of the European powers should be handed over to a supranational authority or League of Nations. However, the proposal on a 'Jewish return' was at odds with the Turkish Empire's Arab population determining its own destiny and had a different rationale. Brailsford, who was among the end of war defectors from the Liberals to the ILP and from 1922 became its most prolific writer on international matters in radical and socialist newspapers, gave an early indication of at least one of the ideological impulses for treating Palestine as an exception. Outlining his ideas on a League of Nations, in a work published in early 1917, he commended the revitalisation of the Turkish Empire through German railway-building and mining and through the development of a Jewish state in Palestine. 'The Ottoman Empire', he declared, 'can plead no right against the civilised world to keep this garden for all time a wasted and disorderly desert. Its native Arabs and Kurds have no loyalty to the Turks, and few moralists would care to defend the right of a handful of degenerate semi-savages to exclude the millions who might live by tilling the soil which they neglect.'[14]

Brailsford's view was not heretical among radicals and Labourites. J.A. Hobson, a close associate of Brailsford, was an influential critic of imperialism, but his opposition to it was also less than total. Although he set out its negative effects in some detail, he did not rule out that there could be a 'sane imperialism'. It was legitimate on the part of 'civilized white nations' to take control of 'lower races' provided that there was a wider interest, 'the safety and progress of civilization of the world' and they were 'acting for the real good of the subject race'.[15] He suggested that whereas this could not occur under a colonialism based on 'a small minority wielding political or economic sway over a majority of alien and subject people' it had been achieved by colonisation in Australia and Canada. From a Social Darwinist perspective, Hobson viewed the settlers' success in transplanting their civilisation into 'the new natural and social environment' as proof of their superiority in the struggle for survival and therefore a step in the path of social progress. He characterised these pure settlement colonies, in which Europeans aimed to build their economy with white labour and replicate the society from which they came, as the 'natural overflow of nationality'.[16] Yet, in the same work, he conceded that the establishment of these colonies had entailed 'the extermination of the lower races, either by war or by private slaughter, as in the case of the Australian bushmen ... or by forcing upon them the habits of civilisation equally destructive of them'.[17] Faced with this contradiction between 'doing good for the subject races' and abiding by the laws of universal social progress, Hobson opted for the latter: 'It cannot seriously be maintained that any group of inhabitants, by virtue of mere priority of occupation or because they have for certain time exercised government over a territory would have a right (save in a strictly legal international sense) to neglect or abuse resources, the utilization of which might be an urgent need to the world at large.'[18]

Charles Buxton would have been familiar with Hobson's argument and used it to justify the Zionist project in Palestine. He, too, was among the middle-class radicals who left the Liberals for Labour and on joining the party's Advisory Committee on Imperial Questions, became one of its colonial experts. 'The rights of Muslims and Christians must on no account be prejudiced', he commented in 1918, 'on the other hand, I cannot admit the contention that the people who for the time being occupy a certain portion of the earth's surface are necessarily entitled to exclude from it others who could use it better for the good of the whole.'[19] This was also the contention of the Labour Zionist party, Poale Zion. The theory of 'constructivism' it propagated, was one of the several syntheses of Marxism and Jewish nationalism debated among left Zionist groups prior to the First World War. From 1920 it became the political line of Poale Zion parties in Europe and defined the orientation of the Labour Zionist movement in Palestine. In 1916, Shlomo Kaplansky, who had been involved in the Austrian Poale Zion, circulated a memorandum to European socialist parties setting out Poale Zion's political philosophy. The essential feature of 'constructivism' was the subordination of the class struggle to the nationalist objective of forming a Jewish nation in Palestine, on the grounds that only when this national entity had been formed would the Jewish working class be able to establish socialism. He reiterated the main points of this argument in a 1922 issue of *Socialist Review*, a journal edited by Ramsay MacDonald.[20]

'The regulation of immigration and the colonisation of sparsely inhabited tracts of land', argued Kaplansky, 'is one of the obligations of international labour democracy' and, therefore, he added, 'a hundred thousand Arabs have no right of possession over Palestine'. He distinguished the 'socialist colonisation policy' of the Labour Zionist movement based on Jewish labour from 'the colonial policy of Imperialism which seeks the exploitation of peoples and countries'. The Jewish labourers were, he asserted, bringing benefits to the Arab peasants: 'in the growing towns the *Fellahin* [peasants] find increasing demand for their products … from the Jews the Arab learns the use of fertilisation and the use of machinery … Wherever the Jewish worker appears on the labour market he brings the demand for a higher standard of life and higher wages.' Only the rich Arab landlord class, claimed Kaplansky, had an interest in obstructing Zionist settlement because their power depended on keeping the Arab masses in a state of backwardness. Referring to the armed clashes of 1920–1921 between Arabs and Jews in Jaffa and Jerusalem, he asserted that the Arabs had no right to 'prohibit the approach of other land and work seeking people to soil which is lying idle'.[21] These were to become familiar themes in Labour Zionist propaganda that Poale Zion propagated in Britain. The party members were active in a few constituency Labour parties but the focus of their activity was to establish friendly relations with the Labour hierarchy. At the 1921 Labour Party conference, a resolution moved by Kaplansky on behalf of Poale Zion backed the policy to develop Palestine 'not upon the foundation of capitalist exploitation but in the interest of Labour'.[22]

MacDonald, who would head the short-lived, minority Labour governments of 1924 and 1929–1931, was among the first leading Labour politicians to declare in favour of Zionism. He toured Palestine in 1922, visiting Labour Zionist projects and holding discussions with Jewish labour leaders. His notes on the journey and his dispatches to the Glasgow-based ILP newspaper, *Forward*, which were subsequently published by Poale Zion as a pamphlet, does not record him meeting with Arabs.[23] If he did, he evidently considered it of little importance.

There followed in MacDonald's wake a long line of Labour visitors, who as hosts of the Jewish trade union federation, the Histadrut, were taken around Zionist settlements, which they duly lauded on their return. Their visits paralleled those of communists and fellow-travellers to the Soviet Union who on the basis of a similarly contrived showcasing of the system also obliged with the fulsome praise expected by their hosts.[24] MacDonald's reports were in the genre of a travelogue, the narrative switching between the viewpoints of a pilgrim and an intrepid explorer. He depicted a stagnant Orient shaken from its stupor by the vitality of the settlers. 'The Jewish town spreads on the sand. The foundation of a new garden city have been laid; in the middle of the sand dunes a big factory is at work turning out stones everyday sufficient to build a house.' He knew of Arab opposition to Zionism which in 1920 and 1921 had led to violence between Jews and Arabs but he put this down to their different levels of development. 'Socialism and trade unionism came with the immigrants and the Jewish workmen demanded a higher standard of life than the Arab. The old Arab leaders saw their position threatened.' He characterised the resulting conflict as between the Middle Ages and the twentieth century to assert that the Arab population 'do not and cannot use or develop the resources of Palestine'.[25] It therefore followed that progress in the Middle East had to be introduced by outsiders, a position that was consistent with the Labour Party's thinking on the colonies.

The support for self-determination that the *War Aims Memorandum* had heralded in the first flush of enthusiasm for Woodrow Wilson's declaration had rapidly waned in the Labour Party. With the Versailles peace agreement ending any prospect of dismantling the imperial system, the party's colonial experts turned their attention to how to manage the Empire. The two main currents of thought on colonial affairs in the Labour Party, formulated most explicitly in relation to Africa, were 'the constructive imperialists', such as Ramsay MacDonald, who were committed to an imperial trusteeship that would lead the colonies in the distant future towards self-government within the Empire and those like Leonard Woolf and Norman Leys who placed a greater emphasis on Britain playing an active role in improving the economy and providing training for self-government.[26] They represented variations on what Porter has called 'ethical imperial ideology', which required of the imperial state a benevolent paternalism that would protect the colonised from capitalism.[27] The Advisory Committee on Imperial Questions, one of several committees set up to assist the party's National Executive Committee (NEC) on policy matters acted as the main discussion forum and although the Committee's influence on the leadership was probably negligible after the early 1920s, its policy papers and the journalistic output of Norman Angell and H.N. Brailsford reflected the various strands in the party's outlook. Their views were often theoretically eclectic and even idiosyncratic. Thus Josiah Wedgwood and Charles Buxton defended the indigenous people's land rights against European settlers in Kenya but not in Palestine, and Brailsford believed that Indians should have greater control over their affairs, but not the

Arabs of Palestine. In truth, Labour's early support for Zionism was only partially anchored in its interpretations of colonialism; it derived much of its momentum from the political culture of the British labour movement.

In Labour's nonconformist heritage, the Arab had only a shadowy presence, while the Israelites were venerated. Sidney Webb is said to have remarked that the men and women who composed the Labour Party were 'at heart primitive Methodists'.[28] James Middleton, the long-serving Assistant Secretary and then General Secretary of the Labour Party, was of that mould. Explaining his sympathy for Zionism, he recalled how scripture lessons at Sunday school had imprinted on his generation the stories of the Israelites. But as he noted, Palestine had 'never seemed more than a Bible picture – somewhat remote in the mind and remote in distance'.[29] For the Zionists, the task was to make it appear within reach, as a pragmatic solution to the allegedly intractable problem of anti-semitism. The Zionist case drew some of its support, including from the labour movement, by proposing a solution to anti-semitism which anti-semites themselves favoured: to remove from society the object of prejudice rather than the prejudice itself.

Herbert Burrows, who was prominent in the Social Democratic Federation and later in the Socialist League, explained to *Jewish Chronicle* readers in 1915 that he thought 'Jews are too clever for trade unions – and too mercurial'. Passing lightly over the circumstances that had led to Jews being concentrated in commerce and in the small workshops of the sweating industry, he explained that 'the staying power of the Jewish race, as evidenced in history, does not seem to have been displayed in regard to their connection with trade unionism. It is due in the first instance to the strong individualism of the Jew and also to his keen ambition. The man of today is the master of tomorrow'.[30] Burrows approved of the Zionist project in Palestine. The anti-semitic *arrière pensée* in the support for Zionism was also articulated in the *New Statesman*'s welcome for the Balfour Declaration. The weekly had greeted the setting up of a Jewish home as a way of making Palestine 'once more prosperous and populous, with a population attached to the British Empire' but hinted at a darker side to its approval: 'The present position of the Jews as unassimilated sojourners in every land but their own can never become satisfactory.'[31] The notion that Jews were unassimilated because they were inherently inassimilable was emphasised by Zionists. Weizmann spoke of Jews being an 'insoluble element':[32] 'We work too hard, we love education too much, we are too enterprising etc., etc. and Palestine with a Jewish population would be the best asset for the Empire.'[33] Thus the qualities that for Burrows rendered Jews alien and undesirable as part of the working class could, Weizmann suggested, render them useful as agents of the British Empire.

The case for Zionism on imperialist grounds proved, however, less effective in winning the support of the British labour movement than the discourse which represented the Labour Zionist project in terms that shared the main tenets of Labourism, or what Stuart MacIntyre has termed 'Labour Socialism'. It was a socialism that was to be brought about not by class struggle, but by an appeal to moral values to create a new society based on 'the productive community ... including entrepreneurs'.[34] This moral community was depicted as transcending not only class but also communal interests and thus capable of uniting the Jewish and Arab masses of Palestine. The 1929 Arab rebellion distilled the Labour Party's interpretation of the Arab-Jewish conflict in the ideological terms of Labour Zionism.

Following the riots, the British government appointed a four-member commission of inquiry headed by a judge, Sir Walter Shaw, to examine their cause. The majority report concluded that although the immediate causes could not be attributed to Arab fears of Zionist settlement, they were a contributory factor. It rejected the Zionist movement's explanation that the Mufti was behind the riots and argued that, given the existing methods of cultivation, Jewish land purchase was putting pressure on the land available to the Arab sector. The Commission, acknowledging the attentiveness of Palestinians to its investigation, concluded that 'villagers and peasants alike are taking a very real personal interest both in the effect of the policy of establishing a national home and in the question of the development of self-governing institutions'.[35] The one dissenter to the report was the Labour MP, Harry Snell. Jewish land purchase, he countered, had not posed a threat to the Arab population, citing in support the Histadrut's assurance that 'the Jewish Labour Movement consider the Arab population as an integral element of this country'. Snell was also dismissive of conceding to Arabs greater powers of self-government, declaring that given the political consciousness of the *fellaheen* they did not have 'constitutional grievances'.[36] Zionist leaders, fearing that any initiative towards self-government in Palestine would put the Arabs in a position to halt Jewish immigration, applauded Snell's stand and so did Brailsford. He mocked the majority's report for portraying a politically conscious peasantry rather than a hapless mass manipulated by Muslim leaders: 'we are told that these illiterate peasants rank above many European races in political consciousness. That, to be blunt, is an effort of the forensic imagination.' The government, he suggested, could help the Arabs made landless to settle in Transjordan. 'The time is coming when it must be recognised that the semi-nomad economy of the Bedouins cannot coexist with intensive culture. Does it follow that this progress should be checked?'[37]

A resolution moved by Poale Zion at the 1930 Labour Party annual conference won approval for Snell's minority report. The Labour Zionist movement was presented by its advocates as the carrier of trade unionism and co-operatives, initiating developments that would bring social progress to the Arabs.[38] Katznelson, a Histadrut leader, elaborated the point in the ILP weekly, the *New Leader*: 'Whenever the Arab workers show any desire to improve their conditions of labour, the Palestine Labour Party comes to their help although this invariably provokes the wrath of the *effendis* [landowner and local notable] and the Mohammedan'.[39] The portrayal of Zionist settlement activity as socialist colonisation, protecting the indigenous people from capitalist exploitation and, at the same time, bringing about economic development, had a strong appeal to Labour's 'ethical imperialists'. But the credibility of the Zionist case was dealt a heavy blow only a few months after its approval at the 1930 Labour Party conference.

The Shaw Report was followed up by a Royal Commission inquiry, appointed by the Labour government and headed by Sir John Hope Simpson, to examine the underlying causes of the Arab discontent. Its report cast doubt on Jewish settlements' alleged benefits for Palestinians and swung the balance in favour of government officials who, like the High Commissioner, Sir John Chancellor, urged measures to placate Arab hostility. While Snell's dissent had allowed the Zionist movement and its supporters to draw some comfort from Shaw's findings, there was none for them in Hope Simpson's. 'The most lofty sentiments are ventilated in public meetings and in Zionist propaganda', the report commented, but 'legal documents binding on every settler in a Zionist colony are not compatible with the sentiments publicly addressed'. Land purchased by the Jewish National Fund (JNF) 'ceases to be land from which the Arab can gain advantage either now or at any time in the future. Not only can he never hope to lease or cultivate it, but … he is deprived for ever from employment on that land'. The expansion of Jewish enterprises was also unlikely to benefit Arab labour because the 'policy of the Jewish Labour Federation is successful in impeding the employment of Arabs in Jewish colonies and Jewish enterprises of every kind'.[40]

Even before Hope Simpson completed his report, MacDonald fretted over the international reaction to any policy shift. He advised his Colonial Secretary, Sidney Webb, who was ennobled to take up the post and became Lord Passfield, that 'the Palestine situation is not one to be dealt with on its own internal aspects, but has to be handled in relation to outside considerations'. The reaction of the Muslim world had to be taken into consideration, 'but we are not improving our grip upon the Muslim world by giving the Palestinian Arabs to understand that pressure from them is to divert our policy in Palestine'. He implied that greater heed should be paid to the Zionist concerns. From 1926, the *Yishuv* had suffered from a severe economic recession, which the following year led to more Jews leaving than entering Palestine. A gradual recovery began in 1929, but MacDonald warned that if political factors turned away Jewish capital from Palestine, 'we shall have to face a very uncomfortable condition of unemployment and agitation, and Jewish pressure will be found all over the world against us'. The Palestine situation would then have reverberations in the US: 'it is of the greatest importance that we should keep American oil interests in good relations with us, if we are to have the railway from Baghdad to Haifa with the pipe line running alongside of it.'[41]

It fell to Passfield to formulate the government's policy recommendations, the White Paper, in the light of the Shaw and Hope Simpson reports. At the time, he was embroiled in a protracted conflict with Kenya's European settlers and their lobbyists in London for proposing, in line with Labour Party policy and the demands of the humanitarian lobby, to introduce in Kenya the principle of 'native paramountcy'. Beatrice Webb speculated in her diary on how such a principle might apply to Palestine: 'this process of artificially creating new communities of immigrants brought from any part of the world is rather hard on the indigenous natives! The white settlers in Kenya would seem to have as much right, on this assumption, to be where they are, as the Russian Jews in Jerusalem!'[42] Nevertheless, there was to be no calls from liberal and left-wing circles for 'native paramountcy' in Palestine which would have required renouncing the Balfour Declaration and the terms of the Mandate. Hope Simpson had a narrower remit and his assessment was that the British administration, in seeking to meet the Balfour Declaration's commitment to establish 'a home for the Jewish people', had neglected the Declaration's other commitment, to protect the interests of the Arab population. Passfield embarked, therefore, on finding a more balanced approach.

Passfield had played an important role in the drafting of the Labour Party's *War Aims Memorandum*, but he was not strongly committed to its support for Zionism. He and Beatrice Webb earlier categorised Arabs among the 'non-adult races', requiring Europeans guardianship before they could attain self-rule. The Webbs 'adhered to the common belief that ethnic groups had distinct moral and intellectual characteristics which were biologically and culturally transmitted from generation to generation.'[43] The Jews, in their hierarchy, were higher up the scale than the Arabs but their alleged individualism and materialism made them lacking in some of the qualities which made the Anglo-Saxons the most disposed to attain socialism.

Not all socialists shared the Webbs' outlook on the Arab world. Charles Ashbee, for example, who had been strongly influenced by the ideas of William Morris, was an admirer of Arab culture and served as an advisor to the Palestine government on arts and monuments. He noted after meeting the Webbs that they 'speak in unclouded satisfaction of there being no Jews in the British Labour Party' and went on to cite Sidney declaring: 'French, German, Russian Socialism is Jew-ridden. We, thank heaven, are free!' Sidney's explanation for Jews avoiding the Labour Party was that, 'There is no money in it'. While Ashbee, despite his mother being Jewish, appears to have been untroubled by the Webbs' anti-semitism, he was critical of their defence of the Labour Party's Palestine policy. He considered them to be ignorant of the country, 'nor do they want to know, that the "poor Jews" may go back to their own country that is good enough for the Webbs'. And, he added, 'The Webbs indeed have a contempt for Islam and the Arab, one so often finds in specialists absorbed in home affairs'.[44]

Ashbee's assessment of the Webbs' attitude to the Arab world was undoubtedly accurate, but the constraints on Sidney in dealing with Palestine resulted not from his prejudices but from the Labour government recoiling from a change of direction in imperial policy. In formulating the government's approach to Palestine, Passfield held, in 1930, a series of talks with a delegation of Palestinian notables, including the Mufti of Jerusalem, Hajj Amin Al-Husseini. MacDonald put in only a brief, courtesy appearance. These talks were the only time during the Mandatory period that the Palestinian nationalist leadership was able to put its case to a leading Labour party figure. By contrast contacts between Labour Zionists and British labour movement leaders were frequent. The Labour Party's Advisory Committee on Imperial Questions and the party's General Secretary routinely sent briefing papers and policy drafts on Palestine-related matters to Poale Zion for comment but on only one occasion did the Committee grant a hearing to a Palestinian Arab representative.[45]

In his meeting with the Palestinian delegation, Passfield argued that the Balfour Declaration had been superseded by the League of Nations Mandate – 'We might have altered the Balfour Declaration but the Mandate is a different thing' – and he went on to add: 'the Jews will never be a majority in Palestine ... The Mandate does not say that Palestine should be made into a Jewish state'. But to his Palestinian interlocutors this was scant reassurance. They countered that the Mandate required that Jewish settlement should take place on condition that it did not harm the other section of the population and yet, as Hope Simpson's report had accepted, 'the position and interest of this non-Zionist section of the population have not been respected'. Land was sold to Jewish settlers, Jamal Effendi Husseini told Passfield, by absentee landlords and also by smallholders: 'sold by their impoverished owners because they have no bank to support them and really no other place to relieve them.'[46] The Palestine government's past attempts to establish a banking system that would provide loans to Arab farmers had been stifled by the Colonial Office and the Treasury, which opposed diverting funds for this purpose. The Fabian in Passfield may have been sympathetic to the Palestinians on this point but, as Colonial Secretary, he remained deaf to the pleas on their behalf. On constitutional reform, the two sides clashed sharply. Passfield was hoping to persuade the delegation to set up an Arab Agency – along the lines of the Jewish Agency – responsible for community affairs and acting as representatives on a Legislative Council. The British had made a similar proposal in 1921. Passfield ruled out a representative assembly making decisions by a majority vote on the grounds that, 'the British government must have the power whether there is a Council or not to do everything that is required by the Mandate'.[47] This set the limit on how far the Labour government was prepared to go to satisfy the Palestinian demand for self-determination.

Passfield's White Paper offered, by way of concession, to slow down the Jewish community's rate of growth. It proposed severely to restrict Jewish landholding to its existing level arguing that apart from land held by Jewish agencies in reserve, 'there remain no margin of land available for agricultural settlement by new immigrants'. State-owned land would not be made available for Jewish settlement 'in view of their actual occupation by Arab cultivators and of the importance of making available additional land on which to place the Arab cultivators who are now landless'. It also proposed a different, more restrictive criterion for immigration. Instead of allowing the entry of Jewish immigrants according to the labour requirements of the *Yishuv*, it suggested that future immigration would have to take into account its potential impact on Arab employment. In effect, Passfield was challenging the evolving economic separatism of the *Yishuv* by seeking to constrain the main colonising instruments of the Zionist movement; its policies of 'conquest of land' and 'conquest of labour', aimed at facilitating the economic absorption of Jewish immigrants. The White Paper reiterated Hope Simpson's point that land acquired by the Jewish National Fund was, from the point of view of the Arab population, 'extra-territorialised'. The land-purchasing arm of the Zionist movement, permitted prospective lessees 'the cultivation of the holding only with Jewish labour'. The resulting loss to the Arab community had led to a growing landlessness, which the government estimated to affect around a third of the rural population. From the collective settlements subsidised by the WZO and from Histadrut-owned enterprises Arab labour was excluded. The Histadrut also insisted, as the White Paper noted, 'on the employment of Jewish labour exclusively by all Jewish employers'.[48]

The protests orchestrated by the Zionist movement and its allies at the White Paper's publication took the government by surprise. Passfield described it as a 'hurricane' and in the face of it, Beatrice's diary reveals that his attitude to Zionism changed from indulgent to hostile. 'Sidney started out with great admiration for the Jew', she wrote, presumably meaning those in Palestine rather than the ones in Europe, of whom he had spoken disparagingly to Ashbee, 'and contempt for the Arab … but he reports that all his officials, at home and in Palestine find the Jews, even many accomplished and cultivated Jews, intolerable as negotiators and colleagues'.[49] British officials were, indeed, more at ease in dealing with Palestinians, whom they regarded as uncomplicated, primitive people. 'Being Orientals,' wrote the head of the Middle East Department at the Colonial Office, 'they will understand an order, and if once they realize that we mean business, may be expected to acquiesce'.[50]

Passfield's White Paper had been approved by the Cabinet but MacDonald at the head of a minority government and in the midst of a severe economic crisis was too weak to resist the hostility it aroused. The Zionist movement was able to use a by-election in Whitechapel, in London's East End, to mobilise its supporters, though this was not the main factor in its ability to secure the government's retreat. The electoral leverage that it could theoretically exercise over the Labour Party *via* the Jewish vote was confined to a handful of places like Cheetham Hill (Manchester), Leylands (Leeds) and in Whitechapel, a constituency in which Jews formed about a third of the electorate. For the by-election campaign, the Palestine Protest Committee was formed to campaign for Barnett Janner, the Liberal candidate and well known Zionist on a platform of opposing the White Paper. Poale Zion gave its backing to the Labour candidate after he committed himself to oppose, if elected, the government's proposed Palestine policy and following a forceful intervention by Ernest Bevin, promising that the twenty-six MPs sponsored by the Transport and General Workers' Union (TGWU) would also vote against the policy if it were put to Parliament.[51] The Labour candidate was elected but with a much-reduced majority, though it is unclear to what extent this can be put down to the White Paper. The Zionist vote was probably split between the Liberal and Labour candidates and the introduction of a Communist candidate also changed the distribution of votes. A Cabinet Committee, convened by Arthur Henderson, subsequently carried out the review which led to the retraction of the White Paper.

The by-election played a lesser part in persuading MacDonald to reconsider the Passfield White Paper than the opprobrium it aroused internationally and particularly in the United States.[52] In any case, the Zionists' defeat of the White Paper boosted their movement in Britain. The EZF had decided not to participate in the Palestine Protest Committee but the surge of activity in response to the government proposals appears to have energised it after a membership decline in the 1920s.[53] The Protest Committee was reported by its secretary to have organised nineteen open-air meetings and two mass meetings with more than 700 in attendance, as well as distributing 10,000 handbills and an equal number of manifestos.[54] Poale Zion also benefited. Its membership in this period was around 600 but Labour Party concern over the Jewish vote in certain constituencies, however small or even mythical, helped to enhance its standing in the eyes of the party bureaucracy. A Poale Zion report of which a copy was sent to the Labour Party's head office, claimed: 'The firm stand of the Poale Zion was largely responsible for the defeat of the enemies of socialism in Whitechapel.'[55]

MacDonald's retraction of the White Paper took the form of a letter to Weizmann in which he set out to clarify the government's policy. He not only reversed the concessions that Passfield had made to Arab concerns but, by removing some ambiguities in British policy, committed the government more firmly to Zionist aims. The government, MacDonald stated, did not intend prohibiting further sales of land to Jews. While restating the wish to settle the Arab landless, he added that 'this obligation in no way detracts from the larger purposes of development' which he defined as 'the most effectual means of furthering the establishment of the National Home for the Jews'. It was a formulation that in all but name declared the *Yishuv*'s paramountcy in British policy. On the economic absorption of Jewish labour, MacDonald retreated from Passfield's proposal to link future immigration to its potential impact on Arab employment. He also explicitly disavowed the criticism of the Histadrut's exclusionary practice, telling Weizmann: 'The principle of preferential and, indeed, exclusive employment of Jewish labour by Jewish organisations is a principle which the Jewish Agency are entitled to affirm.'[56]

A British Labour prime minister's *imprimatur* for the exclusionary practices of the Histadrut was a political triumph for Labour Zionists. The policy of 'Hebrew labour' made them vulnerable to criticism from the international labour movement. MacDonald had earlier hinted at his own misgivings, though in the most pusillanimous terms. After recalling how a few years earlier he had been hosted by the Histadrut to witness the 'extraordinary transformation' it was bringing about in Palestine, he remarked: 'This very question of the wisdom of an exclusive Jewish labour colony, on one side, and an Arab labour policy on the other, occupied hours of our time in a very profitable and pleasant interchange of views.'[57] Passfield was reported by an American Jewish newspaper to have spoken to a group of Zionists more bluntly: 'You cannot, he insisted, make it a rule that in this piece of territory no Arab can work. This causes hard feeling. How would you like it if we said no Jews can be employed in certain sections of England?' Yet, Passfield, too, had recoiled from recommending that the British government intervene, adding feebly: 'we do not prevent the Jews from excluding Arab labour. They can go on doing it but we do not approve of it.'[58]

The Histadrut was not a conventional trade union. Under the control of Mapai, which had been formed by the merger of two Labour Zionist parties in 1930, it became the main state-building institution to which the WZO channelled funds knowing that private capital could not be relied upon to employ Jewish labour in the face of competition from cheaper and, in some sectors, more skilled Arab labour. World Jewry was the largest source of funding for the Yishuv and also for Israel until 1971 when the United States' contribution began to exceed it.[59] With the WZO's patronage, the Histadrut developed a range of institutions to assist the absorption of Jewish labour, which included labour exchanges, banks, co-operatives, a construction company and health care. In these ways, funds from overseas assured Jewish workers a higher living standard than the labour market would have facilitated. The Histadrut leadership's drive to absorb Jewish workers into the Yishuv's economy dictated its attitude to Arab labour and trade unionism.

At the Histadrut's 1927 congress, Ben-Gurion, later Israel's first prime minister, led the opposition against a left-wing Labour Zionist group's proposal for a joint Arab-Jewish trade union organisation. At his urging, the congress resolved that Arabs be excluded from the Histadrut but should be encouraged to organise separately, leaving the way open to a limited degree of collaboration.[60] It was in the Histadrut's interest to co-operate with Arab workers in mixed workplaces, mostly in the British controlled public sector, where Arab labour could not be excluded but, if unorganised, could exert a downward pressure on the Jewish workers' terms of employment. Consequently, from 1932, the Histadrut fitfully promoted and grudgingly resourced the Palestine Labour League (PLL), to provide under its auspices a separate organisation for Arab workers, though it ensured that its activities did not conflict with Zionist objectives.[61] Moreover, the leadership came to recognise that Arab workers' affiliation to the Histadrut could provide an alternative to their unionisation by the

Palestinian Arab Workers' Society (PAWS), which was aligned with nationalists. The PLL also proved useful for the Histadrut to fend off criticism, mainly from the communist movement, over its 'Hebrew labour' policy and its hostility to joint unions for Arab and Jews. 'To counter such criticism and bolster Labour Zionism's internationalist credentials, it helped to be able to point to ongoing efforts to establish contact, and develop friendly relations with the Arab working class in Palestine.'[62]

The British Labour Party was not alone in enthusiastically embracing Labour Zionism. For the European social democratic movement it represented the 'positive colonial policy' that Bernstein, Vandervelde and Jaurès had advocated and had been rejected on the floor of the Second International's Stuttgart Congress in 1907. Kautsky had led the opposition and succeeded by 127 votes against 108 to reaffirm the previous condemnation of colonialism but, as Rebérioux and Haupt note, 'the majority obtained undoubtedly did not correspond to the attitude of the majority of the delegates: the left owed its victory to the personal prestige of Kautsky'.[63] However, at the 1928 Brussels Congress of the Labour and Socialist International, the right-wing reversed that stand, declaring colonialism to have a positive role where 'the immediate abolition of the colonial state would not bring with it any progress towards a national culture, but rather a relapse into barbarism'.[64] On the margin of this Congress but building on its ideological foundations, Poale Zion succeeded to form the Socialist Committee for Workers' Palestine. The Committee counted among its founding members several of the most prominent members of European socialism, including Bernstein, Blum, de Brouckère, Henderson, Huysmans, Lansbury, Löbe, Longuet, Renaudel, Turati and Vandervelde, who became its president. A good deal of Labour Zionism's appeal to these leaders was that its socialist colonisation, by rejecting the dictatorship of the proletariat, represented the antithesis of the Bolshevik model. MacDonald liked its emphasis on constructing the new society rather than on class struggle and Max Adler and Paul Löbe praised it for not requiring violence.[65] Nor would it have escaped their notice that the Zionist movement wanted Palestine to remain within the British Empire. By then the socialist parties of Europe that had participated in government, or anticipated doing so, were only too ready to place the main emphasis on the potential for an enlightened administration of the colonies and, only secondarily, on their right to self-determination. A contemporary observer of the proceedings in Brussels remarked: 'the Labour Party of England, the socialists of France, Holland and Belgium, are against policies which would seriously disturb the basic relations of their home countries with their colonial dependencies.'[66] The Congress's recommendation that socialist parties make use of the colonial system to extend the formation and development of a socialist labour movement was fully in accord with the form of colonisation that Labour Zionism saw itself carrying out.[67]

The Labour Zionist movement in Palestine organised 80 to 90 per cent of all Jewish labour in the country. Dov Hoz, a Labour Zionist leader and founding member of the Haganah, the military arm of the *Yishuv*, explained to the 1929 Labour Party conference that Labour Zionism was 'determined to transplant into the Orient your ideals and our ideals of Socialism and Labour'.[68] The Jewish settler was presented not merely as an outpost of European civilisation in the backward Orient but under the aegis of trade unionism and socialism, the purveyor of the highest achievements of that civilisation. Vandervelde, the Belgian socialist leader, mused that if Palestine became like other colonies 'that would be on whole an insignificant fact. What inspires many with a passionate interest is that Palestine is not like any other colony but, on the contrary, more than any other a land of marvellous social experiments, brimming with idealism'.[69] From this standpoint, Palestinian hostility to Jewish immigration and settlements belonged not to the nationalist awakening of the colonial world but to a backward social order resisting working-class politics and technical advance. In response to the communal clashes that broke out in Palestine in August 1929, which precipitated the British government appointing the Shaw Commission, Vandervelde reiterated the Zionist movement's explanation that they had been caused by the '*effendis* and their fanatics': 'they have succeeded to arouse the fanatized masses and have been able to push them to massacre, to spill blood and to destroy property'. Between the 'Arab *fellah* and the Jewish *chalutzim*', he asserted, 'there is not in the large majority of cases opposition but community of interest'.[70]

British Labour politicians supportive of Labour Zionism focused in the 1930s on the trade union and co-operative organisations it brought to Palestine, which they argued, much like Vandervelde, were establishing Jewish settlements on lines that would also bring development to the Palestinians. This theme appears to have had a still stronger appeal to the post-MacDonald party leadership. After MacDonald left the party, the Trades Union Congress (TUC) General Council assumed a more commanding role over Labour's direction. In face of the severely weakened Parliamentary party, it could assert political influence by the contribution it made to party funds, the bloc vote it could marshal at party conferences and the position it held on the National Council of Labour, where policy decisions were taken.[71] The enhanced importance of the trade unions in the Labour Party's internal workings was reflected in a more pronounced workerism in the party's ideology, in part an effect of the closing of ranks in the wake of MacDonald's 'betrayal' but perhaps also to give voice to working-class resentment at bearing the brunt of the economic crisis. This language of class, part of a broader change in the party's internal culture, depicted workers not as in antagonism to capital but as forming a community anchored in the institutions and ethics of social solidarity.[72] It represented an ideolgical shift that was to be epitomised by Herbert Morrison's vision of Labour Zionism.

Morrison rose to prominence through the London Labour Party, of which he was to be the secretary for thirty-two years. Deeply involved in municipal affairs, his main concern on the party's NEC was domestic matters. As a young man he had been inclined to the ILPs critical position during the war, but went on in the 1920s to follow the party line.[73] His first public intervention on Palestine was to declare from the chair of the Labour Party conference that there was 'no enduring divergence of interests between the Jewish and Arab working populations in Palestine'.[74] Until this time he had shown no particular interest in the issue. In 1934, after he lost his parliamentary seat at the 1931 general election, he visited Palestine for the first time. From then, he became 'passionately pro Zionist', to which his friendship with Dov Hoz, who resided in London for a time, probably also contributed.[75] Morrison's visit to Palestine may have been prompted by his ambition to recapture the seat he had previously held in Hackney. The constituency had a sizeable Jewish population, though votes in Jewish working-class communities in this period were more likely to be won on an anti-fascist than a pro-Zionist basis. A more important motivation appears to have been Morrison's enthusiasm for Labour Zionism. It represented the brand of socialism that he approved.

After being a member of the Marxist Social Democratic Federation in his youth and then of the ILP, Morrison rapidly moved to the right and, according to his biographers, pursued communists with such implacable intensity that by 1928 he was renowned in the party as '"our chief witchfinder"'.[76] In 1936, when recalling his visit to Palestine, Morrison pointedly referred to the Soviet experience in connection with Zionist agricultural settlements, telling Parliament that the latter were 'the greatest example of unselfish, co-operative and human effort ... a finer thing than is happening in any part of Russia'.[77] The settlers' idealism embodied, in his opinion, the spiritual qualities of socialism. 'They are doing it for no money at all ... directly in association with and under the control of the great Jewish trade union organisation, the Jewish Federation of Labour'.[78] He counterposed to communism an ethical socialism in the Christian, humanist tradition, to which labour politicians often laid claim – a socialism that was implemented through an act of moral cleansing. The material improvements by which Labour aimed to improve society 'was not an end in itself but as a stepping stone to the mental and spiritual regeneration of mankind'.[79] Morrison believed that this was being realised in the Zionist agricultural settlements. The settlements were for him a triumph on two fronts. They represented a mastery over nature and the making of Jews into 'first class colonisers, to have the real, good, old, Empire building qualities'.[80] He saw in Jewish agricultural labour, a form of purification, redeeming the anti-semitic projection of the Jew which Morrison took for real. 'I have met many Jews in many countries', he wrote in 1935, 'I know the London Jews very well, but the Palestinian Jews were to me different; so different that a large proportion of them were not obviously Jews at all'.[81]

Labour Party figures saw in the *kibbutzim*, which in the late 1930s had a mere 5.2 per cent of Palestine's Jewish population, the ideal form of co-operative organisation.[82] They were impressed by its collectivism, while for Labour Zionists it was primarily a way of establishing exclusively Jewish settlements.[83] Although many of those who joined the kibbutzim were imbued with socialist ideals, for Ben-Gurion, the aspect that made it deserving of support was its contribution to establishing a separate economy for the Yishuv. 'The kibbutz,' he explained in 1926, 'is the natural way of colonization for the labour movement in this country. But so long as the kibbutz does not solve in practice a number of social and economic problems, it is natural that other ways of colonization will be adopted.'[84] The kibbutzim also had an indispensable strategic role. They were a means of laying claim to territory by forming militarised settlements capable of defending newly and sometimes forcibly acquired land. After 1948, they were used to extend the Jewish presence in the border areas and to break up the remaining Palestinian population concentrations. The kibbutzim, emblematic of Labour Zionism's new society and much celebrated by Western Socialists for its communal and egalitarian values, were the training ground of the Yishuv's and later of Israel's military and political elite. By 1967, although the kibbutzim had only 3.9 per cent of the population, they provided 22 per cent of the officers in the Israeli army.[85]

The Histadrut's 'Hebrew labour' policy was the other important mechanism for excluding Arab labour in favour of Jewish workers. It campaigned for Jewish employers to exclude Arabs, particular from the citrus groves. Glazer divides the campaign into two phases. In the first period, 1927–1932, the Histadrut focused on seeking the removal of Arab labour on the grounds of Jewish unemployment. In the second period, 1933–1936, when an economic recovery was underway, Jewish labour preferred employment in the urban sector over the citrus groves, but the Histadrut maintained the 'Hebrew labour' campaign, insisting that continued Jewish immigration depended on maximising employment opportunities in the Jewish sector. The emphasis of the campaign shifted to the urban areas; mobile units of picketers moved from one enterprise to another, leading at times to physical attacks on Palestinian workers. 'During the peak period of urban pickets – from August 1934 through February 1935 – flying pickets operated in Haifa, Jerusalem and Tel Aviv.'[86] Despite the fact that Hope Simpson's report had made reference to the Histadrut's sectarian conduct, the issue was rarely raised in Britain. The picketers achieved a certain amount of international attention, however, in 1934, when their action directed against orange groves north of Jaffa led to violent clashes with Palestinian workers. The *Jewish Chronicle* reported: 'The entire Jewish population in the neighbourhood of Kfar Saba has voluntarily mobilised for the purpose of picketing Jewish orange groves in Kfar Saba in which Arab labour is employed … The employers argue that they were compelled to use Arab labour because of the shortage of Jewish workers.'[87] By one of the bitter ironies of which the history of the Palestine conflict is replete, this coincided with Nazi initiatives in Germany to boycott Jewish businesses and to exclude Jews from public places. In Bavaria, 'the local branch of the Union of German clothing manufacturers has refused to accept any business offers from "non-Aryan" agents or factory owners, unless they were wounded in the war … Jews hardly dare to enter any public place, even a restaurant or café. The last remaining garden restaurant that has been open to Jews has now been closed to them. Jews are not admitted to the swimming baths.'[88]

For the Zionist movement, the Nazi measures against Jews in Germany were further justification for ensuring the availability of employment for Jews in Palestine though it also involved discrimination on the basis of ethnicity. Defending its use in Palestine, Selig Brodetsky, a professor of mathematics at Leeds University, who would later become the first Zionist president of the Board of Jewish Deputies, declared: 'just as the English working men had a right to expect the English employer to employ English working men, so the Jewish working men had a right to expect the Jewish employer to employ Jewish working men.'[89] This argument would not have been out of place, at the time, in the propaganda of the British Union of Fascists (BUF).

On the rare occasions that Labour politicians confronted Labour Zionism's sectarian politics of seeking to undermine the position of Arab labour in the economy, they sought to explain it not as an aspect of colonisation but as the exclusivity characteristic of craft unionism, a defensive measure by workers against the attempt by capital to lower the price of labour.[90] Some socialists were discomfited, however, by this aspect of Jewish nationalism. Tom Reid, a member from the late 1930s of the Labour Party's Advisory Committee on Imperial Questions, told a member of the Jewish Agency: 'Zionism was not a wise movement for the Jews to foster. It was the same nationalism that we objected to in Hitler.'[91] A degree of disquiet on the left during the early 1930s is also indicated by David Hacohen, who became one of the directors of Soleh Boneh, the Histadrut's construction company. In his autobiography he recalls discussions with socialist students from different countries during his university days in London: 'I had to fight my friends on the issue of Jewish socialism, to defend the fact that I would not accept Arabs in my trade union, the Histadrut; to defend preaching to housewives that they not buy at Arab stores; to defend the fact that we stood guard at orchards to prevent Arab workers from getting jobs there.'[92] For some socialist Jews in Palestine, the Zionist labour movement's boycott of Arab labour and of Arab goods led them to reject Zionism. Connie Seifert departed for Britain where she joined the Communist Party.[93] Ygael Gluckstein was repelled by Zionism for similar reasons and left Palestine for Britain after the war where in 1950, under the name Tony Cliff, he formed, a Trotskyist group. This group evolved into International Socialists and then the Socialist Workers' Party (SWP), though the Palestinian issue did not figure prominently in the political work of any of the mutations. In his autobiography, Cliff recounts that in 1944 shortly before his wife, Chanie Rosenberg, arrived in Palestine, the *kibbutz* she intended to join, belonging to the left-wing Zionist group Hashomer Hatzair, was involved in a clash over land with some Palestinian farmers:

There were four kibbutzim and four Arab villages in this particular valley, surrounding a stony hill. The kibbutzim all decided to oust the Arabs from their villages which were on land the Jewish National Fund had bought from Arab landlords. They therefore formed a long phalanx at the foot of the hill, picked up stones as they climbed up and threw them at the Arabs on the other side. These Arab tenants had cultivated this land for generations and they had received nothing at all from their landlords for their land. They fled in fear and the Zionists took over the whole hill.[94]

Norman Bentwich, a former legal officer in Palestine, questioned the wisdom of the campaign against Arab labour at the 1937 conference of the EZF. Bentwich was a member of Brit Shalom, a small left-wing Zionist group founded in 1926 by Jewish intellectuals, which advocated that the Jews should form a bi-national state with the Palestinians.[95] He called for Jews to employ Arabs as a way of giving reality to co-operation between the two communities, without which, he believed, peace could not be built in Palestine. An editorial in the *Jewish Chronicle* described Bentwich's intervention at the conference as having 'roused a storm of criticism'.[96] Ben-Gurion was among the critics: 'had not Jews in Germany employed non-Jewish workers? Did not Jews in Poland employ non-Jewish Polish workers and what has been the result there?'[97] 'I reply,' wrote Bentwich a few weeks later, 'that we have to uphold a higher ethical standard.'[98] There was, however, no objection to the 'Hebrew labour' campaign, by the leaders of the international socialist movement. A statement, in 1934, by the Socialist Committee for Workers' Palestine, and signed among others by Vandervelde, Blum and Gillies (the British Labour Party's General Secretary), asserted: 'It is demonstrated in practice that the progress of Jewish colonization benefits Arab labourers themselves, and that already now the obstinately pursued effort of the Jewish Labour of Palestine and the General Federation of Labour is leading to more and more splendid results.'[99]

The Arab rebellion's outbreak in 1936 which began with a general strike had the paradoxical effect of entrenching still deeper the British Labour Party's position on Palestine behind the 'workerist' dogma that the Zionist project did not generate a conflict of interest between the Arab and Jewish workers. The general strike, launched in April, was aimed at forcing the British to terminate the Zionist project and would last six months. It began with nationalist youths combining in several towns with political groups to form local committees which called for strikes and shop closures. A national leadership emerged after a few weeks with the formation of the Arab Higher Committee, led by the Mufti of Jerusalem and bringing together prominent figures from the traditional Palestinian elite. The Higher Committee called for a general strike until the British halted Jewish immigration and land purchase and allowed a popularly elected Legislative Council. Soon after the strike began, the Histadrut wound down its picketing campaign against Arab labour, partly to avoid making the situation more difficult for the Palestine government but also because it used the opportunity offered by the withdrawal of Arab labourers to get Jewish workers to take their place. This was particularly significant in the public sector where the Zionist movement worked in collaboration with the British authorities to try to break the strike.

Among British Labour Party leaders, neither the Palestinians' mobilisation for a general strike nor the Histadrut's efforts at strike-breaking appeared to cause any consternation. Their response followed the pattern established during the 1929 outbreak of communal violence. They characterised the Arabs' hostility to Zionism as seeking to obstruct a benign form of colonisation. The explanation for the cause of the rebellion rehearsed the arguments current in Labour circles during the controversies surrounding the Shaw Report and the Passfield White Paper. Harold Laski, at the height of his political influence on the left-wing intelligentsia and, by the 1930s, strongly sympathetic to Zionism pointed to the source of the problem as stemming from 'the *effendi* and such trouble makers as the Grand Mufti'.[100]

In the parliamentary debate on the Arab rebellion, Labour speakers repeating the Labour Zionist political line gave no credence to the Palestinian population having genuine grievances. The benefit to the peasantry, claimed Creech Jones, an up-and-coming expert on colonial affairs in the party, was that by 'Jewish immigration new markets have been found, new land has been reclaimed and the Arab peasant has been released from the money lender because of the capital which has become available'. He suggested that the Palestinians roam the region without commitment to their land or village: 'When they reach Palestine they even neglect their own towns and flock round the Jewish settlements.'[101] The Arab strike was described by Tom Williams, from Labour's front bench in the House of Commons, in terms that placed it beyond the bounds of legitimate trade unionism. After evoking the pacific nature of the 1926 general strike in Britain, he exclaimed: 'these disorders in Palestine can scarcely be characterised as the result of a strike in the sense in which that term is generally understood.'[102] In the same Parliamentary debate, Morrison lavished praise on the settlements and on the spirit of Labour Zionism. 'What are the Jewish trade unions trying to do?' he asked rhetorically, and replied: 'They are trying to bring working men Arabs and working men Jews together in co-operation.'[103] Two days later, Ben-Gurion, writing to his wife from London, was exultant: 'The speeches by Lloyd George, Leopold Amery, Tom Williams, Creech Jones, Herbert Morrison, James de Rothschild and Victor Cazalet were wholly or partly prepared by us ... But the best speech was by Herbert Morrison.'[104]

The main labour movement newspaper, the TUC-funded *Daily Herald*, initially counselled a less partisan approach, warning: 'To dismiss Arab insurgence as the outcome of the work of agitators within or propaganda from without would be dangerously short-sighted.'[105] Yet that was precisely the tenor of its subsequent reports from Palestine filed by A.L. Easterman, a journalist active in Zionist politics and later the political director of the World Jewish Congress. In a series of articles he portrayed the strike as instigated by feudals and overseas fascists, which could be sustained only by intimidation and terrorism. 'I have discovered', he announced in a front-page article, 'full details of a hitherto undisclosed element in the Palestine upheaval – the part played behind the scenes by Fascism, chiefly by Italy. The plot is to further Italian imperial ambitions and turn the Mediterranean into an Italian sea.'[106] The Italian and German governments used the Palestinian Arab rebellion for anti-British propaganda and Zionist sources claimed that they funnelled some money to the Arab Higher Committee but even if this had occurred it was of minor significance – as the protracted nature of the insurgency was to reveal its roots were indigenous. The editorial line of the *Daily Herald* also hardened towards the Arabs when it became evident that the strike had inaugurated an armed rebellion in the countryside. 'They have been promised a Royal Commission to investigate all their complaints and all their grievances ... But, apparently, judging conciliation to be evidence of weakness and coming capitulation, they have gone on from violence to violence, from murder to murder.'[107]

After a period of relative lull between October 1936 and September 1937, the rebellion continued until 1939 involving attacks which inflicted damage on police stations, transport infrastructure and Zionist settlements. Once the rebellion's main base moved to the countryside its leadership fragmented. Local rebel leaders at the head of relatively small bands often operated on their own. Several of them alienated villagers by plundering their food stocks but generally, until late 1938, peasant support for the rebellion held up well.[108] The assessment of the High Commissioner that year was that 'the Rebellion has unquestionably become a national revolt involving all classes of the Arab community in Palestine and enjoying considerable support from the Arabs outside it'.[109] In response, the British increased their military strength from two to eighteen battalions and extended military rule over the whole of Palestine. Neither the resilience of the rebellion nor the brutal military repression deployed to defeat it altered, however, the Labour Party's position. The party orthodoxy on Zionism's beneficial consequences for both Jews and Arabs was maintained. While the British labour leadership clung to this interpretation throughout the controversy surrounding the Peel Commission's report, the *Yishuv*'s Labour Zionist leaders acknowledged among themselves that it was a myth. 'There is no Arab who is not harmed by the Jews' entry into the country', admitted Moshe Sharett, who would become Israel's first Foreign Minister.[110]

The *Daily Herald* described the rebels as terrorists and explained the British army's role as taking on 'an army of Arab gangsters and the perpetrators of countless outrages'.[111] There were some dissenters from this standpoint on the Labour movement's left-wing, who began to discern an emergent nationalist consciousness. Stafford Cripps argued, in 1936, that 'British imperialism can no doubt crush the nationalist aspirations of the Arabs for the time, but when this has been done the problems will remain unsolved'.[112] And Michael Foot, who had been an unsuccessful Labour Party candidate the previous year, ridiculed the argument put forward by Josiah Wedgwood that the Palestinian peasants had no nationalist aspirations: 'The responsibility for the Arab revolt must be laid at the door of crude anti-semitism, scheming Arab landlord, Nazi gold or Italian intrigue. Any red herring is apparently good enough to enable Mr. Wedgwood to shirk the uncomfortable fact that there exists in Palestine a powerful and virulent growth known as Arab nationalism.'[113]

The most forthright support for the Arab revolt was to come from the Communist Party. 'The Arabs are fighting for their liberation and independence', a *Daily Worker* editorial declared: 'But very cunningly the capitalist press is trying to depict them as the paid tools of Mussolini ... Their struggle is not anti-semitic but anti-imperialist.'[114] The newspaper subsequently carried critical accounts of several British military operations. They described the army's house demolitions in Safad and adjacent villages and also in Jaffa, where, the correspondent explained, they affected the 'poorest class of dock labourers and hawkers'.[115] One report described how after some rebels killed two British soldiers by derailing a train in Lydda: 'Tanks were driven into the town, and were used in the deliberate demolition of the poor wooden huts of the Arab workers.' In a village near Ramallah, the report continued, troops expelled the inhabitants and then burned down their houses.[116]

Alongside the military repression, the Conservative-dominated national government was looking for a political solution to bring the rebellion to a close. It appointed a Royal Commission, headed by Earl Peel, to make recommendations. The Report concluded that the Mandate was unworkable and should be terminated by partitioning Palestine into separate Arab and Jewish states, with only Jerusalem's holy places remaining as a British Mandated area. It also proposed that immigration policy instead of being determined by the 'economic absorptive capacity of Palestine', which in line with MacDonald's 1930 letter to Weizmann was administered according to the *Yishuv's* labour requirements, should take into account political, social and psychological factors.[117] This aimed to make the government's immigration policy take into account Palestinian sensibilities. With an eye to the Arab world's opinion, the Commission recommended that no more than 12,000 Jews *per annum* be allowed to enter Palestine over the ensuing five years.

The recommendations were unacceptable to both sides. Leaders of the Palestinian community saw no justification for having part of their land taken from them and the Zionists argued that by placing a limit on the scale of immigration and the area of Jewish settlement, the British would be reneging on their commitments in the Balfour Declaration and the Mandate. Weizmann and his colleagues, nonetheless, privately welcomed aspects of the Peel Report. It gave recognition to the Zionist aspiration for a sovereign Jewish state in Palestine and by putting forward the idea of a population exchange between the two proposed states, it lent legitimacy to the principle of removing Palestinians from their land for the purpose of forming the Jewish state.

Zionists in London nevertheless assiduously lobbied against the Peel Report and they were able to make an impact on the Labour Party's position with regard to it. Ben-Gurion met the party's executive and Weizmann discussed tactics with a group of MPs which included Clement Attlee, the Labour Party leader. Attlee described the Peel Report's assessment that the Mandate had proved unworkable and should therefore be terminated as a 'triumph for Fascism'.[118] The party leadership dismissed once more Arab hostility to Zionism as unrepresentative of the mass of the people. Reiterating the argument that over the years had become the Labour Zionist mantra on the subject, Tom Williams explained to the House of Commons that the Labour Party opposed partition because 'broadly speaking the workers' interests are identical whether they are Jews or Arabs ... We do not think that a comparatively few either feudal landlords or modern capitalists ought to stand in the way'.[119]

Labour leaders maintained that the root of the conflict derived from the contrasting levels of economic development between the Arab and Jewish communities. They believed it could be resolved if the Arabs progressed either by being pulled along in the slipstream of the Jewish settlers' dynamism or, as Morrison urged, through government initiated, 'social and economic legislation steadily lifting the economic, the social and, in the end, the political status of the Arab masses'.[120] Labour's call for Arab-Jewish unity rested on the assumption that the Jewish claim had priority because its trade unionism and socialist aspirations gave it a greater claim to universality. Thus British labour leaders misapprehended the politics of nationalism in Palestine: they conflated it, on the Jewish side, with working-class politics and they denied its popular force on the Arab side by characterising it as the resistance of feudal reactionaries barring the way to progress, which failed to recognise that Palestinian opposition to Zionist settlement had begun to rework traditional village and clan loyalties into a wider, Palestinian identity. There was a much greater readiness among some Conservatives to accept nationalism's over-riding importance in the Arab rebellion. For instance, Ormsby-Gore, the Conservative Secretary of State for the Colonies stated: 'the fact of nationality, the Arab fears of a Jewish national home and the Arab objection to it. That is the fundamental cause and the cause of previous risings, and it is the cause of last year's rising.' Dismissing the Labour Party's position he added, 'the trouble of Palestine is political and not economic'.[121]

In the face of the hostility to partition from both sides, the National government's support for this as a viable proposition waned. The Woodhead Commission appointed in January 1938 to examine the practicality of implementing the Peel Commission's recommendation of partition, advised against it. War with Nazi Germany was now on the horizon and the Cabinet concluded that, given Britian's Middle East interests, the Arab viewpoint could not be ignored. The Palestine policy, outlined in a 1939 White Paper, proposed to restrict Jewish immigration to 75,000 labour certificates over five years and advised the formation of an independent Palestinian state within ten years. In response, Labour's front bench in Parliament rallied behind the Zionist opposition to the White Paper. Morrison described it as 'a cynical breach of the pledges given to the Jews and the world, including the Americans', pointing out that by proposing to hand over sovereignty at the stage when the government anticipated the Palestinian population to be in the majority would lead to a restriction on Jewish immigration and consign Palestine's Jewish population to remain permanently a minority.[122] At the 1939 Labour Party conference a resolution condemning the White Paper was approved with only two hands raised against it.[123] During the war, when Morrison and Noel-Baker took up ministerial positions in Churchill's government they could no longer lead Labour's opposition to the government's Palestine policy but the party continued to press the Zionist case. Dissent among Labour Party members on this issue was rare. An attempt by a Manchester delegate to rally opposition to the Poale Zion resolution, at the 1940 party conference, failed. He had argued that 'the Balfour Declaration very clearly laid it down that there should be no violation of the existing rights of the Arab population in Palestine, but the position is that the Jewish population, has, by reason of the persecution in Europe, increased enormously, and if unchecked it will obviously become a serious matter'.[124]

Sustained opposition to Labour's policy was expressed by Tom Reid in the party's Advisory Committee on Imperial Questions. However, since the late 1920s, this had become a discussion circle among colonial experts with little influence on the party's executive. Significantly, Reid's ideological formation had not been in the labour movement. He had worked in the colonial service in Ceylon and the Seychelles and was a member of the Woodhead Commission that, in 1938, had examined the feasibility of partitioning Palestine. In 1942, in the Advisory Committee's discussion on Palestine, he was the lone, anti-Zionist voice. Reid was opposed to depriving Palestine's Arab majority from attaining self-government either by stalling until there was a Jewish majority or by parcelling out the system of government between Arab and Jewish cantons. 'Why', he asked, 'should sovereignty over the territory of the people of Palestine be given to immigrants against the wishes of Palestine?' He believed that a self-governing Palestine would not be opposed to a restricted immigration, if the Arabs did not feel that it was hitched to the project of turning them into a subordinate minority. Reid described the 'economic absorptive capacity' criterion for permitting Jewish immigration into Palestine, which the 1939 White Paper intended to annul but the Labour Party had continued to support, as 'a joke'.[125] The economy could absorb any number of immigrants, he pointed out, while they were being subsidised from abroad but, on the other side, the Palestinians were being deprived of their livelihood through Jewish land purchase and the boycott of Arab labour. Bentwich, his colleague on the Advisory Committee, despite previously expressing disapproval over the Histadrut's campaign to boycott Arab labour, responded defensively to Reid's criticism, claiming it unduly emphasised 'a wrong tendency on the part of some Labour enterprises'. But Reid held to his position: 'The statement that Jews boycott Arab labour in industries is fair and true ... Jews have even been beaten up by Jews for employing cheap Arab labour.' And to the standard Zionist argument that the Arab masses had become more prosperous as result of the economic development of the *Yishuv*, Reid replied: 'Capitalists often claim that the creation of material prosperity justifies conquest or aggression by force or otherwise. This is not Labour doctrine nor socialism.'[126] He reasoned that some Jewish immigration and sale of Arab land to Jews would be acceptable to a future Palestinian Arab government as long as it was not aimed at securing political domination for the Jewish population. The solution was for Jewish immigrants to 'throw in their lot with the Palestinians instead of trying to set up an exclusive racial or communal economic system'. Reid proposed, therefore, that Palestine be granted self-government after the war on the basis of equal rights for all its citizens, minorities included, and with security assured for the holy places.[127]

The Committee's discussion had no perceptible impact on the Labour leadership's thinking. The party's plan for the post-war world drafted by Hugh Dalton and submitted for approval to the 1944 Labour Party conference proposed a solution that Zionist leaders were wary of openly advocating though it formed an integral part of Zionist thinking.[128] This was to remove Palestine's Arab population or, in the words of Herzl, the founder of the Zionist movement, 'to spirit the penniless population across the border'.[129] Dalton's initial draft even contemplated the expansion of a Jewish Palestine beyond the neighbouring countries of Mandatory Palestine: 'There is also something to be said for throwing open Libya or Eritrea to Jewish settlement, as satellites or colonies to Palestine'.[130]

The statement adopted by the 1944 Labour Party conference made the case for a Jewish state on the basis of the Holocaust: 'there is surely neither hope nor meaning in a "Jewish National Home," unless we are prepared to let Jews, if they wish, enter this tiny land in such numbers as to become a majority. There was a strong case for this before the War. There is an irresistible case now, after the unspeakable atrocities of the cold and calculated German Nazi plan to kill all Jews in Europe. ... Let the Arabs be encouraged to move out as the Jews move in ... The Arabs have many wide territories of their own; they must not claim to exclude the Jews from this small area of Palestine, less than the size of Wales. Indeed, we should re-examine also the possibility of extending the present Palestinian boundaries, by agreement with Egypt, Syria and Transjordan.'[131] The chilling logic of one ethnic group having to make way for another, drew on the stereotypical depiction of the Arabs as wondering nomads bereft of attachment to their land and collective life.

'Reactions to the resolution have been widespread and bitter', the High Commissioner reported from Jerusalem. 'The Arab population who have been inclined to regard Zionist propaganda abroad with little more than irritation, are now thoroughly alarmed at what they regard as this new manifestation of its effectiveness. They are genuinely shocked and dismayed'. He attached to his dispatch a letter from the 'learned men (*Ulama*), landowners and elders' that reflected their hurt and anger: 'Is it really the concern of Arabs to bear the aggression on Jews by the Nazis? ... Why other countries will not bear this burden, and why should Arabs, who are not concerned in the aggression be involved.'[132]

Zionist leaders had been consulted on Dalton's formulation and although delighted by the Labour Party's statement on Palestine they were nonetheless anxious to downplay the 'transfer' idea.[133] They had always maintained that there was plenty of room for Jewish immigrants and that, therefore, the Zionist project posed no threat to the Arab inhabitants. Berl Locker, who had been prominent in the Histadrut and was, in this period, the London representative of the Jewish Agency, sought to take the heat out of the controversy without Labour retracting its 'transfer' proposal. Thus in a letter to the party's general secretary he reiterated the more diplomatic formulation that a transfer of the Arab population was 'not a prerequisite condition for a large-scale Jewish immigration' while adding that 'it would be wrong to take out the transfer clause; its removal might be interpreted as an admission that the Labour Party's proposal involves an injustice to the Arabs.'[134]

The predominant motive behind Labour's 'transfer' proposal was that something had to be done for the Jews in the light of the Nazi extermination programme, but the party's International Subcommittee had discussed the idea as early as July 1941 before that had been set in motion. At a meeting convened by the committee, Locker, representing the Jewish Agency, was asked by Noel Baker if the Zionists' aspiration to settle three to four million Jews in Palestine assumed the 'transfer' of its Arab population. He replied that it did not, though he did not want to rule it out as an option, adding that the 'transfer' he had in mind would be 'by voluntary agreement between us and the Arabs and we would no doubt be ready to help in the economic resettlement of Arabs'.[135] The presumptuousness of this proposal, given that the Jews in Palestine, at this stage, formed only a third of its population, hints at Locker's confidence that he was talking among friends and ones not averse to the idea of carving out a bit of the imperial estate to fellow Europeans. Dalton's draft was subsequently considered at five meetings of the International Subcommittee without any objections to his Palestine proposal being recorded. Only a couple of years earlier, an exchange of populations between India and Pakistan had been dismissed by Brailsford as 'a proposal as difficult to realise as it is repugnant'.[136] Yet it was not only the Holocaust that gave momentum to the 'transfer' idea and overrode doubts about the ethics of uprooting people. From mid-1944, as the Allied armies advanced towards Germany, liberating one country after another, displaced civilians, defeated soldiers, escapees from forced labour camps and refugees began to make their trek home or to safer areas. With the end of war imminent, official circles anticipated further movements of large numbers of people.[137] Against this background, Dalton thought of making ethnic divisions correspond to national boundaries as a mere tidying up operation. 'Such movements of population', he wrote, 'will be a small affair compared to the gigantic "general post" which Hitler has set going all over Europe, and to the vast post-war problems of the repatriation of prisoners and exiles'. He added: 'If two families don't get on, there is a better chance of peace if they are put to live in separate houses.' Noel-Baker's rejoinder did not contest the desirability of such a solution but cautioned that whatever was done by way of transferring populations, 'Europe will never be ethnologically perfect' and hence minorities had to be defended.[138] As the war against fascism entered its final phase, the Labour Party's support for Zionism derived part of its conviction from the desire to restore order in the post-war world on the basis of ethnically homogenous states.

At Labour's annual conference in May 1945, Dalton reiterated the Labour Party's 1944 declaration on Palestine, calling on the Allied powers to agree to an increase in Jewish immigration to Palestine and the setting up of a Jewish state. This was Zionism's high tide in relation to the Labour Party. It marked a significant achievement for Zionist politics and especially for Poale Zion, whose campaigning and lobbying activities had been instrumental in aligning the Labour Party's Palestine policy with the Zionist cause.

Notes

1 Anti-semitic references to 'rich Jew' were common in the Social Democratic Federation's newspaper *Justice* and in the guild socialists' *New Age*. P. Colbenson, 'British Socialism and Anti-Semitism, 1884–1914' (PhD thesis, Georgia State University, 1979).
2 Labour Party, *War Aims Memorandum* (London: Labour Party, 1917).
3 *The Manchester Guardian* (18 August 1918). Sargent indicates that Schneier Levenberg (see Chapter 2) was of the view that the commitment on Palestine was drafted by Webb but more significant is that there was no objection to it from any leading Labour figures. See A. Sargent, 'The British Labour Party and Palestine 1917–1949' (PhD thesis, Nottingham University, 1980), p. 14.
4 A. Reid and H. Pelling, *A Short History of the Labour Party* (Basingstoke: Palgrave, 2005), pp. 206–207.
5 A.J.P. Taylor, *The Trouble Makers* (London: H. Hamilton, 1957), p. 156.
6 E. Bennett, 'Lausanne – and After', *Foreign Affairs* (December 1922), p. 119.
7 *The Herald* (10 January 1918); *The New Statesman* (17 November 1917).
8 *The Call* (4 April 1918).
9 British Library of Political and Economic Science, Passfield Papers, Beatrice Webb, Diary, vol. 34, 18 March 1917.
10 E. Manela, *The Wilsonian Moment* (Oxford: Oxford University Press, 2007), p. 25.
11 C.F. Brand, *British Labour's Rise to Power* (Stanford: Stanford University Press, 1941), p. 90.
12 A. Mayer, *Wilson vs. Lenin, Political Origins of the New Diplomacy, 1917–1918* (Cleveland: Meridian Books, 1964) p. 316.
13 Quoted in Mayer, *Wilson vs. Lenin.*, p. 316.
14 H.N. Brailsford, *A League of Nations* (London: Headley Brothers, 1917), p. 165.

15 J.A. Hobson, *Imperialism, A Study* (London: Allen & Unwin, 1961), pp. 235–237.
16 Ibid., p. 7.
17 Ibid., p. 252.
18 Quoted in J. Townshend, 'J.A. Hobson: Anti-Imperialist?', *International Review of History and Political Science*, 19 (1982), 33.
19 *The Herald* (19 January 1918).
20 S. Kaplansky, 'Jews and Arabs in Palestine', *Socialist Review* (March 1922).
21 S. Kaplansky, *The Jews and the War* (The Hague: Poale Zion, 1916).
22 *Labour Party Annual Conference Report* (hereafter LPACR) 1921, p. 198.
23 National Archives, London, (hereafter NA), MacDonald Papers, 30/69/819, 'Visit to Palestine: Jottings', J.R. MacDonald, 1922; J.R. MacDonald, *A Socialist in Palestine* (London: Poale Zion, 1922).
24 K. Morgan, G. Cohen and A. Flinn, *Communists and British Society 1920–1921* (London: Rivers Oram Press, 2007), p. 218.
25 MacDonald, *A Socialist in Palestine*, p. 13.
26 S. Howe, *Anti-colonialism in British Politics* (Oxford: Clarendon Press, 1993), p. 47.
27 B. Porter, *Critics of Empire* (London: Macmillan, 1968), p. 117.
28 National Art Library, Victoria and Albert Museum, Charles Ashbee, *Memoirs*, vol. 5, 14 January 1924, p. 102.
29 S. Levenberg, *The Jews and Palestine: A Study in Labour Zionism* (London: Poale Zion, 1945), p. 199.
30 *Jewish Chronicle* (1 October 1915 and 5 February 1904).
31 *New Statesman* (7 November 1917).
32 Quoted in L. London, *Whitehall and the Jews, 1933–1948* (Cambridge: Cambridge University Press, 2003), p. 275.
33 C. Weizmann, *Letters and Papers*, Series A, vol. 7 (Oxford: Oxford University Press, 1975), p. 220.
34 S. MacIntyre, 'Socialism, the Unions and the Labour Party', *Bulletin of the Society for the Study of Labour History*, 31 (Autumn 1975), 108.
35 *Report of the Commission on the Palestine Disturbances of August 1929*, Cmd. 3530 (London, 1930) p. 129.
36 *Report of the Commission on the Palestine Disturbances*, p. 176.
37 H. Brailsford, 'Caesar and the Appeal of Massacre', *The Menorah Journal* (May 1930) reprinted in General Federation of Jewish Labour, *Documents and Essays, On Jewish Labour Policy in Palestine* (Greenport: Greenwood Press, 1975), p. 138 and p. 141.
38 Ahmad Sa'di discusses the origins and development of the Zionist explanatory framework in 'Modernization as an Explanatory Discourse of Zionist-Palestinian Relations', *British Journal of Middle Eastern Studies*, 24:1 (1997), 25–48.
39 *New Leader* (14 March 1930).
40 Sir J. Hope Simpson, *Palestine. Report on Immigration, Land Settlement and Development*, Cmd. 3686 (London: HMSO, 1930) p. 54.
41 John Rylands Library, Manchester University, Manchester, Ramsay MacDonald Papers, RMD/1/9/16, MacDonald to Passfield, 24 July 1930.
42 N. MacKenzie and J. MacKenzie (eds), *The Diary of Beatrice Webb*, vol. 4 (London: Virago, 1985), p. 190.
43 J.M. Winter, 'The Webbs and the Non-White World: A Case of Socialist Racialism', *Journal of Contemporary History*, 9:1 (1974), 181.
44 Ashbee, *Memoirs*, vol. 5, p. 102.
45 George Mansur, the former secretary of the Arab Labour Federation, gave evidence to the Peel Commission on labour conditions and the Histadrut. It took nine months for him to get a hearing from the Advisory Committee on Imperial Questions. The

following year, in 1939, he appeared on a political platform with an anti-semite, which was brought to the attention of Labour Party headquarters. There were no further meetings with him. Reginald Reynolds, who knew him well, rejected the charge that he was anti-semitic. R. Reynolds, *Beware of Africans* (London: Jarrolds, 1955), p. 24.

46 NA, CO 733/184/2, Arab Delegation to London, May to June 1930.
47 NA, CO733/184/1, Arab Delegation to London, January to May 1930.
48 Palestine, *Statement of Policy His Majesty's Government* (Passfield White Paper) Cmd. 3692 (London: HMSO, October 1930).
49 N. MacKenzie, *The Letters of Sidney and Beatrice Webb*, vol. 3 (Cambridge: Cambridge University Press, 1978), p. 335.
50 Quoted in B. Wasserstein, *The British in Palestine* (London: Royal Historical Society, 1978), p. 115.
51 Labour Party Papers (henceforth LPP), Labour History Archives, People's History Museum, Manchester, JSM/210/79, Poale Zion, 'Whitechapel by-election' n.d., Middleton Papers.
52 G. Sheffer, 'Intentions and Results of British Policy in Palestine: Passfield's White Paper', *Middle Eastern Studies*, 9:1 (1973), 43–60.
53 D. Cesarani, 'Zionism in England, 1917–1939' (PhD dissertation, University of Oxford, 1986), p. 131.
54 Central Zionist Archives (hearafter CZA), Jerusalem, Palestine Protest Committee, A241/1, Letter from English Zionist Federation, 10 November 1930; 'Report of Activities Covering the Period from November 19th to December 2nd'.
55 Poale Zion, 'Whitechapel by-election'.
56 *Hansard*, Commons, v. 248, cc. 751–757, 13 February 1931.
57 *Hansard*, Commons, v. 245, c. 117, 17 November 1930.
58 Modern Records Centre, University of Warwick Library, Papers of the Transport and General Workers' Union, MSS 126/EB/Wh/1/8, transcript of article, n.d. circa 1930,
59 J. Benin, 'The United States-Israel Alliance', in T. Kushner and A. Solomon (eds), *Wrestling With Zion* (New York: Grove Press, 2003), p. 43.
60 Z. Lockman, *Comrades and Enemies, Arabs and Jewish Workers in Palestine, 1906–1948* (Berkeley: University of California Press, 1996), p. 107.
61 D. Bernstein, 'From Split Labour Market Strategy to Political Co-optation: The Palestine Labour League', *Middle Eastern Studies*, 31:4 (1995), 775–771.
62 Lockman, *Comrades and Enemies*, p. 109.
63 M. Reberioux and G. Haupt, 'L'attitude de L'Internationale', *Le Movement Sociale*, 45, (October 1963), p. 19.
64 *Bulletin of the Labour and Socialist International*, series 2, no.3 (September 1928), p. 11.
65 Institute of Social History, Amsterdam, Braunthal Papers. Adler quoted in Braunthal to Erlich, December 1935, Letter, no. 48; Löbe quoted in J. Glasneck, 'Die Internazionale Sozialdemokratie und die Zionistische Palastina-Kolonisation in den Jahren 1929/30', *Wissenschatliche Zeitschrift der Martin Luther Universitat*, 26:4 (1977), p. 48.
66 L. Lorwin, *Labour and Internationalism* (London: Allen and Unwin, 1929), p. 441.
67 *Bulletin of the Labour and Socialist International* (September 1928).
68 LPACR, 1929 p. 213.
69 E. Vandervelde, *Le pays d'Israel* (Paris: Rider, 1929), p. 211.
70 Comité Socialiste pour la Palestine Ouvrière, *Bulletin*, No.4 (November 1929).
71 P. Addison, *The Road to 1945* (London: Pimlico, 1994), p. 47.
72 The gender implications are discussed in P. Graves, *Labour Women: Women in British Working-Class Politics 1918–1939* (Cambridge: Cambridge University Press, 1994), p. 185.

73 B. Donoughue and G.W. Jones, *Herbert Morrison: Portrait of a Politician* (London: Weidenfeld & Nicolson, 1973), p. 112.
74 LPACR, 1929, p. 153.
75 Ibid., p. 435.
76 Ibid., p.98.
77 Hansard, Commons, v. 313, c. 1387, 19 June 1936.
78 *Jewish Chronicle* (6 November 1936).
79 Hansard, Commons, v. 313, c. 1387.
80 Ibid., v. 341, c. 2005, 24 November 1938.
81 *Daily Herald* (12 September 1935).
82 A. Ben-Porat, *Between Class and Nation* (New York: Greenwod Press, 1986), p. 160.
83 G. Shafir, *Land, Labour and the Origins of the Israeli-Palestinian Conflict 1882–1914* (Berkeley: University of California Press, 1996); B. Kimmerling, *Zionism and Territory: the Socio-territorial Dimensions of Zionist Politics* (Berkeley: University of California Press, 1983), and M. Shalev, 'Time for Theory: Critical Notes on Lissak and Sternhell', *Israeli Studies*, 1:2 (1996), 170–188.
84 Quoted in Y. Shapiro, *The Formative Years of the Israel Labour Party* (London: Sage, 1976), p. 220.
85 G. Kaufman, *To Build the Promised Land* (London: Weidenfeld and Nicholson, 1973), p. 118.
86 S. Glazer, 'Picketing for Hebrew Labour: A Window on Histadrut Tactics and Strategy', *Journal of Palestine Studies*, 30:4 (2001), 46.
87 *Jewish Chronicle* (20 April 1934).
88 Ibid. (6 April 1934).
89 Ibid. (7 December 1934).
90 J.C. Wedgwood, *The Seventh Dominion* (London: The Labour Publishing Company, 1928), p. 86; For Brailsford, excluding Palestinians from Jewish agricultural co-operatives required no special pleading: 'These backward, illiterate and very dirty people could not mix in the family life of these colonies on an equal footing', *New Leader*, 2 January 1931.
91 M.J. Cohen, *Retreat from the Mandate* (London: Elek, 1978), p. 48.
92 Quoted in A. Bober (ed.), *The Other Israel: The Radical Case Against Zionism* (New York: Anchor Books, 1972), p. 12.
93 *The Guardian* (12 March 1998).
94 T. Cliff, *A World To Win* (London: Bookmarks, 2000), p. 13.
95 *Jewish Chronicle* (28 May 1937).
96 Ibid. (4 June 1937).
97 Ibid. (28 May 1937).
98 Ibid. (4 June 1937).
99 Comité Socialiste pour la Palestine Ouvrière, Bulletin, No. 8, February 1934.
100 *New Statesman* (20 June 1936). Labour Zionist claims that the development it was bringing about would sweep away the ruling class and liberate the impoverished masses was not borne out in the post-1948 period, when Mapai (the Israeli Labour Party) was in power. Lustick points out that in 1953, Shlomo Avineri, an Israeli political scientist and member of Mapai, criticised his party for cultivating the support of the privileged stratum of the Palestinian minority in Israel: 'the representatives of the Arab minority who have supported the policies of Mapai in both the First and Second Knessets were not representatives of the working class or of agricultural labourers, or of the fellahin. To a man they are representatives of the effendi class – large landowners, Sheiks, heads of hamulas, notables, and religious leaders – Muslim, Christian, and Druze ... It is ironic that our support in the Arab sector

derives from precisely the most reactionary circles' (quoted in I. Lustick, *Arabs in a Jewish State* (Austin: University of Texas Press, 1980), pp. 203–204.
101 *Hansard*, Commons, v. 313, c. 1353, 19 June 1936.
102 *Ibid.*, v. 313, c.1326.
103 *Ibid.*, v. 313, c.1326 and 1388.
104 D. Ben-Gurion, *Letters to Paula* (London: Valentine, Mitchell, 1971), pp. 100–101.
105 *Daily Herald* (13 June 1936).
106 *Ibid.* (18 September 1936).
107 *Ibid.* (8 September 1936).
108 J. Norris, 'Repression and Rebellion: Britain's Response to the Arab Revolt in Palestine of 1936-39', *Journal of Imperial and Commonwealth History*, 36:1 (2008), 25–45.
109 NA, CO935/21, Sir Harold MacMichael to Colonial Office 24 October 1938.
110 B. Morris, *Righteous Victims* (New York: Vintage Books, 2001), p. 136.
111 *Daily Herald* (27 June 1936).
112 *Manchester Guardian* (8 September 1936).
113 *Ibid.* (15 September 1936).
114 *Daily Worker* (28 May 1936).
115 *Ibid.* (18 August; 17 September 1936).
116 *Ibid.* (30 July 1936).
117 Royal Commission Report, *Palestine*, Cmd. 5479, (London: HMS, 1937) p. 299.
118 Quoted in Cohen, *Retreat from the Mandat*, p. 35.
119 *Hansard*, Commons, v. 326, c. 2337 and 2344, 21 July 1937.
120 *Ibid.*, v. 347, c. 2137, 23 May 1939.
121 *Ibid.*, v. 326, c. 2242, 21 July 1937.
122 *Ibid.*, v. 346, c. 2142, 23 May 1939.
123 *LPACR*, 1939, p. 256.
124 *Ibid.*, 1940, pp. 173–174.
125 LPA, LPP, Labour Party Advisory Committee on Imperial Questions (henceforth LPACIm.Q), Memo. No.238E 'Comment on the Report on Palestine', September 1943.
126 LPA, LPACIm.Q, Memo. No.238B 'The Palestine Problem', September 1943.
127 LPA, LPACIm.Q, Memo. No.238E, 'Comment on the Report on Palestine'.
128 N. Masalha, *Expulsion of the Palestinians: The Concept of 'Transfer' in Zionist Political Thought, 1882–1948* (London: I.B. Tauris, 1992); Morris, *Righteous Victims*, pp. 139–143.
129 Quoted in E. Said, *The Question of Palestine* (London: Vintage, 1982), p. 13.
130 LPA, LPP, International Department, draft, 'Post-War Settlement', 12 November 1943, Box Foreign/Defence Policy 1935-1945.
131 Report of the 43rd Annual Conference of the Labour Party (London: Labour Party, 1944).
132 NA, CO733/463/5, Letter. High Commissioner to Colonial Office, 29 May 1944.
133 C. Simons, *International Proposals to Transfer Arabs from Palestine, 1895–1947* (New Jersey: Tavistock Publishing House, 1988), p. 189. In July 1941 at meeting of Labour Zionist leaders with the Labour Party's International Committee, Locker made clear that he supported the voluntary 'transfer' of Arabs and 'we would no doubt be ready to help in the economic resettlement of Arabs'. Minutes. International Sub-Committee, Labour Party, 11 July 1941. Levenberg Papers, Box 'Zionism'.
134 LPA, International Department, Locker to Gillies, 15 May 1944, Box 5.
135 Levenberg Papers, Minutes of Meeting between Poale Zion and the International Sub-Committee of the Labour Party held at Transport House, 11 July 1941, Box 'Zionism'.
136 H.N. Brailsford, *Subject India* (London: Gollancz, 1943), p. 88.

137 'Between them Stalin and Hitler uprooted, transplanted, expelled, deported and dispersed some 30 million people in the years 1939–43. With the retreat of the Axis army the process was reversed'. T. Judt, *A History of Europe Since 1945* (London: Pimlico, 2007), p. 23.
138 LPP, LPA, LP/International Department Foreign and Defence Policy 1935–1945, Hugh Dalton's draft 'Post-War Settlement', 12 November 1943 and Ph. Noel-Baker 'Notes on Mr.Dalton's Outline Sketch of the Principles upon which a Declaration of Post-War International Policy should be based', n.d.

2 Zionism and Anglo-Jewry

Poale Zion's effectiveness in gaining labour movement support partly depended on the wider Zionist movement's campaign to win over Britain's Jewish community. In 1930, well before Zionism came to dominate Anglo-Jewry's political outlook, Lloyd George was advised, when addressing the Jewish electorate in Whitechapel, that it 'would like to hear something brief and personal about Palestine'.[1] In this period, declarations along these lines by prominent politicians would have been understood by most East End Jews as a gesture of friendliness and not as an explicit endorsement of the Zionist project. Zionism was a late arrival among nationalisms and no more the 'natural' expression of ethnic identity than other nationalisms.

Before the Second World War, Zionism struggled to find a foothold in the Anglo-Jewish community, whose politics and culture were defined by immigrants from Eastern Europe. There had been a steady flow of Jewish immigrants to Britain from the middle of the nineteenth century but from 1881 a series of pogroms in the Russian Empire led to the arrival of much larger numbers. By the early 1920s, about two million Jews had migrated to the United States and the Jewish population in Britain increased from about 60,000 to 300,000, changing the size and character of Anglo-Jewry. 'It converted', Schneier Levenberg, the leading intellectual of Poale Zion in Britain, later noted, 'what was by then an increasingly middle class and religiously latitudinarian community, acculturated to British habits and ideals, into one composed predominantly of proletarian, Yiddish speaking immigrants, mainly Orthodox in religion but with pockets of radical, even revolutionary, secularists'.[2] The immigrants provided the workforce mainly in the consumer goods industries such as clothing, furniture, footwear and jewellery, which from the mid-nineteenth century had begun to develop in small workshops in London and, similarly, in Manchester, Leeds, Liverpool and Glasgow.

Numerous Jewish voluntary schools and charity organisations were set up to support the new arrivals' influx into the ranks of the poor. The Board of Jewish

Guardians that had been formed in 1859, by the three main synagogues in London, extended its charitable work to provide a more co-ordinated method of poor relief in the community. Chaim Bermant, the novelist and commentator on Anglo-Jewry, describes a proliferation of community organisations in Leeds at the turn of the century which applies equally to other concentrations of Jewish immigrants. 'The benevolent societies multiplied as rapidly as the population, with one to help the aged and another the orphaned, a third for mothers during their confinement, a fourth for penniless brides and a fifth for newcomers.'[3] Much of the financial support for these philanthropic activities came from legacies and special gifts by wealthy individuals. For the small wealthy elite, philanthropy was a source of prestige but also a way to mould the community to its liking. In the midst of anti-semitic agitation over the influx of Jewish immigrants in the 1880s, this elite feared for its own place in British society. The Board of Guardians, with other voluntary organisations which dispensed charity, intervened. 'Their first reaction was to try and stop immigration; their second was to try to settle those immigrants who seemed economically viable and, if they could, to deter or return the rest.' In all, concludes Lipman, 'between 1880 and 1914 the Board sent back some 17,500 cases – probably representing altogether some 50,000 individuals'.[4] Some of the refugees were offered assistance to move on to the United States. At the same time steps were taken, wrote the journalist Lucien Wolf, 'partly by the utilisation of existing machinery and partly by the creation of new societies and agencies, to civilise and anglicise the foreign Jews who had already established themselves in the East End'.[5]

Most of the immigrants escaped this acculturation process by working and living alongside fellow immigrants. Weizmann, who was born in Russia and came to Manchester in 1904 to take up a post in the Chemistry Department of the University, wrote later: 'by far the largest part of the community was made up of Russian Jews who were, as usual, very poor, very Jewish and, to me, very attractive.'[6] They were not, however, greatly interested in Zionism and it is doubtful if the future Zionist leader and first president of Israel, despite his warms words, paid much heed to them. A leading English Zionist critical of the movement's direction charged, in 1932, that 'a man's value to Zionism was to be measured only by the size of his financial contribution'.[7] It was among the middle-class and often English-educated Jews that Zionism gained its first activists and its pre-Second World War social base.

The handful of political collaborators whom Weizmann had gathered around himself in Manchester was from the more prosperous section of the Jewish middle class, confident of their status in British society but conscious of their cultural distance from it. Charles Dreyfus was a city councillor, chairman of the local Conservative Party and one of the founders of a dyestuff manufacturing company that later formed a part of ICI; Simon Marks and Israel Sieff were successful businessmen who went on to become directors of Marks and Spencer.

Harry Sacher, another associate, was a journalist with the *Manchester Guardian*. Shortly before the Balfour Declaration's announcement Sacher confidently predicted the Zionists sweeping aside the old elite: 'the little Jewish oligarchy or plutocracy which most of the non-Jews were content to accept as the mouthpiece of Jewry has been cast down by the same hurricane which has swept away the Grand Dukes.'[8]

Weizmann, who became the President of the Zionist Federation in 1917, indicated two ways of working in Britain: one focused on 'Zionist revival of the masses in the ghettos' and the other on 'interesting certain circles of wealthy Jews in specific Palestine projects and Palestine issues'.[9] Weizmann and his colleagues opted for the second, 'cultivating the sympathies of the advantaged ... to bring Zionism into association with the most important of Anglo-Jewry's established institutions'.[10] The 'advantaged' that they attracted came mostly from the emerging entrepreneurial and professional classes, the *nouveaux riches*.[11] They were mostly the offspring of economically successful immigrants, who went on to university to become lawyers and doctors or combined the business acumen learnt from their parents with knowledge of the society in which they had grown up. Although numerically small before the Second World War their economic power and status in mainstream British society fuelled their ambition to wrest the leadership of Jewish communal affairs from the traditional leadership, drawn from the few wealthy families who headed the main Anglo-Jewish institutions and represented the community in official circles. For these early Zionist activists, Jewish nationalism provided, comments Stuart Cohen, both a doctrine and the justification for building the EZF as an institutional base that could rival the Anglo-Jewish Establishment. 'Hence they could regard their roles in the EZF as a convenient, and perfectly justifiable means of reconciling their personal ambitions (which were unabashedly parochial) with their Jewish national conscience.'[12]

Leslie Lever, Sidney Hamburger, Michael Fidler were contemporaries who had several of the sociological characteristics common to this group. Bill Williams has written insightful biographies on both Hamburger and Fidler, tracing their lives against the background of the sociological transformation of Anglo-Jewry.[13] Lever and Hamburger were born in Britain to immigrant parents, Lever becoming a successful lawyer and Hamburger a wholesaler in domestic electrical appliances. Both became active in communal affairs, in the Manchester Labour Party and in local government, their ascent in the three hierarchies being mutually reinforcing. Lever became a city councillor in 1932, eventually an alderman and then, in 1950, a member of parliament. At various times, he was also president of the Representative Council of Manchester and Salford Jews, chairperson of Manchester Poale Zion and vice-president of the Zionist Central Council.[14] Sidney Hamburger was elected in 1941 to the executive of the Association of Young Zionist Societies and, in the following year, to Manchester's Jewish Representative Council. In 1946 he was elected as a Labour Party city councillor and held a number of important positions in the council's post-war reconstruction of Salford, becoming the mayor in 1968.

Michael Fidler developed different political loyalties but he similarly combined prominence in Manchester's Jewish communal life with a career in local and national politics. In 1932, Fidler became a manager in his father's waterproof garments factory and, in 1943, a secretary to the employers' federation of that industry. He was, by the end of the war, also on the executive of the Representative Council of Manchester and Salford Jews and a member of the Board of Jewish Deputies. Although Fidler was sympathetic to Israel's establishment, as chair and founding member of the Federation of Jewish Youth Societies (FJYS), he 'resisted affiliation to the English Zionist Federation out of fear that the cultural activity of the FJYS would be submerged by Zionist zealotry'.[15] The subsequent evolution of Fidler's politics broadly illustrates the key changes in the ideological orientation of the Anglo-Jewish middle class. In 1945 he left the Liberal Party to become a right-leaning independent councillor for Prestwich, an area of post-war Jewish middle-class settlement. In the mid-1960s he joined the Conservative Party and was elected to Parliament in 1970 for Bury and Radcliffe. He also rose in the communal hierarchy. Soon after the 1967 Arab-Israeli War, Fidler was elected president of the Board of Deputies, the principal representative body of Anglo-Jewry, against a candidate who was more closely identified with the 'Zionist caucus' on the Board. Yet as his biographer explains: 'He found himself, very probably willingly, riding the crest of a Zionist wave, as intent as anyone in the "Zionist caucus" to align the British state behind Israeli aspirations.'[16] In 1974, Fidler founded the Conservative Friends of Israel.[17] This at a time when support for Zionism in the British labour movement began to ebb.

In the inter-war years, many Jews left the working-class areas of the larger cities for the suburbs. Most of those who moved were small workshop owners, managers, traders or clerks. In the suburbs, they developed a social network distinct from the radical politics and Yiddish culture associated with the first generation immigrants. Newly formed synagogues were often the first landmark and they reflected social as well as religious aspirations. Hamburger attributed the dwindling membership of his synagogue in a Salford suburb to it 'having ceased to be a House of Prayer and become, instead, a reflection of the financial status of our heads of business houses'.[18] The Jewish middle class was both less religious and more status conscious than the first generation of immigrants. Williams has highlighted the role of the provincial Jewish Literary Societies among the 'ambitious and socially aspiring' youth.[19] From their more senior members, there were perennial complaints on the lines that the societies were 'sailing under false colours, because they are in reality social and dance clubs'.[20] The Maccabi Association, emphasising the importance of physical education, played a similar social function. It, too, tended to develop its branches in more prosperous Jewish neighbourhoods. Their 'low-brow' social events, as some in the community saw them, were building cohesion among suburban Jewry, constituting the cultural milieu in which the new middle class was shaped and from which Zionists recruited into their own societies.

The EZF had 234 affiliated bodies in the early 1920s, which included some synagogues and friendly societies as well as youth and women's organisations. There were also Zionist groups which did not affiliate. Individual membership of the Federation required the payment of the *shekel*, a small annual fee which entitled members to vote for delegates to the World Zionist Congress. The *shekel* was 'not only a symbol of adherence to the Zionist movement', explained the *Zionist Review*, the Federation's main publication, 'but also forms its principal source of income'.[21] In 1929, on the occasion of the organisation's thirtieth anniversary, it claimed 30,000 members. Later reports gave a far lower membership figure by excluding affiliated organisations.[22]

The largest of the affiliated bodies was the Federation of Women Zionists (FWZ), the umbrella organisation for groups in various parts of the country. In 1939, 40 per cent of Jewish women were said to have belonged to a Zionist society in Edinburgh, 25 per cent in Liverpool and 24 per cent in Newcastle. In Manchester and London, where there were more active and longer established male-dominated Zionist organisations, women tended to be marginalised: the percentage of organised women was less than 1 per cent in Manchester and 13.4 per cent in London.[23] The FWZ's recruits reached 6000 by 1944. A memorandum submitted to its executive reported that the Zionist women's societies were chiefly successful in the 'middle-sized Jewish communities' where so-called 'drawing-room meetings' played an important role. Many of the groups were conceived as extending the traditional caring role of women. The secretary of the Brighton society informed the national executive in 1926 that 'more than 50 per cent of the members were non-Zionists and interested only in the movement as Welfare work in Palestine'.[24] In the late 1930s, women's groups were called on to promote the purchase of Palestine produce to counter the economic depression in the *Yishuv*.[25] According to the Federation's assessment, the women membership was 'for the most part composed of the older age groups'.[26] Its efforts to involve younger members failed. Only a year after *Zionist Review* had claimed that the youth movement of the FWZ 'continues to flourish particularly in the provinces',[27] it was wound up, after the executive concluded that it had 'proved itself to have fulfilled no real need amongst the young women and girls'.[28]

By contrast, the setting up of Zionist societies in universities was considered a success by the EZF. Although their membership was small, 'some of the second generation of native Zionist leaders first attained prominence at the university societies'.[29] The EZF's activists, given their own class background, found themselves more at ease with the Jewish middle class, as Levenberg would disparagingly note, but it was also the stratum that they found to be responsive. Jewish workers were generally unconvinced of Jewish nationalism's relevance. 'Zionism offers nothing to the Jewish workers who intend to remain in this country', exclaimed Israel Dublansky, an official of the Waterproof Garment Workers' Union.[30] In most industries where Jews were a significant part of the workforce the firms were largely Jewish owned. In the rubber-proofing sector, which was based in Manchester, it was estimated that in the mid-1930s, 90 per cent of the firms and 40 per cent of the 8000 workforce were Jewish. The patronage of Jewish employers through communal bodies encouraged ethnic loyalty among the employees but this was periodically disrupted by workers' discontent. The strikes in the rubber-proofing sector in 1934, 1937 and 1945 were supported by Jews and non-Jews. The question that concerned Jewish workers, Dublansky argued, was 'what measures and policy should they support which will improve their immediate needs and hold out prospects for their future?'[31]

Zionists repeatedly expressed frustration at Jewish workers' indifference to their cause. At the Manchester Zionist conference in 1938, a delegate deplored 'the apathy of Jewish workingmen to Jewish affairs and the upbuilding of Palestine'.[32] Reflecting on this period, Levenberg complained that the people 'who were connected to the Labour Movement in the "old home" are still thinking in terms of Bundism, Anarchism, etc. ... They have no time or no desire to "check up" on what has happened since they left Russia or Poland'.[33] Culturally, they were still linked to the *shtetl* (Jewish village, or small community in Eastern Europe). Harold Rosen growing up in the inter-war years in East London recalled that 'Yiddish was the language you lived in'. The father of one of his friends advised: 'Forget Hebrew, it's for the Zionists. Yiddish is the language of the Jewish proletariat.'[34]

From 1933 until the war, when fascism was in the ascendance in Europe, left-wing politics exercised a stronger pull on the Jewish working class than Zionism. Even *shekel* holding and membership of the Federation did not necessarily mean active involvement in a Zionist organisation, though fluctuations in membership figures are nonetheless indicative of ideological shifts. Rubinstein, in an analysis of international trends in the Zionist movement's membership figures, points out that in the face of rising anti-semitism across Europe in the 1930s, support for Zionism had remained weak. In Poland, it had the backing of about 25–30 per cent of the Jewish community, less than for the Bund, the Jewish socialist organisation, which held the view that Jewish workers should struggle for economic improvements and socialism alongside non-Jewish workers. In the mid-1930s of the Jewish communities in Hungary and Romania 1.3 per cent and 2.6 per cent, respectively, were *shekel* holders. 'Until just before the outbreak of the Second World War although support for Zionism did indeed rise, it simply failed to capture the support of more than a minority of Jews anywhere.'[35]

In Britain, in this period, the left's anti-fascist mobilisation had a particularly strong appeal among Jewish working-class youth. In Manchester, the Young Communist League's Cheetham branch, with a membership of 200 and one of the largest in the country, was mainly Jewish.[36] An activist in the Zionist movement urged the stepping up of propaganda work for the recruitment of pioneers for Palestine, to 'attract young Jews who at present put all their efforts into left-wing politics'.[37] It was, however, not only left-wing politics that was limiting the influence of Zionism. Anglo-Jewry's traditional elite, the so-called 'Cousinhood' or 'Grand Dukes' who wanted the Jewish population to retain its distinct religious identity while adopting British social norms, were not the spent force that Sacher had claimed. To them Zionism was as much an anathema as left-wing ideologies. They patronised the Jewish Lads' Brigade and a variety of local youth clubs, for which the Association of Jewish Youth acted as the parent organisation and whose leadership emphasised that the clubs were 'British'.[38] Basil Henriques, from a wealthy banking family and educated at Harrow and Oxford was, for several decades, a prominent figure in the Association. In 1915 he had set up the Oxford and Bethnal Green Boys' Club, modelled on Baden Powell's boys scouts, with the aim of spreading the public school ethos of 'sportsmanship and good citizenship' to the Jewish lower orders. Henriques' wife worked along parallel lines in the National Organisation of Girls Clubs, which were inspired by the idea that in the Jewish community the middle-class woman should act as the role model: 'sharing the refinements of culture and knowledge which have been absent through no fault of their own, from the education of her less fortunately placed sisters.'[39]

In response to the activities of Oswald Mosley's BUF, community workers at two East End Jewish youth clubs took the initiative to make contact with non-Jewish clubs. In 1936, the Cambridge and Bethnal Green Jewish Boys' Club opened its doors to non-Jews. A historian of Jewish youth organisations remarks that the 'Jewish community by and large was opposed to the idea', but he apparently has in mind the community leaders because he revealingly adds, 'although no objections were received when parents were notified of the plan'.[40] By 1938, the club had 320 Jewish and 80 non-Jewish members and held both Jewish and Christian services. The *Jewish Chronicle* commented that the 'joint club seems to be working out very well'.[41] The Oxford and St. George's Old Boys' Club, with which Henriques was associated, followed suit and though it apparently pleased neither the Orthodox (Henriques identified with Liberal Judaism) nor the Zionists, the non-sectarian initiative appears to have been in tune with the political mood in the East End.

Poale Zion was acutely conscious of the gulf between Zionism and the Jewish working class. Although the only Labour Zionist organisation in Britain, its following was small. It gave the size of its membership for the 1930s as 450–500; increasing to 1,500 during the war and reaching a peak, in 1948, at 2,200.[42] These figures do not include however the organisation's women and youth wings which would bring the total peak membership to about 5000. Poale Zion claimed support from some of the Jewish trade unions in a few light industries such as the bakeries, shoe-making, mantle and cigarette manufacture,[43] but their support seems to have come from the union leaders rather than from the membership. There were also sympathisers among the Workers' Circle branches, a network of friendly societies formed in 1912 by refugees from the failed 1905 Russian revolution which combined providing benefits in sickness and death with political discussion and education. Its seventeen branches, largely autonomous from each other, had a combined membership in the inter-war years of around 3000, but declined somewhat with the approach of war when some of its members entered the armed services.[44]

Poale Zion activists viewed themselves as the vanguard of the wider Zionist movement in Britain. Levenberg's impatience with what he considered to be the EZF's lack of ideological clarity was fairly characteristic in this respect. He alleged that 'the policy of General Zionists was to avoid problems, to make everything smooth'.[45] The problem, he thought, could be traced to Herzl's first collaborators in England, who had been infected from its inception by pragmatism: 'a casual attitude to matters of Zionist principle; the refusal to think hard; the disinclination to foster learning and ideological inquiry.'[46] Levenberg's yardstick was the intellectual climate in Eastern European Jewish circles in the 1920s and 1930s and, especially, the ideological conflict between Marxism and Zionism, which had defined his outlook and from which he believed Poale Zion's doctrine had emerged as a superior synthesis.

Levenberg had been a journalist for a Polish Zionist newspaper before finding employment with the Jewish Agency in London in 1936. On his death in 1997, at the age of 90, the *Jewish Chronicle* recalled a 'deeply private, even secretive person', who had 'never fully integrated into Anglo-Jewish society'.[47] His distance from the mainstream Jewish community was that of an intellectual and Zionist activist. During his long life he held several official posts in the Zionist movement. Whatever post he took up, nurturing the relationship between Zionism and the British labour movement was Levenberg's lifelong preoccupation and he painstakingly chronicled that relationship to publicise every Labour Party and trade union declaration favourable to the Zionist cause.[48] He held rigidly to the Labour Zionist mantras and many of his speeches and articles cover the same themes, prominent among which was the lamenting of Anglo-Jewry's lack of commitment and idealism. A writer on Jewish community life described Levenberg as 'a man who commands great respect but who gives very boring speeches',[49] yet he was often an acute observer of the Jewish community.

Among the voluminous papers he has left behind mostly in the form of drafts and briefing papers for Zionist publications and organisations there are only a few fragments on his youth. He was born in Latvia into a middle-class family that had been forced to resettle in Kursk outside the Pale of Settlement because of the Tsarist regime's drive to reduce Riga's Jewish population. The Levenberg family moved to the suburbs, some distance from the small impoverished Jewish quarter, probably to suit his father's trade. Latvia came under Soviet rule between 1917 and 1924 but this appears to have had little impact on

Levenberg. He felt isolated both at school, where he was the only Jewish pupil, and in his neighbourhood. Ethnicity and class set his family apart and his recollections indicate no sympathy for the surrounding community. He remembered them as 'people of peasant stock, ignorant, bigoted and clearly displaying anti-Jewish prejudice'.[50] When he went to study law at the University in Riga, he came into contact with a vibrant political culture among the city's 35,000 Jewish population. He joined the Labour Zionist movement. The fascist takeover in Latvia, in 1934, caused Levenberg to flee to Poland where he worked for a Yiddish language, Poale Zion newspaper. It was on his return from an assignment in Palestine that he stopped off in England and was taken on by the research department of the Jewish Agency. London had already become, he observed, 'the centre of Zionist politics and important manoeuvres'.[51]

By the early 1930s, Labour Zionism was the main political force in the Yishuv but the Zionist movement in Britain was in the hands of the 'general' or bourgeois Zionists. In Levenberg's view 'the then leaders of the British Zionist Federation had no understanding of the social aspirations of the working class. To them socialism was an alien creed: they refused to mix pure Zionism with ideas of proletarian revolution.' He detected 'a wall of animosity between official Zionist leaders and the poor workers – many of them newcomers to the British Isles.'[52]

The lack of Zionist activists able to connect with the working class was brought home to Levenberg by the 1938 petition campaign which he considered, nevertheless, to be 'one of the most glorious chapters' in the history of Poale Zion. The petition launched under the slogan, 'Open the Gates of Palestine for the victims of Hitler' was aimed against the British government's attempt to placate Arab opposition to Zionist settlement plans by restricting Jewish entry to Palestine.[53] 'We collected about a quarter of a million signatures but could have had a million' Levenberg recounted, 'But we were let down, the number of *chavarim* who took part in the actual work was extremely limited. The Zionist Federation was indifferent ... The Zionist movement has never understood how to speak to the "man on the street" ... Our people did not live among these masses.' He added, however, by way of mitigation that at a time when East End Jews were under threat from fascists, Poale Zion's response 'was too constructive; those Jews who were under the influence of Communism were perhaps more under the influence of the destructive side. Some of them wanted to destroy the whole world.'[54]

The difficulties that Poale Zion had in expanding its membership in the 1930s was due largely to its insistence on resolving the problem of anti-semitism by Jewish settlement in Palestine, which offered an uncertain solution in a distant land and at a time when the Anglo-Jewish working class felt threatened on its own doorstep by unemployment, deskilling in the clothing industry and Mosley's fascism. The general Zionists nevertheless won some converts to their cause partly through their single-mindedness and organisational skills and partly through their involvement in fundraising for Jewish refugees which, from 1933, increasingly dominated communal life.

The election of Selig Brodetsky, at the end of 1939, as the first Zionist president of the Board of Deputies came before the main surge of grassroots support for Zionism. It resulted largely from the EZF's improved campaigning ability at a time when the election of deputies involved little community participation and the deputies themselves felt frustrated by the leadership's lack of accountability and wanted a change at the top. The Board was ripe, therefore, for the Zionist takeover. Despite its standing as the main representative body of British Jews the elections of its deputies and leadership were not democratic. As the historian Cecil Roth observed: 'contested elections were rare; ambitious candidates for office often paid membership dues of the bodies which they were supposed to represent; pocket constituencies were easy to find.'[55] Thus the Zionist success in increasing their representation on the Board of Deputies reflected their single-mindedness in a context of disarray rather than mass support. 'There were in the East End and in the large cities numerous small synagogues,' observed Bermant, 'which still had members on paper if not at their services, and which, if they paid their minimum subscription to the Board, could nominate deputies. They were, in short, rotten boroughs. These were taken over by the Zionists and the Board was packed.' Among the incongruous representations that this produced, Bermant cites the case of the former chairman of the Zionist Federation who was elected for the Leeds Chassidic Synagogue though he was 'neither from Leeds nor a Chassid'.[56]

Brodetsky probably also benefited from the higher profile that the Zionists had acquired in this period due to the refugee crisis. The philanthropic activities in support of the refugees fleeing from Nazism gave them the opportunity to integrate their state-building project into the mainstream fundraising activity of the Jewish community. From 1933 onwards the focus of philanthropy changed from assisting Anglo-Jewry to supporting refugees, including those going to Palestine. The Zionists eased their way in, entering into an uneasy collaboration with representatives of the old elite. Poale Zion joined in. It hoped to develop Jewish working-class support for Zionism by holding collections in Jewish-owned factories, but these required the employers' co-operation and even then the amounts collected were dwarfed by the contributions of bourgeois benefactors. In 1939, collections at ninety-nine factories in Leeds over a three-month period raised £350, while a banquet at the Savoy Hotel in the same year to mark the climax of the Jewish National Fund Week raised £32,000 (equivalent, in 2011, to about £11,000 and £1 million respectively).[57]

It was in this period when Poale Zion established closer working relations with the mainstream Zionist movement over fundraising that it affiliated to the EZF. This brought to the Federation's work in Britain a more outward-looking orientation and it allowed Poale Zion, with its highly active cadres, to wield more influence than the size of its membership would suggest. A year after its affiliation, Poale Zion succeeded in having five of its six candidates elected to the EZF's various committees and the following year all ten of its candidates were elected.[58]

Zionist Review, the publication of the EZF, also assumed a sharper, more political edge from 1942 when Levenberg became its editor. It signalled Poale Zion's integration into the Zionist mainstream in Britain, which had been boosted by Brodetsky's election to the presidency of the Board of Deputies. Prior to the war, Levenberg had defined his party's relation to the Board as 'one of silent opposition'.[59] The deputies' priorities had been historically synonymous with those of the Anglo-Jewish elite: to protect Jewish religious practices and to defend Jews, at home and abroad, from anti-semitism. There were similar, nominally representative bodies in towns such as Manchester and Leeds which had sizeable Jewish populations. The communal elite generally mediated between the community and the wider society discreetly, through official channels, hoping to avoid public hostility. Its timidity in the face of BUF incitement against the Jewish community was in the spirit of its traditional mode of operating: it was disapproving of confronting fascism through popular mobilisation. Thus, as has been often highlighted, in the lead up to the 'Battle of Cable Street', in October 1936, when the Jewish People's Council (JPC) had called for halting the fascists from marching through London's East End, the president of the Board of Deputies, Neville Laski, advised the Jewish community to stay away from the mobilisation.

The Board's timorousness was not confined to the anglophile anti-Zionists. Leslie Lever, a Poale Zion member and Labour councillor, supported the Labour Party line that, out of respect for free speech, a planned fascist meeting in north Manchester should be allowed to go ahead despite a petition signed by 3,500 residents in the Cheetham area calling for it to be banned.[60] Jewish communists were the leading force both in the JPC and in the ex-Servicemen's Movement Against Fascism and Anti-Semitism but Poale Zion, along with two left-wing Zionist youth groups, joined these campaigns.[61] It was alert to the attraction of communist militancy to Jewish working-class youths and to an extent shared the frustration which some of them felt with the Anglo-Jewish elite's concern for respectability. 'In spite of their wealth and the positions they occupy in various spheres of public life,' complained Zionist Review, 'these people are terribly afraid lest one should question their loyalty. They consider Zionism as a danger to their status and are obsessed with the idea of "double loyalty".'[62] Yet Zionists participated in the Trades Advisory Council (TAC) which was similarly 'obsessed' with conforming to British social norms. The organisation launched in 1938, sought to counter anti-semitism by controlling the behaviour of the Jewish community, particularly in commerce. Thus it went quite a long way in accepting the anti-semitic slur that it was the behaviour of Jews that was causing anti-semitism. There were several Zionists active in the TAC, including its General Secretary, Maurice Orbach, a Poale Zion member, who in 1945 became a Labour

MP. The desire to abide by British values was as prevalent among Zionists as among those they deprecated for 'assimilation'. The two groups differed over Zionism but they had a shared commitment to work through the established channels of British society. And even the difference between them tended to blur with the growing importance, in communal activities, of assisting the refugees fleeing fascism.

Levenberg and other Labour Zionist leaders were critical of 'general' Zionism's lack of political clarity and the Federation's focus on fundraising, arguing that Zionism required a broader and deeper commitment than philanthropy, but their own appeal to the Anglo-Jewish working class was mainly for funds. The editor of the *Jewish Chronicle*, a sympathiser of the right-wing Revisionist Zionists, saw the irony. He pointed to Ben-Gurion lauding the achievements of Labour Zionism in Palestine, while 'we are still reminded week by week, and almost day by day, in the insistent appeals for one Palestine fund or another that the Yishuv is umbilically dependent upon finance from capitalist systems in other parts of the world'.[63] Labour Zionism's success in securing land and employment in Palestine for Jewish immigrants, required financial support from the Zionist movement's largely *petit bourgeois* rank and file and from wealthy business people around the world.[64] Support for the refugees elevated the importance of philanthropic work, enhancing its function as a source of power and status for the larger patrons.

Between 1933 and the end of 1938, of the estimated 150,000 Jews who left Germany about 42,500 emigrated to Palestine. Approximately, 11,000 sought refuge in the UK in that period and a further 4,000–5,000 went on from Britain to other countries.[65] The entry of each refugee was conditional on a British citizen or refugee organisation guaranteeing that the individual would be provided with financial support and, therefore, not be a burden on the state.

To provide refugees entering the UK with financial support, the Central British Fund for German Jewry (CBF) became the principal co-ordinating body. In March 1936, it was re-formed as the Council for German Jewry, to expand and coordinate more effectively the work of assisting the mass emigration of German Jews. The organising committee from which the council emerged was British-based, with the Zionists and non-Zionists receiving an equal number of seats on both the governing Council and the Allocation Committee.[66] There were tensions between the two political factions over the allocation of funds for refugee work. A writer in the *Zionist Review* in 1938 complained that most Zionists had donated more to the Council's appeal on behalf of Austrian Jewish refugees than to the Zionist settlement project in Galilee. 'According to Zionist belief and experience, regulated colonisation in Palestine is the only durable or radical answer to persecution in the Diaspora. In other words, the Galilee campaign is itself the most beneficial aid which can be rendered to Austrian as to other beleaguered Jews in Europe.'[67] This was part of a relentless promotion of Palestine as the most realistic and desirable destination for Jewish refugees. The German Jewish immigration into Palestine brought manpower and financial assets to the Yishuv's economy only a few years after the Zionist goal had appeared to falter. In 1925, the Yishuv's economy entered into recession and in 1926 and 1927, with unemployment increasing, more Jews were leaving than entering Palestine. Thereafter, however, Jewish immigration into Palestine increased first moderately and then, following the Nazi accession to power, quite steeply. In 1933, there was a four-fold increase with 30,000 Jewish immigrants arriving and, in 1935, that figure reached almost 60,000. British restriction on Jewish entry in response to the Arab rebellion reduced the numbers entering, by 1937, to about 10,500.[68] The Zionist focus on opening Palestine to unlimited immigration co-existed uneasily and, at times, openly collided with other schemes to assist the victims of Nazism.

In Britain, the resulting tensions affected not only the Council for German Jewry but more widely the efforts of Jewish as well non-Jewish groups to persuade the government and the public to be supportive of refugees seeking sanctuary in the UK. The formation of the Council had been prompted by the passing of the Nuremberg Laws in September 1935, which deprived German Jews of citizenship rights, forbidding them to marry or to employ non-Jews. The Council's public appeal for funds was joined by Keren Hayesod, the Zionist movement's principal fundraising organisation, in return for being guaranteed a share, equivalent to its average income in other years. The joint appeal raised nearly three-quarters of a million pounds in less than eighteen months but the political differences and personal animosities persisted in the fundraising work.[69] Weizmann, mistrustful of some of the Council's non-Zionist members and their collaborators, wrote in venomous terms of their efforts to resettle German Jews in places other than Palestine. 'Hitler is doing his utmost to destroy the Jewish community within Germany, and these Jewish bodies are continuing and completing his work, by dispersing the remnants and scattering them to the four corners of the earth.'[70] In private, Weizmann was prepared to concede that Palestine could not immediately absorb all the refugees but since the Zionists aimed to exert maximum pressure on the British to increase the numbers allowed into Palestine he did not want this publicly aired.

The compromise formulation hammered out by the founding committee of the CBF was to regard Palestine as 'the chief country to which it is possible to plan emigration on a considerable scale, *but not the only one*'.[71] For the Zionist leaders this was not sufficient. They wanted 'the plight of German Jewry as a bargaining point through which they could elicit more immigration certificates from the British government'.[72] Moreover, if the number of German Jews given entry to Palestine came out of the existing immigration quota permitted by the British, this would affect both the class and political complexion of the Jewish settlers. Weizmann was concerned that professionals were over-represented among the German immigrants. 'Soon', he wrote from Jerusalem, at the end of 1935, 'every street in town will look like Harley Street – the number of doctors is incalculable. What these poor people will do simply cannot be imagined.' He worried that such people were not nation-building material: 'How poor little Palestine is to absorb and digest all this flow of humanity, and emerge out of it all with a healthy structure, Heaven only knows.'[73] Weizmann and his colleagues did not want German Jews taking up quota places at the expense of Polish Jews, who were more likely to be workers and Zionists.[74] And yet a further source of contention with the non-Zionists was the latter's plan to set up a bank which would help German Jews wishing to emigrate, to liquidate their assets and transfer a part of the assets' value to Palestine in the form of German exports. The Zionist leadership was party to this agreement and faced criticism at the time from anti-fascists, and even from within the Zionist movement, for undermining the economic boycott of Nazi Germany. Weizmann objected to the proposed bank not out of principle but on the grounds that it would give rise to a new organisation which would promote colonisation outside the Jewish Agency's control. He warned of 'new tin gods, new salaries, new overhead charges, and another attempt towards weakening the central authority'.[75]

The Zionist advocacy of Palestine as the solution to the refugee crisis gained more vocal backing among humanitarians and the European labour movement as the number of refugees escalated. From 1933 until the end of 1938, alongside the 11,000 refugees that entered Britain, France accepted 250,000 and Holland, which only had a population of 8.5 million, also took 11,000.[76] In this period social democratic parties and their federation, the Labour and Socialist International, drew the attention of their members primarily to the 'political refugees' who were socialist and communist activists. The TUC provided financial help and legal advice to German and Austrian refugee trade unionists seeking to settle in Britain. The Socialist Party in France imposed an annual one-franc levy on each member for its 'Solidarity Fund for the Victims of Fascism'.[77] Such initiatives testified to the sympathy in the labour movements of the liberal democracies for those fleeing fascism, but while they addressed some appeals to their governments to liberalise entry conditions the refugee flight also provoked alarm in their ranks.

The first wave of refugees from Nazism had arrived in countries still deep in recession. France, the largest recipient of German refugees had, in 1935, 12.6 per cent of the working population unemployed and about half the workers had reduced hours of work. In Britain the unemployment rate fluctuated between 9 and 12 per cent until the outbreak of the war. The arrival of Jewish refugees in these conditions was exploited by the far right to gain influence through xenophobic and anti-semitic campaigns which in turn affected labour organisations. The Confédération Générale du Travail (CGT) supported some demonstrations which marched to the slogan 'France for the French'.[78] In 1938, TUC leaders sought tight control over the entry of refugees into Britain. In a submission to the government, made jointly with refugee organisations, they asked that the admission to employment of refugees 'should be permitted provided that one of the organisations supported the application and the conditions of employment were not worse than those accepted by nationals'.[79]

In this climate, no socialist party was prepared to advocate accepting unrestricted numbers of refugees. Johan Albarda, leader of the Social Democratic Party in the Dutch Parliament, remarked: 'It cannot be disputed that a Government which accorded the right of asylum on the most generous scale might create serious difficulties for its own country'; and Lansbury, as leader of the Labour Party, rejected the suggestion from one of his own MPs that Britain should allow the mass entry of Jewish refugees.[80] A resolution, in 1934, by the Socialist Committee for Workers' Palestine, signed by among others Vandervelde, Blum and Gillies, the general secretary of the British Labour Party, pointed to Palestine as the solution. Immigration controls in the US, anti-semitism and overcrowding in Eastern Europe, imposed strict limits, it said, on work and asylum opportunities for Jews fleeing their countries of origin. In these conditions, 'Palestine offers Jewish immigration possibilities which are increasing in the same proportions as the difficulties elsewhere'.[81]

At various times the possibility of the British Empire, the neutral countries and Britain taking larger numbers of Jewish refugees was mooted. Discussions on the absorption of refugees distinguished between 'individual infiltration', where the authorities of the receiving country scrutinised the acceptability of each applicant for entry, and 'mass resettlement'. Until 1938, official circles in the liberal democracies had believed that the situation could be managed through 'individual infiltration' if the exodus from Germany could be restricted to manageable limits and if the policy of confiscating refugee property were modified'.[82] The Nazis' annexation of Austria, which had a Jewish population of 180,000, proved such assumptions to be illusory but refugee policy continued to be based on 'individual infiltration'. In July 1938, a conference initiated by President Roosevelt and attended by representatives of thirty-two countries met at Evian to discuss the refugee crisis. The scale of the problem became still graver later that year. First, German Jews seeking to emigrate were subjected to further restrictions on the proportion of their property that they could take with them and, then, the Nazi takeover of the Sudeten areas of Czechoslovakia and the Kristallnacht pogroms caused still more refugees. The Zionist movement saw the ensuing public concern as an opportunity but also as a potential threat. It could not be totally dismissive of the possibilities of the allied and neutral countries opening their borders to desperate refugees but it continued to insist that the priority should be to assist them to reach Palestine. In 1938, Ben-Gurion warned with ruthless logic that if Jews in the democracies were confronted with having 'to choose between the refugees, saving Jews from concentration camps, and assisting a national museum in Palestine, mercy will have the upper hand and the whole energy of the people will be channelled into saving Jews from various countries. Zionism will be struck off the agenda … If we allow a separation between the refugee problem and the Palestine problem, we are risking the existence of Zionism'.[83]

The question of finding sanctuary for the large numbers of Jewish refugees would become a matter of public debate in Britain, first in 1938 following Kristallnacht, then in 1942, after the Western press began to publish information on the Nazi's mass extermination programme, and again after the war, from 1945 to 1947. Following Kristallnacht, public sympathy for Jews increased and several public figures and pro-refugee groups demanded a more open admission policy from the government. Two pro-refugee advocates arguing in 1939 for such an approach 'alike on moral and economic grounds' observed: 'The change in public opinion effected by the November pogroms was deep and widespread; it even served to call a halt among some of those who had shewn anti-semitic tendencies.'[84] This offered an opening to try to persuade the British public of the need substantially to increase the numbers of refugees that should be allowed into Britain.

Sir John Hope Simpson, who had chaired the 1930 Royal Commission Report on Palestine that was critical of Zionist settlement in this period, backed the humanitarian lobby's campaign to liberalise the entry of Jewish refugees to Britain, France and some of the neutral countries. He pointed out that if these countries agreed to take 'a quarter of the potential refugees from Germany at once, and accommodate them, if necessary in camps, until they could be dispersed to countries of ultimate settlement, a substantial step would have been taken towards the solution of the problem'.[85] The Liberal Party's executive, on a visit to the Prime Minister, had argued that 'the British Government would have widespread popular support in offering asylum to large numbers of refugees from the Nazi regime'.[86] Wedgwood, an ardent supporter of the Zionist cause, thought Britain or Palestine could accommodate the refugees. But for the Zionist movement increasing the flow of refugees to Britain was of little interest. Thus, in December 1938, after the British government had ruled out Palestine taking 10,000 Jewish children from Germany, Weizmann rejected Malcolm MacDonald's offer that Britain would take them.[87]

At the end of 1938, *Zionist Review*, too, acknowledged the surge of public sympathy for the refugees: 'There has been a welcome attempt on the part of the British press and Government to canalise the sympathy which the tragic events in Germany have evoked on the part of the British people. That pity, we know, was nation-wide.'[88] The EZF launched a petition campaign calling on the government 'to open the gates of Palestine'. 'Letters were sent out', Levenberg later recounted, 'to all Jewish organisations, Trade Unions, Labour Party branches, to the Liberals and Conservatives'. The campaign's headquarters in Whitechapel displayed pictures depicting the persecution of Jews in Germany.[89] 'There are two special features', commented *Zionist Review*, 'which render the Petition movement particularly valuable at the present time. It is, in the first place, an instrument of Zionist education. The Petition movement also canalises the general sympathy which is now being expressed on behalf of Jewry into a constructive channel; it is having the effect of keeping Palestine boldly in the forefront of a solution to the Jewish problem'.[90] The petition, which was submitted to the government with 210,000 signatures, had succeeded to generate, the *Jewish Chronicle* reported, 'a considerable volume of propaganda activity and to enlist the support of trade unions, the Liberal Party organisations and the Co-operative movement'.[91]

There was strong support from the Labour Party for Palestine being opened up for the refugees. Noel-Baker argued that in the light of the successful resettlement, in the decade following the First World War, of 1.5 million refugees from Turkey in such relatively poor countries as Greece and Bulgaria, the Jewish refugees could be accommodated in Palestine or other parts of the Empire. He did not propose Britain.[92] A few days later, in a Parliamentary debate, Morrison suggested that in the face of international pressure to resolve the refugee problem the government should opt for letting refugees into Palestine rather than Britain: 'I do not underestimate the fact that there are limitations as to how far that can be permitted in this country without serious political effects in certain parts'.[93] The party leadership probably felt comfortable with this position. It allowed Labour to suggest a solution without causing alarm in the labour movement over Jewish refugees' potential impact on the labour market and the anti-semitism which that might provoke.

The left of the labour movement did not advocate an alternative policy. The British Communist Party only had a membership of around 15,500 in 1938,[94] but its influence in the trade unions extended beyond its own members. In this period, the party's stated aim was the broadest unity on the left and of the working class, an objective which tempered its internationalism on the refugee issue. The *Daily Worker*, addressing itself to the intergovernmental committee formed by the Evian conference, asked for frontiers to be opened for 'genuine political refugees'.[95] The same term was employed by social democratic parties and implied a narrower category than the Jewish refugees. In the wake of Kristallnacht, Page Arnot, one of the Communist Party's intellectuals, declared: 'It is no use shifting the responsibility by hoping and asking that the Soviet Union should open its frontiers. That is for them to decide; and we cannot shirk our duties in this way.' But he promptly proposed another way of shirking them by suggesting that the government in addition to providing accommodation for refugees in Britain should be 'taking up the question with the Dominion Governments of the Empire'.[96] Palestine could not provide the solution because Jewish immigration would 'greatly increase unemployment and intensify Arab-Jewish antagonism'.[97] As far as Britain's contribution was concerned, the Communist Party opted for the government's 'individual infiltration' response, rather than mass entry. 'A demand has got to be made', declared the *Daily Worker*, 'to speed up the work of the Home Office and the Foreign Office with regard to the admission of refugees'.[98] It was hardly a clarion call for international solidarity. Still more striking is how little weight the party accorded to the situation of Jewish refugees in its agitation work. Even in its campaign against the BUF, the Communist Party did not link the opposition to fascism and anti-semitism to a demand to lift the restriction on the number of refugees allowed into Britain.

The leaders of the Jewish community were also reticent about pressing for Britain to relax its entry conditions. Jewish organisations collaborated with the Home Office in implementing the policy of 'individual infiltration' and, accordingly, the Council for German Jewry acted as the financial guarantor for the refugees it had approved. A deputation from the Council consisting of three Zionists, including Weizmann, and three non-Zionists, met the prime minister a few days after Kristallnacht to explore what measures could be taken to assist German Jews. The minutes of the meeting recorded: 'the Council recognised the difficulties of the Government and they would not think of suggesting that the doors should be widely thrown open.'[99] It was a conclusion that suited the Zionists and it also met the non-Zionists' concern that a large increase in the number of refugees entering Britain might arouse anti-semitism. For those who entered, Bolchover observes, the Anglo-Jewish community went to great lengths to disperse around the country and 'advised them to keep a low profile, so as to avoid the impression of a substantial and menacing Jewish body within England'.[100]

In the year leading up to the war, the sympathy generated by the events of 1938 for the Jewish victims of Nazism was fragile and did not give rise to a coalition of forces in favour of the mass immigration of Jews into Britain. Over the course of 1938, in response to pressure from humanitarians and public opinion, the government did, however, relax its entry controls. It also speeded up the admission procedures; it admitted nearly 10,000 unaccompanied children from Germany and took over the funding of refugee settlement and re-emigration from voluntary organisations. Entry to the UK was authorised for up to about 50,000 refugees between May 1938 and the end of January 1939. Louise London estimates that even then only 'perhaps one applicant in ten succeeded in gaining entry'.[101] The political groups which might have influenced the government to allow the entry of a much larger number allied themselves with the policy of 'individual infiltration'. This was the stance, each for its own reasons, of most of the humanitarian lobby, the Labour Party, the trade union movement, the Communist Party and of the Zionist and non-Zionist organisations in the Jewish community. The only other political solution on which, with the exception of the communists, they were in agreement was that the refugees be allowed to go to Palestine. They paid little heed to the Arab viewpoint and were either indifferent to the refugees' impact on Palestine or blithely assumed it would be beneficial. Eleanor Rathbone, an independent MP and a leading women's rights campaigner, who was moved by the persecution of Jews to become one of the leading humanitarian advocates for the refugees exclaimed: 'Would it matter to the progress of civilisation if all the Arabs were drowned in the Mediterranean?'[102]

And Angell and Buxton, prominent humanitarians, thought that it was not unreasonable for the indigenous people to make way for a persecuted people whom they considered to belong to European civilisation. 'Vast spaces outside Palestine', they wrote, 'are open to them for development, or for their wanderings.'[103]

The widespread feeling of revulsion in Britain over Kristallnacht had opened a window of opportunity for a few months for left-wing and humanitarian groups to move public opinion in a direction that might have induced government action in favour of the mass resettlement of Jews in Britain, if only on a temporary basis as Hope Simpson had suggested. But this did not translate into sufficient political pressure and Kristallnacht and the accompanying sympathy for the plight of European Jewry faded quickly in public consciousness, as Kushner has described. He puts it down to a combination of factors: the intrusion of other events, repression by the collective consciousness of an event 'that ran counter to the liberal assumption that in post-emancipatory society anti-semitism was the fault of the Jews' and 'the abandonment of the issue as matter of public concern by democratic governments'. There were several contradictory as well as overlapping ideological responses at work. By 'early 1939 a detailed investigation found the "very ordinary" response that '"the Jews really brought it all on themselves"'.[104] According to a survey by the British Institute of Public Opinion, also in this period, which was prior to the publication of the government's White Paper announcing its intention to restrict immigration to Palestine, 'sixty percent said that they favoured the continuation of Jewish immigration to Palestine; twenty-six percent expressed no opinion; only fourteen percent gave negative replies'.[105] And, in July that year, an opinion poll showed that only 26 per cent 'were totally opposed to the entry of refugees' into Britain.[106] Opinions were fluid and contradictory on how to resolve the Jewish refugee crisis but public support, in 1939, was swaying towards the policies of allowing a limited number of refugees into Britain and opening Palestine to further Jewish immigration. These views broadly reflected the responses advocated by the principal political protagonists over the refugee issue. The Zionist option prevailed because the political resolve to find sanctuary, on the scale required, in Britain and in the other liberal democracies was lacking.

It was not until 1942 that the Nazi's treatment of Jews again came to command public attention in Britain. It took 'constant repetition of the Jewish plight, prominent reporting and the reinforcement of an official announcement to make any lasting impression. This occurred only once in the war, on either side of the Atlantic – at the end of 1942.'[107] Among pro-refugee groups and the Jewish community there was already despondency. In February, the *Struma*, a ship carrying Romanian Jews to Palestine, sank after the British High Commissioner made clear that the passengers would be denied entry to Palestine. When the ship had docked in Istanbul, the Turkish authorities had ordered it to be towed out of the harbour, after which it sank with 759 passengers, including 150 children.[108] The dire situation of European Jewry became still more evident from the end of

June 1942 when British newspapers began disseminating reports on the Nazi's programme to exterminate the Jewish population of Poland. Official confirmation of it came in December, in the form of a statement to Parliament by Anthony Eden, the foreign secretary.

On the day of Eden's speech, Rathbone attacked government policy: 'Few people realise the rigidity of the regulations by which the Home Secretary now controls the entry of refugees to this country and the corresponding regulations affecting the colonies.'[109] There were appeals to come to the aid of Jewish refugees by the Archbishop and prominent humanitarians. Sir Neill Malcolm, former League of Nations High Commissioner, wrote in *The Times*: 'Is it really true that in the whole world no room can be found for them?'[110] 'Seldom, if ever,' wrote Rathbone, 'have the emotions of British men and women irrespective of class or party, been more deeply stirred by a tragedy which did not affect them personally'. She pointed to a Gallup Poll which had asked 2,450 adults in Britain: 'Do you think that the British government should or should not help any Jews who can get away?' Seventy-eight per cent replied 'Yes'. 'Over half of those so replying wanted admission to be extended to "as many as can come"'.[111]

By this stage the numbers of Jews able to escape from Nazi-occupied Europe was down to a trickle but there were still hopes that the Germans might strike a deal to allow some Jews to emigrate. Zionist leaders, therefore, wanted to ensure that in any campaign to rescue Jews Palestine would figure as the principal destination. Their aim, as in 1938–1939, with the petition campaign, was to canalise public sympathy in the direction of demanding unrestricted or, at the very least, increased Jewish immigration into Palestine. When Rabbi Solomon Schonfeld, a leading figure in the ultra-Orthodox community in Britain tried to have a motion put in Parliament, in early 1943, calling on the government 'to find temporary refuge in its own territories or in territories under its control', it was scotched by the Zionists. They objected to the motion because it did not specifically refer to Palestine and because they did not want a political initiative to succeed which bypassed the Board of Deputies at a time when it was under Zionist leadership.[112] Such shenanigans were of marginal influence however; the Zionist position was, in any case, gaining support in this period among Anglo-Jewry. They were able to draw strength from and reinforce a sense of abandonment among Jews, resulting mainly from the Allies' inability to halt the Nazi genocide and from the fact that, notwithstanding the fight against Nazism and condemnation of its racism, the anti-fascist governments appeared ineffectual in the face of the catastrophe engulfing European Jewry.

The sense of desperation in the Jewish community was expressed by *Zionist Review*: 'Hundreds of meetings have taken place in all parts of the country. The Churches, the Labour Movement, the Liberal Party, Women's organisations, Co-operative Guilds and various other bodies have all raised their voices on behalf of Jewry threatened with extermination ... What has been done as a result of all these representations? Very little!'[113] A meeting of the Board of Deputies was reported to have deprecated 'the reluctance of the British Government and other Governments of the United Nations to take action for rescuing Jews threatened with extermination'. Brodetsky complained not only of the restrictions on entry to Palestine but that 'No change was made in the regulations governing the admission of refugees to this country'.[114] Although the liberalisation of entry into Britain had not been an important demand for the Zionists, it served their purpose to emphasise the lack of progress in finding other avenues of escape, to underline that Palestine alone offered refuge provided that Britain allowed it. In response to pro-refugee campaigning groups and public concern on the two sides of the Atlantic, the US and British governments convened a conference on the island of Bermuda in March 1943 to discuss what measures could be taken with respect to refugees. The allies continued to rule out negotiating a release of Jews from Nazi control through an agreement with Hitler.[115] The number of escapees to neutral Spain, Switzerland and Sweden may have still increased if Britain and the US had encouraged these countries to adopt a more open-door policy with the promise that the refugees would be resettled elsewhere after the war, but such a commitment was not made.[116] The *Jewish Chronicle* noted that the practical outcome of Bermuda was 'depressingly small' and added: 'Once more Jewish Palestine shines in the enveloping darkness as the one sure haven, the only one, from which distraught and broken Jewry will not be turned back.'[117] A leading Zionist remarked more bluntly: 'The Bermuda Conference has proved conclusively that there was no other place for Jews but Palestine'.[118]

The National Jewish Committee (NJC) of the Communist Party of Great Britain (CPGB) felt particularly vexed in this period by the increasing sympathy among Jews for the Zionist demands. The Committee had been set up to rally the Jewish community behind the communist movement's demand that the Western Allies come to the aid of the Soviet Union by opening a second front. The NJC took on the task of countering the Zionist focus on Palestine which was alleged by communists to be holding back Jews from the fight against fascism. To reveal the Zionists' 'diversionist' politics, the NJC analysed the political content of the articles carried by *Zionist Review* between January and July 1943. During 'the most critical months of the war', it complained:

> Jewish war effort in this country – no mention. The question of the Second Front – no mention. The question of mobilising Jewish organisations for the war – no mention. Jews in the USSR and help for the Soviet Union – paltry two and half pages. Rescue of Jews – fourteen pages. Fight of the Jews in Warsaw ghetto – three pages. Fight against Anti-Semitism occupies two pages! War effort of the Jews in Palestine – three pages ... 157 pages are devoted to the question of Palestine, Zionism, Zionist Education ... A fine war time record!'[119]

The NJC was however forced to acknowledge that Zionism was gaining ground among Jews. 'Zionist ideas have gripped the imagination', it stated in late 1943.[120] The Jewish community was coming round to accepting the Zionist argument in favour of Palestine as its hopes of any other solution to save European Jewry faded. The sense of vulnerability was probably accentuated by the intensification of domestic anti-semitism from mid-1943 and by the dispersal of Jewish working-class communities, which accelerated during the war and was eroding their political life and sense of solidarity. Those who moved to the suburbs tended to be more receptive to appeals invoking ethnic identity.

Zionist leaders also detected the shift in attitudes in the Jewish community. At the instigation of the WZO, the EZF launched a membership drive at its annual conference in January 1943. In each district membership committees were to be assisted by full-time organisers, with the centre giving financial support from three to six months. The aim was 'that each member shall be pledged to bring in at least ten new members in the course of a month' and that the overall membership be increased to 50,000.[121] That figure was not reached but most of the Federation's wartime membership growth took place in 1943, a year for which it reported an increase from 5,500 to 20,000. By the beginning of 1946, it was to increase to 31,000, about 10 per cent of the adult Jewish population.[122]

There was no serious challenge to the Zionist message that Palestine should accommodate most of the European Jews seeking a safe haven. The government disputed the numbers that Palestine could take but not the idea that it be the main refuge. A few humanitarians continued to call for a relaxation of Britain's entry conditions but just as no political party, so no section of Anglo-Jewry mounted a campaign for it. In late 1943, Alfred Hyamson, who by dint of being steeped in English patriotism had a slightly jaundiced view of Zionism, observed that in the Jewish community when it came to formulating policy on the refugees, 'the Zionists form the only party and monopolize practically all the platforms. Consequently, whether the Zionist claim is justified or not, there seems to be no alternative for anyone who wishes to give practical assistance'.[123] For many Jews, support for Zionism was born out of resignation rather than enthusiasm. They regarded Palestine, notwithstanding the British-imposed quota on immigration, as still the most likely country to accommodate the refugees. The sentiment that it was a place of refuge *faute de mieux*, did not please Zionist activists. At the EZF's Annual Conference in 1944, a delegate complained that 'the Zionist consciousness of the new members was not on a very high level'.[124] Similarly, a report to the executive of the FWZ on its affiliated societies in twenty-one towns observed that while the membership had grown considerably there was not 'very great depth in the movement', which it attributed 'to the tendency to overstress the child rescue approach, making the issue a charitable one'.[125]

Wartime conditions impeded political activities and while Zionists found the Jewish community to be receptive to their message that Palestine be opened to the refugees, translating that into organisational gains, through increased membership and activism, met a number of obstacles. In early 1942, the Women's Zionist Society of north Manchester reported a decline in activity as a result of 80 per cent of the members having been evacuated.[126] The German air raids in 1940 and 1941 also disrupted Jewish community life in other cities and particularly in East London. Already prior to the war Zionist societies had found organising meetings and groups in the capital, where two-thirds of Britain's Jewish population lived, more difficult than in the smaller provincial centres, though this was not due just to air raids. By far 'the greatest difficulty', *Zionist Review* reported shortly before the war, 'has been encountered in the wealthiest districts in London ... Residents in these districts rarely go to the ordinary propaganda meetings and have no interest in organisations as such.' It pointed to these residents' contribution to the JNF, for which a blue collection box was distributed to households, as the one redeeming feature. Yet, a few months later a leading Zionist complained that 'in London only 20 per cent of the Jewish population had J.N.F. boxes'.[127] The influx of German and Austrian refugees probably added little to the strength of Zionist organisations.

The 50,000–80,000 Jewish immigrants who fled fascism from Germany and Central Europe to Britain from the mid-1930s were predominantly middle class. Many found employment but they did not easily integrate into Anglo-Jewish life.[128] Bermant has commented that 'though their contribution to British life as a whole has been out of all proportion to their number, their impact on the Jewish community, when one recalls that they came to form some 10 per cent of it, has been less marked'.[129] Unlike the Eastern European immigrants, their social life revolved more around the café than the synagogue. To the Zionists, the majority of the German and Austrian Jewish refugees were 'assimilated' and could not be regarded 'a nationally conscious element'.[130] Although such a characterisation tended to imply that, by contrast, the Jewish working class, which was mostly of Eastern European origin and more steeped in cultural and religious traditions, was nationalist, in fact, support among it for Zionism had remained patchy and restrained throughout the war.

Levenberg observed that Jewish workers 'did not consider Palestine as a land for immigration ... They are fully occupied with the daily struggle for life.'[131] He was troubled by Zionism's failure to rally the Jewish population behind its political demands, which was all the more striking in this period when much of European Jewry's survival was in doubt. He began a talk in 1941 by remarking, 'It is often asked why is Zionism not a mass movement here?'[132] and during his long life, it was a question to which he repeatedly returned. He was inclined to see it as resulting from the Jewish community's acculturation in British society. It had adopted a 'practical and pragmatic' approach: 'the belief in fair play; the belief in moving slowly but surely towards the target.'[133] Even political parties and trade unions in Britain, he pointed out, were not mass movements. 'The trade unions are a tremendous political force, they have very efficient machinery but the participation of the rank and file is extremely limited.'[134] If this was clutching at straws, Levenberg could nevertheless justifiably claim that Poale Zion's work in the more limited sphere of the Zionist Federation and in the Labour Party had been successful.[135]

Several delegates at the 1943 annual conference of the Zionist Federation were reported as having noted that 'there was no Zionist movement in the East End'.[136] But only a small minority in the Jewish working class influenced by communist ideas opposed Zionism and once the scale of the Nazi extermination became known and the survivors were reported to be languishing in the Displaced Persons' camps, the majority appears to have come round to be broadly sympathetic to Zionism. This is the picture that emerges from a survey carried out in 1947–1948. Of the 40,000 questionnaires sent out to Jewish households only 3,346 responses were received and, among these, men and the 41–50 years age group were over-represented. Although it was not a rigorously conducted survey, it nonetheless gives a rough indication of the trends in the community. 872 described themselves as non-Zionists and only 3 as anti-Zionists, while 492 classed themselves political Zionists and a further 1,419 as non-political Zionists, which was understood to mean belonging to Zionist societies not linked to any of the political parties in the *Yishuv*. A further indication of strong Zionist sentiment was that, among the respondents, *Zionist Review* had 515 readers, exceeded only by the *Jewish Chronicle*.[137]

The Zionist case also appears to have won sympathy right across British society. An opinion poll in March 1939 had indicated 60 per cent to be in favour of continued Jewish settlement in Palestine and only 14 per cent to be opposed to it.[138] There were no surveys on the subject in wartime but some contemporary observers detected increased support for Zionism in humanitarian and liberal-minded circles. A survey carried out by the FWZ in early 1943 claimed that 'there was growing sympathy among more intelligent and progressive peoples with the idea of a Jewish National Home in Palestine', adding that it was 'a strange paradox, that side by side with increasing anti-Semitism in this country, there was an increasing understanding of the Jewish problem'.[139] Orwell, too, identified contradictory public responses: 'It so happens that the war has encouraged the growth of anti-Semitism and even, in the eyes of many ordinary people, given some justification for it'. He pointed to Jewish traders being blamed for wartime commodity shortages in the clothing and food sectors, where Jewish traders were concentrated, and to the feelings of resentment that Jews were the only people certain to benefit from an Allied victory. 'Consequently, the theory that "this is a Jewish war" has a certain plausibility, all the more so because the Jewish war effort seldom gets its fair share of recognition.' At the same time, on the issue of Palestine, 'it had become *de rigueur* among enlightened people to accept the Jewish case as proved and avoid examining the claims of the Arabs'. He thought this was 'primarily because the Jews were in trouble and it was felt one must not criticise them'.[140] Orwell's conflation of the Zionist with the 'Jewish case', also illustrates the extent to which in intellectual circles Zionism had come to be readily equated with the collective voice of Britain's Jews.

Anglo-Jewry's progressively more supportive attitude to Zionism developed in tandem with its sociological transformation. As the Jewish middle class expanded, class politics had a diminishing appeal, leading to a decline in support among Jews for the CPGB and to extinguishing any prospect that Poale Zion could develop into a distinct political force. The community's embourgeoisement ensured that the so-called 'general' or bourgeois Zionism would dominate its outlook.

The Jewish dispersal from the East End, and the corresponding break-up of its working-class community, was accelerated by the Blitz, which had destroyed two-thirds of Stepney,[141] but the trend had been set in motion earlier and was mainly due to economic changes. A survey for the Trades Advisory Council carried out in 1943/1944 in a period of severe unemployment reported:

> in 1939 there were well over 10,000 clothing establishments in London, including furriers, dry cleaners, repairers, etc., and the great majority were small firms employing less than ten people. Since the beginning of the war the total number of establishments had been reduced by over 40%. Among others a great number of Jewish firms were liquidated and it is estimated that over one-third of those in clothing establishments went out of business.[142]

Small firms in which Jewish workers were concentrated had been the most affected by the call-up for military service of workers, the shortages in materials and the increased dominance of large manufacturers. At the same time more aspiring families were moving from the inner cities to the suburbs in Manchester, Leeds and Glasgow.[143]

This move towards the suburbs and middle-class status continued to gather pace after the war. Jewish workers moved out of what had been their staple trades, though this did not apply to the same degree to Jewish employers. 'Not only have the latter sometimes emerged as economic magnates in these same fields, but they also remained in very large numbers as owners of medium and smaller sized workshops or factories.'[144] Two-thirds of the respondents in a survey conducted by Krausz in Edgware in 1962–1963 were self-employed while the figure for the general population was 7.4 per cent.[145] The Jewish middle class also expanded by a growing number of the younger generation entering the professions, particularly medicine and law. In Edgware, 57 per cent belonged to the professional or managerial categories. In the general population that figure was just over 39 per cent.[146] Edgware, along with Hendon and Finchley, reflected the new Jewish middle class's move to the northern and northwest suburbs of London. Synagogues opened and closed reflecting the movement of their congregation and though in the suburbs they remained the focal point of Jewish social life, they functioned within a network of relations less dense than those which had characterised the old working-class neighbourhoods.

The membership growth of Zionist organisations was not sustained after 1948. The *shekel* owners, those who for an annual payment of two shillings were able to cast a vote in the election of delegates to the Zionist Congress, numbered 46,000 in 1946 but declined over the following four years by 10,000. The number who voted in this period, which indicates a greater degree of political commitment, remained the same, about 11,000, leading Freedman to conclude that 'while popular enthusiasm for the cause may have declined since the establishment of the State of Israel, a hard core of Zionists has persisted unchanged'.[147] The community was wary of Zionist politics. The anti-semitic outburst in the wake of Irgun's execution of two British sergeants and, following Israel's establishment in May 1948, the allegation that British Jews had 'dual loyalties', elicited a defensive response.[148] Harold Laski's intervention that 'he would feel safer if there was a Jewish government sitting in Tel Aviv with the right to interest itself in the Jews of England, just as the Vatican had a right to interest itself in the Roman Catholics', is unlikely to have been widely shared.[149]

In September 1950, the annual report of the Zionist Central Council of Manchester and Salford noted that the level of fundraising reached that year had been less than the previous year. It attributed the decline 'to the fact that there has not been inculcated a Zionist background into the minds of prospective donors in their youth'.[150] It also became clear that relatively few Jews were prepared to make *aliya* (emigrate to Israel). From Britain, only 3,000 settled in Israel during the first five years of the state's existence.[151] Levenberg later spoke of a 'missing generation': 'The British Zionist movement suffers from the present political apathy. Although interest in Israel and Zionism are strong, they only come to the fore at times of crises.'[152] He linked the lack of active involvement in Zionist politics in the 1950s to a weakening of Jewish identity. At times he attributed this to the 'neglect of Jewish education in the western countries' which he claimed had brought about 'assimilation, disintegration and indifference to the Jewish heritage'.[153] While some Zionist leaders, including Ben-Gurion, still looked to liquidating the Diaspora through emigration to Israel, Levenberg believed this to be unrealistic and argued that, in any case, Jewish communities still had an important political role to play in support of Israel: 'Task number one is to keep Jewish communities strong and powerful, and task number two is to help build the State of Israel. These two tasks are interdependent ... if the Jewish communities are weak, if the Jewish communities are crumbling they cannot help the State.'[154]

Zionist politics in Britain was drawing into its orbit increasing numbers of the newly expanded middle class. The *shekel* holders' election of delegates to the Zionist Congress continued to show in the 1950s and 1960s strong support for Poale Zion but its appeal was based less on its claims to be socialist than on its link to the governing party in Israel, Mapai and, from 1968, the Israeli Labour Party. Labour Zionism's base in the community was narrow and for all practical purposes Poale Zion operated as a part of the EZF with special responsibility for liaising with the British Labour Party and trade unions. In 1949 its newspaper reported 'a healthy growth in membership ... by the London and provincial branches'[155] but this boast was undermined a few months later by a correspondent asking: 'Is it not a fact that only about one-fifth of the total membership of the Party actually responds to Party dues, turns up at lectures and talks, subscribes to the *Jewish Vanguard*, etc., and that the remainder, about 2,500, are simply "paper members"?'[156] Another member wrote that the party 'has degenerated into a very loose association of people who belong to it out of a feeling of loyalty'.[157]

Poale Zion, claimed a 1948 Communist Party appraisal of Jewish political organisations, was 'mainly composed of middle class people'.[158] This characterisation made at a time when the CPGB, in line with the Soviet leadership, was not hostile to Zionist efforts to establish a Jewish state, appears to be fairly accurate. It is consistent with a more recent academic assessment that almost all the leading figures in Poale Zion, even in the 1930s, were lower middle class or small business employers.[159] What had condemned the party to decline after the war, however, was not that its activists were predominantly lower middle class, but that to retain a distinct identity it addressed itself to a rapidly shrinking working class. 'The East End of London', a writer in the *Jewish Vanguard* in 1950 commented, 'with its colourful Yiddish posters, its memories of the Ghetto and its ragged proletariat is slowly but surely disappearing. The sons and daughters of the former Galician "fabricants" in the East End are moving to the suburbs of London … It is becoming more and more bourgeois, more addicted to pleasure.' The article concluded that Poale Zion's old political role had become redundant: 'With Jewish immigration to England practically at a standstill and assimilationist tendencies steadily gaining momentum, the material on which to draw a separate Socialist Party is drying up'.[160] Labour Zionism had failed to attract a significant Jewish constituency when there had existed a larger Jewish working class and several Jewish trade unions but the writer was nonetheless right to sense that the sociological changes in the community ruled out better prospects for it in the future. Support for socialist ideas in Anglo-Jewry was diminishing. Poale Zion's work in factories was confined to fundraising for the Israeli trade union federation. Its national rather than class appeal is illustrated by the Leeds Histadrut Committee reporting in 1951 that voluntary deductions were in place for 60 per cent of the town's Jewish factory workers, an arrangement that depended on the employers' collaboration.[161]

The one role that continued to distinguish Poale Zion from the rest of organised British Zionism was the lobbying it carried out in the Labour movement. The concentration of Jews in a dozen or so constituencies enabled Poale Zion to continue to present itself to the Labour Party as an electoral asset, despite its small membership. The existence of a 'Jewish vote' was widely presumed to exist in relation to issues of particular importance to the community. As in the pre-war period there were only a handful of parliamentary constituencies in which, theoretically, a sufficient concentration of Jewish electors could combine with a sufficiently marginal seat, to be able to determine the outcome, though only if Jewish electors voted on the basis of the 'Jewish issue'. The statistical data on the degree of swing in constituencies with sizeable Jewish electors which could be attributed to the MPs stand on 'Jewish issues', show in every case, Crewe remarks, such minute deviations from the norm that they are 'more remarkable for their slenderness than their existence and could easily be explained by quite different factors'.[162] It was, however, in the interest of Poale Zion to suggest that a Jewish vote over Palestine and later Israel existed and this was given some credence in the Labour Party. During the 1950 general election, the general secretary, Morgan Phillips, told the party's candidate in Willesden that Morrison, Sam Watson and Alice Bacon had 'all made friendly references to the social democratic society which was developing in Israel', which 'should help you considerably in countering the campaign against us amongst the anti-Bevinist section of the Jewish electorate'.[163]

By the 1950s, Poale Zion's ageing and dwindling membership had ruled out any prospects the organisation might once have had of developing a mass base in the Jewish community. Its work was confined to distributing propaganda, initiating resolutions in a handful of constituency Labour parties and campaigning among *shekel* holders in the Jewish community for the Labour bloc in the World Zionist Congress. It had always been a 'weak transplant' in Britain but its decline was nonetheless symptomatic of the process by which Jewishness was being reconstructed in terms of middle-class values.[164]

The sociological transformation of the Jewish community did not by itself make mainstream Zionism the political beneficiary. For the most part, the new middle class accommodated its Jewishness as a peripheral part of a more individualised, suburban lifestyle. In relation to British party politics this was reflected in the community's shift to the right in terms of voting preference. The not altogether reliable survey carried out in 1947, referred to earlier, indicated that about a third of Jewish respondents classed themselves as Labour or Socialist supporters, one-fifth as Conservatives and a third as Liberals.[165] By contrast, a study of Jewish voters in Finchley in the 1959 general election, indicated that they favoured Conservatives over Labour in a ratio of 3 to 1. In the 1964 election, in the same constituency, the ratio was two to one.[166] The Jewish community's embourgeoisement would also alter its interaction with Zionist politics.

An important source of Jewish identity was the persistence of anti-semitic prejudices on all levels of British society. In a fairly attenuated form anti-semitism was present in everyday, popular discourse though without seriously impeding Jewish participation in the labour market or civic life. As Levenberg acknowledged: 'The defeat of Nazism, the settlement of Jewish DPs' problem; the weakening of anti-semitism; the growing economic prosperity, all this made the Jewish problem less acute than in the past'.[167] The attitude of the more assimilated, middle-class Jew was articulated by a letter in the EZF's newspaper which, concurring with one of its reviewers declaring that Anglo-Jewish writers were overly 'preoccupied with the suffering of either the Warsaw or the Hendon ghetto', stated: 'Of course we don't care: of course we are apathetic towards them. Why shouldn't we be? ... I enjoy good books and good theatre, but I don't want to waste my limited time on writers merely because they happen to be Jews or because they write about Jews.'[168] Alongside a decline in anti-semitism, Zionism, which depended on ethnic identification by Jews, was declared to be on the wane, too, by an in-depth sociological survey of post-war Anglo-Jewry.

Krausz's study of Leeds' Jewish community, covering mainly the late 1950s, argued that Zionism was:

> definitely on decline, as is clearly shown by the following: (a) a sharp decline in membership, e.g. the Leeds Zionist Society's membership has gone down from 400 to 150; some of the youth groups have disappeared...a number of adult societies exist only on paper ... (b) even in fund raising there is an overall lessening of enthusiasm.

He added that the amount of funds collected was only maintained and occasionally increased 'due to the extra effort of some of the leaders'.[169]

The Zionist Federation's meeting in 1958 (by then renamed the Zionist Federation of Great Britain and Ireland) should have been attended according to the organisers by 1,278 delegates, but, observed the *Jewish Chronicle*, 'even the opening session could boast only half the number, while the ordinary session had to be content with one-tenth'.[170] Yet a high proportion of the community continued to be involved in Zionist activities in a more passive and less overtly political way. In 1958, 63.5 per cent of Jewish families in Leeds contributed to the JNF.[171] In Edgware, where Krausz looked at the newly suburbanised Jewish middle class, 50 per cent contributed funds for Israel regularly and 41 per cent occasionally.[172]

The Zionist movement's efforts to gain political support in Britain had always contained a strong emphasis on fundraising. Between 1920 and 1929 it raised on average £17,000 per year[173] (equivalent to about £600,000 in 2011). The joint appeal of five Zionist organisations, of which the main two were Keren Hayesod and the JNF, raised in the three-year period between 1944 and 1947 more than £1.7 million (equivalent to about £37 million in 2011). 'In 1948, the year of the establishment of the State of Israel, the Appeal reached £1,750,000.'[174] Fundraising was a collective activity which tended to overarch doctrinal divisions between Liberal, Reform, Orthodox and ultra-Orthodox and between the Zionists and non-Zionists. Some tension over the focus of charitable activities nevertheless persisted. In 1953, Neville Laski, a former president of the Board of Deputies, who had been opposed to the setting up of a Jewish state, complained that the community 'had the greatest difficulty in obtaining money for Anglo-Jewish welfare work and for carrying on their communal affairs in an orderly manner, though funds for Israel were readily available'.[175]

The Joint Palestine Appeal (JPA) formed separate committees for each trade thereby drawing in provincial businessmen. The large inequalities of wealth, as well as the diminishing significance of the Jewish working class in the community, were apparent in the contributions. In 1950, when the JPA aimed to raise £2 million (about £45 million in 2011), Poale Zion's collection for it from

Jewish factory workers in Leeds, over a five-month period, raised £127 which was less than it had been in 1939. By contrast a gathering of business leaders of the furniture and timber trade at the home of Isaac Wolfson, owner of the mail order chain, Great Universal Stores, and of around 2000 retail outlets, raised £70,000 in a single evening. The 'large sums raised by the Joint Palestine Appeal', the Zionist Central Council of Manchester noted, 'are provided in the main by substantial contribution from business people'.[176] In 1961, the *Zionist Year Book* reported that English Jewry had raised through the two main funds, Keren Hayesod and the JNF, about £35 million since Israel's foundation in 1948. The FWZ contributed, over the same period, an additional £2.5 million.[177]

Krausz's belief that Zionism in the 1950s and early 1960s was on the decline ignored its diffusion beyond conventional forms of political activity. A sense of collectiveness centred on Israel was, to borrow Billig's words, 'embedded in habits of thought and life', of the Anglo-Jewish middle class, which made nationalist consciousness 'banally habitual' and thereby apparently 'natural'.[178] Participating in Zionist meetings and rallies had little attraction to the community's expanding middle class but charitable work in support of Israel provided an alternative associational activity which was respectable, uncontroversial (in the eyes of mainstream British society) and provided a basis for cohesion. The 'fairly strong interest in Israel' that was observed among the new Jewish middle class in Edgware, in the early 1960s, was an important component of its class formation.[179] It was an identity that contained a good dose of middle England. Krausz, in his study of Leeds' Jewish community, observed: 'The prayer for the State of Israel is recited in the synagogue after the Prayer for the Queen. Most religious and lay speakers stress the importance of Israel and sing the national anthem after "God Save the Queen".'[180]

While Anglo-Jewry's Jewishness was redefined mainly by Zionism, its Englishness was reshaped to mirror the social conservatism of English suburbia. An aspect of this was the community distancing itself by relation to more recent immigrants. The Board of Deputies and the *Jewish Chronicle* expressed opposition to discrimination against black immigrants but, as a 1969 report on British attitudes to race noted, there was from the Jewish community little institutional involvement in combating anti-black racism.[181] The vice-chairman of the Board of Deputies expressed the view, in 1965, that immigration should be stopped for at least five years and then reviewed, warning that in 'any future recession if there were an army of skilled unemployed in this country, then their fury would be unleashed not against the Negroes but against the Jews'.[182] An inquiry carried out for the Board of Deputies into Jewish attitudes to the black community met with indifference. Of the 800 questionnaires distributed to youth groups, synagogal and other bodies, only forty were returned.[183] A columnist in the *Jewish Chronicle* claimed that the liberal sentiments of the Board of Deputies and the *Jewish Chronicle* were not representative of the community: Anglo-Jewry was 'well integrated and assimilated and shares the attitudes and prejudices of most Englishmen, which is to say, it regards the coloured immigrants as a social menace'.[184] The phrasing was intentionally provocative but not unfounded. In the mainstream of the Jewish community there was a coded, unselfconscious, ideological realignment on the basis of 'whiteness'. An aspect of this was the Jewish middle class's indifference to black people with whom they had little contact. Jewish working-class residents, on the other hand, in ethnically mixed Hackney, were found by a study in the late 1970s to hold similar racist views of their black neighbours as found among non-Jewish, white, inner-city residents.[185]

Whereas the 'Cousinhood' had promoted the Jewish community's Anglicisation, the new entrepreneurial class that took over the leadership position encouraged its Zionisation, principally by spearheading a permanent philanthropic mobilisation in support of Israel. Wolfson's ascendancy was characteristic of this changeover. Aris desribes him as part of 'a newer generation of self-made entrepreneurs of Russian and Polish origin for whom Judaism and Zionism were inextricably mixed'.[186] The 'mix', however, also had other ingredients. 'Wolfson has always been a devout Jew,' Aris explains, 'but his Zionism is of a more recent date. Up to about 1948 he was too busy building the business to devote much time or money to the Zionist cause, but after discreet and gentle pressure from Israel (now Lord) Sieff of *Marks and Spencer*, who explained that a businessman of his standing in the community could not really remain on the sidelines, Wolfson's attitude changed.'[187]

Lavy Bakstansky, the general secretary of the Zionist Federation for forty years, acknowledged the movement's embrace by the rich and powerful. He explained it, tongue in cheek, as resulting from the social mobility of Zionism's former petty bourgeois supporters: 'the Second World War witnessed a redistribution of capital, and some of the former boys of "Fulbourne Street" [a street of small retailers in Whitechapel] are today among the Jewish magnates in trade and industry. Here is a case of an "investment" yielding magnificent dividends.'[188] To Levenberg this appeared less attractive and he hoped that Zionism could remain allied to socialist values in Britain's Jewish community and in Israel. But he had moments of doubt, writing in the early 1960s: 'One of the negative features of Anglo-Jewish life is the exaggerated and sometimes nauseating respect for material wealth. A charitable explanation of this phenomenon is the need to obtain contributions for the various fundraising bodies.'[189]

Manchester's Zionist Central Council had noted that the large sums raised by the Joint Palestine Appeal 'are provided in the main by substantial contributions from the business world'.[190] In 1960, the Appeal's organisers considered publishing in the local Jewish press the names of those who contributed over £25.[191] Philanthropic activities were simultaneously a demonstration of commitment to Israel and to being middle class. The FWZ, which in the 1960s had a membership of 17,000 and, according to Bermant, was the most active group within the Zionist movement, organised fundraising through coffee evenings, whist drives and fashion shows. It derived 'the mass of its members from the more expensive suburbs, and if they meet away from home they do so in surroundings which they feel are in keeping with their place in society. In London, the Hilton is almost the lady Zionists' home-from-home, and in the provinces they assemble in the local equivalent'.[192]

Wolfson, Sieff, David and Charles Clore, Bernard Delfont, Max Rayne, Gerald Ronson and Michael Sobell were the leading philanthropists from the Jewish *nouveaux riches*. They were either British-born or had come to Britain young, and had acquired enormous wealth through either the retail sector, the entertainment industry or property development. Their extensive patronage of philanthropic activities in support of Jewish institutions in Britain and in Israel established their position at the apex of Anglo-Jewry while their economic status and association with the British political and cultural elites gained them civic honours (all were ennobled). 'It is difficult for a Jewish working-man or woman', Levenberg lamented, 'to "fit in" into a communal life, where dinners, receptions, and cocktail parties play such a great part.'[193] The Jewish middle class, professionals and smaller retailers, integrated by contrast more easily into the fundraising organisations and activities that dominated communal life. In 1956, a *Jewish Chronicle* report placed Manchester's Jewry among the most active in the country, adding: 'Social life is real and productive. Charity is its Kingpin.'[194]

The post-war growth in Jewish schools also contributed to forging a mutually enhancing connection between Jewish ethnic identity and middle-class aspirations. In the community's collective memory, education, though not exempt from anti-semitism, had provided one of the few avenues for social advancement. From the late nineteenth century, Jewish community leaders had looked to the state schooling system to acculturate to English ways the immigrants who came to Britain. Religious education was provided outside school hours through the *cheder* (room), which consisted of a private tutor giving religious instruction to a group of children for between ten to fifteen hours per week. The religious authorities kept a vigilant eye on this form of instruction. Their own intervention took the form of the Jewish Religious Education Board which had the support of the Chief Rabbi. The classes it funded were attended mainly by the poor who could not afford to pay for private tuition and, mostly, by girls for whose religious education families were generally more reluctant to pay.[195]

In the inter-war years there were a dozen full-time Jewish voluntary schools, four in the provinces and the rest in London, which provided a general as well as a religious education. They struggled to maintain their numbers. In London, four times as many Jewish children attended schools controlled by the London County Council.[196] In 1938, the president of the main Jewish school in Manchester 'saw no enthusiasm among the younger generation of Jewish parents for the idea of a Jews' School'.[197] A comment piece in the *Jewish Chronicle* that year concluded that, the 'lack of support by Jewish parents to the Jewish day schools makes it abundantly clear that these efforts are still regarded by them as pioneer ventures'.[198]

The 1944 Education Act initially discouraged separate denomination schools by introducing provisions for religious organisations to give instruction during school hours: 'one of the results was that an increasing number of parents came to regard this minimal instruction as adequate and did not feel obliged to send their children either to Jewish Day Schools or to Synagogue Classes'.[199] The act, however, also allowed for new schools to be established and then to avail themselves of local authority funding. Once the community could find the capital for the start-up cost the way was open to set up its own schools. The momentum and the funds came from the recently suburbanised and increasingly prosperous middle class. Prior to the war aspiring Jewish parents generally saw the mainstream state schooling as the best way to advance their children's future but in the 1950s, the Jewish community was encouraged to seek a separatist solution by religious leaders and Zionists. They both saw the expansion of day schools as a way to counter the trend towards assimilation.

'The danger of assimilation that Anglo-Jewry faces is indeed a grave one', announced a commentator in the *Jewish Chronicle* in 1956, discerning evidence for the possible extinction of Britain's Jewish community in a survey conducted among Jewish students the previous year. This indicated that 10 per cent were 'quite likely' to marry out of the faith and a further 36 per cent thought it 'possible though unlikely'.[200] A decade later it was estimated on a 'very conservative assumption' that 25 to 30 per cent of Jewish men and women married out.[201] Indicating the alarm over this, the chairman of the youth club committee of the Jewish Marriage Education Council, which had been set up in 1947 to propagate 'traditional values', warned of the 'new morality' bringing about a 'serious weakening' of Jewish marriages and family life.[202] Out-marriage signalled the decreasing force of anti-semitism in British society but religious as well as Zionist leaders perceived it primarily as a threat to Jewish survival. They saw the remedy in the extension of Jewish schooling though they had divergent approaches to how this should be carried out.

At a conference in 1956, ultra-Orthodox rabbis condemned attempts by the Zionist Federation to set up day schools in Britain. They doubted the Zionists' commitment to religious education complaining that the Zionist Congress's decision that year to launch a worldwide campaign for Jewish day schools was a belated acknowledgment that intermarriage was rampant. It amounted, they alleged, to an admission that 'Zionist ideology does not afford protection against the consuming germ of assimilation'.[203] There was further complaint from ultra-Orthodox quarters that the United Synagogue's leadership had approved financial support for Zionist Federation schools in preference to ultra-Orthodox schools.[204] The collaboration over schools between the United Synagogue, the main Orthodox bloc, and the Zionists, developed out of concern on the leadership level that assimilation was endangering the future existence of the Jewish community. It led, in 1958, to the reopening on a new site in Camden, of the Jews' Free School, the most famous of Anglo-Jewish schools. The Zionist Federation Educational Trust made a donation of £50,000 and undertook to cover 30 per cent of the annual budget of the school's religious department.[205]

The expansion of Jewish voluntary schools from the 1950s provided one of the means by which middle-class aspirations could be delivered through religious and nationalist indoctrination. The new 'Other' in the form of the black immigrant population encouraged the Jewish middle class to emphasise a Jewishness that was also English. Bermant described how an initiative to persuade the Zionist organisation to set up the Clapton Jewish Day School was 'helped by local circumstances': 'There is a sizeable coloured population in the area, and this tends to encourage families to take their children out of the State schools and into the private ones. Once the coloured families begin to move out of their ghettoes and into the suburbs, the other Jewish day schools may enjoy a similar boost.'[206] The head of a Jewish primary school in northwest London expressed dismay in 1978, over 'Jewish parents who only a couple of generations ago were themselves immigrants refusing to agree to send their children to this or that school simply because they don't want their children to mix with those of coloured immigrants'.[207]

From 1954 up to 1963 the total number of children attending full-time Jewish day schools roughly doubled to reach 8896. Of the thirty-eight schools, only eight were secondary schools. By 1977, there were forty primary schools and seventeen secondary schools providing for 12,800 pupils. Thus about 30 per cent of children born between 1956 and 1965 received full-time Jewish primary or secondary day-school education.[208] The proportion of Jewish children who received some religious instruction was much higher. Estimates in the 1960s varied between 60 and 80 per cent[209] but this did not involve the same degree of exposure to Zionist indoctrination as in the day schools, particularly at the secondary level where the teaching of Hebrew often relied on teachers recruited from Israel.[210] An Israeli historian commenting on the collaboration in schooling between the Zionist Federation and the Embassy in the 1950s, notes: 'The ZF [Zionist Federation] resurrected and redefined itself by creating a nation-wide system of Jewish-Zionist education, which became its most significant achievement during the period.'[211]

The extent to which support for Israel was promoted in Jewish schools varied but the general ethos was Zionist and, by 1961, the Zionist Federation had six of its own day schools. Some of the schools were fee paying but most were state funded, though parents were generally expected to make a financial contribution to the provision of religious instruction. The charge was lower in schools which were subsidised by the Zionist Federation.[212] In 1971, the Zionist Federation claimed that 4,500 children were taught in Zionist schools.[213] In almost all the Jewish schools children were immersed in Zionist ideas for which, in addition to Hebrew language classes, visits to Israel came to form an increasingly important supportive role. Tours organised for youth as the 'Israel Experience' were described by the head of the Youth and Pioneer Department of the WZO, in 1996, as 'an educational tool, a hands-on experience, aimed first and foremost at bringing individuals closer to the historic heritage, which has Israel as its centre, and in this way to tie them to Judaism, to Israel and to Zionism'.[214] In these ways, the communal youth milieu extending from the school to extra-curricula activities was made markedly more nationalist, from the late 1960s than it had been for the generation drawn into anti-fascist politics in the late 1930s and during the war years. Socialist ideas, even in the diluted form of left-wing Zionism, lost out. In 1961, an army major and Labour Zionist stalwart was brought to London from Israel to try to revive the youth wing of Poale Zion. 'I very soon gave up dreaming of a mass movement,' he declared two years later, and shortly before his return: 'I am content with the 400 members we have now in London, Leeds, Manchester and Liverpool.'[215]

The 1967 war is widely identified as pivotal in the development of Anglo-Jewry's commitment to Israel. As a measure of the groundswell support the war unleashed, Williams points to the Joint Palestine Appeal receiving £2.25 million in 1963 but £60 million in 1967 and an average of £10 million a year thereafter.[216] Without doubt the community's mobilisation behind Israel's war effort represented a public demonstration, above all to itself, of its identification with Israel and this in turn helped to strengthen Zionism's political hold on the community. But the groundwork had been laid over the previous two decades. Zionism's ideological conquest of the Anglo-Jewish community succeeded because it received the embrace, on the one hand, of the religious hierarchy, for whom ethnic separatism (in which religiosity was an important component) was the last line of defence against secularism[217] and, on the other, of the suburban Jewish middle class, which through its schools, youth groups and charities, was able to turn ethnic identification into a mechanism of empowerment and internal cohesion, without jeopardising its Anglicisation.

Notes

1. 'Lloyd George' in *Encyclopaedia Judaica* vol. 11 (Jerusalem, 1971), p. 413.
2. Levenberg Papers, Untitled report compiled on behalf of Board of Deputies, 1977, Box 5, File 1.
3. C. Bermant, *Troubled Eden: An Anatomy of British Jewry* (London: Valentine, Mitchell, 1969), p. 50.
4. V.D. Lipman, *A Century of Social Service, 1859–1959* (London: RKP, 1959), pp. 98, 100.
5. L. Wolf, *Essays in Jewish History* (London: The Jewish Historical Society of England, 1934), p. 359.
6. C. Weizmann, *Trial and Error* (London: Hamish Hamilton, 1949), p. 149.
7. Quoted in M. Berkowitz, *Western Jewry and the Zionist Project 1914–1933* (Cambridge: Cambridge University Press, 1997), p. 73.
8. *Jewish Chronicle* (8 June 1917).

9 C. Weizmann, *Letters and Papers*, Series A, vol. 5, Series A, vol. 5 (Oxford: Oxford University Press, 1975), p. 319.
10 S.A. Cohen, *The English Zionists and British Jews* (New Jersey: Princeton University Press, 1982), p. 128.
11 B. Williams, '"East and West": Class and Community in Manchester Jewry, 1850–1914', in D. Cesarani (ed.), *The Making of Modern Anglo-Jewry* (London: Blackwell, 1990), p. 18.
12 Cohen, *English Zionists*, p. 127.
13 B. Williams, *Sir Sidney Hamburger and Manchester Jewry* (London: Valentine Mitchell, 1999): B. Williams, *Michael Fidler (1916–1989), A Study in Leadership* (Stockport: R&D Graphics, 1997).
14 *Jewish Chronicle* (5 August 1977).
15 Williams, *Fidler*, p. 53.
16 Williams, *Hamburger*, p. 177.
17 *Jewish Chronicle* (27 September 1974).
18 Quoted in Williams, *Hamburger*, p. 56.
19 Williams, *Hamburger*, p. 28.
20 *Jewish Chronicle* (23 October 1925).
21 *Zionist Review* (March 1938).
22 Ibid. (7 January 1944); Paul Goodman, *Zionism in England, 1899–1929* (London: English Zionist Federation, 1929), p. 42.
23 London Metropolitan Archives (hereafter LMA), Federation of Women Zionists, Executive, Minutes 14 June 1939, LMA/4175/01/01/004-006.
24 LMA, Federation of Women Zionists, Executive, Minutes, 1 December 1926, LMA/4175/01/01/004-006.
25 LMA, Federation of Women Zionists, Small Executive and Propaganda Committee, Minutes, 6 April 1938, LMA/4175/01/01/004-006.
26 *Zionist Review* (28 January 1944)
27 Ibid. (30 September 1938).
28 LMA, Federation of Women Zionists, 14 June 1939, Minutes of the Executive LMA/4175/01/01/004-06.
29 Cohen, *English Zionists*, p. 129.
30 *Jewish Chronicle* (14 December 1934).
31 Ibid. (14 December 1934).
32 Ibid. (8 July 1938).
33 Levenberg Papers, Levenberg, 'Poale Zion – Past, Present and Future', summary of talk, 13 August 1941, Box 1, File 1.
34 H. Rosen, *Are You Still Circumcised? East End Memories* (Nottingham: Five Leaves Publication, 1999), p. 63.
35 W.D. Rubinstein, 'Zionism and the Jewish People, 1918-1960: From Minority to Hegemony', *The Jewish Journal of Sociology*, 43:1/2 (2001), 10.
36 S. Gewirtz, 'Anti-Fascist Activity in Manchester's Jewish Community in the 1930s', *Manchester Region History Review*, 4:1 (1990), 17.
37 *Jewish Chronicle* (8 July 1938).
38 Ibid. (26 February 1937).
39 Ibid. (18 March 1938).
40 S. Bunt, *Jewish Youth Work in Britain* (London: Bedford Square Press of the National Council of Social Services, 1975), p. 130.
41 *Jewish Chronicle* (9 December 1938). In 1942, Henriques formed the anti-Zionist organisation the Jewish Fellowship to encourage Jews to define themselves by religion.

42 Membership figures are given in Labour Party Annual Conference Reports.
43 *Jewish Vanguard* (19 January 1951).
44 Labour History Archive (hereafter LHA), CPGB Papers, 'Our Attitude to Zionist Activities and the War', National Jewish Committee, 10 October 1943.
45 Levenberg, 'Poale Zion – Past, Present and Future'.
46 *Jerusalem Post* (21 April 1959).
47 *Jewish Chronicle* (6 June 1997).
48 S. Levenberg, *The Jews and Palestine: A Study in Labour Zionism* (London: Poale Zion, 1945).
49 S. Brook, *The Club: The Jews of Modern Britain* (London: Constable, 1989), p. 371.
50 Levenberg Papers, Levenberg, draft paper, 'Memories of an Earlier Refusenik' n.d. circa early 1970s, Box 'Zionism'.
51 *South Africa Jewish Frontier* (August 1962)
52 *Jewish Vanguard*, 'Sixty Years of Poale Zion' (25 February 1966).
53 Two years earlier, the Jewish People's Council, had gathered 100,000 signatures in only forty-eight hours to petition the Home Secretary to ban the BUF's planned march in the East End. See Elaine R. Smith, 'Jewish Responses to Political Anti-Semitism and Fascism in the East End of London, 1920–1939', in T. Kushner and K. Lunn (eds), *Traditions of Intolerance, Historical Perspectives on Fascism and Race Discourse in Britain* (Manchester: Manchester University Press, 1989), p. 64.
54 Levenberg, 'Poale Zion – Past, Present and Future'.
55 C. Roth, 'Postscript from London', *Contemporary Jewish Record*, 8:1 (1945), 76.
56 Bermant, *Troubled Eden*, p. 102.
57 *Zionist Review* (20 April 1939 and 15 June 1939).
58 N. Jackson, 'Poale Zion in War-Time', *Jewish Labour*, November –December 1943.
59 Levenberg Papers, Levenberg, draft article, no title, n.d., File 1/1.
60 *Jewish Chronicle* (19 June 1936).
61 Ibid. (4 September 1936).
62 *Zionist Review* (23 July 1943).
63 *Jewish Chronicle* (24 October 1941).
64 M. Shalev, 'Jewish Organised Labour and the Palestinians: A Study of State/Society Relations in Israel', in B. Kimmerling (ed.), *The Israeli State and Society, Boundaries and Frontiers* (New York: State University of New York, 1989), p. 99.
65 *Hansard*, Commons, v. 341, c. 1314, 21 November 1938.
66 N. Bentwich, *They Found Refuge* (London: The Cresset Press, 1956), p. 20.
67 *Zionist Review* (April 1938).
68 *Survey of Palestine* (Jerusalem: Government Printer, 1946), p. 185.
69 *Jewish Chronicle* (28 May 1937).
70 C. Weizmann, *Letters and Papers*, Series A, vol. 17 (New Brunswick: Transaction Books, 1968–1986), p. 88.
71 Quoted in D. Silberklang, 'Jewish Politics and Rescue: The Founding of the Council for German Jewry', *Holocaust and Genocide Studies*, 7:3 (1993), 341. Emphasis added by Silberklang.
72 Silberklang, 'Jewish Politics'.
73 Weizmann, *Letters and Papers*, vol. 17, pp. 72–73.
74 Silberklang, 'Jewish Politics', p. 345.
75 Weizmann, *Letters and Papers*, vol. 17, p. 122.
76 N. Angell and D. Buxton, *You and the Refugee* (Middlesex: Penguin Books, 1939), p. 225.
77 *International Information*, 17 November 1938.
78 R. Schor, L'opinion francaise et les étrangers en France, 1919–1939 (Paris: Publication de la Sorbonne, 1985), p. 564; *Report of the Proceedings at the 70th Annual Trade Union Congress* (London: TUC, 1938), p. 208.

79 *Report of Proceedings at the 70th Annual Trade Union Congress.* The stance of trade unions was not uniformly restrictionist, see T. Kushner, *The Holocaust and the Liberal Imagination* (Oxford: Blackwell, 1994), pp. 77–81.
80 Communications on the Conditions of Political Prisoners, LSI, 18 October 1933; Hansard, Commons, v. 304, c. 2101, 25 July 1935.
81 Comité Socialiste, Bulletin, no.8, February 1934.
82 Sir John Hope Simpson, *The Refugee Problem, Report of a Survey* (London: Oxford University Press, 1939), p. 516.
83 Quoted in A. Bober (ed.) *The Other Israel: The Radical Case Against Zionism* (New York: Anchor Books, 1972), p. 171.
84 Bober, *The Other Israel*, p. 248.
85 Hope Simpson, *The Refugee Problem*, pp. 548–549. His recommendation was supported by Angell and Buxton, *You and the Refugee*, p. 257.
86 A.J. Sherman, *Island Refuge* (London: Paul Elek, 1973), p. 178.
87 N. Rose (ed.), *Baffy, the Diaries of Blanche Dugdale, 1936–1947* (London: Valentine, Mitchell, 1973), p. 118.
88 *Zionist Review* (24 November 1938).
89 Levenberg Papers, Levenberg, 'How Started the Petition Campaign', n.d., Box 'Articles'.
90 *Zionist Review* (22 December 1938).
91 *Jewish Chronicle* (30 June 1939).
92 Hansard, Commons, v. 341 c. 505, 14 November 1938 and c. 1438, 21 November 1938. After the Nazi annexation of Austria, Wedgwood had tabled a motion in the Commons to relax entry to Britain for Austrian refugees up to a period of 6 months and to give British citizenship to those deprived by the German government of their Austrian citizenship. Labour MPs voted for this motion but with the knowledge that government benches would defeat it. Hansard, Commons, v. 333, cc. 1003–1009, 22 March 1938.
93 Ibid., v. 341, cc. 2003–2005, 24 November 1938.
94 A. Thorpe, 'The Membership of the Communist Party of Great Britain, 1920–1945', *The Historical Journal*, 43:3 (2000), 783.
95 *Daily Worker* (3 August 1938).
96 Ibid. (29 November 1938).
97 Ibid. (15 July 1938).
98 Ibid. (30 November 1938).
99 Sherman, *Island Refuge*, p.171. The Council for German Jewry succeeded the Central British Fund for German Jewry in March 1936.
100 R. Bolchover, *British Jewry and the Holocaust* (Cambridge: Cambridge University Press, 1993), p. 50.
101 L. London, *Whitehall and the Jews, 1933–1948* (Cambridge: Cambridge University Press, 2003), p. 131.
102 Quoted in S. Pedersen, *Eleanor Rathbone and the Politics of Conscience* (New Haven: Yale University Press, 2004), p. 262.
103 Angell and Buxton, *You and the Refugee*, p. 135.
104 Kushner, *The Holocaust and the Liberal Imagination*, p. 55.
105 B. Wasserstein, *Britain and the Jews of Europe, 1939–1945* (Oxford: Oxford University Press, 1979), p. 23.
106 Ibid., p. 57.
107 Kushner, *Holocaust and the Liberal Imagination*, p. 138.
108 *Jewish Chronicle* (6 March 1942).
109 Quoted in V. Gollancz, *Let My People Go* (London: Gollancz, 1942), p. 6.

110 Ibid., p. 7.
111 E. Rathbone, *Rescue the Perishing* (London: National Committee for the Rescue of Jews from Nazi Terror, June 1943), p. 18.
112 Letter from Solomon Schonfeld, *The Times*, 6 June 1961; *Zionist Review* (19 February and 5 March 1943).
113 *Zionist Review* (26 February 1943).
114 Ibid. (26 February 1943).
115 Wasserstein, *Britain and the Jews of Europe*, pp. 189–192.
116 London, *Whitehall*, p.211.
117 *Jewish Chronicle* (7 May 1943).
118 *Zionist Review* (23 July 1943).
119 Hull University Library, Reginald Bridgeman Papers, National Jewish Committee 28 August 1943, DBN 26/2.
120 LHA, People's History Museum (hereafter PHM), CPGB Papers, 'Our Attitude to Zionist Activities and the War', Discussion Paper at an enlarged meeting of the National Jewish Committee on 10 October 1943, CP/CENT/CTTE/02/02.
121 *Zionist Review* (26 February 1943); LMA, Executive, Federation of Zionist Women, Minutes, 17 February 1943, LMA/4175/01/01/007.
122 *Zionist Review* (25 January 1946).
123 A. Hyamson, 'A Letter from London', *Contemporary Jewish Record*, 6:5 (October 1943), p. 485.
124 *Zionist Review* (4 February 1944).
125 LMA, Minutes, Federation of Women Zionists, Honorary Members, 13 June 1945. LMA/4175/01/01/007.
126 LMA, Federation of Women Zionists, Report of the Conference at Southport 27 January 1942, LMA/4175/01/01/007.
127 *Zionist Review* (23 February 1939 and 20 April 1939).
128 Bolchover, *British Jewry and the Holocaust*, p. 51.
129 Bermant, *Troubled Eden*, p. 74.
130 Levenberg, 'Looking Back', *Zionist Review*, 11 September 1942.
131 Levenberg, 'Poale Zion – Past, Present and Future'.
132 Ibid.
133 Levenberg Papers, Levenberg, 'Anglo-Jewry: Light and Shadows', ms., n.d., Box 'Articles'.
134 Levenberg, 'Poale Zion – Past, Present and Future'.
135 Levenberg Papers, Report of the British Poale Zion submitted to the World Zionist Conference of the Ichud Olami, July 1964, Box 5, File 1.
136 *Zionist Review* (22 January 1943).
137 R. Henriques, *Survey of Jewish Interests* (Bedford: Rush and Warwick, 1949), p. 17.
138 S. Levenberg, 'Zionism in British Politics' in P. Goodman (ed.), *The Jewish National Home* (London: J. Dent and Sons, 1943), p. 115.
139 LMA, Federation of Women Zionists, Minutes, Council Meeting, 3 February 1943, , LMA/4175/01/01/007.
140 G. Orwell, 'Antisemitism in Britain', *Contemporary Jewish Record*, 8:2 April (1945), p. 166.
141 A. Levy, 'In Search of the East End', *Jewish Chronicle* (9 January 1948).
142 N. Barou, *The Jews in Work and Trade* (London: Trades Advisory Council, 1948), p. 10.
143 B. Williams, *Manchester Jewry* (Manchester: Archives Publications, 1988) p. 98; N. Grizzard and P. Raisman, 'Inner City Jews in Leeds', *Journal of Jewish Sociology*, 22:1 (1980), 21–33.
144 E. Krausz, 'The Economic and Social Structure of Anglo-Jewry', in J. Gould and S. Esh (eds), *Jewish Life in Modern Britain* (London: Routledge and Kegan Paul, 1964), p. 31.

145 E. Krausz, 'The Edgware Survey: Occupation and Social Class', *The Jewish Journal of Sociology*, 11:1 (1969), 79.
146 Krausz, 'The Edgware Survey', p. 76.
147 M. Freedman, 'Demographic and Other Statistical Aspects', in M. Feldman (ed.), *A Minority in Britain* (London: Vallentine, Mitchell and Co., 1955), p. 123.
148 M. Edelman and Norman Bentwich, 'The Problem of Dual Loyalties: Laying the Bogey', *Jewish Chronicle* (2 July 1948).
149 *Jewish Chronicle* (24 September 1948).
150 Manchester Central Reference Library, Zionist Central Council of Manchester and Salford, 21st Report, September 1950, p.17.
151 *Jewish Chronicle* (29 October 1954).
152 Levenberg, Draft, 'Board of Deputies and Zionism' n.d., File 5/1.
153 Levenberg, 'The Jewish Agency's Education Policy' draft, January 1955, File 4/4.
154 Levenberg Papers, Levenberg, 'Israel and the Diaspora'. Address delivered at the National Congress of the World Jewish Congress (British Section), 9 December 1951, Box 'Zionism'.
155 *Jewish Vanguard* (18 February 1949).
156 Ibid. (10 June 1949).
157 Ibid. (10 June 1949).
158 *Jewish Clarion* (March 1948).
159 G. Shimoni, 'Poale Zion: A Zionist Transplant in Britain', in P. Medding (ed.), *Studies in Contemporary Jewry*, vol. 2 (London: Bloomington University Press, 1986), p. 259.
160 *Jewish Vanguard* (3 March 1950).
161 Levenberg Papers, Report of the Histadrut Committee to the Administrative Committee of the Joint Palestine Appeal, January 1951, Box 'Zionism'.
162 I. Crewe, 'Is there a "Jewish vote" in Britain', *Patterns of Prejudice*, 18:1 (1984), 47.
163 Labour Party Papers (hereafter LPP), Labour Party, Palestine/Israel Documents 1945–1951, M. Phillips to D. Weitzman, 2 February 1950.
164 Shimoni, 'Poale-Zion'.
165 Henriques, *Survey of Jewish Interests*, p. 17.
166 G. Alderman, *Modern British Jewry* (Oxford: Clarendon Press, 1998), p. 338.
167 Levenberg Papers, Levenberg, 'Return to Political Zionism', draft, May 1956, Box 'Articles'.
168 *Jewish Observer and Middle East Review*, 10 August 1962.
169 E. Krausz, *Leeds Jewry* (Cambridge: The Jewish Historical Society of England, 1964), p. 115.
170 *Jewish Chronicle* (4 April 1958).
171 Krausz, *Leeds Jewry*, p. 59.
172 Krausz, 'The Edgware Survey', p. 159.
173 Levenberg Papers, Levenberg, 'Trends in British Zionism, An Historical Survey', n.d. c.1950s, Box 'Articles'.
174 *Zionist Year Book*, 1959–1961, p. 322.
175 *Jewish Chronicle* (13 November 1953).
176 Levenberg Papers, Report of the Israel Histadrut Committee submitted to the Joint Palestine Appeal, January 1951, Box 'Zionism'; *Jewish Chronicle* (3 March 1950); Report of the Zionist Central Council of Manchester and District, 1 July 1952 to 30 June 1953, p. 27.
177 *Zionist Year Book*, 1961–1962, p. 301.
178 M. Billig, *Banal Nationalism* (London: Sage, 1997), p. 63.
179 Krausz, 'The Edgware Survey', p. 159.
180 Krausz, *Leeds Jewry*, p. 115, n. 4.

181 E. Rose, *Colour and Citizenship, A Report on British Race Relations* (Oxford: Oxford University Press, 1969), p. 376.
182 Jewish Chronicle (9 April 1965). Anglo-Jewish attitudes to the black community from which this reference is taken is discussed in G. Alderman, *London Jewry and London Politics 1889–1986* (London: Routledge, 1989), pp. 118–119.
183 Jewish Chronicle (17 October 1969).
184 Ibid. (5 November 1976).
185 Y. Ginzberg, 'Sympathy and Resentment, Jew and Coloureds in London's East End', *Patterns of Prejudice*, 13:2–3 (1979), 39–42.
186 A. Aris, *The Jews in Business* (London: Jonathan Cape, 1970), p. 72.
187 Ibid., p. 117.
188 Jewish Chronicle (2 February 1962).
189 Levenberg, 'Anglo-Jewry: Light and Shadow', n.d. c.1965, Box 'Articles'.
190 Manchester Central Reference LibraryAnnual Report of the Zionist Central Council of Manchester, 1952–1953.
191 Manchester Central Reference Library, Joint Palestine Appeal Committee, 1951–1962, Minutes Book, entry for 25 February 1960.
192 Bermant, *Troubled Eden*, p. 118.
193 Jewish Vanguard (3 January 1968).
194 Jewish Chronicle (8 June 1956).
195 Ibid.(30 April 1937).
196 C. Herschon, *To Make Them English* (Bristol: Palavas Press, 1983), p. 64.
197 Jewish Chronicle (15 July 1938).
198 Ibid. (19 August 1938).
199 E. Conway, 'The Future of Jewish Schools' in P. Bander (ed.), *Looking Forward to the Seventies* (Buckinghamshire: Colin Smythie, 1968), p. 285.
200 Jewish Chronicle (15 December 1956).
201 A study of the US Jews concluded that 70 percent of the children of mixed marriages are not brought up as Jews. 'We simply cannot afford', commented the Jewish Chronicle's report, 'to lose so large a proportion of Jewry', Jewish Chronicle (11 March 1966). A British study pointing to an increase in out-marriage on basis of the decline in synagogue marriages was published a couple of years later.
202 Jewish Chronicle (4 September 1964 and 23 May 1969).
203 Ibid. (10 August 1956).
204 Ibid. (20 March 1959).
205 G. Black, J.F.S. *A History of the Jewish Free School, London since 1732* (London: Tymseder Publishing, 1998), p. 210.
206 Bermant, *Troubled Eden*, p. 133.
207 Jewish Chronicle (3 March 1978).
208 Herschon, *Make Them English*, p. 97; I. Fishman and H. Levy, 'Jewish Education in Great Britain', in J. Gould and S. Esh (eds), *Jewish Life in Modern Britain* (London: Routledge & Kegan Paul, 1964) p. 76. The estimate for 1949 comes from Rose L. Henriques's survey based on 3,400 returns of Jewish Chronicle readers, Jewish Chronicle (2 September 1949) and is probably less reliable than the figures collated by J. Braude, the source for Herschon and also for Fishman and Levy. Braude reported that of the 57 Jewish day schools in 1977, 20 were state aided (with an enrolment of over 6,800) and 37 schools were independent. See J. Braude, 'Jewish Education in Britain Today' in S. Lipman and V. Lipman (eds) *Jewish Life in Britain, 1962–1977* (New York: K.G. Saur, 1981) p. 126; O. Valins, B. Kosmin and J. Goldberg, *The Future of Jewish Schooling in the United Kingdom* (Institute of Jewish Policy Research, 2002), www.jpr.org.uk (accessed 25 May 2011), p. 2.

209 Fishman and Levy, 'Jewish Education', p. 73; *Jewish Chronicle* (23 May 1969).
210 A survey based on over 2,000 respondents carried out in 1995 exploring British Jews' attitude to Israel found that, for young people, visiting the country was significant in developing a strong attachment to it. B. Kosmin, A. Lerman and J. Goldberg, *The Attachment of British Jews to Israel* (London: Institute for Jewish Policy Research, 1997), p. 13.
211 N. Aridan, *Britain, Israel and Anglo-Jewry 1949–1957* (London: Routledge, 2007), p. 233.
212 *Jewish Chronicle* (1 September 1961).
213 *Ibid.* (9 April 1971).
214 Shlomo Gravetz quoted in E.H. Cohen, *Youth Tourism to Israel* (Clevendon: Channel View Publications, 2008), p. 9. The prime purpose of these tours is to demonstrate the Jewish connection to the land and demonstrate Zionist achievements. The Palestinian and Muslim connections are almost entirely ignored. It has become the standard for Israeli tourist promotions to acknowledge the Palestinian presence only by reference to the Bedouins, who are depicted as exotic primitives. An article in the *Jewish Chronicle* (20 May 2011) in promoting the 'Seven Wonders of Israel Tour' aimed at post-GCSE Jewish youth has as 'wonder' no. 6, a visit to 'Israel's Bedouin minority'. Under the subheading 'Bedouin Tents' the writer enthuses: 'Most Israel tours take participants to a Bedouin village, to learn about Bedouin life, taste Bedouin cuisine and sleep in a Bedouin tent'. This at a time when the Israeli army was destroying Bedouin settlements in the Jordan valley and in the Negev. See H. Sherwood, 'The Israelis keep bulldozing their village, but still the Bedouin will not give up their land', *The Guardian* (3 March 2011). 75,000 Bedouins, formally Israeli citizens live in unrecognised villages which lack basic services such as piped water, electricity and sewage network. (See N. Gordon, *Israel's Occupation* (Berkeley: University of California Press, 2008), p. 261, n.79).
215 *Jewish Observer and Middle East Review* (28 June 1963).
216 Williams, *Fidler*, p. 177.
217 Kosmin, Lerman and Goldberg found 'a strikingly clear pattern of strengthening attachment to Israel as the degree of commitment to traditional Judaism rises'. *Attachment of British Jews*, p. 10.

3 British communists and Palestine

Despite its relatively small membership in relation to the Labour Party, the Communist Party of Great Britain took a leading role in anti-colonial campaigns. While the Labour Party between the wars put forward policies to reform the Empire through economic development and administrative training in the colonies, the international communist movement advised communist parties to support nationalist struggles seeking to throw off imperial rule. There were subsequently fluctuations in the communist movement's position on the role of the bourgeoisie in the colonies and on whether the colonial working masses were the only truly progressive force, but the importance attributed to anti-imperialist struggles, not least to create more favourable conditions for the Soviet state, did not waver. The Comintern, which had been set up in 1919 to co-ordinate the work of communist parties, expected the CPGB to play a leading role in the struggle against British imperialism. The party's support for anti-colonialism and opposition to race discrimination which communists held to be endemic to colonial rule drew to it a number of leading nationalists from Asia and Africa, among them Nehru and Kenyetta and activists for black rights, such as George Padmore and Paul Robeson.[1] Internationalism was always much more central to the political work and identity of communists than it was for Labour Party members.

British rule in Palestine and the deepening conflict from the 1920s between Arab nationalism and Zionism figured prominently in communist publications and contained critical insights that were missing in social democratic accounts. CPGB policy on developments in Palestine, as on all foreign policy matters, ultimately conformed to the lead given from Moscow, but its internal deliberations and even public pronouncements were nevertheless subject to conflicting pressures and revisions. This was particularly the case in the late 1930s and during the war when the CPGB struggled to reconcile its opposition to Zionism with winning the Jewish community's support for its anti-fascist mobilisation. Following the Second World War, when the Zionist movement entered into conflict with Britain, the international communist movement abandoned its previous opposition to Zionism. Until then the CPGB constituted the only significant voice among intellectuals and the labour movement to articulate the Arab nationalist point of view.

Several of the key historical turning points in the Arab-Zionist conflict occurred when the party was at the height of its influence: the 1936–1939 Arab rebellion, the publication of the Peel Commission's partition proposals in 1937, the UN vote on partition, in 1947, and the war in Palestine that followed. CPGB membership stood at 2,500 in 1930, but then rose through the party's most sectarian phase to 7,500 at the beginning of 1936. Over the following five years, with the international communist movement widening its appeal in the fight against fascism by adopting Popular Front tactics, the membership grew to 56,000 in 1942.[2] The Communist Party newspaper, the *Daily Worker*, which began in 1930 with a circulation of about 10,000, peaked around 120,000 at the beginning of 1948 before going into a steady decline. The party also ran a number of publications to disseminate its ideas on the left, retaining an effective network of activists among trade unionists and intellectuals until the end of the Cold War. 'For some forty years', writes Samuel, 'the CPGB exercised a gravitational pull on the British left, a field of force whose influence it was impossible to escape'.[3]

Communist policy on Palestine also affected the party's relationship to the Jewish working class and to its own Jewish members. Srebrnik, in a detailed study of the relationship between the CPGB and the Jewish East End, argues that from 1935 until 1947, with an interruption while the Nazi-Soviet Pact lasted, communist and Jewish working-class politics coincided. Their mutually supportive relationship is indicated by the relatively high proportion of Jews among the party's membership, particularly in London. 'Communism thrived for a time as a specifically *ethnic* means of political expression.'[4] Jewish communists were, in his view, 'left-wing nationalists', whose attraction to British communist politics was strongest during the latter part of the war and in its immediate aftermath. In the 1945 general election, Phil Piratin, one of two successful Communist parliamentary candidates, won in Stepney, in the heart of the Jewish East End and the party went on to win, later that year, ten seats in the London borough council elections. These triumphs marked the end rather than the beginning of the communists' electoral advance. As a result of the decline in the East End's Jewish working class, at the time of Piratin's victory in Stepney, the electoral register had about 51,000 eligible voters, which was about half the number on the 1939 register.[5]

After the war, Anglo-Jewry's increasingly middle-class composition was an important factor in its diminishing support for communism but, in Srebrnik's view, the relationship between the CPGB and the Jewish community was doomed from its inception because of Marxism's inability to recognise the force of nationalism. Ethnicity, he suggests, trumps other forms of collective identity because it is generated through 'private forms of communication' which he argues, quoting the political scientist, Jean Blondel, 'appear to shape the ideology of individuals more profoundly than do public forms of communication'.[6] It is, Srebrnik asserts, a more fundamental form of social relation because it is constituted through day-to-day contact rather than formal channels such as newspapers or political rallies. Thus the politicisation of ethnicity, consisting of the mobilisation of 'private' sentiments for political ends has, he alleges, a built-in advantage and will, therefore, ultimately win out. To support this view, he arbitrarily ascribes to the 'private' realm an eclectic selection of sociological characteristics which are supposed to demonstrate the primacy of ethnicity over class: 'Because ethnicity is ascribed at birth, it has temporal priority over other allegiances; furthermore, the "concatenation of residential and occupational segregation gives a decisive advantage to the development of ethnic rather than class solidarity".'[7] None of these factors, however, either individually or in combination necessarily assures the primacy of ethnicity. Class formation is always mediated through multiple determinations, with politics playing the decisive role in how collective identities crystallise in that process.

Srebrnik's own historical account bears this out. The communists were more successful than the left-wing Jewish nationalists, Poale Zion, because the politically most active section of Jewish workers was persuaded that the communist-led mobilisation around class grievances would be more effective than if workers organised on the basis of ethnicity. This was the appeal of the party's main campaigns in the East End: for deeper air raid shelters, better housing on affordable rents, the opening of the Second Front and organising street protests against the BUF. The Communist Party's readiness to confront fascism was, undoubtedly, its principal attraction to most Jews but the importance of ethnicity in their political alignment, arose not from their 'private' realm but in response to anti-semitism. It was when the communist movement no longer seemed to offer an adequate response to anti-semitism that Zionism began to make headway among Jewish workers and tension over Palestine developed between the Communist Party and many of its Jewish supporters.

For Srebrnik, however, Marxism's deficiency in relation to the national question made it only a question of time before the ethnic identity of the Jewish working class would assert itself and prise it from the Communist Party. 'Marxists', he asserts, 'were particularly obtuse in their analysis of the predicament Jews faced in the modern world', an obtuseness that was to be compounded by Stalinist orthodoxy on the national question.[8] On this basis Srebrnik forecloses any need to examine the CPGB's analysis of Zionism. Yet, notwithstanding the sclerotic impact of Stalinism on the international communist movement, the CPGB's reports and policy declarations on Palestine from the late 1920s until 1947 provided a critical insight into Zionist settlement and the British colonial rule that oversaw it.

The violent clashes which broke out between Jews and Arabs in August

1929, and led to 249 deaths, provoked the first extensive commentary on the Palestine conflict in the communist press. The bloodshed began from a dispute over the control of the Western Wall in Jerusalem's Old City, a holy site to both Jews and Muslims, and spread to several towns. The response of communist parties followed the line set by the Comintern, which was, in turn, guided by Moscow. In the summer of 1929, the Comintern initiated its most sectarian phase, characterising social democratic parties as a form of 'social fascism' that served as an instrument of the capitalist class 'for the paralysing of the activity of the masses in the struggle against the regime of Fascist dictatorship'.[9] Thus communist accounts of the communal clashes in Palestine and the British Labour government's measures to repress them were used to demonstrate the validity of this thesis. 'The Palestine crisis', declared J.T. Murphy in *The Communist Review*, 'provides a further glaring example of the integration of Social-Democracy with Fascist imperialism ... the Labour Government flung troops, aeroplanes, battleships into the situation with a promptitude which commanded the admiration of all the bourgeois forces'.[10] *Inprecorr*, the Comintern's publication, after pointing to the Zionist labour leaders' affiliation to the social democratic Second International, argued: 'The chief task which the Zionist socialists set the members and supporters of their party is to carry out the seizure of the land.' It noted that the Palestine Communist Party opposed 'the expropriation of the small peasants' land by the Zionists' and supported the 'brotherly union of the Arab and Jewish workers in the fight against the base action of the social imperialists'.[11] A more detailed and considered examination of the 1929 clashes appeared in *Labour Monthly*, the journal edited by the CPGB's chief ideologue, Palme Dutt.

Under the initials J.B. the article disputed attempts to characterise the violence as due to 'imperialist intrigue'. The underlying reasons lay in British rule effecting 'a fundamental transformation of the social structure' through its patronage of the Zionist movement. Jewish land purchase from the Arab big estate owners placed large sums at the disposal of this landed class, strengthening feudal power in the villages but further impoverishing the Bedouins and the poor peasants, the *fellahin*. 'The Zionist colonisation signified for the semi-nomadic Bedouins, who make up almost a fifth of the Arab population, that they were forced out of their usual pasture lands.' The peasants, in addition to the increased taxation imposed by the colonial authorities, saw their purchasing power diminish as Jewish immigration drove up non-agricultural prices. 'Thus the Government and the Zionist colonists, after having completely ruined the *fellahin* and the Bedouins, have made out of them an army of reserve labour of the cheapest kind.' They, along with the artisans, ruined by imported goods, were forming an urban proletariat. But, as workers, they faced obstacles to becoming organised by the Zionist trade union's refusal to accept Arab members: 'The Congress of the Jewish Trade Union organisation, "Histadrut", rejected an appeal for admission to membership put forward by a delegation of over 2,000 Arab workers.' Some Arab agriculture labourers employed in Jewish-owned orange groves were similarly rejected in 1928. It was in these circumstances, J.B. concluded, that the Arab working class and the other discontented groups came under the leadership of the 'treacherous feudal-bourgeois leaders bent on strengthening their alliance with imperialism'. It warned that Arab leaders were 'diverting the spontaneous movement of the masses into the channel of a Nationalist struggle and deceiving their followers'.[12]

The alternative the writer pointed to, was for the working class to assume the leadership of the struggle for national independence, based on the unity of Arab and Jewish workers. The article commended the Palestine Communist Party's stance which, in accordance with the 'class against class' line of the Comintern, sought to expose the Arab nationalist leadership and 'to promote the organisation of international trade unions on the basis of the identity of interests among Arab and Jewish workers'.[13] The communist proposal for an international union was in opposition to the purely Jewish-based Histadrut which, by the early 1930s, was the main institutional base of Labour Zionism in the *Yishuv*.

The Labour Zionist movement's commitment to acquiring land exclusively for Jewish use and its 'conquest of labour' strategy, by which it put pressure on Jewish enterprises to employ only Jewish labour, were criticised by communists though J.B. rejected the notion that Jewish workers in Palestine formed some kind of a labour aristocracy, arguing that they, like the Arab inhabitants, were deprived of the franchise and their wages had been 'levelled down and approximated to the wages of Arab workers'.[14] In reality, Jewish workers received a subsidy through the social insurance schemes of the Histadrut that was funded by the WZO. In the British-controlled public sector, Jewish workers were generally more highly paid than Arab workers often by the device of allocating them the more highly skilled tasks.[15]

In 1933, a writer for *Inprecorr*, diagnosing the background to the Arab strikes and demonstrations which broke out in October, pointed to a tendency for peasants to be 'ousted to an increasing extent from the Jewish plantations' and remarked that the Jewish 'national socialist organisations', Mapai and Poale Zion, had been particularly active in this work.[16] The *Daily Worker* portrayed the Arab strikes and demonstrations as aspects of the class struggle by Arab workers against British imperialism. It made no mention of the position of the Jewish labour organisations. An editorial envisioned the unity of Arab and Jewish workers to fight the British administration which 'with the help of Zionism is striving to construct an imperial citadel'.[17]

The prospects for cross-communal class solidarity were put to a test three years later. In April 1936, the Arab Higher Committee gave voice to the anti-colonial orientation of a rapidly spreading Palestinian strike movement by demanding a halt to Jewish immigration and to land sales to Jews. The strike lasted six months and inspired armed bands in the countryside to attack British military posts and property. It was not until the summer of 1939 that the colonial authorities completely crushed the rebellion. The *Daily Worker* covered the rebellion with frequent and supportive reports stressing that the Palestinians were struggling against British imperialism. It highlighted the RAF bombing of rebels and the troops killing, arresting and evicting villagers. Under the headline, 'Arab Village Sacked and Burned', it described an army punishment raid on the town of Lydda in response to the derailing of a train.[18] 'At Safad,' another dispatch reported, '32 Arabs have been arrested and six houses in the town and adjacent villages have been demolished'.[19] Zionist leaders and their supporters in the British Labour Party were maintaining that the rebellion was fascist instigated. A front-page article in the TUC-owned *Daily Herald*, under the headline, 'Italy Stirs Up Arab Riots', claimed: 'Secret agents, chiefly Italian, are behind the recent outbreak of terrorism in Palestine, in which 19 Jews have been killed.'[20] In Parliament, Herbert Morrison concluded that the 'trouble in Palestine has been created not by the masses of the Arab people at all, but through a minority of certain classes of the Arabs, probably mostly by the agents of Herr Hitler and Signor Mussolini'.[21] The Communists rejected this analysis.

A *Daily Worker* article conceded that it was part of Italian policy to foment trouble in the colonies of her rivals, but added: 'The talk of Italian money, however, sidetracks the real issues, by making this question the primary reason for the present unrest.'[22] An editorial declared: 'The Arabs are fighting for their liberation and independence. But very cunningly the capitalist press is trying to depict them as the paid tools of Mussolini.'[23] Jim Shields giving the main report on Palestine, at the party's Central Committee meeting in June 1936, was similarly dismissive of Italian and *effendi* influence to explain the rebellion.[24] The CPGB leadership embraced the Arab demands for a halt to Jewish immigration, the cessation of the sale of Arab lands and the constitution of a legislative assembly.[25] The Labour Party took the contrary position. It backed the British military repression to quell the rebellion and made no mention of the formation of representative government. The two parties differed both on the causes and the solution to the rebellion but, above all, in their assessments of the impact of Zionism on the Palestinian population.

British Labour leaders accepted the Labour Zionist explanation that Jewish settlement was opening up new markets as well as introducing improved farming methods and trade union organisation to the Arabs but Jim Shields, in his report, contested this interpretation. He attributed the Arabs' hostility to their 'acute unemployment problem which has arisen from the small peasants being evicted from the farms and driven from the land'.[26] The dynamics of this process was analysed in greater depth in *Labour Monthly*, by Thomas Hodgkin, who later became an academic and African specialist. He wrote pseudonymously as 'British Resident', possibly an ironic reference to the fact that he was expelled from Palestine in 1936, after resigning from his post in the Palestine Administration over the British response to the Arab rebellion.[27] Unless the Arabs succeeded in halting immigration and land sales, argued Hodgkin, they would become numerically outnumbered and lose the power to achieve political independence.

'Economically the Arabs are already dominated by the Jews who control the country's industries and share with the British control of its finance.'[28] Jews owned only a tenth of the land held by the Arabs but it was, he observed, mostly in the plains, some of the most fertile areas in the country. The average Arab landholding had declined by 1930 to about half the minimum subsistence area required and was decreasing still further as a result of Zionist land purchase. 'The process of Jewish settlement frequently involves for the Arab tenants the miserable round of sale by absentee landlords, inadequate compensation, expensive lawsuits dragging out over many years, police evictions, accompanied sometimes by shooting, and finally drifting to the towns.'[29] Although the Arabs tended to see, mistakenly, argued Hodgkin, Zionism as their main enemy rather than as an integral part of British imperial policy, their objection touched on a more fundamental contradiction. Their interests clashed, he explained, not with Jewish immigration *per se*, or with the sale of lands to Jews *per se*, but with these being controlled by the British government, in the interest of Zionism and of Britain, and to thwart Arab aspirations for independence. British imperialism was therefore the main enemy of the Arabs and Hodgkin reiterated the communist view that the solution lay in the coming together of Arab and Jewish workers, 'in a powerful, united Labour and Trade Union movement'.[30]

Communists and Labour Party politicians were at one in calling for this unity but whereas Labour tended to argue that the Arab *effendi* fomented the hostility between Jewish and Arab workers to keep the masses from the progressive influence of Jewish workers, according to communists, the enmity was generated by British imperialism using Zionism to drive a wedge between the two communities. In both perspectives, the cause of the division was extraneous to the working-class struggle and the resulting conflict was merely a temporary impediment to the development of class consciousness. The communists were, nevertheless, unlike Labour, critical of the Histadrut for excluding Arab workers from its ranks and from Jewish enterprises but they, too, failed to confront the sociological and political implications of a trade unionism that subordinated class to nationalist objectives. Communist analyses of the Palestine situation were constantly to invoke either the potential for the unity of Arab and Jewish workers or, more often, to judge this process to be well underway and gaining momentum. An editorial in the *Daily Worker* claimed that, in the period leading up to an Arab strike in 1933, 'Arab and Jewish workers have shown increasing signs of coming together'.[31]

During the 1936 Arab rebellion, a feature article in the *Daily Worker* again reported that Jewish and Arab workers 'find themselves more and more drawn together in the common struggle against bellicose Zionism and Arab Feudalism and against the arch enemy, British Imperialism'.[32] The action of Arab lightermen in assisting the evacuation of several hundred Jewish workers in the midst of the communal violence that erupted in Jaffa, in April 1936, was cited as evidence of class solidarity.[33] The Histadrut's role in undermining the Arab strike, though condemned by the Palestine Communist Party[34] did not fit into this picture and went unreported. At a time when the Comintern affirmed the need for the broadest possible unity among workers, communists were not inclined to dwell on the Histadrut pursuing national not class interests or on the consequent, sectarian gains of Jewish workers. There is no indication that the communist movement grappled with the idea that the Jewish working class, through its trade union, might be an integral part of the Zionist colonising project. The Communist movement's Marxism furnished no insight into the specificity of settler colonialism, depicting the *Yishuv* in crude instrumentalist terms as a tool of British imperialism which underrated its popular base and failed to grasp its specific structure. Even Hodgkin's more sophisticated elaboration of the official line characterised the Zionist movement's political orientation entirely by its connection to British imperialism and accorded no weight to its internal dynamics.

Once the Arab Higher Committee called off the strike, communist interest in the rebellion declined but, in June 1937, when the Peel Commission's Report was published, the party returned to the theme that British imperialism was fanning hatred between Arabs and Jews. Ivor Montagu, a film-maker and CPGB member, described the Commission's partition proposal that there be an Arab and a Jewish state as a 'classic example of "divide and rule".'[35] The Central Committee, too, saw it as hindering Jews, Christians and Muslims to develop common citizenship and demanded 'the termination of the Mandate; the recognition of an independent Arab state with full rights of citizenship for the Jews; and the institution of a democratically elected Legislative Assembly'.[36]

The democratic reforms demanded by the Arab nationalist leadership were seen by the party as conducive to building the unity of Arab and Jewish workers. The CPGB adhered to the line, laid down in 1935 by the Comintern's 7th Congress, that the national bourgeoisie was a progressive force. The decision was part of the communist movement abandoning its previous line for a Popular Front-style alliance aimed at uniting all progressive forces. Issie Panner, one of the party's specialists on Jewish affairs, writing under the pseudonym Rennap translated this into the Middle East context. In January 1939, he demanded that the Mufti be allowed by the British to represent the Palestinian side at a conference that was planned to take place in London, on the grounds that the Mufti, unlike the moderate leadership the British preferred, had the backing of his people.[37] A few months later, however, he warned that 'the Grand Mufti's entanglements with fascism' could bring the Palestinians worse oppression than British imperialism.[38]

British communist leaders knew that their stance on Palestine was attentively followed by Jewish party members and by the more politicised section of the Jewish working class. In the Central Committee's discussion of the 1936 Arab rebellion, Ted Bramley, a London organiser, observed: 'we have been driven to the situation of discussing this question because of the apparent revolt of the Jewish population in this country, against the line of our Party'. Another Central Committee member, Finlay Hart, the veteran Scottish communist, complained that Zionists were exploiting the strong national sentiment among the Jews. He reported that at meetings with Jewish workers, the party was being challenged to say where a national home for Jews could be established: 'Their fear of fascism which is bringing them closer to our party, makes them think they must have some place where they can work without interference in the world.'[39]

The Arab rebellion coincided with fascism making further advances in Europe and with Anglo-Jewry's deepening involvement in efforts to find funds and safe haven for Jewish refugees. The CPGB detected increasing competition in the Jewish community from Zionism. Its response was to draw attention to Birobidjan, the Jewish autonomous region in the Soviet Union,[40] and 'to make clear that the struggle of the Arabs is not against the Jews but is one against British imperialism'.[41] Despite such gestures, the party continued to face criticism from its Jewish members and sympathisers. A letter in the Daily Worker complained that an article in the paper on the Arab revolt was 'a violent attack upon the Jews and one which would rejoice Mosley and his Blackshirts'.[42] Three other letters hostile to the party line were published which suggests that many more were received. The regular column, 'Worker's Notebook', commented: 'There has been and there continues to be considerable confusion in the minds of our Jewish comrades in this country about the policy of the CP so far as the situation in Palestine is concerned.'[43] Three years later 'confusion' was still being reported. Jim Roche told the Central Committee, in June 1939, that the majority of the Jewish population in Leeds was under the influence of Zionism: 'there are people who supported us financially in the past, who are sore with the Party because they have the impression that the Party's attitude is the same as the fascists' except that we don't believe in oppressing them'.[44]

Communist assessment in the 1930s of Zionism's appeal to Jews had its mirror inverse in the Zionist perception of communist influence. A correspondent in the Young Zionist, in December 1932, complained that, among Jewish working-class youth, Zionism 'had made no headway. The tendency in the best part of our Jewish working class ... is to join the Communist Party.'[45] This concern was again raised in 1939. A worker for the East London Zionist Association claimed that the younger elements of the community 'are being gradually won over by extreme left views'.[46] In the light of such concerns, the Young Zionist counselled a more activist approach to oppose fascists in the East End. Poale Zion militants felt affinity with the anti-fascist mobilisation but they also saw their involvement as a way to prevent the Jewish community coming under the influence of communists, who were the leading force in the anti-fascist campaign.

The CPGB's support for the Arab rebellion and its anti-Zionism was a source of unease among some of its Jewish members. The leadership responded by setting up a Jewish Bureau to oversee the party's activities in the Jewish community. For most left-wing Jews the communists' anti-fascist activities and trade union work were generally of weightier consideration than their position on Palestine. 'The Jews in East London', recalls Joe Jacobs, who was a party activist in the area, 'were not yet in favour of Zionism'. To Jacobs, class was the over-riding issue: 'Jewish workers had to identify themselves with workers everywhere to organise for the overthrow of the capitalist system.'[47] His contemporary, Mick Mindel, a communist trade union organiser in the garment industry, is recalled by his grand nephew as 'aware of Zionism churning away, but he only ever saw it out of the corner of his eye'.[48] Many Jewish party members refused to accord much importance to Zionism and, during the war, the party met some resistance when it wanted some of them to focus their political work in the Jewish community.[49] They would have seen it as work of lesser importance because of the party's view, shared by its Jewish members, that Zionism was a movement of the Jewish middle class.[50]

The Communist Party's position on Palestine did have a limited influence on the left of the Labour Party. It was two trade unionists close to the Communist Party who moved a resolution, at the 1936 Labour Party Conference, attacking the British role in Palestine. Palme Dutt commented approvingly in the *Daily Worker*: 'The role of British imperialism and Zionism, and the struggle of the dispossessed Arab masses were explained by Alex Gossip and Lester Hutchinson on behalf of the Furnishing Trades' resolution for unity of the Arab and Jewish masses against British imperialism.'[51] From the Labour Party, Arthur Creech Jones conceded that criticism of Zionism had some support in Labour Party ranks. He referred, in 1939, to 'many comrades who feel the Arabs are being prejudiced by the establishment of a National Home in Palestine'.[52] At the Labour Party conference the following year an anti-Zionist amendment was moved in terms similar to communist pronouncements.[53]

Communist Party attacks on the Histadrut for excluding Arab workers certainly made an impression among its own followers. When the *Daily Worker* claimed that Jewish culture and ideas on trade unionism 'helped in raising the organisational and cultural level of the Arab workers'[54] – an argument used by Labour Zionists and by their British Labour Party supporters – a reader from the East End asked whether the columnist was aware 'that the Histadrut (Palestine TUC) leadership has not only debarred Arabs from entering the trade unions, but incites the Jewish against the Arab worker'.[55] Throughout the 1930s, communists argued against the Zionist case particularly within the Jewish community and encouraged Jewish comrades and sympathisers in this task. At a Poale Zion Conference the intervention by a member of the Workers' Circle, a Jewish Friendly Society, was headlined in the *Daily Worker*: 'Uproar at Meeting as Zionist Lie is Nailed'. The report claimed that a Workers' Circle member showed how the Arab unrest 'was the logical outcome of British Imperialist-Zionist policy of fomenting hatred between Jews and Arabs'.[56]

The communist movement condemned the British government's 1939

White Paper, which proposed, in addition to restricting Jewish immigration into Palestine, that the two communities participate in the Mandatory administration with a view to evolving, over a ten-year period, towards an independent Palestinian state. Rennap described the restriction on immigration as proof that the Zionists 'have been tricked by British imperialism' and characterised the offer of involving Jews and Arabs in the administration as amounting to a token political representation which would not lead to the Arab-Jewish co-operation needed for self-government. Instead, the two communities had to demand 'that a democratically elected assembly of the peoples of Palestine be called as soon as possible'.[57] The realisation of this ideal unity of the two peoples against imperialism served as the basis, over the following five years, for criticising the Zionist and the Palestinian nationalist leaderships in about equal measure. The party implicitly abandoned its earlier distinction between Arab and Jewish nationalism, which had pointed to the Zionist project facilitating imperialist involvement in the Middle East because of its dependence on British military protection and the ethnic enmity it generated.

In a series of interventions, Rennap set out how Arabs and Jews could bypass both the Arab nationalist leadership, in particular the Mufti, who had declared his allegiance to Hitler, and the Zionist leaders, Ben-Gurion and Weizmann, who 'hitched their wagons to the Imperialist kite instead of trying to come to terms with their Arab neighbours'.[58] He believed that beyond the political elite on either side, there lay pure class interest which given the 'correct' lead would be able to unite the two ethnic groups in common opposition to British imperialism. Rennap also detected signs of a non-sectarian leadership from left-wing Zionists and the Palestine Communist Party. The converse of this 'vanguardist' understanding of political forces was a constant underestimation of the extent to which the Zionist movement, by contrast to the Mufti and the traditional Palestinian leadership of religious and landed notables, controlled and incorporated its social base. The Zionist leadership's power was anchored in the bureaucratic structures of the Histadrut and the *kibbutzim* which organised Palestine's Jewish community in antagonistic relation to the Palestinians.

The idea that Zionism could be detached from its social base in Palestine and the consequent exaggerated importance given to the small number of left-Zionists advocating a bi-national solution made sense only on the basis of *Yishuvism*, which had been given currency earlier by the Jewish section of the Palestine Communist Party.[59] It derived from the notion that the *Yishuv*, having matured into a stable, national community, was largely autonomous from the Zionist movement and had the potential by virtue of its technical capacities and social organisation to be the most advanced political force in Palestine. This argument began to surface in Rennap's interventions from 1939, when he described Palestinian Jewry as an 'oppressed people' and called on them to defend the Histadrut.[60]

With the Nazi attack on the Soviet Union, in July 1941, British communists' priority was to rally the maximum support for the anti-fascist struggle and, in particular, behind its campaign for the Allies to open a second front to relieve the German military pressure on Soviet forces. The CPGB's Jewish Bureau was renamed the National Jewish Committee (NJC), a subcommittee of the party's International Affairs Committee, and the scope of its work was expanded. Among its tasks was to publish a monthly newspaper, the *Jewish Clarion*. The Committee estimated that there were 360,000 Jews in Britain of whom 250,000 were in London and added: 'in the East End 60/70,000 Jews constitute 15% to 18% of the population covered by the East London Sub-District of the party.'[61] The NJC was assigned to counter the influence of Zionism within Anglo-Jewry.

The Zionist organisations' growth in the Jewish community, which had accelerated in the 1930s, expanded further during the war years. Poale Zion saw its membership of only 450 in 1939, grow to 1,500 by 1945, and its propaganda activities also increased.[62] Sam Alexander, a member of the NJC who also served on the Executive of the Workers' Circle, reported in early 1948 that the 'Zionist Federation has a membership of 30,000 (many of whom are members of more than one affiliate)'.[63] This was out of a Jewish population that had reached 450,000. The size of Zionist organisations' membership gives, however, only a very general impression of political attitudes in the Jewish community. Internal Communist Party papers identified two widely prevalent attitudes. One was passivity. The NJC noted: 'it is a characteristic feature of Jewish life at the present time and especially since the advent of Fascism and its growth in the past decade, to avoid open and organisational association with progressive movements. Many Jews and Jewish organisations fear that to do so would add grist to the mill of anti-Semitism'.[64] The other prevalent attitude, according to the party, was sympathy for Zionism, which it believed had gained ground during the war and especially from the summer of 1942, as increasing numbers of reports of the Nazi extermination programme reached the Jewish community.

The NJC called on party members to 'challenge Zionists everywhere, first and foremost on the part they are playing individually and organisationally in the war effort in such a way as to bring out the diversionist character of Zionism'.[65] In practice, however, a less combative approach was adopted. The NJC sought to reassess the party's traditional hostility to Zionism, motivated by the feeling that without such a step communists would be hindered in winning over the Jewish community. It commented: 'our approach to the problem of Palestine and to questions related to it have appeared negative and unsympathetic, thus widening the breach between us and those who have been affected by Zionist propaganda. In these circumstances it [is] necessary to examine anew our estimation of the problem of Palestine and of related questions such as immigration, land purchase etc. in the light of the need for greatest unity in the fight against fascism'.[66]

The party experienced some difficulties in recruiting Jewish party members to carry out the more intense organisational and propaganda work among Jews that it believed was required for the wartime, anti-fascist mobilisation. Heppell distinguishes a divergence between generations among Jewish party activists. The older immigrants tended to have a strong sense of ethnic identity and prior to the war had taken on the party's 'Jewish work'. The younger, more assimilated Jewish members generally felt greater commitment to their position in the party than to their links to the Jewish community.[67] This difference became less relevant during war. Jack Gaster, the son of the Sephardi community's Chief Rabbi was estranged from his family and had no involvement in specifically 'Jewish work' of the party until the war when he became chairperson of the NJC.[68]

The leadership might have been expected to welcome the dissolution of Jewish identity but the CPGB, for its anti-fascist strategy, required 'Jewish work' and to this end William Gallacher dispensed with the idea that communists aimed to make class-consciousness supersede all other forms of collective identity. He turned Jews' commitment to their ethnic identity into a measure of their political reliability: 'However a Jewish man or woman has been educated or brought up, if they are not loyal to their own people, their loyalty to others will always be in question.'[69] Rennap, using the historical materialist explanation of anti-semitism, sought to account for the viscosity of ethnicity. Jewish distinctiveness, he explained, was formed in the interstices of the feudal order. Barred from handicraft work and land ownership, Jews were forced into trade and usury. Although capitalism tended to integrate 'Jewish' activities into the economic mainstream, Jews often remained concentrated in their old occupations that survived from the previous social order. In the period of imperialism, this provided the opportunity 'to divert mass struggle against capitalism into mass persecution of Jews'.[70] So far Rennap followed the standard Marxist explanation of the time, however; instead of anticipating further economic development bringing about the inevitable assimilation of Jews he pointed to the persistence of their 'national characteristics and consciousness'. In 1946, Alf Sherman, in an internal party document, attacked this thesis. Demonstrating fealty to Stalinist dogma with the same zeal as he would to neo-liberalism thirty years later, he nevertheless landed some telling blows. He dismissed the argument that it required Jews to work among their 'own people' as unnecessary opportunism since winning support for communism from the Jewish working class and petty bourgeoisie, far from posing any special difficulties, met with more success than from the rest of the population.[71] Jews made up about 10 per cent of the party's membership around this time, a far higher proportion than their share of the population.[72] Sherman's more basic objection was that Gallacher and Rennap were legitimising ethnic separatism. He attacked them for ignoring that Jews, by Stalin's definition, were not a nation since they had neither a common language, nor a common economic life, nor a common territory. In fact, Stalin's position was not an inoculation against Jewish separatism as the Soviet promotion of Biro-Bidjan showed, but Sherman's criticism is nonetheless revealing of how far Gallacher and Rennap had retreated from the earlier communist position. Their implicit acceptance of the idea that Jews were inassimilable was conceding one of the central tenets of Zionism (and of anti-semitism).

This affirmation of Jewish distinctiveness ran with the grain of the communist propaganda directed at Anglo-Jewry which from 1943 also narrowed its objection to Zionism. Dutt concurred with the approach. 'With regard to the reactionary character of Zionism,' he told the NJC, 'the task is one of very patient enlightenment and not primarily polemical propaganda'.[73] But the party took no steps to initiate the 'patient enlightenment'. This is illustrated by its position, at the end of the war, on the resettlement of the Jewish Displaced Person. The CPGB knew that the Zionist appeal in the Jewish community derived in large measure in presenting Palestine as the only practical solution for finding homes for the Jews of continental Europe liberated from the concentration camps. The party leadership did not exclude Palestine once it became 'free and independent' but balanced this by stating: 'Britain is allowing 190,000 Poles, most of whom are fascists, free entry to what would be a far smaller number of Jewish victims of fascism.'[74] This statement had no practical consequence because it was not translated into a political campaign around the demand for allowing more Jews in to Britain. Yet, the party was not a stranger to taking on campaigns to move public opinion. It had done so during the war, not only in support of Britain opening a second front against Hitler to relieve the pressure on the Soviet Union but also to advocate that the British government should reopen negotiations with the Indian nationalist movement. The party reported that in response to its initiative on India, 'a well-organised and thorough going campaign has resulted in resolutions being passed by the most important factories, trade union branches, shop stewards' committee and local Labour Parties'.[75] The following year, the party lent its support to a campaign over the Bengal famine. No similar mobilisation was attempted by the CPGB in support of its call for more Jewish Displaced Persons to be allowed into Britain. It was not a priority for the party and therefore not an issue over which it was prepared to risk working-class hostility.

The NJC, in an internal document, struck a different note from the party leadership in the summer of 1945. Welcoming the Soviet supported resolution passed shortly before, at the World Trade Union Conference in London, which had stated that the Jewish people 'must be enabled to continue the rebuilding of Palestine as their National Home', the NJC asked the party 'to reassess the present position of Palestine and the Middle East'. It claimed that the Yishuv, with a population of 600,000, 'has assumed the character of a firmly established community and as such is entitled to full rights'. It alluded to Stalin's definition of a nation, remarking that the Yishuv 'was established on a territory (however small that is), with an economic life (more advanced and cohesive than that of many older communities), a common language (Hebrew – with a very prolific cultural life) and a common psychological background' and called for 'the Jewish community to enjoy the rights of self-government'. The Committee still proclaimed that 'the principles of Zionism have always been and remain reactionary and unscientific', but without further explanation went on to state that the Yishuv established by the Zionist movement had to be assessed independently of its political ideology. 'The Jews of Palestine', it declared, 'constitute the most progressive force in the Middle East'. The document left open 'the future status of Palestine' but called on the abrogation of the 1939 White Paper's limitation on the number of Jews allowed to settle in Palestine and on the sale of land to Jews, on the basis that these measures constituted 'an infringement of the democratic rights of the Jews in Palestine'. Of the democratic rights of the Palestinians it made no mention, concluding: 'We realise that this new approach may be interpreted as a betrayal of the Arab national struggle or as an acceptance of Zionism'.[76]

Indicating fierce debates behind the scenes, Gaster by the turn of the year rowed back closer to the leadership's position. His wobbling reflected the difficulty of reconciling the party's policy with the growing sentiment in the Jewish community that Palestine should be kept open for Jews seeking refuge. In *Labour Monthly*, Gaster argued that Jews had brought about economic development in Palestine but also recalled that Arab workers had been largely excluded from this 'by the Zionist policy of Jewish exclusiveness'. He reiterated that the main anti-colonial force was the Arab struggle for independence and that the Jews in Palestine should end the sectarian practice of excluding Arab labour from Jewish industry and agriculture. Some of the Displaced Persons he argued should be permitted into Palestine but on condition that this was not done with the Zionist aim 'of continued Jewish immigration until a Jewish majority can impose a Jewish State on an unwilling Arab minority'. The unity created between Arabs and Jews in the economy would he suggested lead to a 'joint Arab-Jewish state'.[77] In the absence of any significant anti-Zionist political force within the Yishuv to act along these lines, Gaster's proposals amounted to empty pieties. The Yishuv's *raison d'être* was economic separatism and, short of being forced by political pressure or military defeat, there was not slightest prospect of it yielding to appeals for Arab and Jewish unity.

The same month that this article appeared, the party submitted a statement on Palestine to the Anglo-American Committee of Inquiry, which Bevin had initiated in a last-ditch effort to find a settlement to the conflict. The statement had a different emphasis on Jewish entry into Palestine from Gaster's article, though he, along with Piratin, attended its submission to the Committee. It recommended that the international community should assist Displaced Persons to return to their country of origin. Those who were unwilling to do so should be allowed entry elsewhere, 'not under sufferance but as honoured guests'. When Piratin was asked at the Committee hearing whether this meant that American immigration laws should be changed, he replied: 'And our British arrangements'. The party, on this occasion, ruled out Palestine taking the Displaced Persons: 'no country or countries have the right to impose upon another country that is not free or able to express an opinion through democratic representative institutions, the acceptance of immigrants'. It also claimed that a Jewish state in Palestine, 'would put the Jewish people in the position of being the instrument of international and imperialist power politicians in the Middle East' and, inflame elsewhere, 'latent anti-semitic tendencies by giving credence to the idea that Jews are "foreigners"'. Thus the party leadership did not follow the NJC's 'reassessment' and did not repeat Gaster's call for 'a joint Arab-Jewish state' which implied shared sovereignty, at a time when the Jews of Palestine were only half the size of its Arab population. The CPGB's statement also held back from committing itself to any particular political form for the future state opting, instead, for the more general formulation that the Mandate should be terminated and the two communities be left to settle 'freely and democratically', enabling Arabs and Jews to live 'as free and equal citizens'.[78]

For a time this stood as the official line but in the meanwhile, the NJC had second thoughts and declared 'that the Arabs however backward they are in comparison with the Jews both socially, culturally and economically, [they] are at the moment more progressive than the Jews of Palestine'.[79] The NJC's inconsistencies and divergence from the party leadership's line occurred in the absence of a clear lead from the Soviet leadership. Moscow, during the war and in its immediate aftermath, had left the management of communist policy in the Empire to the British party. In 1947, however, the Soviet Union took the decisive step of reversing the communist movement's past opposition to the setting up of a Jewish state and the following year, when the Arab states declared war against the newly established state, the communist press castigated Arab leaders as representing imperialist interests.

The new policy was announced by the Soviet foreign minister, Andrei Gromyko, in an address to the UN General Assembly on 14 May 1947, on the basis that 'not a single West European state had succeeded in protecting the elementary rights of the Jewish people and shielding them from the violence of the fascist butchers'.[80] Gromyko proposed that the interest of Arabs and Jews could be safeguarded in an 'integral Arab-Jewish democratic state' but if that was unattainable then Palestine should be partitioned to form two states, one for the Arabs and the other for the Jews. The link between the persecution of Jews in Europe and the solution to be sought in Palestine was one that communists had previously rejected.[81] But the Soviet Union had begun to link them by encouraging the emigration of Jews to Palestine from the emerging Soviet bloc countries. 'The mass departure of approximately 280,000 Jews by land and sea from the Soviet bloc countries could only have occurred with the knowledge and consent of Moscow.'[82] The Soviet leadership had come to regard the Zionist militias' armed conflict with the British and the establishment of a Jewish state arising from that conflict as an opportunity to weaken Britain in the Middle East. This was the underlying rationale for the CPGB's attitude to developments in Palestine.

There had been acts of terrorism against the British authorities in Palestine since 1942 from two small right-wing Zionist groups but, from October 1945, these activities escalated as they came under the coordination of the Haganah, the main military arm of the Yishuv. 'The newly united resistance movement immediately attacked British communications throughout the country.'[83] Behind this development, Gaster discerned 'a sharpening conflict between the leading Zionists, who are increasingly identified with the Jewish bourgeoisie and are willing tools of British imperialism and the rest of the Jewish community'.[84] Meyer Vilner, the leader of the Palestine Communist Party (PCP) from which the Arab members had split off in May 1943, argued in a statement to the CPGB that Jews and Arabs could form a partnership on the basis of a bi-national state and in opposition to British imperialism. What made this new orientation possible was, he claimed, the growth of a proletariat, on the Arab side, and the Histadrut's decision to readmit into its ranks the Communist Party, on the Jewish side, which he implied would change the Histadrut's previous sectarian and exclusionary practices.[85] In reality, it was the PCP's willingness to alter its political line that allowed its readmission into the Histadrut. Without explicitly reversing its opposition to further Jewish immigration, the PCP expressed its readiness to help build the Yishuv and to oppose the 1939 White Paper's 'anti-democratic and racial laws', which were the clauses aimed at restricting the Jewish population from becoming the majority community in Palestine.

In June 1946, when the British responded to attacks by Zionist militias by carrying out searches and mass arrests, a statement by the CPGB's Central Committee pointed to the arrest without charge of some 2,000 Jews, 'including leaders of the Palestine Jewish community, Jewish agency, Trade Union and Co-operative'. These leaders, characterised by the party in the past as reactionaries seeking to turn the Jews of Palestine into the tools of British imperialism, were now described as men and women who 'occupy the same positions and command the same respect, in Palestine, as the leaders of similar organisations do in Britain'.[86] A shift in position was also evident in the resolution on colonial affairs that the CPGB leadership proposed to the 19th Party Congress, held in February 1947. The previous Congress had called for a joint struggle by Arabs and Jews 'to end the Zionist policy of Jewish exclusiveness in industry and agriculture' and for Jewish immigration to be subjected to Arab-Jewish agreement.[87] By contrast, the Central Committee's resolution pointed to imperialism as the source of oppression but made no reference to Zionism. It provoked a party member to complain that it was 'vague': 'No mention is made in the resolution as to our view on Jewish immigration, Zionism and questions appertaining to the problem.'[88]

The vagueness disguised the adoption of Yishuvism. The international communist movement characterised the armed attacks on the British military presence in Palestine as progressive on the basis that it came from the Yishuv not from the Zionist movement. Hyman Levy, one of the CPGB's prominent Jewish intellectuals, explained that the Yishuv had succeeded in bypassing the Zionist movement to emerge as a progressive, anti-imperialist force. In Palestine, he explained, 'the movement leftwards has proceeded apace, and now the recognition of the new State by the U.S.S.R. has clinched the situation ... The struggle in Palestine has taken on a clear anti-imperialist character for the masses of the Jewish people, while the role of the Zionist leadership intriguing with imperialism has become exposed.'[89] Thus, following the Soviet agreement to partition in October 1947, the communist movement finally transferred the mantle of anti-imperialism from Arab nationalism to Zionism, a political about-turn that was disguised behind a spurious distinction between the politics of the Yishuv and the Zionist movement.

In the wake of the UN General Assembly's vote, in November 1947, to divide Palestine into two states (with Jerusalem as a separate entity under international control), fighting broke out. A Daily Worker editorial under the title 'Who is to Blame?' explained: 'The offensive is being waged by the Arabs who are using armaments supplied by the British for that purpose ... The shedding of Jewish blood must cease and the Government must be compelled to abandon its imperialist policy. '[90] Arab suffering, however, did not elicit similar sympathy. On 26 April, the Daily Worker reported a 'big Arab evacuation' from Haifa and two days later that Palestinians were fleeing from Jaffa, following a mortar attack by Irgun. Yet an editorial attributing responsibility for the war to Bevin, the British foreign minister, declared: 'In this situation the sympathy of all men and women will go out to the struggling Jewish community which although severely menaced is fighting to maintain its right as a people to uphold the decision of the United Nations.'[91]

On 15 May, when the British Mandate ended and Ben-Gurion declared the establishment of the state of Israel, King Abdullah of Transjordan ordered his troops into Palestine, ostensibly as part of the Arab League's plan to liberate Palestine. 'This reactionary war,' commented the CPGB's Central Committee, 'conducted by the chieftains of the Arab League under British control is entirely against the interests of the Arab masses, who in all countries of the Middle East are striving for freedom from imperialist domination'.[92] In the pages of the Daily Worker, the Arab war effort was depicted as devoid of popular support. A report alleged that demonstrations in Arab capitals in favour of the war were staged and were in contrast to 'the marked apathy shown by the Arab people throughout the war'.[93] The Arab armies were described as containing 'everything except those very Arab people of Palestine who are supposed to be fighting'.[94] And those that fought, an editorial explained, did so 'weakly and finally ran away because the heart of the common people was not in the war'.[95]

During the first half of the war the Daily Worker emphasised that Israel was adhering to the partition determined by the UN. Derek Kartun, the paper's foreign editor, who travelled with the Haganah during some of the fighting, argued that Israel's two strengths were, first, the people's determination and, second, 'precisely that it has conformed all along with the decisions of the United

Nations'.[96] Yet when Zionist forces assumed control over most of Jerusalem, which was not in accordance with the UN partition plan, the *Daily Worker* did not interpret it as a violation of a UN decision but as a response to UN bias, to a situation where 'far from genuine internationalisation being in sight, Count Bernadotte [the UN Mediator] is intent upon giving Jerusalem to King Abdullah'.[97] It is the newspaper's coverage of the flight of the Palestinian Arabs, however, which gives the clearest view of the way the CPGB and the international communist movement sought to portray the war.

On the day that Israel declared its independence, Kartun wrote: 'The struggle for an independent, democratic State is not being made any easier by the policy of the Jewish administration towards the Arabs. For there is little doubt that the Haganah cannot be absolved of responsibility for the unhappy flight of the Haifa Arab population.' The Jewish Agency had said, he noted, that it would welcome back the Arabs who had fled from the towns and villages. 'But', he added, 'it is known privately that Jewish leaders are not displeased to see the Arab population of Israel drastically reduced'.[98] In another report, he remarked that some Jewish leaders 'would gladly see Israel totally without an Arab population'.[99] These sobering reflections on what amounted to ethnic cleansing proved to be isolated expressions of disquiet over the Zionist treatment of the Palestinians. Kartun, himself, did not accord much significance to this aspect of the war. Thus on reaching the Arab town of Safad – according to him the first correspondent to do so after it had been over-run by the Haganah – he made no comment on the absence of the town's former inhabitants. He appears to have been enraptured by the capture of the citadel which dominated the Arab quarters: 'it is almost incredible', he enthused, 'that an army without mountain artillery and heavy air support could ever have taken this fortress', and apparently to reassure his readers that the Haganah's operation was not only a remarkable military feat but also fully justified, he added that Safad was 'well within the boundaries' of the UN defined Jewish state.[100]

In August 1948, most of the British press, in response to urgent appeals from the UN and by the British government, began to give prominence to the Palestinians who had been forced to flee their homes during the fighting. 'A human disaster', wrote *The Times*, 'comparable to the San Francisco or Japanese earthquakes, tidal waves, and flood is the grim description of the plight of 300,000 helpless people, given by Sir Raphael Cilento after his six-day tour for the United Nations of the Arab refugee camps. They are faced with food shortage, with the risk of an epidemic disease and with terrible uncertainty.'[101] The *Daily Worker*, by contrast, struck a sceptical note: 'The Foreign Office is seeking by means of a brand-new formula to rouse world opinion against Israel and to fortify as far as possible the shaky position of the Arab states in the Palestine dispute'. The article alleged that the Arabs were made homeless by British policy: 'The 80,000 Arabs in Jaffa, for instance, were persuaded to leave the city before the entry of Jewish forces, largely as result of British propaganda to the effect that the Jews would slaughter them if they stayed.'[102] A fortnight later, the paper charged that the commander of the Arab Liberation Army, Fawzi El Kawji, had in many areas terrorised Palestinian Arabs into flight 'and is thus very largely responsible for the present Arab refugee problem'.[103] By this stage, the only military force the *Daily Worker* was prepared to exonerate from causing Palestinians to abandon their homes was the Israeli army that captured the villages from which they fled. Its report on Nazareth pointing out that the inhabitants had stayed, made no reference to the fact that the likely cause for this was Israel's fear that the expulsion of its predominantly Christian population would incur Western disapproval. Instead, the correspondent interpreted it as evidence of the Zionist authorities pursuing 'a policy of conciliation and friendship', concluding: 'This is characteristic of the policy of the Israeli provisional government and army in all occupied Arab towns and villages'.[104]

The military clashes that began in December 1947 did not end, and then not completely, until January 1949. Throughout this period, *Labour Monthly*, which normally carried the party's analyses of international developments, made only one brief reference to the war. Its editor, Palme Dutt, had been an exponent of the CPGB's opposition to partition and to the formation of a Jewish state. The declaration, in March 1947, of the Conference of Empire Communists which he had helped to formulate, confirmed this opposition only shortly before Gromyko announced the Soviet acceptance of the principle of partition.[105] Dutt counselled in a letter to the Palestinian communist leader, Emile Touma, that the two positions should not be counterposed, adding: 'The diplomatic task of the Soviet Union and the political task of our parties do not always coincide in concrete details.'[106] Although this seemed to imply that the communist movement did not have to follow the Soviet lead, Dutt was an implausible champion for an independent stance. He was not always in step with policy turns initiated in Moscow but he invariably fell in line, most notoriously in 1939, following the Soviet-Nazi pact, when by contrast to Harry Pollitt, the CPGB's leader up to then, he pressed for the adoption of Moscow's line that both Germany and Britain were imperialist powers and therefore there was no reason to prioritise the struggle against fascist Germany. When that line was reversed in 1941, with the Nazis' attack on the Soviet Union, Dutt changed his position accordingly. By comparison, the CPGB ideological summersault over Palestine was much less contentious on the left. In *Labour Monthly*, Dutt briefly echoed the new policy, stating that an aggressive war had been revived in the Middle East 'through Britain's subsidised puppets with British arms and officers against the Jewish state and the United Nation's decision'.[107] He paid no heed, however, to the UN vote on 11 December 1948, demanding that Israel allow the return of the refugees. Following the vote he claimed that the collapse of the Arab League 'quickens the anti-imperialist consciousness of the Arab masses to recognise their true enemy, not in the Jewish people, but in imperialism'.[108] The Zionist movement, at the point at which it seized state power, did not exist as a political actor in Dutt's analysis. His few lines on Palestine, in the midst of a war with major international implications, were calculated to say the minimum, indicating Dutt's unease that support for partition and the establishment of Israel would reflect poorly on his and *Labour Monthly's* standing, particularly among communists and nationalists in India.

The Soviet intervention on the side of the Zionists was not confined to declarations. Some Jews heading for Palestine were allowed to leave the Soviet bloc countries and the supply of rifles, machine guns and heavy weaponry from Czechoslovakia, after the Communist take-over in that country in March 1948, was acknowledged by Ben-Gurion to have played an important part in changing the balance of forces in favour of the Haganah. The weapons were paid for with $100,000 raised by the Zionist movement in the United States.[109] There was also assistance from the Hungarian Communist Party which in 1945–1948 formed part of a coalition government before taking total control. The branch in Hungary of the strongly pro-Soviet, Labour Zionist group, Hashomer Hatzair secured training from the Hungarian army for 1,500 of its volunteers for the Haganah and, until early 1949, the Hungarian authorities even as they were seeking to rein in the Zionist movement's internal political influence allowed *aliya* to be organised and for Jews from neighbouring eastern European countries to pass through the country on their way to Palestine.[110]

Following the 1948 Arab-Israeli war, the CPGB called for the UN resolution to be fully implemented by the setting up of a Palestinian Arab and a Jewish state, but its campaigning was limited to demanding that the British government recognise the state of Israel. It continued to omit reference to the UN Security Council resolutions, passed in November and December 1948, which required Israel to withdraw its forces to the positions they held on 14 October and to repatriate the Palestinian refugees. The near silence on the fate of the Palestinians by British communists – who in the past had taken a leading part in campaigns on rights to national self-determination – contributed to removing the issue from political debate in Britain. Efforts to draw attention to the refugees' plight were left to a few humanitarians and still fewer Arab sympathisers. The CPGB's support for the Zionists during the war contributed to the public indifference to the fate of Palestinians and helped to consolidate Zionism's influence over the left-wing of the Jewish community. By the early 1950s, the CPGB, in accordance with the Soviet position, became increasingly critical of Israel for its close relations with the West but its ritualistic denunciation of Zionism, was tainted by the officially inspired anti-semitism in the Soviet Union which further diminished the party's standing in the Jewish community.

Notes

1 J. Callaghan, 'The Communists and the Colonies: Anti-Imperialism between the Wars', in G. Andrews, N. Fishman and K. Morgan (eds) *Opening the Books: Essays on the Cultural and Social History of British Communism* (London: Pluto Press, 1995), pp. 12–13.

2 K. Morgan, 'The Communist Party and the Daily Worker 1930–1956', in Andrews, Fishman and Morgan, *Opening the Books*, p. 144; H. Pelling, *The British Communist Party* (London: A. and C. Black, 1975), p. 104; J. Eaden and D. Renton, *The Communist Party of Great Britain since 1920* (Basington: Palgrave, 2002), p. 84.
3 R. Samuel, 'Staying Power: The Lost World of British Communism', *New Left Review*, 156 (March/April 1986), 110.
4 H. Srebrnik, 'Sidestepping the Contradictions: the Communist Party, Jewish Communists and Zionism 1935–48', in Andrews, Fishman, Morgan (eds), *Opening the Books*, p. 136
5 *East London Advertiser* (25 May 1945).
6 H. Srebrnik, *London Jews and British Communism 1935–1945* (Ilford: Valentine, Mitchell, 1995), p. 148.
7 Ibid., p. 149.
8 Srebrnik, 'Sidestepping the Contradictions', p. 124.
9 K. McDermott and J. Agnew, *Comintern: A History of International Communism from Lenin to Stalin* (Basingstoke: Macmillan, 1996), p. 238.
10 J.T. Murphy, 'Growth of Social Fascism in Britain', *The Communist Review*, 2:1 (1930), 29.
11 *Inprecorr* (9 August 1929).
12 J.B., 'The Class Character of the Palestine Rising' Pt. 1, *Labour Monthly*, 12:3 (1930), 159–162.
13 J.B., 'The Class Character of the Palestine Rising' Pt. 2, *Labour Monthly*, 12:4 (1930), 249.
14 Ibid., 245.
15 B. Smith, *The Roots of Separatism* (London: I.B. Tauris, 1993), Ch. 7.
16 *Inprecorr* (17 November 1933).
17 *Daily Worker* (30 July 1933).
18 Ibid. (30 July 1933).
19 Ibid. (18 August 1936).
20 *Daily Herald* (13 May 1936).
21 *Hansard*, Commons, v. 347, c. 2138, 23 May 1939.
22 *Daily Worker* (21 May 1936).
23 Ibid. (18 August 1936).
24 LHA, CPGB Papers, Central Committee, Minutes, 5 June 1936.
25 *World Views and News* (20 June 1936).
26 CPGB Papers, Central Committee, Minutes, 5 June 1936.
27 T. Hodgkin, *Letters from Palestine 1932–1936* (London: Quartet, 1986).
28 British Resident, 'The Events in Palestine', *Labour Monthly*, 18:7 (1936), 411.
29 British Resident, 'Is Palestine Prosperous', *Labour Monthly*, 18:11, 688.
30 British Resident 'Open Letter to Socialist Zionist', *Labour Monthly*, 20:4 (1938), 248.
31 *Daily Worker* (30 November 1933).
32 Ibid. (8 May 1936).
33 Ibid. (8 and 21 May 1936).
34 M. Budeiri, *The Palestine Communist Party* (London: Ithaca Press, 1979), p. 96.
35 *Daily Worker* (10 July 1937).
36 *Daily Worker* (17 July 1937).
37 I. Rennap, 'The Arab-Jewish Conference', *Labour Monthly*, 21:1 (1939), 54.
38 I. Rennap, 'The Position in Palestine and the Path to Peace', *Labour Monthly*, 21:5 (1939), 309.
39 CPGB Papers, Central Committee, Minutes, 5 June 1936.

40 Daily Worker (7 and 20 May, 10 July 1936), in Preface to I. Rennap, Anti-Semitism and the Jewish Question (London: Lawrence & Wishart, 1942).
41 CPGB Papers, Central Committee, Minutes, 5 June 1936.
42 Daily Worker (27 April 1936).
43 Ibid. (26 June 1936).
44 CPGB Papers, Central Committee, Minutes, 24 June 1939.
45 G. Alderman, London Jewry and London Politics 1889–1986 (London: Routledge, 1989), p. 97.
46 Cesarani, 'Zionism in England', p. 160.
47 J. Jacobs, Out of the Ghetto (London: Calverts North Star Press, 1978), p. 208.
48 J. Freedland, Jacob's Gift (London: Penguin Books, 2006), p. 283.
49 J. Heppell, 'A Question of "Jewish Politics"? The Jewish Section of the Communist Party of Great Britain 1936–1945', in C. Collette and S. Bird (eds), Jews, Labour and the Left (Aldershot: Ashgate, 2000), p. 105.
50 CPGB Papers, Letter of the National Jewish Committee of the Communist Party, 10 October 1943, CP/CENT/CTTE/02/02.
51 Daily Worker (27 April 1936).
52 LPACR, 1939, p. 256.
53 LPACR, 1940, p. 173.
54 Daily Worker (21 May 1936).
55 Ibid. (26 May 1936).
56 Ibid. (27 May 1936).
57 I. Rennap, 'The White Paper on Palestine', World News and Views, 19:30 (3 June 1939).
58 Rennap, 'The Position in Palestine', 311.
59 J. Franzen, 'Communism versus Zionism: The Comintern, Yishuvism, and the Palestine Communist Party', Journal of Palestine Studies, 34:2 (2007), 6–24.
60 Franzen, 'Communism versus Zionism', 16.
61 CPGB Papers, National Jewish Committee, 'Letter of the National Jewish Committee of the Communist Party', 10 October 1943, CP/CENT/CTTE/02/02.
62 Labour Party Annual Conference Reports contain membership figures for Poale Zion, which was an affiliated organisation. See also N. Jackson, 'Poale Zion in Wartime' (Jewish Labour, November-December 1943).
63 Jewish Clarion (March 1948).
64 Sheffield University, Zaidman Papers, National Jewish Committee, 'The Jewish Question', n.d., circa early 1945, 118/4/2(i).
65 CPGB Papers, National Jewish Committee, 'Our Attitude to Zionist Activities and the War', Discussion paper at the enlarged meeting of the NJC on 10 October 1943, CP/CENT/CTTE/02/02.
66 Zaidman Papers, National Jewish Committee, 'Party Work Amongst Jews in Britain', 9 November 1943, 118/9f/xix.
67 Heppell, 'Question of Jewish Politics', p. 109.
68 G. Cohen, 'From "Insufferable Petty Bourgeois" to Trusted Communist: Jack Gaster, the Revolutionary Policy Committee and the Communist Party', in J. McIlroy, K. Morgan and A. Campbell (eds), Party People Communist Lives (London: Lawrence & Wishart, 2001), p. 201.
69 W. Gallacher, 'Preface' to I. Rennap, Anti-Semitism and the Jewish Question (London: Lawrence & Wishart, 1942).
70 Gallacher, 'Praface', p. 29.
71 Zaidman Papers, 'Jewish Nationality – A Pernicious Illusion'. It was written under the pseudonym 'Avis'. Zaidman April 1946, 118/9f/14-15. Showing the same logical consistency, Sherman defended his invitation to the openly racist, French far-right

leader, Le Pen, to a private meeting on the fringe of the 1987 Conservative Party Conference: 'If we condemn French or English people's desire for a French France or English England as "racist" are we not conceding the notorious "Zionism" is racism slogan of the Communist-Arab-Moslem dominated UN?' (Jewish Chronicle, 2 October 1987).

72 K. Morgan, G. Cohen and A. Flinn (eds), Communists and British Society 1920–1921 (London: Rivers Oran Press, 2007), p. 188.
73 Zaidman Papers, National Jewish Committee, 'The Third Annual Enlarged Meeting', 13–14 January 1945, 118/9f/xxi.
74 CPGB Papers, Report of the Executive Committee, 19th National Congress, Covering period December 1945 to November 1946, CP/CENT/CONG/05/03, p. 41.
75 British Library, India Office Collection, Special Branch Report, L/PJ/12/454 'India League Campaign Following the Breakdown of Negotiations with India' not dated, circa June 1942. The organisation of factory ballots to pressure the British government to agree to Indian self-determination is referred to in the CPGB's publication, World Views and News, 2 May 1942, 224.
76 CPGB Papers, 'Statement to the International Affairs Committee from the National Jewish Committee', n.d., circa summer 1945, CP/IND/DUTT/15/7.
77 J. Gaster, 'Palestine', Labour Monthly, 28:1 (January 1946), pp. 27–30.
78 'European Jewry and the Palestine Problem: Statement Submitted to the Anglo-American Committee of Inquiry by the CPGB' (CPGB, January 1946, London).
79 CPGB Papers, Information Document Prepared by the National Jewish Committee, January 1947, CP/IND/DUTT/15/7.
80 I. Strizhov, 'The Soviet Position on the Establishment of the State Of Israel', in Y. Ro'i (ed.), Jews and Jewish Life in Russia and the Soviet Union (Essex: Frank Cass, 1995), p. 309.
81 CPGB, 'European Jewry and the Palestine Problem'.
82 A. Kochavi, Post-Holocaust Politics: Britain, the United States and Jewish Refugees (Chapel Hill: University of North Carolina Press, 2001), p. 227.
83 N. Lucas, Modern History of Israel (London: Weidenfeld and Nicholson, 1974), p. 223.
84 Gaster, 'Palestine', p. 29.
85 CPGB Papers, M. Vilner, Memorandum, 4 November 1945, CP/IND/DUTT/15/7.
86 Jewish Clarion (July 1946).
87 Ibid. (December 1945).
88 World Views and News (January 1948).
89 Jewish Clarion (July 1948).
90 Daily Worker (3 April 1948).
91 Ibid. (28 April 1948).
92 Ibid. (22 May 1948).
93 Ibid. (20 July 1948).
94 Ibid. (29 July 1948).
95 Ibid. (19 November 1948).
96 Ibid. (29 June 1948).
97 Ibid. (2 August 1948).
98 Ibid. (15 May 1948).
99 Ibid. (24 May 1948).
100 Ibid. (20 May 1948).
101 The Times (9 August 1948).
102 Daily Worker (4 August 1948).
103 Ibid. (17 August 1948).
104 Ibid. (11 August 1948).
105 Jewish Clarion (March-April 1947).

106 CPGB Papers, Dutt to Touma, 4 June 1947, CP/IND/DUTT/15/7.
107 P. Dutt, 'Notes of the Month', *Labour Monthly*, 30:8 (1948), 225.
108 *Labour Monthly*, 31:2 (1949), 38.
109 Pappe, *Ethnic Cleansing*, p. 44; Morris, *Righteous Victims*, pp. 193 and 215. The Czechoslovak communist assistance despite following Moscow's line was subsequently used to discredit and remove the Czech party's general secretary, Rudolf Slansky, and several other Jewish party members. They were accused at their show trial in 1952, in which most of the principal defendants were Jewish, of being 'Zionist agents' in terms that were unmistakably anti-semitic. See F. Fejtő, *Les Juifs et L'Antisemitisme dans les Pays Communistes* (Librairie Plon, 1960, Paris) pp. 64–69.
110 R. Győri Szabó, *A kommunizmus és a zsidóság az 1945 utáni Magyarországon* [*Communism and Jews in post-1945 Hungary*] (Budapest: Gondolat, 2009) pp. 87 and 106. As Győri Szabó makes clear, the Hungarian Communist Party in this period also engaged in anti-semitic incitement, thinly disguised as attacks against speculators and black marketers, to try to increase its popular support. From 1949, the purging of 'Zionist elements' in the party was used for the same purpose.

4 Post-war social democracy and Israel

The CPGB's defection from the side of Palestinians along with their rejection of Arab nationalism meant that the Palestinians lost their only ally in Britain. Although the party's influence had been confined to the relatively small anti-colonial left its policy shift represented a significant narrowing of the opinions available to the politically more engaged section of the British public. During 1948, British press coverage of the Arab-Israeli war was mostly tucked away in brief reports even in the more serious newspapers. The expulsion of the Palestinians by Zionist forces began in late December 1947; it would cause about 300,000 refugees by the time of the Israeli state's establishment on 15 May the following year. Yet, it was not until the second week of August 1948 that the British press, encouraged by UN officials, gave prominence to the unfolding crisis. A *Jewish Chronicle* editorial observed: 'this week *The Times*, the *Observer*, the *Economist*, the *News Chronicle*, and the *Daily Express* have simultaneously drawn attention to the fact that there are some 300,000 Arab fugitives from Jewish-occupied territory.'[1] The leader-writer expressed concern over these reports, a few of which appeared to suggest that if it was right for some 200,000 Jewish Displaced Persons in Europe to enter Palestine as immigrants then it was only right that the Palestinian refugees should be allowed to return. The *Jewish Chronicle*'s anxiety soon abated. The refugees remained in the camps and the British media's interest in their fate all but disappeared for almost two decades.

    The earlier terrorist campaign by Zionist military groups which aimed at forcing the British to lift the restriction on Jewish immigration into Palestine had triggered some intense discussion in the press but left a confused picture. At the end of 1946, Mass Observation in its tracking of public opinion found that even 'at the peak point of interest in Palestine, there is little evidence of more than a rudimentary knowledge of the situation among the majority of the people'. It noted a 'vague anti-semitism' and a feeling that Britain should let the two sides 'scrap it out' but also some sympathy both for the Arabs and for the idea that Jews should have a 'national home' somewhere.[2] Following the Irgun's hanging of two

British sergeants in July 1947, there was an outbreak of antisemitic attacks against Jewish shops in Manchester, Eccles and Liverpool and against a gathering of Jewish ex-servicemen in East London[3] but Mass Observation found that 'the hanging incident had not had any pronounced lasting effect upon opinion'.[4] Again, public opinion on Palestine was amenable to being guided but it was beset by conflicting signals.

On coming to power in July 1945, the Labour government had to address, in relation to Palestine, two immediate concerns: first, to preserve British military presence in the Middle East and, second, to resettle the Jewish DPs gathered in the allied controlled zones of Germany, Austria and Italy. In the first few months of liberation over 3.8 million displaced people, many of them Jews, returned to their countries of origin but among those still in camps, mainly in the American zone, and awaiting resettlement, were the survivors of the Nazi extermination programme and Jews seeking refuge from Poland and Russia.[5] The Attlee government's decision on taking office to stand by the 1939 White Paper's limitation on Jewish immigration set the Labour Party's leadership in conflict with the Zionist movement. It was a repeat of the confrontation which had occurred in 1930. Again the US government's stance would prove decisive. Although Zionists alleged an antisemitic attitude on the part of the Labour government's foreign secretary, Ernest Bevin, he was pursuing a policy which was perfectly explicable in terms of Britain's strategic interest. Indeed, in 1930, when the Passfield White Paper had threatened to inflict a by-election defeat on the Labour candidate in Whitechapel, Bevin had shown similar pragmatism. He intervened at the time with government ministers to get the proposal on limiting Jewish immigration retracted as the Zionist movement demanded.[6] But as foreign secretary in the post-war Labour government, Bevin was set on a collision course with the Zionist movement. He was well aware of the Gordian knot he had to confront in the Middle East. 'The tragedy of the Balfour Declaration,' he ruefully reflected in 1945, 'was that it was unilateral. Neither its British authors, nor its American and British supporters, had taken account of the Arabs.'[7]

The Arab question for Bevin was not primarily a humanitarian issue though he could not ignore that aspect. The Middle East, a Foreign Office briefing paper reminded the Cabinet, 'is a focal point of communications, a source of oil, a shield to Africa and the Indian Ocean, an irreplaceable offensive base'.[8] British officials regarded the Suez Canal and its military bases alongside it as vital to the Empire. Palestine's importance was enhanced, therefore, after the war by uncertainty over Britain being able to renew its military agreement with Egypt and by fear of Soviet power extending southwards by exploiting Arab discontent with the despotic, conservative rulers on whom British influence in the Middle East depended. Bevin had good reason, therefore, to continue the policy of restricting Jewish settlement in Palestine. But his resolve was to be undermined by the combination of Britain's heavy economic and military dependence on the US, and President Truman's policy on Palestine ceding ground to the Zionist movement as a result of domestic political pressure.

The issue that brought Palestine to the fore in Anglo-American relations was the Zionist demand that 100,000 Jews in the DP camps be immediately admitted to Palestine. The quota fixed by the 1939 White Paper was nearly exhausted by the end of the war but the figure of 100,000 was partly symbolic. The Zionist leadership had spelled out in 1942, in the Biltmore Programme, that its aim was the formation in Palestine not merely of a 'Jewish home' but of a Jewish state.[9] It wanted, therefore, the British to remove all restrictions on Jewish immigration to Palestine. In the run up to the 1944 US presidential elections, a well-organised Zionist campaign was able to secure sympathetic statements in support of this demand, from Roosevelt, on the Democratic side, and from leading Republicans. This 'would seem to prove', reflected the political philosopher Hannah Arendt, who had escaped to the US from Nazi persecution a few years earlier, 'that the great majority of voting Jews in America are regarded as pro-Palestinian and that, so far as there is "a Jewish vote," it is influenced by the programme for Palestine to the same degree as the Polish vote is influenced by American foreign policy toward Poland'. American Jews, even the non-Zionists, she noted, had a more positive attitude towards the Palestine project than was the case among 'assimilants' in Europe. In the US, she explained, Jewish interest in Palestine 'is only natural, needs no excuses, in a country where so many national splinter groups show loyalty to their mother countries'.[10] The Zionists' claim of fertilising the desert and introducing modern techniques would have also resonated with the mythology of the American frontiersmen. 'Zionism after all,' mused Richard Crossman in 1946, 'is merely the attempt by the European Jew to rebuild his national life on the soil of Palestine in much the same way as the American settler developed the west'.[11] He did not pursue the analogy to the outcome that it suggested for the indigenous people.

A journalist who travelled to Cincinnati, Ohio, at the end of 1945, to appraise the mood of a Jewish community removed from the political maelstrom, found that many Reform Jews who had previously opposed Zionism were going over to the Zionist camp, 'as the situation in Palestine deteriorates and as reports continue to pour in of reviving anti-Semitism in Europe'.[12] The membership of the Zionist Organisation of America reached around 950,000 out of a Jewish population of 5 million. It had over four hundred local emergency committees and, with substantial funding, a 'central office was set up in New York and fourteen special departments, each under experts in their respective fields, were immediately established'. The new structure showed impressive results: in 1944 'ten per cent of the 3,300 columns reprinting Zionist press releases were found in the general American press. By 1945 this number increased to twenty-five per cent giving a total of 4,000 columns.'[13] The Congressional elections later that year made Truman particularly attentive to Zionist lobbying believing that it could sway Jewish electors in New York, which had a Jewish population of about 2 million. Thus the Attlee government's efforts to associate Truman with a Palestine policy aimed at retaining the support of Britain's Arab allies ran up against a powerful, countervailing force in the US.

Differences between London and Washington manifested themselves first over the approach to the DPs in Europe. Truman, on taking over the reigns of power from Roosevelt, commissioned Earl Harrison, a lawyer and academic, to report on their conditions in the camps run by the Allies. Harrison described a harrowing situation. Three months after V-E Day, he found Jews still wearing their pyjama-like camp garb or SS uniforms, guarded behind barbed-wire fences in 'some of the most notorious of the concentration camps, amidst crowded, frequently unsanitary and generally grim conditions, in complete idleness, with no opportunity except surreptitiously to communicate with the outside world'. The approximately 100,000 Jews in the British and American zones, less than 10 per cent of the remaining DPs were grouped by the country from which they originated with the result, Harrison observed, that the special needs of the Jewish survivors were not addressed. He recommended, as an immediate step, that Jews who could not be rehoused should be placed in separate camps and be accessible to Jewish agencies. Attlee in a letter to Truman rejected these proposals on the grounds that the separate treatment of Jews would cause resentment among other DPs but more probably because of fears that such measures would facilitate Zionist propaganda work. Still more unacceptable, from the British government's point of view, was Harrison's recommendation that there be a 'quick evacuation of all non-repatriable Jews in Germany and Austria, who wish it, to Palestine'. Although he counselled the US and British governments to accept 'reasonable numbers' into their countries, he indicated his agreement with the Jewish Agency's call that 'one hundred thousand additional entry certificates be made available' for entry to Palestine.

Harrison suggested that this would be in line with the thinking of the newly elected Labour government citing, in support, from the 1944 Labour Party conference statement that 'it is morally wrong and politically indefensible to impose obstacles to the entry of Palestine now on any Jews who desire to go there'.[14] Truman responded by urging the Labour government to allow 100,000 Jewish DPs into Palestine but he was rebuffed by Attlee and Bevin, who in government could not turn a blind eye, as their party had in the past, to Arab opposition. Bevin still wanted, however, to involve the Americans in finding, and possibly imposing, a solution and he secured Truman's agreement to an Anglo-American Committee of Inquiry to make policy recommendations on the basis of conditions in Palestine and by reference to the problem of Jewish immigration. Bevin had anticipated that the Committee would devise a plan which could be implemented without greatly upsetting the balance of forces that underpinned the British presence in Palestine. The Committee composed of six Americans and six British, chosen by their respective governments, visited Austria to assess the situation at the Jewish DP centres and conducted hearings in

London, Washington, Cairo and Jerusalem. The Committee, encouraged by Bevin's prior commitment that if its recommendations were unanimous they would be accepted, managed to agree on a set of proposals. It included that 100,000 Jewish DPs be issued with entry certificates to Palestine and that Arabs and Jews should form self-governing communities within a unitary state, administered by the British, 'pending the execution of a trusteeship agreement under the United Nations'.[15]

Soon after the inquiry's completion, Richard Crossman, a former Oxford don and recently elected Labour MP, who had served on the Committee, published his account of its deliberations, under the title *Palestine Mission*. In the opinion of the American historian Wm. R. Louis: 'For perception of the Arab as well as the Jewish side of the case, *Palestine Mission*, stands above all other contemporary writings of the committee. Crossman's insights were penetrating and imaginative. During the course of the investigation he became a convinced Zionist for intellectual as well as humanitarian reasons, and his ideas about socialism played an important part in the transformation of his attitude.'[16] This assessment grossly exaggerates Crossman's perspicacity but *Palestine Mission*, by explaining his conversion to Zionism, does offer an unusually detailed exposition of some of the key elements in social democratic thinking on Palestine in the immediate post-war years. There were other post-war Labour politicians, most notably Herbert Morrison, Arthur Greenwood and Harold Wilson who like Crossman gave voice to the Labour Party's pro-Zionist orientation but none wrestled with the Palestine issue with the same intellectual intensity.

In *Palestine Mission* Crossman began from the premise that the Zionist project had to be assessed by relation to its own aims, which implied attributing secondary importance not only to the issue of the DPs but also to Zionism's impact on the Palestinian Arabs. He baldly asserts that Britain 'cannot assist the Jews in Palestine without violating Arab rights' and for him, echoing Weizmann, this was the lesser injustice though one that he believed would be mitigated by Jewish settlement bringing social and economic advances to the region. But his interpretation of Zionist settlement's impact on the Palestinians fails to dispel the impression that his anticipation of there being a trade off for them between rights and benefits is chimerical. Recalling a visit to a commune of the Labour Zionist group, Hashomer Hatzair, that had been established by the removal of Palestinians from the land, Crossman dismissively remarks on 'the filthy tin-can settlement where the Arab peasants, evicted from the Plain of Esdraelon, huddle', without registering the slightest sympathy for them.[17] And after a meeting with Palestinian notables in Beisan, 'a filthy town', he remarks that in that area 'land sales are still going on, and one-third of the land has been lost already'.[18] He notes this merely to explain the notables' hostility to the Jews rather than as an indicator of its wider implication for the Palestinian peasantry. 'Looking at the position of the Palestinian Arab, I had to admit that no western colonist in any other country had done so little harm, or disturbed so little the life of the indigenous people.'[19] For him the Mandate was being manipulated in the Palestinians' favour, notwithstanding the fact that it incorporated the Balfour Declaration and therefore the commitment to the building of a Jewish 'home'. He reached this improbable conclusion on the basis of 'anti-Jewish bias' in the attitude of British officials, which he contrasted to their benign paternalism towards the Palestinians.[20] It confirmed for him that the Zionists were addressing a graver and historically more intractable injustice, which he felt was borne out by the situation he faced; on the one hand, the Jewish DPs desperate for a home and, on the other, Palestinians to whom Jewish settlement on their land had done 'little harm'.

Crossman recounts that after his colleagues had met some of the Holocaust survivors in Austria, the 'abstract argument about Zionism and the Jewish state seemed curiously remote'.[21] Yet notwithstanding the emotional impact of this visit on him, he remained unconvinced of the Zionist claim that Palestine offered the solution to antisemitism. A 'Jewish Commonwealth will neither solve the Jewish problem nor reduce anti-Semitism. Only for the tiny minority of Jews who actually go to Palestine will it afford a solution.' For those who remained in other countries, the 'vast majority', Zionism would satisfy 'an inner need' but constitute 'an added menace'.[22] The more immediate and pragmatic consideration for supporting the entry of the Jewish displaced into Palestine, which the Zionists demanded and Earl Harrison had endorsed, was that the DPs themselves wished to go to Palestine. What the DPs wished could not be abstracted, however, from the options open to them. As the *Economist* had pointedly observed: 'If a Jewish DP is asked whether or not he wants to go to Palestine, his answer will depend upon the alternatives offered. If the only alternative is a palliasse at Belsen, he is bound to say yes.'[23] For the Jews liberated from the Nazis only to languish in DP camps, it became evident that an international solution to their plight based on several countries offering them sanctuary was unlikely.

Many of the displaced had made their way home or to other countries but the number of Jews in United Nations Relief and Rehabilitation Administration (UNRRA) camps increased from 18,000 at the end of 1946 to over 167,000 by mid-1947.[24] Some of the Jewish returnees fled from outbursts of antisemitism in Poland and elsewhere in Eastern Europe, their departure, as indicated in the previous chapter, encouraged by the communist authorities. A survey, conducted among the survivors of Dachau soon after their liberation, indicated that 15 per cent desired to go to Palestine, whereas 65 per cent wished to return to their home countries.[25] Later surveys in DP camps would show much higher proportion wanting to enter Palestine.[26] In the intervening period hundreds of Zionist envoys from Palestine, mainly from the Labour Zionist groups, were sent to persuade them. 'Each party tried to put its people in control of the committees that governed the DP camps and assumed that the refugees would continue to support them once they arrived in Palestine.'[27] Crossman, describing the state of mind of the DPs in Austria, scoffed at the idea that their preference for going to

Palestine could be put down to propaganda, but he conceded that they had little choice: 'Even if there had not been a single foreign Zionist or a trace of Zionist propaganda in the camps these people would have opted for Palestine ... For nine months, huddled together, these Jews had had nothing to do but to discuss the future. They knew that they were not wanted by the western democracies.'[28]

The Anglo-American Committee's report made only a token appeal to the US and British governments, 'to find new homes for "displaced persons"' in association with other countries, but it assumed that this would not happen, by declaring: 'We know of no country to which the great majority can go in the immediate future other than Palestine.' Adding, with less nuance and candour than Crossman in his book: 'Furthermore that is where almost all of them want to go.'[29]

Crossman acknowledged that the decision over the 100,000 displaced Jews being allowed to go to Palestine was not merely about finding homes for the displaced. It would be difficult on such grounds, he noted 'to remove the legitimate Arab objection that democracies should practise humanity as well as preaching it to Moslems'.[30] The real issue was whether the US and Britain should support the formation of a Jewish state and for this he sought justification not merely on humanitarian grounds which, he knew, could be met by other than the Zionist solution but on the basis of a deeper, more compelling historical necessity. Yet, the necessity that he presents merely reiterates the well-rehearsed nationalist rhetoric of Zionism. 'The Jew who opposes the national home and tries to convert Judaism into a religious sect is denying the greatest Jewish achievement of our age and suppressing a part of his own personality. ... In the twentieth century a people without a nationhood is a people without virility.'[31] Ironically, this 'greatest Jewish achievement' is no more than the nation state that many other ethnic groups had already attained. In terms almost identical to those used by the Belgian socialist leader Vandervelde two decades earlier, Crossman declares that he could not support a Jewish state if it were merely a 'national home', but if it is 'a socialist commonwealth, intensely democratic, intensely collectivist and strong enough to fend for itself'.[32] He cites a passage from the diary that he kept during the Commission's work, in which he toyed with the idea that the *Yishuv* 'will develop into the finest piece of Western socialism since Vienna', only to remind himself that 'no one suggested that the Vienna socialists should go out and occupy the mountain homes of the Greeks in the Peloponnesus'.[33] He anticipated danger to the 'national home' coming not from Zionist land acquisition and economic separatism which he considered to be part of its revolutionary impact on the Middle East and, 'in the long run', beneficial to the Arabs, but because the Jewish settler was 'arrogant, tactless and uncomprehending of the Arab point of view', qualities which he failed to link to the power relation intrinsic to the colonising enterprise.[34]

Crossman's 'Arab point of view' is the timeless, Oriental outlook. In his reconstruction of the two conflicting nationalist forces in Palestine, the Zionists are the harbingers of a future free of antisemitism and modelled on socialism, while the Palestinian Arabs are presented as devoid of any historical project. They embody the past: obdurate villagers, clinging to their outmoded ways. Crossman refers fleetingly to Albert Hourani, but makes no reference to the argument he had presented to the Anglo-American Committee. Hourani, born to Lebanese parents in Manchester and later a renowned Middle East scholar, was working for the Arab Office in Jerusalem when he presented his testimony to one of the hearings of the Anglo-American Committee. The British High Commissioner commented that his presentation 'did something to prove the existence of the Palestinian Arabs'.[35] It indicated moreover the existence of a progressive Arab nationalism which Crossman chose to disregard.

Hourani argued that the Zionist demand for 100,000 Jewish refugees to be allowed into Palestine was 'not to solve the refugee problem for its own sake, but to secure political domination in Palestine'. He recalled that 'responsible Zionists have talked seriously about the evacuation of the Arab population, or part of it, to other parts of the Arab world'. Even partition would not be sufficient for some sections of the Zionist movement, it would merely serve as a stepping-stone for further expansion. Jews could live in Palestine with full rights as citizens but Zionism's aim to carve out a state was unacceptable to the indigenous population and the wider Arab world. This was not an isolated stance by a liberal-minded Arab intellectual. Arab states made several proposals between 1946–1947 'in favour of integrating the Jews living in Palestine in what would have effectively been a bi-national state, they also made a proposal about the Jewish refugees then in Europe'.[36] An important current of thinking in the Arab world was quite prepared for Palestine to share in the burden of accommodating Jewish refugees but only if that was decoupled from the Zionist project. Transforming Palestine's Arab character, Hourani pointed out, could be carried out only 'by violence or by securing an artificial domination supported from outside'.[37] The contrast with Crossman, on this point, could not have been sharper. They had very different understandings of what was entailed in imperial rule. The Labour politician saw imperialism not as a complex of power relations organised around economic exploitation but as a policy responsible for shoring up the Arab ruling classes though, curiously, not in facilitating Zionist settlement activity. He therefore predicted that a socialist Jewish state in bringing to its neighbours 'the ideas and the techniques of western civilisation' would accelerate 'the downfall of the medieval social order' and 'in so doing it will grow into the life of the Middle East, and grow away from its present dependence on the west'.[38]

Crossman's belief that Labour Zionism could become a reforming force in the British Empire was fuelled by the notion, widely held in Labour Party ranks after the war, that with a socialist government in London, the Empire could be reformed in a socialist direction. The Labour Party's handbook for speakers advised: 'Imperialism is dead, but the Empire has been given a new life. Socialist planning is developing it not for personal profit, but for the Common Weal.'[39]

Bevin had justified in similar terms the setting up of the British Middle East Office in Cairo with a development division to provide technical assistance for economic modernisation in the region and with the aspiration that this would translate into a 'peasants not pashas' approach to development. The policy lacked, however, the capital investment to launch any substantial development schemes and, in any case, was eclipsed by concern over potential Soviet and nationalist threats to British bases in the Middle East which depended on the 'pashas'.[40] It also depended on a close alliance with the United States. In 1947, Crossman, Michael Foot and Ian Mikardo drafted a pamphlet entitled *Keep Left* which, with the support of fifteen Labour MPs, sought to remind the government of its socialist commitments. It also built on the idea that the British Empire could evolve into a socialist force. They argued that Britain should ally neither with the US nor the Soviet Union but form closer ties with continental Europe and the Commonwealth. The longing for this 'third force' politics imagined as a social democratic modernising project bringing development to the colonial world tallied with Crossman's enthusiasm for a Jewish state in Palestine: 'Jewry and the British Commonwealth are linked by a common fate. "One World," neither Communist nor anti-Communist.'[41]

To Crossman's deep disappointment, the Anglo-American Committee's recommendations were shunned by the British government. Although the Committee presented them as a compromise between the opposing sides, the Palestinians were being asked to give up half their land for the prospect of self-government in the remainder, while the Zionists would secure the immediate benefit of increasing the *Yishuv*'s population by 100,000. Oliver Stanley, a Conservative and former secretary of state for the Colonies, described it as 'a compromise in which one side got all the action and the other side just got the words'.[42] Bevin, too, saw that allowing 100,000 Jewish DPs to enter Palestine immediately without even the precondition that the Zionist military groups disarm was not going to secure Arab acquiescence and would require a military commitment that Britain could not afford. Truman's opportunist backing for the proposal to allow 100,000 Jewish DPs to enter Palestine, while ignoring the Committee's other recommendations, provoked Bevin's outburst at the Labour Party conference in 1946, that 'this was proposed with the purest of motives. They do not want too many Jews in New York.'[43] Bevin's point would have been more telling if his own government had offered entry to Britain to a substantial proportion of the remaining displaced Jews. The government in this period was struggling to supply workers for agriculture and such industries as construction, coal mining and textiles. In March, a committee of Cabinet-rank ministers estimating the labour shortage to be one million, commented: 'all the evidence suggests that there is little hope of restoring the balance between requirements and supply for some time to come.'[44] By July 1948, 163,000 working aliens had been recruited through official schemes and 50,000 on individual permits. The recruits were mainly former members of Polish troops and their dependents but also Ukrainians and Yugoslavs.[45] Piratin, in a Communist Party pamphlet, echoing the party's executive's report two year earlier, asked rhetorically why Poles had been recruited into Britain to fill gaps in the labour force and yet the government claimed to have no room 'for a few thousand Jewish refugees who have been the greatest victims of Fascism, and whose political and social outlook is in accordance with our own'.[46] A Labour Party internal document hinted at the official thinking behind recruiting from the DPs nationalities other than Jews. It explained that the government 'does not encourage these elements to form groups in this country which by developing political organisation, may endeavour to exert pressure on the Government ... European volunteer workers are therefore split-up on arrival on the basis of occupation and without any attempt to preserve racial or cultural entities'.[47]

In 1946, a further attempt had been made to find a common position with the US on Palestine through a modified version of the Anglo-American Committee's recommendations. The package of proposals in the so-called Morrison Grady plan was mocked at the time for putting forward a proposal that the Colonial Office must have had in draft form before the Anglo-American Committee had been appointed. Its constitutional proposals were a throw-back to the 1919 Government of India Act which made a futile attempt to divert the Indian nationalist movement from the main levers of the central state into occupying itself with road repair and sewage disposal on the provincial level. On the model of the diarchy introduced by that Act, the Morrison Grady plan envisaged the formation of an Arab and a Jewish province, each with some executive powers and an elected assembly but with Britain retaining overall control. On the contentious issue of immigration, this would mean, Morrison explained, that 'as long as the economic absorptive capacity of the province was not exceeded, the Central Government would authorise the immigration desired by the provincial government'.[48] The Morrison Grady plan was, however, more than a throwback to the past, it was an admission that the beneficial effects of Zionist settlement for the Arabs had little to show for it and, therefore, the imperial state had to assume a more interventionist role.

Morrison explained to Parliament that the joint committee of experts he and Truman's nominee, Henry Grady, had headed in order to consider the Anglo-American Committee's recommendations, recognised that the poor living standards of the Palestinian Arabs should be addressed. The problem they faced was the product of the previous two decades. As Zionist economic separatism developed, the gap between the two communities' living standard had widened. Past attempts by British officials in Jerusalem to assist the Arab sector had been over-ruled in London to avoid imposing an additional burden on British tax payers. The Arab farmers' difficulty in accessing loans, raised by the Palestinian delegation to London in 1930, touched on only one aspect of the authorities' neglect of the Arab sector which, unlike the *Yishuv*, did not have access to alternative financial resources. The Palestinian community's schooling, that was largely dependent on government funding, also faced serious under-investment. Heading the 1930 Royal Commission enquiry, Sir John Hope Simpson had noted that for the financial year 1928–1929, the Zionist Executive's budget for less than 20,000 Jewish school children exceeded the Palestine government's expenditure for a potential school-age population five times that size.[49] At the Mandate's termination, in May 1948, 'about half of the 800 Arab villages had no schools at all' and the limited schooling available failed to provide scientific and technical training.[50]

At the Mandate's deathbed, Morrison and Grady were promising that Britain and, still more, the US would assume responsibility for delivering economic development to the Palestinians. The joint committee suggested that the US grant 50,000 million dollars for this purpose.[51] Morrison still clung to the illusion that the conflict between Zionism and the Palestinians stemmed from their different levels of development and could be resolved by assisting the Palestinians to close that gap. The idea that the Zionist movement's sectarian practices, which it required for nation-building, would prove to be acceptable to the Palestinians as long as they experienced economic improvements was, probably, the most enduring myth in Labour's pro-Zionist mindset.[52] Unsurprisingly, the Morrison Grady plan was rejected by both Arabs and Zionists. President Truman, too, refused to accept it. 'The opposition in this country to the plan', he wrote to Attlee, alluding to Zionist lobbying, 'has become so intense that it is now clear it would be impossible to rally in favour of it sufficient public opinion to enable this government to give it effective support'.[53] It was the last British-led initiative at constitutional reform. In February 1947, the government decided to refer the Palestine issue to the United Nations.

Without US backing, Britain had neither the military nor the economic resources to impose a solution. Yet, in 1944, the British government spent £4.5 million in Palestine on maintaining law and order, 'nine times the sum budgeted for health, six times the sum spent on education'.[54] The Morrison Grady plan was unveiled against the background of Zionist military groups stepping up their terrorist campaign to lift the restriction on Jewish immigration and the British army increasing its repression. Shortly before the plan was announced the underground, right-wing Zionist group, Irgun Zwei Leumi, blew up the King David Hotel in Jerusalem where the secretariat of the British administration was housed. Ninety-one people were killed.

The escalation of the conflict was to deepen the rift between the Labour government and its pro-Zionist backbench MPs. Criticism of the Labour government's Palestine policy was coming mostly from the Labour Party's left-wing. They alleged that the policy to placate Arab opinion was driving the moderate Zionists, willing to co-operate with Britain, into the hands of extremists. A group of MPs which included Crossman, Jennie Lee, Michael Foot, Sidney Silverman and Woodrow Wyatt, in a letter to Attlee complained: 'In Palestine and the Middle East the pledged policy of the Labour Party has been sacrificed to the needs of imperial defence as seen by the C.I.G.S. [Chief of the Imperial General Staff].' Labour's left-wing in this period believed that Bevin's strategy in the Eastern Mediterranean was infected with what the letter's signatories called 'the anti-red virus', cultivated in the United States. They commended, as the antidote, the 'middle way between the extreme alternatives of American "free enterprise" economics and Russian totalitarian socio-political life'.[55] There were to be some differences among members of this group on where exactly 'the middle way' ran, with Crossman deciding fairly early that it should be closer to the US. The Labour left's commitment to building a 'third force', nevertheless, continued to define its position on foreign affairs, while Labour Zionism by virtue of its social democratic politics was seen as a natural ally. By contrast, the emerging anti-colonial movements – be they in Africa or the Arab world – were not seriously considered in this context. At the 1945 general election, Orwell commented, 'the avoidance of imperial issues was quite astonishing. When foreign affairs were mentioned at all, the reference was almost invariably to the U.S.S.R. or the United States'.[56]

Although the issue of granting independence to the colonies, and most notably to India, was debated among Labour's imperial affairs specialists, the self-determination of colonial people did not become an integral part of the party's political outlook until after the launch, in 1954, of the Movement for Colonial Freedom (MCF). The party's left-wing was no exception in this respect. Its weekly newspaper, *Tribune*, in a 1948 editorial headed 'Let's Stay in Africa', acclaimed the virtues of empire: 'Africa offers huge material resources which can be exploited for the benefit of Britain and the world.'[57] The advent of a Labour government was portrayed as turning to progressive ends the international division of labour inherited from imperialism. The 'new Commonwealth', a subsequent issue declared had to be a 'great partnership in planned enterprise. Only thus can the economic menace to the colonies be countered. Only thus can Britain remain a great power.'[58] Britain could then take on a new pacific role in the international arena. 'Mr. Bevin's policy in the Middle East could fulfil a function far beyond that of imperial interests or even nationalist Labour policy. It could be nothing less than the buffer that can prevent the clash between America and Russia.'[59]

Denis Healey, on the right of the party, similarly reasoned that 'democratic socialism will only survive as an alternative to these two extremes if Labour Britain survives as a world power'.[60] And *Tribune* called on the government to facilitate the setting up of a Jewish state by partitioning Palestine in the name of democratic socialism, 'the noblest cause worth fighting for'. The party, before coming to power, the paper recalled, had been 'committed on the subject of Palestine as on no other issue of foreign politics', adding: 'The reason for that commitment was also plain. The core of the Zionist movement in Palestine itself was – and still remains – Socialist and Labour.'[61]

The monthly journal, *Socialist Commentary*, was less overtly partisan over Palestine. It was positioned on the right of the party, and proved to be an intellectual seedling for the Gatskellites.[62] One of its editors, Rita Hinden, had been the leading influence in the work of the Fabian Colonial Bureau which she and Creech Jones had set up, in 1940, to develop the party's thinking on colonial issues. Hinden had been active in the Zionist youth movement in Palestine in the late 1920s, but left to study at the London School of Economics and settled in England. Allan Flanders, her co-editor on *Socialist Commentary* and later an influential voice on the party's right on industrial relations, recalled Hinden becoming 'more and more disenchanted with the nationalist streak in Zionism'.[63] Her erstwhile collaborator, Creech Jones, who after visiting Palestine in the early 1930s had become committed to the Zionist goal also claimed to have modified his view when, as Colonial Secretary, he worked alongside Bevin. In a letter to the historian Elizabeth Monroe, in 1961, he reflected that 'in all the confused and unreal discussion in Europe and America and among Jews, the Arabs just did not exist … I confess that before the war I too was somewhat contemptuous of the Arab case though if I had been otherwise I still would have supported the idea of a Jewish Home in Palestine'. He had disagreed with the Biltmore resolution, in which the Zionist leadership laid claim to the whole of Mandatory Palestine, as well as with the 1944 and 1945 Labour Party resolutions, which had called for the 'Arabs to move out' and for the removal of 'the present unjustifiable barriers to immigration'. These were, he told Monroe, 'too extravagant, unjust and impracticable'.[64]

Socialist Commentary published a couple of contributions from Labour Zionists but several more from their longstanding political opponents, the Jewish Bund. The Bund did not survive the Nazi and Soviet wartime occupations of Poland, its main pre-war base, but a small number of activists escaped to the West and continued the organisation in a skeletal form. 'The Jewish immigration into Palestine alongside other countries would be much stronger', an exiled Bundist writer argued, 'if it were dissociated from the declared purpose of establishing a Jewish state'.[65] Palestine would not be able to solve the problem of antisemitism, because 'the majority of Jews will remain dispersed in many countries and in those countries the Jewish question will have to be solved on the spot and antisemitism extirpated'.[66] An editorial, probably written by Hinden, opted in 1946 for a bi-national state, and criticised the government's rejection of the Anglo-American Committee's recommendations. After the United Nations decision in 1947 to partition Palestine and the subsequent outbreak of war, *Socialist Commentary*'s position became indistinguishable from that of the party's left-wing. In July 1948, during the first truce in the war, an editorial unperturbed by the fact that over 400,000 Palestinians had been turned into refugees opined: 'However sympathetic one is towards Arab susceptibilities and aspirations, one cannot seriously claim that a Jewish state in this little strip of coastland is doing a grave injustice to the Arab peoples in their far flung lands.' The risk of Arab leaders being pushed into the Soviet embrace, it argued, should not be overestimated and after criticising past approaches for their 'failure to realise the strength of Arab nationalist aspirations', it reverted to Labour's usual substitute for recognising those aspirations, by proposing an injection of economic development into the Middle East.[67]

Labour's left-wing remained critical of Bevin's Palestine policy right until Britain's formal recognition of Israel in 1950, which it believed had been delayed by the Foreign Office out of pique.[68] Left-wing MPs began to dissent in the summer of 1946 over the decision to counter the Zionist militias' attack against British targets, with the arrest of personnel linked to the institutions of the Yishuv.[69] The following year Crossman and Mikardo lamented that the British withdrawal would take place without prior arrangements for an orderly transfer of power and, on the final vote to relinquish British rule in Palestine, they were among a group of thirty Labour MPs who voted against the government.[70] The problem for Bevin was that in the absence of a UN-led army to take over the reigns of power an orderly handover would have required devolving power to the armed forces of the two communities, a *de facto* implementation of the UN-decreed two-state solution for which he did not want to be held responsible in the eyes of the Arab world.

Bevin's priority after the Arab states declared war on the newly established Israel was to defend the position of Britain's closest regional ally, King Abdullah of Transjordan, whose Arab Legion was furnished with British officers and arms. Abdullah's aim to annex the part of Palestine that the UN partition plan had designated as the Palestinian Arab state suited Britain. The Foreign Office did not aspire to a major revision of the UN partition. It would have liked to see the UN's allocation of the Negev to the Jewish state altered and hoped that Abdullah would gain control of at least its southern part for the British army to have a land bridge between Egypt and the Arab east.[71] The King had ambitions of his own. He yearned to expand his impoverished territory into Palestine's more fertile and populous land and the 1948 war offered him that opportunity. In the coalition of Arab armies that declared war on Israel, Abdullah's Arab Legion, officered and equipped by the British, was the strongest force and for the military campaign to liberate Palestine it had been assigned the leading role but Abdullah adhered to a prior understanding with Zionist leaders (though one that did not include Jerusalem) that he would not attack the UN-designated Jewish state.[72] Bevin did not want it otherwise as he made clear when he set limits to the deployment of British officers serving in the Arab Legion: 'In the event of hostilities breaking out between the Arab Legion and the Jewish State within its frontiers as laid down by the Assembly', Bevin commented, 'we shall of course have to order all regular British officers to withdraw from and remain outside Palestine.'[73] The British government's 'pro-Arab' stance, as seen by its critics, was narrowly circumscribed by the imperial strategic interest and this did not extend to defending the establishment of a Palestinian Arab state in accordance with the UN partition resolution. Yet, when Zionist military attacks from the end of 1947 to mid-1949 forced Palestinians to abandon their towns and villages, it would fall to

Bevin to take the lead in drawing the British public's attention to their desperate plight.

The expulsion of Palestinians began in early December. The UN partition resolution was followed by a three-day Arab strike and sporadic violence against Jewish buses and shops. By mid-December, the Haganah had shifted to an aggressive reprisal strategy which, in Morris's words, included 'blowing up houses used by Arab terrorists and expelling their inhabitants'.[74] Pappe estimates that these early assaults, in which Irgun and the Stern gang were prominent, caused by the end of January 1948 the deaths of 1,500 Palestinians and the forcible expulsion of about 75,000, mainly from the cities of Haifa, Jaffa and west Jerusalem.[75]

The British media depicted the early phase of the war as a series of tit-for-tat killings but showed no cognizance of Palestinians being bombed and intimidated out of their homes. The reporting was too sanitised for the Executive Committee of the Histadrut which feared that the international community's backing for the UN partition would wilt if the prowess of Zionist forces was underrated. It complained that reports of the war were 'greatly reducing Arab losses from Jewish defenders'. The *Manchester Guardian*, despite being a long-standing advocate of the Zionist cause, was moved to remark that a 'good deal of Jewish "defence" seems to consist of savage reprisals on innocent Arabs' and it characterised the Histadrut 'boasting that they killed more Arabs than is admitted by official communiqué' as 'distasteful'.[76] The reporting of Labour newspapers also spared the reader from information on the scale of Palestinian deaths and dispossession. The *Daily Herald*, which around this time had a circulation of around two million, began to transmit news of the destruction inflicted on Palestinian society only from April 1948. That month it reported on the Irgun's massacre of villagers in Deir Yassin and on the flight of women and children from Tiberias, though neither event drew any editorial comment. Its correspondent described Palestinians fleeing Haifa but implied that they had brought this on themselves. He claimed, apparently on the basis of Zionist sources, that when the Haganah took the city a German SS colonel responsible for training the Arab armies was captured.[77] There was no further mention of the colonel either during or after the war but the following day the high commissioner, presumably to explain the British army's failure to intervene, reportedly told London that the Haifa battle had been 'the direct consequence of continuous Arab attacks on Jews during the past four days' and that there had been 'no massacre'.[78] The *Daily Herald* did not explain that the Haganah followed up its bombardment of the town by firing on the people amassed around the gates of the port, trying to flee. *Tribune* described the Haganah's capture of the city as 'efficient and effortless'.[79]

The *New Statesman*'s commentary on the 1948 war was written mainly by Crossman and by Jon Kimche, an activist in the Zionist movement who was well connected to its leadership. Crossman advocated the withdrawal of British troops and the partition of Palestine. In his accounts, as Kishtainy points out: 'the war was likened to the Spanish Civil War; the Jews with Republicans; Ben-Gurion with Churchill. The Palestinians were described by Crossman as pilferers demolishing "as thoroughly as Arabs in the past demolished Roman cities and crusader castles".[80] In the *New Statesman*, the Palestinian perspective was confined to the letters page despite the presence in London of two able, Arab nationalist intellectuals, Edward Atiyah and Albert Hourani.[81] Kimche sent some dispatches from Palestine and is also likely to have been the source of most of the unsigned commentaries in *Tribune*. One such, in early May 1948, reflected the Zionist leadership's confident assessment of the armed opposition it faced. It described the volunteer forces from Syria, Iraq and Egypt as having been 'utterly routed' and normality returning to all areas except Jerusalem. In stark contrast to later mythology that the Israeli state emerged as a miraculous triumph against overwhelming odds, it calculated that 'Arab forces available for immediate invasion are only the Transjordan Legion under its British Commander-in-Chief and one under-strength Iraqi motorised brigade. The Arabs are thus in no state for organised attack.'[82] Reports in the *New Statesman* recycled key elements of the Zionist propaganda. 'I watched the Arabs leave Haifa and Jaffa,' Kimche wrote, without a hint at the Zionist military assault that was its cause, 'and I watched Jewish farmers with tears in their eyes say good-bye to Arabs at Hedera with whom they have been working for thirty years.'[83]

In February 1948, forty Labour and one Liberal MP urged the British government 'to terminate all military assistance to the Arab states which have defied or have threatened to defy the decisions of the United Nations'.[84] They, like the CPGB in this period, raised no objection, however, to the newly established Israeli state departing from the UN partition plan when seizing by armed force areas that had been allotted to the Palestinian-Arab state. The Foreign Office, alarmed at the regional consequences of the disaster inflicted on the Palestinians, took steps to draw attention to the situation of the refugees, though Bevin had initially considered the Palestinian population's expulsion from the area designated for the Jewish state by the UN as not entirely unwelcome. 'It might be argued', he wrote, 'that the flight of large numbers of Arabs from the territory under Jewish administration had simplified the task of arriving at a stable settlement in Palestine since some transfers of population seems [sic] to be an essential condition for such a settlement'.[85] Over the following months London's assessment changed in response to the growing concern of UN and British officials over the potentially destabilising impact of the refugee influx into Arab states and into the parts of Palestine outside Israeli control.

For the UN, Sir Raphael Cilento estimated the number of refugees, in mid-August 1948, to be between 250,000–300,000 distributed between Lebanon, Syria, Egypt and the Nablus-Tulkran-Ramallah area under Transjordan's control. There were more than 40,000 infants under two years old, 55,000 between two and five years old and 12,500 pregnant women. Sixty-four per cent were in very crowded, unsanitary conditions in private houses and the rest in tents or entirely without shelter.[86] In eastern Palestine and Transjordan, the British Middle East

Office warned a few weeks later: 'the situation is largely out of control. Here there are tens of thousand without cover of any sort, living on famine rations, in some cases on as little as half a pound or less bread and as much fruit as they can procure.'[87] In December, the UN reported that both Egyptian and neutral observers estimated the death rate among the refugees in Gaza to be 120 per day. 'Pneumonia, dysentery and weakness from malnutrition and infants account for a large part of the mortality rate.'[88]

By early 1949, the total number of refugees was thought to be around 750,000, of which 80 per cent were estimated to be women and children, 'many of whom are widows and orphans'.[89] A nurse from the British Red Cross described deteriorating health among the 20,000 refugee population of a camp in the Jordan Valley: 'Queuing for treatment begins very early and the waiting patients are a pitiful sight with their sore eyes, infected ears, multiple abscess on body, and the mothers with their babies, undernourished little scraps, too weak to cry, with very thin arms and legs, wizened faces and distended abdomens.'[90] Officials in the various Middle East capitals repeatedly reminded the Foreign Office that Arab countries were struggling to manage the refugee influx. They evidently feared that politicians and administrators far removed from the situation might believe that the refugees would somehow be absorbed by their new environment. That Arabs simply roamed the desert, unattached to a particular locality was a common stereotype in the West and one that Zionist propaganda had helped to sustain. Weizmann only a few years earlier wrote that if any Arabs 'do not wish to remain in a Jewish state, every facility will be given to them to transfer to one of the many and vast Arab countries'.[91]

A British official in Transjordan commented that 'on the whole the greatest kindness and hospitality have been shown to the refugees by the villagers and town people who are enduring great discomfort from overcrowding as a result'. He was apprehensive, however, that the Transjordan government, 'which had such meagre financial and administrative resources' had to accommodate 'poverty stricken refugees equal to fifty percent of the normal population'.[92] The UN's relief which relied on voluntary national contributions by states 'has been shamefully slow and meagre', the *Manchester Guardian* observed, and did not get off the ground until September 1949.[93] Sir Alec Kirkbride, the British representative in Amman, pointed out that it was the Arab states 'which footed the entire bill for the upkeep of the refugees during the first six months'.[94] While the refugees were clinging to the hope of returning to their homes, British and UN officials began to turn their thoughts to how they could be resettled in the areas they had found refuge. The Foreign Office was fully aware that 'the homes and property of Arab refugees from Jewish areas have in many cases been destroyed, occupied or looted'[95] and a Memorandum on the refugees had concluded that it was 'most unlikely that more than a few will ever be able to return'.[96]

British officials recognised that the Arab countries would not be able to provide sufficient farming land or other opportunities for gainful employment without major, external financial investment. Sir John Troutbeck, head of the British Middle East Office in Cairo, told London that Iraq would not be able to resettle the refugees and their presence in the Jordan Valley would pose problems by generating competition for water and land.[97] Such prognoses fuelled fears in London that the failure to resolve the Palestinian refugee problem would open the way to communism by fanning Arab resentment against Britain and the West. A British major, after witnessing in Nablus refugees sheltering under trees in miserable conditions, reported that they 'blame Great Britain for their plight and their hatred for us plus America and the Arab League is unbelievable'.[98] The refugee issue threatened to affect British strategic interests. The Foreign Office saw immediate assistance as demonstrating 'our sympathy for Arab peoples, to counteract some of the disillusionment and consequent ill-feeling towards ourselves and the Western world which has arisen in Arab countries as a consequence of recent events'.[99] For the longer term, the Labour government adopted two approaches. One was to press for the Israeli government to allow the return of Palestinian refugees, the other was to secure resources for the development plans that had inspired the setting up of the British Middle East Office. British officials solicited US backing for funding development schemes in the Middle East, 'to raise the economic potential of each country as a means of absorbing the refugees'.[100] Neither of these aims was achieved but they indicate the basis of Bevin's 'pro-Arab' policy. He was not committed to a Palestinian state, even of the size laid down by the UN partition plan but it was in Britain's interest to find a solution to the refugee problem that might go some way to calm Arab anger over Palestine.

In January 1949, Bevin had to defend the government's Middle East policy to a largely hostile House of Commons. He pleaded for greater understanding of the Arab point of view: 'there is so much propaganda on the other side and I think it is sometimes forgotten that the Arabs are in the world'. For the Arabs, who have been 'occupying Palestine for more than 20 centuries, to be turned out of their lands and homes to make way for another race is a profound injustice ... 500,000 Arabs have been driven from their homes. In Jaffa, which was an Arab town of 70,000 allotted to the Arabs by the Assembly Resolution of 1947, there are now, so I am informed, only 5,000 Arabs'. When the left-wing MP Sidney Silverman interrupted to say that the Israeli Government 'far from driving anybody away, they did their utmost to persuade them to stay', Bevin replied: 'The fact is that 500,000 Arabs are gone; they are refugees; and I do not think they walked out voluntarily ... the marvel to me is that the conscience of the world has been so little stirred over that tragedy.'[101]

Behind the scenes the government tried to get the media to take a greater interest in the refugees in part to win international and, particularly, US aid for their upkeep, but also to supplement the government's financial assistance with voluntary contributions from the British public. The Foreign Office, after contacting a number of newsreel companies in mid-August 1948, recorded that 'photographs of Arab refugees will be shown at many cinemas in England next week'.[102] A few months later it was still lamenting 'the remarkably little public understanding anywhere outside the Middle East of the gravity of the problem', and was pursuing British Movietonenews to cover the refugees' situation in Transjordan.[103] Civil servants doubted that a government fundraising appeal would be successful. In October 1948, the idea was discussed by the Foreign Office but deferred because the 'Catholic Voluntary Societies had already issued an appeal without noticeable success'.[104] There was further agonising about whether a government appeal was appropriate. One objection was that it might be seen as an attempt to buy off Arab hostility to the Jewish state and another was that it would be difficult to make an appeal 'in a non-partisan manner i.e. without making statements which could be represented as anti-Jewish propaganda'.[105] Sir Edward Spears, a former Conservative MP and brigadier-general, who was chairperson of a small, pro-Arab pressure group, the Committee for Arab Affairs, pressed the Foreign Office, in April 1949, to reconsider a public appeal arguing that 'opinion is really being aroused on the subject' and it was important to keep the question before public opinion, especially during the meeting of the [UN] Assembly'.[106]

Spears and other pro-Arab establishment figures appear to have tired of waiting and launched their own appeal, the Anglo-Arab Relief Fund. Another group, the Committee for Christian Relief in the Holy Land, was formed with the encouragement of Bevin. Headed by Lord Altrincham and sponsored by the Archbishop of Canterbury, it secured support from a few MPs and trade union leaders. It aimed to raise £500,000. Bevin had put his name to the Committee's appeal and wrote to William Lawther, president of the TUC, and Arthur Deakin, general secretary of the Transport and General Workers' Union, suggesting that trade unions assist the fundraising by organising pay packet deductions.[107] This initiative went unheeded as did appeals to other quarters. In March 1950, a Foreign Office official noted that the Committee was being wound up. It had raised £1,500 (equivalent to about £38,000 in 2011) of which more than two-thirds went on expenses.[108] For eliciting public sympathy the Palestinians had proved to be the wrong refugees. The Committee suggested that its appeal had failed either because British people had a negative association with the politics of the Holy Land or because they had thought that the UN had the problem in hand.[109] It was an explanation which still begged the question why it was that these perceptions prevailed given the developments on the ground.

Part of the explanation lies in how common the uprooting of people became at the end of the Second World War, making it appear normal, part of a tidying-up operation after the years of havoc and devastation. 'There was a feeling among Western policy makers,' writes Judt, 'that the League of Nations, and the minority clauses in the Versailles Treaties, had failed and that it would be a mistake even to try and resurrect them.' Ethnic Germans who had lived in eastern Europe for generations were forcibly moved as were several million other ethnic minorities,

Poles, Ukrainians, Turks, Slovaks and Hungarians. 'The term "ethnic cleansing" did not yet exist, but the reality surely did and it was far from arousing wholesale disapproval or embarrassment.'[110] Nor was this confined to Europe. In the autumn and winter of 1947–1948, 5.5 million Hindus and Sikhs fled to India and 5.8 million Muslims fled to the newly established Pakistan.[111]

An additional factor anaesthetising Western sensibilities to the Palestinians' plight, was that it resulted from a conflict involving an ethnic group whose suffering had already some popular acknowledgement against another that was widely believed to merely roam the desert.

The expulsion of Palestinians had began in December 1947 but for the first eight months the war was reported as a series of armed skirmishes with only rare references to their impact on the civilian populations. The UN's publicity officer complained that, 'although he had sent numerous films of Arab refugees to the Unites States none of them was ever shown. Feature articles on the same subject were also neglected by all United States newspapers except the *New York Times*.'[112] The Foreign Office was similarly frustrated with the British media and although it arranged some news coverage, the crucial factors for mobilising public concern were lacking: intense media focus and grassroots political agitation. In March 1949, when the UN received pledges of $25 million dollars, two-thirds of them by the United States, to aid the approximately 700,000 Palestinian refugees, the United Jewish Appeal supported by the American Zionist movement launched a $250 million appeal focussing on the resettlement in Palestine of 200,000 Jewish DPs. $26 million was raised the first day.[113]

In Britain, the leading force in international solidarity since the 1920s had been the left-wing of the labour movement, in particular communists and the more internationally minded trade union and Labour Party activists, many of whom had previous association with the ILP. It was largely due to their campaigning efforts that during the war the labour movement raised, in less than two years, £567,000 for the Help for Russia Fund and a further £39,000 for the United Aid for China.[114] The left-wing also campaigned on the 1943 Bengal famine, which was estimated to have claimed at least two million lives. The India Aid Committee, in which Krishna Menon of the India League took a leading role, appealed for funds and organised protest meetings, highlighting India's demand for self-rule as the solution to its repeated famines. Several Trades Councils and trade unions ranging from the National Union of Railwaymen to the National Union of Agricultural Workers sent resolutions demanding that the TUC press the government to provide urgent relief. Walter Citrine, the TUC leader, suggested to the Essex Federation of Trades Council that the India Aid Committee was 'controlled by people of Communist sympathy' but the General Council heeding the strong feelings expressed by the rank and file called that year for full dominion status for India under a government elected on a free vote.[115]

No similar mobilisation took place on behalf of the Palestinian refugees. It was heartbreaking, complained a delegate to the Liberal Party Assembly in 1949, that this gathering 'should disperse without any reference to the tragedy of the Arabs in Palestine'.[116] There was a still more glaring omission over this issue at the Labour Party conference. Between the party's 1917 declaration in favour a 'Jewish home' in Palestine and the 1949 annual conference, the party had declared its commitment to Zionism on eleven occasions but, in the wake of the Palestinians' dispossession and dispersal, not a word was uttered on their fate at that conference. Bevin in a long speech to the delegates on foreign affairs referred to the Middle East only to give the anodyne message that 'we have been trying to stimulate a great economic development'.[117] Three other speakers referred to Palestine but none mentioned the refugees. The party had wholeheartedly embraced the Labour Zionist argument that Jewish settlement would bring progress to the Palestinian population and had repeatedly characterised Arab opposition to Zionism as incitement by feudal leaders who feared that they would be swept aside by a peasantry introduced to modernity. Set against this caricature the reality of more than half a million Palestinians surviving as refugees under tents and trees evidently proved uncomfortable to explain.

Zionist Review, under the editorship of the Labour Zionist, Levenberg, was quick to suggest another, overtly racist narrative to snuff out any sympathy that the Palestinians' plight might arouse: 'The Western world tends to think of the Arab as a falcon-eyed, warrior on a white horse. That Arab is still around, but he is far less numerous than the disease-ridden wretches who lie in the hot streets, too weak, sick and purposeless to roll over into the shade.'[118] *Tribune's* explanation for the defeat of the Arab forces, drip-fed to its readers over several months, reflected the Zionist propaganda claims at various phases of the war. In early May 1948, the paper had still envisaged a 'parallel state' for the Palestinians in accordance with the UN plan but after the Arab states had declared war on Israel and two truces had broken down, Kimche reported from Tel Aviv that, 'Palestinian Arab leaders who remained behind in Jewish territory now say bluntly that the Mufti's self-appointed and extremist "Palestine Arab Committee" (which gained power partly by terrorising political opponents) would never have attained its influence but for British advice'.[119] Kimche did not divulge what the 'advice' was or how it had played such an important role in empowering the Mufti. Once the latter was marginalised as a political force *Tribune's* criticism was directed at the Arab League, which it explained 'began to degenerate the moment it discovered that the only factor able to hold it together was hatred of the Palestine Jews and fear of the social-democracy they were importing into the Middle East'.[120]

In July 1948, Kimche had speculated that 'a genuine settlement' would enable the Palestinians to return to their homes, but by mid-August the Israeli leadership was determined to prevent a mass return of refugees[121] and supporters of the new state set out to show that the refugee crisis had been engineered by the Arabs. An unsigned report in *Tribune* alleged that the Palestinian leaders, having fled to Cairo and Beirut with 'much of their wealth', gave 'orders for a mass evacuation of Haifa, Jaffa and other towns'.[122] The article also gave 'Arab rumour' as the cause of people fleeing: 'Over one third of all the Palestinian Arabs have fled or lost their homes (mostly fleeing on wild Egyptian or Syrian advice), and are now refugees.'[123]

Crossman, who a couple years earlier had argued that a Jewish state would be advantageous to the Arabs, now maintained that the manifestly different outcome was due at least as much to the Arabs themselves as to the Zionist forces. The latter had 'wiped out villages where there had been resistance', but the Arabs 'on the orders of their own leaders and assisted by the British army fled to neighbouring countries hoping to return behind the victorious armies'.[124] In Parliament, he put forward another explanation though still insisting that the Palestinians were largely responsible for their plight: 'When the Iraqi army went they took the Arabs with them. In many cases they fled through fear. I do not think they were ever pushed out by the Jews. They were frightened out, for many of them had murdered Jews for months.' For Crossman the Arabs 'murdered' and the Jews 'pushed' in defence but he agreed, nonetheless, that the refugees' position was 'desperate and tragic'. He cited with approval the Israelis' suggestion that the refugees should be resettled in Transjordan: 'They say how stupid it would be to move them back. After all, these villages were only mud huts anyway. They were terribly bad villages full of vermin.'[125] The derogatory reference to Palestinian settlements not only belittled the scale of the suffering inflicted on their inhabitants, it also obscured the substantial value of the assets expropriated by the Israeli state. 'Abandoned [Palestinian] property,' noted an early study on the topic, 'was one of the greatest contributions toward making Israel a viable state.'[126]

There were some critics of Labour's pro-Zionist stance during the war but they were few and struggled to make an impact. A *Tribune* reader complained 'I do not once remember the Arab point of view being presented by you editorially',[127] and the paper conceded that it had received several letters 'protesting against what the objectors obviously regard as our exaggerated interest in and support for the Jewish case in Palestine'.[128] The left-wing publisher Victor Gollancz set up an organisation, the Jewish Society for Human Suffering (JSHS), to raise funds on behalf of the Palestinian refugees. Addressing the Jewish community as part of his appeal, he emphasised that as a Jew he felt a particular responsibility to take action:

> imagine that you are yourself one of those starving and dying people – just as, five years ago, some of us tried to imagine that we were our own fellow Jews who were being gassed and cremated ... Have we then no responsibility in the face of this horror – no extra, no specially Jewish responsibility, over and above our common human responsibility? ... I am very far from implying that all this misery is the result, either immediately or in the final analysis, solely of Jewish actions. But two things are certain. These women and children would not be dying of starvation and exposure if the Israeli State had never been founded; and the Israeli state was founded exclusively for the salvation and rehabilitation of Jews.[129]

The JSHS was reported in the *Jewish Chronicle* to have raised during the first six months of its existence, the only period for which a record survives, 'over £10,000' (equivalent to about £250,000 in 2011).[130]

With armistice agreed between King Abdullah and Israel in April 1949, Palestine ceased as an internationally recognised political entity, gobbled up by Israel on one side and Transjordan, which then became Jordan, on the other. The Palestinians received little media attention from the end of 1949. There was no political party or group in Britain willing to adopt their cause and articulate the moral outrage that would have fixed the refugees in public consciousness. Their situation cropped up in Parliamentary debates on the Middle East throughout the 1950s in relation to British Treasury contributions to the United Nations' fund for the refugees and, more prominently, in response to armed border clashes between the Israeli military and Palestinian fighters operating from the refugee camps. For London these confrontations were a source of concern: they could spark a wider conflict in the region, enflame anti-Western feelings and provide openings for Soviet influence. But the Palestinians' right to self-determination which the UN partition plan had recognised, if only on a truncated scale, disappeared from Western political discourse on the Middle East.

Bevin's omission of any reference to Palestine in his speech to the 1949 Labour Party conference was designed to avoid controversy. It was a tacit acknowledgement of the unpopularity of his Middle East policy in the party ranks, where the government was widely perceived to have traded Labour's traditional support for Zionism for a strategy that had led to a humiliating withdrawal from Palestine and to a weakening in Britain's position in the Arab world. In the Parliamentary debate on the government's policy a few months earlier, *The Times* estimated that about fifty Labour MPs abstained when the opposition pressed for a vote.[131] Labour Party critics increasingly focused on what they alleged was Bevin's unnecessary delay in according official recognition to the state of Israel. The government withheld recognition until April 1950, eight months after it had been granted by the US. The delay was a gesture to Arab sentiments but also to press Israel to be more conciliatory in its negotiations with the neighbouring states and over the readmission of Palestinian refugees. But Dalton signalled at the 1949 Labour Party conference that the government was preparing for reconciliation, even without any Israeli concessions on the refugee issue, by announcing that the party's National Executive was sending a delegation to Israel at the invitation of the Histadrut.

The delegation led by the Labour Party's chairperson, the leader of the National Union of Mineworkers, Sam Watson, lavishly praised the new state. 'A new Social Dynamism based on progressive democracy and Socialism is being created in a manner akin to that of Britain and the Scandinavian countries.'[132] In the *Daily Herald*, Watson described Jewish pioneers fructifying the barren land, an image that the party had helped to popularise in the 1930s. 'We saw men and women living in tents without water or electricity. They had not been told they must settle in the desert; they chose to go there because they considered hardship a duty.'[133] Of the many more Palestinian refugees living just across the border, also in tents and without electricity, there was not a word either in the delegation's report or in Watson's article. The Labour Zionist discourse was again in full flight, cut loose from the encumbrance of facing up to the consequences for the indigenous inhabitants of the Jewish state's creation.

Following the Attlee government's defeat, the 1952 Labour Party conference provided the opportunity to demonstrate Labour's collective support for the newly established Israel and to distance itself from the Palestine policy associated with Bevin. The resolution approved by the conference spoke of 'the important role Israel is playing in the advancement of democratic socialism in the Middle East' and looked to Britain to advance friendly relations between Israel and the Arab countries.[134] As Britain's global position faced challenges from communism and anti-colonial movements, Labour viewed Israel as a potential ally in the Middle East. 'Properly armed,' Wyatt argued in *Tribune*, 'the Israeli Army could form the nucleus of a Western defence of the Middle East.'[135] The party's 1952 foreign policy statement emphasised that Britain's alliance with the US, based on NATO, was 'not only an instrument for solving temporary problems but as the expression of common inheritance linking the peoples on both sides of the North Atlantic Ocean'.[136] In this racialised vision of the world order, Israel belonged to the West. It has, Wyatt stressed, 'a steadily mounting population of Europeans. Her soldiers are European-trained with European intelligence and discipline.'[137]

A difference opened up over Middle East policy between the Conservatives and Labour, with the latter's return to opposition. The two parties agreed that the Soviet Union presented the main threat to British influence and oil interest in the region but diverged on the how closely this issue was tied to Britain's position on the Arab-Israeli conflict. The Conservatives favoured Israel making concessions over its territorial gains to facilitate a climate in which London could strengthen its alliance with the Arab states, whereas for the Labour leadership support for Israel was the over-riding priority. It believed that Western economic assistance was the key to holding the Soviets at bay as well as persuading the Arab world to accept its existing borders with Israel and absorb the refugees. The Labour leader, Hugh Gaitskell, argued in 1955 that Britain had to change its approach of supplying weapons in equal amounts to the Arabs and the Israelis because the Russian supply of MIG fighters to Egypt through Czechoslovakia was upsetting the balance of forces responsible for keeping the peace.[138] The Labour Party also expressed disapproval of the widely publicised speech by the prime minister, Anthony Eden, at the lord mayor's banquet in Guildhall, in which he suggested that a territorial compromise should be sought between the Arab state's negotiating position founded on the borders of the 1947 partition and Israel's insistence on retaining, minor border modifications apart, the territory it was in control of at the time of the 1949 armistice agreement.[139] Despite Nasser showing flexibility by welcoming Eden's proposal as a 'very good basis' for negotiations, Morrison echoed the Israeli response that the Arab states had rendered the UN partition plan null and void by their rejection of it, in 1947, and their subsequent declaration of war.[140]

Labour leaders also echoed the Israeli position on the Palestinian refugees, though Israel continued to defy the UN resolution requiring their return. 'The blame largely rests on the Arab states,' Morrison alleged when discussing the refugees. 'They would sooner have a grievance than a solution.'[141] Arab governments undoubtedly used the refugees' plight to try to restore their nationalist credentials after the failure of their military intervention in Palestine, but the dynamics unleashed by the refugee presence and the political organisations they formed were largely beyond their control. Officials and aid workers who dealt firsthand with the refugees bore witness to the scale of the problems they posed. In an assessment of their impact on the Arab countries, the US representative in Amman noted that Palestinians in Iraq were regarded 'as foreigners and unwelcome' in the rural areas. 'They would be another unassimilated, discontented minority group unwilling to fit in as the lowest agricultural labour at serf level.' However, aid projects targeting them for resettlement on new land were likely to arouse among the local population, 'fierce resentment that no government could withstand'. And in Lebanon, a continuing Palestinian presence, he warned, 'would upset the sensitive balance which exists between Moslems and Christians'.[142] The prospects of Palestinians being accepted were generally believed to be much better in Transjordan but the British representative there cautioned that its ability 'to absorb another 700,000, most of them destitute, is doubtful'.[143] Moreover, the absorption of the refugees did not hinge only, as Morrison imagined, on the Arab countries which hosted them. In the camps social and political organisations began to articulate the demands and hopes of their inhabitants. 'With few exceptions the slowly declining morale of the refugees is upheld by one dominating idea,' reported the American Friends' Service Committee, a Quaker organisation responsible for distributing aid to just over a quarter of the refugees in camps, 'namely, that they be allowed soon to return to their former homes.'[144]

The testimonies of those working among the refugees refute the facile argument that the Arab states could easily have absorbed the refugees had they wanted to. Not only did they lack resources but a policy of absorption would have had to overcome resistance from their own populations as well as from the refugees. As Rosemary Sayigh's extensive interviews in Palestinian camps in Lebanon show, the peasantry's sense of identity linked them first and foremost to their land and village, which is why they wanted to return to them, and they could not be placated by resettlement elsewhere.[145]

Hugh Dalton expressed compassion for the situation of the refugees, describing it in Parliament, as 'the most shocking element of the Middle East'. But he dismissed the argument that Israel should accept them back as 'totally impracticable'. It seemed to him unreasonable for the Arabs to want the land taken by Israel, 'barely more than 12,000 square miles in area' given that 'the Arab States have more than 2,500,000 square miles'.[146] When he had drafted the Labour Party's 1944 proposal that the Arabs should be 'encouraged to move out' he could not have imagined the brutal way in which that was to be executed and yet, even when acknowledging the misery of the refugees, he still thought that provided the Palestinians had *lebensraum*, they should be indifferent to where that was in the Arab world. It does not appear to have occurred to him that what had been destroyed were the lives of individuals and communities, a culture and a society and that the resulting humiliation and anger would impact on and be articulated through the emerging nationalism in the Arab world.

As Hourani had warned, transforming the Arab character of Palestine could only be carried out by force against the indigenous population. His prediction proved considerably more accurate than the public claims of the Zionist leadership. Ben-Gurion had told the Anglo-American Committee of Inquiry that a future Jewish state would serve all its citizens 'without any difference between Jews, Arabs and others, to care for their security, to work for their welfare'.[147] The declaration of independence, on 14 May 1948, similarly stated that Israel 'will uphold the full social and political equality of all its citizens, without distinction of race, creed or sex'. The commitment to liberal principles proved incompatible with the task of consolidating the state in accordance with Zionist objectives. The defence of the armistice lines and the settlement of Jewish immigrants, 'part of the ingathering of exiles' which brought 680,000 Jews into the country in the first two and a half years of the state's existence, led to a harsh regime of military control over the Palestinian population remaining in Israel.

A third of the recently arrived Jewish immigrants in the newly established Israel were settled in urban areas from which their Palestinian inhabitants had been forced out during the war. On the eve of the 1948 war, of the total land surface of Palestine less than 7 per cent and of the cultivable area around 12 per cent were under Jewish ownership.[148] Palestinian-owned land was legally redefined by the Israeli government as 'abandoned' and transferred into the hands of the state to ensure its control over economic resources. 'According to a statement in 1980 from the Custodian [of Absentee Property], about 70 per cent of Israel's total territory was "absentee land" – that is rightfully the property of Palestinian refugees.'[149] This land expropriation affected not only those who had been turned into refugees but also about half of the 160,000 Palestinian population remaining in Israel on the pretext that between 1948 and 1950 they had temporarily left the country or had moved to a different locality.[150] Additional Palestinian land was expropriated 'in the interests of public safety' and for 'public purposes'.[151] An editorial in the liberal Israeli newspaper, *Haaretz*, described the land acquisition in this period as 'wholesale robbery in legal guise'.[152]

From October 1948 the Palestinian population remaining in the newly founded Israel was put under military administration. They were regarded by the government as a potential 'fifth column' and placed under strict surveillance. Crossman called them 'a privileged and pampered minority', claiming they were 'both prosperous and disloyal'.[153] Their disloyalty he presented as provoking the army's iron fist, while their prosperity he attributed to the Histadrut. 'By enormously improving their economic conditions, the Histadrut is removing any incentive for them to leave the country: by treating them as fifth columnists, the military authorities are nurturing their resentment'.[154] But there was no significant discord between these two arms of the state. The Histadrut gave priority to Jewish workers through its control of labour exchanges. It also discriminated in their favour in its own factories, a practice it continued even after the Military Administration was terminated in 1966. 'Of the thousands of Histadrut-owned firms and factories', Lustick observes, 'not one was located in an Arab village in 1977'.[155] The military, for its part, disadvantaged Palestinians in the labour market by restricting their mobility.

The aim was to take over Arab villages particularly in the border regions and establish Jewish settlements in their place to prevent the return of Palestinians. 'Of the 370 new Jewish settlements established between 1948 and 1953, 350 were set up on absentee property.'[156] Attempts by refugees to regain their land and property by crossing the border from their camps in Lebanon, Jordan, Syria and Gaza became the principal source of armed clashes after the armistice agreements. The records of the United Nations Mixed Armistice Commission which monitored the situation along the border indicated, according to Elizabeth Monroe who visited the area in 1953, that 'there are far more Arab incursions than Jewish incursions' but 'where the Arabs nearly always cross the border in ones and twos ... the Jewish incursions are military operations'. Palestinians crossing the border – termed 'infiltrators' by the Israeli authorities – were driven, she pointed out, by desperation. In Jordan only one-third of the refugees were receiving United Nations rations, leaving between 120,000 and 150,000 on occasional handouts by charities. 'Your Arab sees, on his former land, ungrazed fields and unweeded groves, he sees newcomers endowed with plenty of tools and cattle and seed and water-pipes, and, hungry and destitute, he crosses the border to snatch what he can.'[157] A more recent study, by Morris, drawing on Israeli documentation suggests that between 2,700 and 5,000 Palestinians were killed in crossing over the border into Israel: 'the vast bulk of the infiltration, 90 per cent and more, through 1949–1956, was economically or socially motivated. Most of the infiltrators came to retrieve their possessions and crops and, thereafter, to steal.'[158]

For Wyatt, reporting for the left-wing *Tribune*, as for Watson, the right-wing miners' leader, the Palestinians' plight was for the UN to sort out, their focus and of the left generally was on Israel and the threats it faced. The refugees' desperate state which drove them to risk their lives crossing back into Israel did not figure in Wyatt's reports, which were subsequently republished in a pamphlet form. He explained that Palestinians attempting to return to their lands and homes had been beaten and 'fired on indiscriminately by way of warning', adding in Colonel Blimp mode: 'Such methods may be effective as a deterrent but to the Arabs, who put thieving, smuggling and crossing borders into the same category as we would put exceeding the speed limit in a built up area, they appear outrageous.'[159]

In the first few years following the expulsion of the Palestinians there were, according to Morris, between 10,000 and 15,000 instances of 'infiltration' which tapered off to about half that number by 1956. They were the main source of armed clashes pitting the Israeli army and border police against the Palestinian refugees and, later, armed groups, the *fedayeen*. Palestinian 'incursions' which caused damage to property and in some cases death or injury in Jewish border settlements were met with Israeli army reprisals to deter further attacks and reassure Israeli citizens about settling in these regions, which they were being encouraged to do primarily for strategic reasons. The Israeli army's repeated resort to disproportionate force often directed against entire Palestinian villages by way of collective punishment provoked some censure from Western governments and the UN but the response of its supporters, including on the British left, was generally mooted and indulgent.

In October 1953, Israel escalated the scale of its reprisals. Following the killing of an Israeli mother and her two children by someone suspected of having come from the Jordanian-controlled village of Quibya or its surrounds, an Israeli commando unit led by Ariel Sharon, who in 2001 would become the prime minister, attacked the village to avenge the deaths. The inhabitants were killed by gunfire and grenades inside their houses, which were then blown up, burying the injured and dead. Sixty-nine bodies were recovered, two-thirds of them women and children.[160] The atrocity was referred to the Security Council and condemned by both Britain and the US. In Parliament, the only response from the Labour opposition came from two of its MPs, both committed Zionists, Sidney Silverman and Barnet Janner.[161] They complained that international attention was too narrowly focused on the Israeli attack and should take into account Arab attacks. In the *New Statesman*, Crossman placed less emphasis on Israel committing the massacre than on the hypocrisy of the great powers in condemning, what he called the 'action': 'Not that it is my intention to defend the Israeli action any more than I would defend Field-Marshal Montgomery's demolition of whole villages during the Arab revolt of 1937.'[162]

In the second half of 1954 there was a decline in violent incidents along the Gaza border but they increased in January involving Egyptian intelligence personnel and troops. There was also a Palestinian attack killing two Israeli farmers. At the end of February, Israel mounted an attack on Gaza killing thirty-seven Egyptian soldiers and two Palestinians, including a seven-year-old boy.[163] *Tribune* did not comment on the raid but it portrayed the British government's intervention at the UN condemning the Israeli attack, as a 'stab in the back' and 'unctuous', adding: 'Only a power which is completely free from responsibility for the present state of affairs in the Middle East has the right to criticise Israel for the Gaza incident ... Britain does not have that right.'[164]

Outside the Parliamentary Labour Party, in the wider Labour movement, discussion of the Middle East continued to be dominated by declarations of unstinting admiration for Israel. Criticisms were rare and triggered immediate response from Zionists and their allies in the party. Poale Zion, commending the value of visits to Israel by leading Labour personalities, observed that 'of all those who have visited Israel over the past seven years only one has returned hostile and she is in a special category'.[165] The exception was the MP, Edith Summerskill. Addressing the Socialist International Congress in 1955, as chairperson of the Labour Party, she expressed admiration for Israel's welfare state but added that 'they could have shared it more widely among the Arab population'. She also raised the suffering of the Palestinian refugees. 'The misery and hopelessness of the Arab refugees in their camps is in striking contrast to the life of Israelis just across the border. The bitterness of losing their country is accentuated by the fact that so many of them have also lost the only thing that they have in the world, their home.'[166] Unusually for a Labour politician, Summerskill reiterated the UN resolution calling on the Israeli government to allow Palestinians to return to their property in Israel if they wished to or, alternatively, to receive compensation. On the eve of the 1955 party conference, Arthur Greenwood, a member of the Labour Party's NEC, responded by pointing out that Summerskill was expressing a 'personal view' and that the resolution on the Middle East to be voted on by the party's annual conference 'should do much to correct the wrong impression created by Dr. Summerskill's speech'.[167]

As Greenwood had anticipated, the NEC's resolution was passed. It expressed appreciation for 'the great constructive achievement of Mapai and approves the policy of the National Executive to strengthen in every possible way, the friendly ties between the British and Israel Labour Movements'.[168] Watson, speaking later in the conference called the Histadrut 'the greatest trade union organisation the world has ever seen ... which owns and controls one-third of the Israeli economy' and declared Israel to be 'a beacon of light in the Middle East'.[169] Hayim Pinner, the editor of the *Jewish Vanguard*, Poale Zion's newspaper, informed the Israeli ambassador in London: 'from Israel's point of view this was the best Labour conference since 1944. All the public references to Israel were extremely friendly.'[170]

The conference took place in the aftermath of Labour's second post-war election defeat amidst mutual recrimination between the left and right wings of the party over who was responsible for losing the election. In addition, Bevan, Gaitskell and Morrison, heading rivals camps, were vying for the party leadership.[171] Support for Israel, however, was unaffected by these divisions. While in the 1950s such foreign policy issues as German rearmament, Britain developing its own independent nuclear deterrent and the 'special relationship' with the US were highly contentious, reflecting the ideological divide between the party's left and right, on the Middle East the two wings were broadly united. Although Pinner warned of antisemites and also of '"left wingers", "pacifists" and "anti-colonialists" who are particularly vulnerable to suggestions of "Arab Socialism" and "Progressives" whom they ought to support',[172] the scale of the opposition was nothing like he implied.

Only a half dozen or so members of the Parliamentary Labour Party favoured the Arab states' point of view and they were on the right-wing of the party. The most well known of this group were Christopher Mayhew, Richard Stokes, Edith Summerskill and George Brown. They continued to identify themselves with Bevin's policy objective of defending British interests in the Middle East by cultivating Arab allies though, after Bevin's death, this was an ineffectual minority position in the party. Solidarity with Israel was seen by most right-wingers as part of the struggle against communism in the developing world, while for the left it was primarily a way to assert social democracy as a development model for the Middle East, though this conception too harboured the idea of paving the way for a non-communist form of socialism. The two wings had a common dislike of the rulers of the Arab states not because of their collaboration with Western interests, but because they were considered an obstacle to social progress. Even on the party's left, Arab nationalism's confrontation with Israel was generally perceived to be outside the framework of anti-colonialism. But beyond the parliamentary party and the mainstream labour movement the first, albeit small, chink in this consensus on the left emerged in response to Israel's military confrontations along its border with Palestinian refugees and armed groups, giving some substance to Pinner's fears.

Peace News, a publication of the Peace Pledge Union, a pacifist organisation, adopted an anti-colonial stance from the mid-1950s. It became closely linked with the MCF, bringing together Bevanites, pacifists, communists and radicals of different sorts to demand that Britain takes immediate steps towards decolonisation. The MCF was refused affiliation to the Labour Party on the grounds that it had communist members but within a couple of years it gained the backing of about one-third of Labour MPs and a substantial number of constituency Labour parties and trade unions.[173] Its campaigns focused on independence struggles in Britain's African colonies, the mainstay of what remained of the Empire, but it also helped to organise public protests against Eden's military intervention in Suez.

A *Peace News* editorial argued that the tragedy of Palestine was that British imperialism had used Jews for its own strategic purposes and this had led to another people being turned into refugees. It emphasised that: 'The Jews were of course in no way to blame for the act of bad faith by the British' but sidestepped the separatist polices of Zionist movement, to appeal to the two sides to resolve their differences. 'On the side of the Arabs there must be a readiness to forget the double dealing of the past' and of Israel it demanded full citizenship rights for Palestinians, arguing that they 'should no longer be shut up in their villages in the same way as were the Jews in their ghettos in Eastern Europe'.[174] A subsequent report in *Peace News* condemned Ben-Gurion as the 'arch-apostle of massive retaliation' and called for the refugees to be allowed to return to Israel in accordance with UN resolutions.[175] The newspaper did not call for Palestinian self-determination but was sympathetic to the Arab nationalist point of view. In 1956 it opposed the attack mounted by Britain and France in collusion with Israel to recapture the Suez Canal expressing the view of many in the Labour Party.[176]

Michael Foot's account of the Labour leadership's conduct during the war over the Suez Canal is that Gaitskell, after initially outdoing the Tories in suggesting ways of putting pressure on Egypt, mounted, with Bevan, an effective moral and legal case against what turned out to be a disastrous war. He describes it as 'the most brilliant display of opposition in recent Parliamentary history'.[177] It was however an opposition over means not ends. Labour leaders were no more prepared to acknowledge than the Tories that British imperial power had operated the Suez Canal on blatantly exploitative terms. Despite the contribution of Egyptian labourers to the building of the canal, Egypt had received no income from it until 1937 and only 7 per cent of the Canal Company's profits thereafter.[178] On the injustice of this imperial legacy Bevan, who only a few years earlier had championed further nationalisation in Britain, commented: 'That does not establish Egypt's right to exploit the canal in her own narrow national interest.'[179] Gaitskell was equally dismissive of Nasser's argument that since the World Bank, at US and British prompting, had withdrawn its offer to fund the Aswan Dam, Egypt had to find the revenue for its construction by acquiring a greater share of the canal's commercial exploitation. The Labour leader was opposed to Nasser assuming control over the canal and cited Egypt's ban on Israeli shipping as evidence that the Egyptians could not be trusted to maintain the Suez Canal as an international waterway. His condemnation of the government was for failing to work through the UN. The government had vetoed the Security Council's resolution against Israel's offensive in the Sinai, and had launched the Anglo-French military intervention without UN authorisation. The Labour leadership strongly suspected that Britain and France had colluded in the Israeli attack to be able to retake control of the Suez Canal zone under the pretext of separating two warring sides.[180] The Israeli objectives were to expand its border into Sinai and thereby take control of Sharm el-Sheik, where Egypt was blocking its shipping to Eilat, and also to weaken Nasser by inflicting on him a military defeat.[181] In the event, all three invading forces were compelled to withdraw under international and mainly US pressure. The American reasoning was that even if the invasion achieved its objectives the resulting Arab hostility would open the way to greater Soviet influence in the region.

The Suez debacle weakened Britain's and France's standing in the region and reinforced Egypt's alliance with the Soviet Union. It also deepened Arab hostility to Israel. Morris notes: 'What many Arab leaders had long claimed had now been "proved" – Israel was the imperialists' cats-paw in the Middle East.'[182] Nasser, by contrast, emerged triumphant and the resulting radicalisation led to Arab political leaders bidding for popularity with promises of bringing down the Israeli state. The soaring belligerence helped Israel to secure further military hardware from its Western allies. It also led the British Labour leadership to rapidly set aside its criticism of Israel. The Labour Party's condemnation of the military intervention in Egypt did not weaken its resolve to defend Israel's existence. Not only did that remain the touchstone of Labour's Middle East policy but it envisaged that defence entirely on the terms demanded by the Israeli government. Reflecting on Gaitskell's attitude, Foot observes: 'for all his acceptance of much of the nationalist case, Arab nationalism never had for him the tug which his understanding of Israeli emotions could exercise'.[183] Within a few months of the Suez crisis, Morrison criticised the US for pressuring Israel to withdraw its troops from the Sinai, while Bevan reiterated the Labour leadership's opposition to a territorial compromise between Israel and its Arab neighbours. 'We say now,' Bevan declared, 'that there can be no compromise on the frontiers of Israel as between the 1947 and 1948 lines.'[184]

Peace News was not alone, in this period, in grappling with the hostility between Israel and its Arab neighbours and with the claim, which most of the left had accepted pre-1948, that a Jewish state would simultaneously resolve the problem of anti-semitism in Europe and bring economic development to the Middle East. In 1959, Crossman addressed this issue in a lecture series delivered in Israel, in which he sought to summarise the political outlook of Weizmann, whom he had greatly admired. Crossman explained:

> One of the central themes of his Zionist philosophy was that the National Home was not only a Jewish need, it was also essential to the renaissance of the Arab world. It was his notion that Israel should become the pilot plant in which should take place those experiments in agriculture, in the reconquest of the desert, in the industrialisation of a backward area and in collective living required to revive the vanished glories of Middle Eastern civilisation. Not one tittle of this vision has come true.

Crossman could have added that this notion had been most assiduously promoted by Labour Zionism and that the British Labour Party and he, himself, as recently as 1946, had subscribed to it. However, he preferred another tack. The flaw lay, he insisted, not in the vision or even in its implementation but in the Arab states' response to Israel, which 'has been slowly degenerating into something remarkably similar to Christian anti-semitism'.[185]

To his Israeli audience, gathered to celebrate the achievements of Weizmann and Zionism, the depiction of Arab nationalism as analogous to European fascism, would have been a welcome as well as a familiar argument. Crossman also gave vent to its corollary: the belittling of Arab and specifically Palestinian nationalist grievances. Most of the refugees, he claimed, 'sit idly in the UNRWA camps today', while the Palestinians remaining in Israel, whom in 1949 he had described as a 'pampered and privileged minority', were, he now professed, justifiably discriminated against: 'Ten years after the war ended, these Arab villagers are still a "fifth column" inside Israel, and one cannot be surprised that the Army and police insist on treating them as such.'[186] Crossman was notoriously inconsistent in his political allegiance but, as his biographer recalls, the one cause to which he held steadfast was Zionism.[187] His last and uncompleted literary project would be the official biography of Weizmann.

However, in 1970, in the face of Israel consolidating its occupation of the West Bank and Gaza, Crossman appeared to be reappraising his position. A decade earlier, in his final lecture in Israel, he had argued that 'rather than increase its Arab population, any Israeli Government will deny itself extensions of territory. Ironically enough, the exclusiveness of Israeli nationalism is the best guarantee the Arabs possess against the threat that Israel will ever launch an expansionist war.'[188] Would he now, post-1967, conclude that 'not one tittle of this vision' had come true either? In the form of an open letter printed on the *New Statesman's* front cover, he sought reassurances from Israel's foreign minister, Abba Eban. Crossman claimed that Zionism had been sustained by two aims: first, to provide 'a long-term cure for anti-semitism' and secondly, to 'transform the Middle East within a generation'. Israel's existence, he asserted, had enabled Jew and non-Jew to live in the West 'on terms of genuine equality', by breaking the cycle of cause and effect between Diaspora inferiority complex and anti-semitism. His explanation that Israel's existence halted the supposed psychological basis of ethnic enmity by overcoming Jewish inferiority complex, implied that the Jews were the cause of their own persecution, a standard anti-semitic argument. But if his argument was flawed on this score, it was still less convincing on Israel's supposed transformative effect on the Arab world. And it is clear that it was this that disturbed Crossman and had provoked his letter. He had hoped that Israel would foster in the Middle East a political force independent of the two main military blocs. Instead, its confrontation with the Arab world had led to an unprecedented level of great power involvement and militarisation in the region, with the US on one the side and the Soviets on the other. Israel, he warned, by seeking security through territorial expansion, was becoming imbued with the militaristic ethos of a Prussian state. 'Your hold over the West Bank must grow even more oppressive the longer its lasts. Yet your government feels compelled by military necessity to plant a settlement at Hebron, an area which could not possibly remain Israeli in any peaceful solution.'[189]

Eban, born in South Africa and educated in England, was on the more moderate wing of the Israeli Labour Party and was adept at presenting to the international community even the most belligerent Israeli policies in benign terms.[190] Responding to Crossman, he rejected the charge of Israel becoming militaristic, linking the iron fist policy towards its Arab neighbour with the old tropes of Labour Zionism. Israel was 'a fighting nation without becoming a warrior nation': 'We may show you a pilot who shot down eight aircraft bringing in the fruit from a kibbutz orchard.' On the Occupied Territories he indicated his 'present cabinet colleagues' were ready to find a solution in which 'the majority of the two million Palestinian Arabs on both sides of the river would be citizens of an Arab state … whose structure, name and regime they would be free to determine'.[191] Of the Jewish settlements in the West Bank, however, he said nothing. If Crossman was unconvinced he did not show it. He belonged to the generation of left-wing politicians to whom the fight against fascism had inspired a deep loyalty to Israel. Nevertheless, by 1970, he could no longer maintain that Israel was bringing economic progress to the Middle East nor that it was strengthening the non-aligned forces.

Notes

1 *Jewish Chronicle* (13 August 1948).
2 Mass Observation Archives, Sussex University, File Reports 2342, 'Note on Popular Attitudes to Palestine and Arab countries', 6 November 1946.
3 D. Leach, 'Explosion at the King David Hotel', in M. Sissons and P. French (eds) *Age of Austerity* (Harmondsworth: Penguin Books, 1964), p. 74; S. Carruthers, *Winning Hearts and Minds* (London: Leicester University Press, 1995), p. 63.
4 Mass Observation, File Reports 2515, 'Report on Attitudes to Palestine and Jews', September 1947.
5 Y. Grodzinsky, *In the Shadow of the Holocaust* (Monroe: Common Courage Press, 2004), p. 65.
6 A. Bullock, *Life and Times of Ernest Bevin*, vol. 1 (London: Heinemann, 1960), p. 457.
7 *The Times* (14 November 1945).
8 Quoted in F.S. Northedge, 'Britain and the Middle East', in R. Ovendale (ed.) *The Foreign Policy of the British Labour Government* (Leicester: Leicester University Press, 1984), p. 149.
9 Morris claims that 'implicit in Biltmore [is] that the state would encompass only part of Palestine', in *Righteous Victims* (New York: Vintage Books, 2001), p. 169. There was, however, no hint in the programme of leaving any part of Palestine under Arab sovereignty. As Arendt noted, 'the Jewish minority granted minority rights to the Arab majority'. H. Arendt, *The Jewish Writings* (New York: Shocken Books, 2007), p. 343; See E. Childers, 'The Worldless Wish: From Citizens to Refugees', in I. Abu-Lughod (ed.), *The Transformation of Palestine* (Evanston: Northwestern University Press, 1971), pp. 176–177.
10 Arendt, *The Jewish Writings*, p. 368.
11 R. Crossman, *Palestine Mission* (London: Hamish Hamilton, 1947), p. 41.
12 *The Economist* (8 December 1945).
13 R. Stevens, *American Zionism and U.S. Foreign Policy* (New York: Pageant Press, 1962), p. 21.
14 Earl Harrison, 'The Treatment of Displaced Jews in the United States Zone of Occupation in Germany, 1945', www.ess.uwe.ac.uk/documents/harrison_report.htm (accessed 16 February 2011).
15 The Anglo-American Committee of Inquiry, 1947, http://avalon.law.yale.edu/subject_menus/angtoc.asp (accessed 1 February 2012).
16 Wm. R. Louis, *The British Empire in the Middle East 1945–1951* (Oxford: Clarendon Press, 1984), p. 400.
17 Crossman, *Palestine Mission*, p. 168.
18 Ibid., p. 159.
19 Ibid., p. 176.

20 Ibid., p. 192.
21 Ibid., p. 84.
22 Ibid., p. 80.
23 *The Economist* (10 November 1945).
24 B. Wasserstein, *Vanishing Diaspora* (Cambridge, MA: Harvard University Press, 1996), p. 27.
25 Godzinsky, *In the Shadow*, p. 41.
26 Wasserstein, *Vanishing Diaspora*, p. 21.
27 T. Segev, *The Seventh Million* (New York: Hill and Wang, 1993), p. 136.
28 Crossman, *Palestine Mission*, p. 87.
29 Report of the Anglo-American Committee of Inquiry (1946), www.mideastweb.org/angloamerican.htm (accessed 16 March 2011).
30 Crossman, *Palestine Mission*, p. 54.
31 Ibid., p. 80.
32 Ibid., p. 177.
33 Ibid., p. 148.
34 Ibid., p. 176–177.
35 Quoted in A. Nachmani, *Great Powers Discord in Palestine* (London: Frank Cass, 1987), p. 170.
36 G. Achcar, *The Arabs and the Holocaust* (London: Saqibooks, 2010), p. 53.
37 A. Hourani, 'The Case Against A Jewish State in Palestine: Albert Hourani's Statement to the Anglo-American Committee of Inquiry of 1946', *Journal of Palestine Studies*, 35:1 (August 2005), 80–90.
38 Crossman, *Palestine Mission*, p. 211.
49 Labour Party, *Labour Party Handbook for Speakers 1948–49* (London: Labour Party, 1948).
40 P.W.T. Kingston, *Britain and the Politics of Modernization on the Middle East 1945–1958* (Cambridge: Cambridge University Press, 2002).
41 Crossman, *Palestine Mission*, pp. 214, 211.
42 *Hansard*, Commons, v. 426, c. 980, 31 July1946.
43 *LPACR*, 1946, p. 165.
44 Quoted in K. Paul, *Whitewashing Britain, Race and Citizenship in the Post-war Era* (Ithaca: Cornell University Press, 1997), p. 69.
45 Paul, *Whitewashing Britain*, pp. 68, 74.
46 P. Piratin, *For Peace in Palestine* (London: CPGB, 1946).
47 LHA, Healey Papers, International Department, November 1947, Box 10, File: Displaced Persons, ID/JR29/11/47.
48 *Hansard*, Commons, v. 426, c. 967, 31 July 1946.
49 Immigration, Land Settlement and Development in Palestine (Hope Simpson) Report, Cmd.3686 (London: HMSO, 1930), p. 79.
50 N. Shepherd, *Ploughing the Sand: British Rule in Palestine 1917–1948* (London: John Murray, 1999), p. 15.
51 H. Truman, *Memoirs of Harry S. Truman*, vol. 2, (New York: Da Capo Press, 1956), p. 152.
52 For how this tradition has been continued under New Labour, see J. Stern-Weiner 'Supporting Occupation – Gordon Brown in Israel', *New Left Project*, 1 August 2008 www.newleftproject.org/index.php/site/article_comments/supporting_occupation_-_gordon_brown_in_israel/ (accessed 14 June 2011).
53 Truman, *Memoirs*, p. 152.
54 Leitch, 'Explosion in the King David Hotel', p. 61.
55 LHA, Labour Party, International Department, Letter to Attlee, 29 October 1946, Box 4. File: Labour Party Foreign Policy 1946.
56 *Tribune* (8 March 1946).

57 *Tribune* (20 August 1948).
58 Ibid. (11 February 1949).
59 Ibid. (18 October 1946).
60 D. Healey, *Cards on the Table, An Interpretation of Labour's Foreign Policy* (London: Labour Party, 1948), p. 4.
61 *Tribune* (12 March 1948).
62 S. Haseler, *The Gateskelites: Revisionism in the British Labour Party, 1951–1964* (London: Macmillan, 1969), Ch. 4.
63 A. Flanders, 'Rita Hinden' in J. Bellamy and J. Saville (eds), *Dictionary of Labour Biography*, vol. 2 (Basingstoke: Macmillan, 1974), p. 179.
64 Rhodes House, Oxford University, A. Creech Jones Papers, Creech Jones to Elizabeth Monroe, 23 October 1961, Box 32, File 6.
65 *Socialist Commentary* (March 1946).
66 Ibid. (May 1945).
67 Ibid. (July 1948).
68 W.K. Pattison, 'The Delayed British Recognition of Israel', *Middle East Journal*, 37:3 (1983), 424.
69 *Hansard*, Commons, v. 424, c. 1898, 1 July 1946.
70 Ibid., v. 445, cc. 1227, 1243, 11 December 1947; *Daily Herald* (11 March 1948).
71 NA, H. Beeley, Memo, 31 December 1948, FO371/75346; I. Pappe, *Britain and the Israeli Conflict* (Basingstoke: Macmillan, 1988), p. 58.
72 A. Shlaim, *Collusion Across the Jordan* (Oxford: Clarendon Press, 1988).
73 NA, Bevin to Minister of Defence, Letter, 13 May 1948, FO800/477.
74 B. Morris, *The Birth of the Palestinian Refugee Problem Revisited* (Cambridge: Cambridge University Press, 2004), p. 75.
75 I. Pappe, *The Ethnic Cleansing of Palestine* (Oxford: Oneworld, 2006), pp. 40, 72.
76 *Manchester Guardian* (2 January 1948).
77 *Daily Herald* (23 April 1948).
78 Ibid. (24 April 1948).
79 *Tribune* (30 April 1948).
80 K. Kishtainy, *The New Statesman and the Middle East* (Beirut: Palestine Research Centre, 1972), p. 71.
81 Kishtainy, *The New Statesman*, p. 72.
82 *Tribune* (7 May 1948).
83 Ibid. (18 June 1948).
84 *Manchester Guardian* (27 February 1948).
85 Quoted in Morris, *Righteous Victims*, p. 39.
86 NA, Sir Ralph Cilento to UN International Children's Emergency Fund, 13 August 1948, FO371/68677.
87 NA, British Middle East Office to FO, 7 September 1948, FO371/68678.
88 NA, United Nations 'Relief for Palestinian Refugees, Survey of Operations to Date', 4 February 1949, No.iii/13, FO371/75418.
89 NA, FO Minutes, 2 February 1949, FO371/75420.
90 NA, Report from Red Cross, 'A Day in the Life of a British Red Cross Nursing Sister in a Refugee Camp in Transjordan', 17 March 1949, FO371/75423.
91 C. Weizmann, 'Palestine's Role in the Solution of the Jewish Problem', *Foreign Affairs*, 20: 2 (January 1942), p. 334. The development in Zionist thought of the idea of removing the indigenous people and its eventual implementation are discussed by Nur Masalha, *Expulsion of the Palestinians: The Concept of 'Transfer' in Zionist Political Thought* (London: I.B. Tauris, 1992) and *A Land Without a People* (London: Faber & Faber, 1997).
92 NA, Report by E. Pirdie, 7 October 1948, FO/371/68680.

93 *Manchester Guardian* (25 March 1949).
94 NA, Foreign Office, Minutes, 8 March 1949, FO371/75421.
95 NA, C. Mayhew to D. Rees-Williams, 27 October 1948, FO371/68681.
96 NA, British Middle East Office, Memorandum on Refugees, 7 September 1948, FO371/68678.
97 NA, J. Troutbeck to FO, Letter, 22 November 1948, FO371/68682.
98 NA, Report by Major Hackett-Paine, 25 August 1948, FO371/68677.
99 NA, B. Burrows to Council of British Societies for Relief Abroad, Letter, 3 September 1948, FO371/68677.
100 NA, Minutes of talks with US expert Mr. McGhee about Palestinian refugees, 15 April 1949, FO371/75424.
101 *Hansard*, Commons, v. 460, cc. 933–934, 26 January 1949.
102 NA, Mr. Burrows, Memo., FO, 13 August 1948, FO371/68677.
103 NA, J.S.G. Bead, Middle East Department, Foreign Office, Circular, 15 October 1948, FO371/68680.
104 NA, Minutes, 13 October 1948, Refugee Department, Middle East Section FO371/68680.
105 NA, Lord Altrincham to FO, 17 March 1949, FO371/75421
106 NA, Sir Edwards Spears to FO, Letter, 8 April 1949, FO371/75424. Sir Edward Spears and the Committee for Arab Affairs is discussed by R. Miller, *Divided Against Zion* (London: Frank Cass, 2000), pp. 16–17.
107 NA, Bevin to W. Lawther and A. Deakin, Letter, 24 December 1949, FO371/75441
108 NA, J. Sherringham, Memo., 11 April 1950, FO371/82235
109 NA, R. Williams-Thompson to Bevin, 6 April 1950, FO371/75454
110 T. Judt, *Postwar: A History of Europe Since 1945* (London: Pimlico, 2007), pp. 25–27.
111 L. James, *The Making and Unmaking of British India* (London: Abacus, 1998), pp. 535–635.
112 NA, British Embassy to Eastern Department, 17 February 1949, FO371/75419.
113 *Manchester Guardian* (31 March 1949) and *New York Times* (25 March 1949).
114 *TUC Annual Congress Report*, 1943 pp. 136–137, 335.
115 Modern Record Archives, Warwick University, TUC Papers, W. Citrine to General Secretary, Essex Trades Council, 15 February 1944, Mss 292/954/23.
116 *Manchester Guardian* (31 March 1949).
117 *LPACR*, 1949, p. 190.
118 *Zionist Review* (20 August 1948).
119 *Tribune* (23 July 1948).
120 Ibid. (9 September 1949).
121 B. Morris, 'The Crystallization of Israeli Policy Against a Return of the Arab Refugees: April-December, 1948', *Studies in Zionism*, 6:1 (1985), 85–118.
122 *Tribune* (9 September 1949).
123 Ibid. (23 July 1948). In a riposte to the standard Zionist depiction of the Arab flight in April and May 1948, Morris writes: 'the Arab evacuation of each area was precipitated and triggered in a one-to-one correspondence by Haganah/IDF attack or fear of imminent attack.' B. Morris, 'The Eel and History: A Reply to Shabtai Teveth', *Tikkun*, 5:1 (1990), 81.
124 *New Statesman* (15 January 1949).
125 *Hansard*, Commons, v. 460, cc.994–995, 26 January 1949.
126 D. Peretz, *Israel and the Palestine Arabs* (Washington: The Middle East Institute, 1958) p.143. Fischbach in a more recent study notes: 'By 1954, one-third of Israel's entire Jewish population lived on refugee property, including 250,000 new immigrants housed in urban refugee housing. One advantage to utilizing abandoned refugee housing was that it was much cheaper than constructing new homes. Settling

immigrants in new housing amounted to between $7,000 and $9,000 per family in 1950, compared to $750 per family for repairs to existing Palestinian homes in the villages plus another $750 for animals and farm equipment.' M. Fischbach, *Records of Dispossession* (New York: Columbia University Press, 2003), pp. 73–74.
127 *Tribune* (11 June 1948).
128 Ibid. (17 December 1948).
129 Gollancz Papers, V. Gollancz, 'Jewish Aid for Arab Refugees', Mss.157/3/JS/2/1.
130 *Jewish Chronicle* (6 May 1949).
131 *The Times* (27 January 1949).
132 LHA, Labour Party, Report, Labour Party Delegation to Israel, 29 December–13 January 1950, p. 10.
133 *Daily Herald* (31 January 1950).
134 LPACR, 1952 p .134.
135 *Tribune* (30 June 1950).
136 Labour Party, *Labour's Foreign Policy* (London: Labour Party Publications, 1952) p .4.
137 W. Wyatt, *The Jews at Home* (London: A Tribune Pamphlet, 1950) p. 23.
138 *Hansard*, Commons, v. 548, c. 68, 24 January 1956.
139 *The Times* (10 November 1955).
140 E. Childers, *The Road to Suez* (London: MacGibbon and Kee, 1962), p. 141; *Hansard*, Commons, v.547, c.852, 12 December 1955.
141 *Hansard*, Commons, v.547, c.846, 12 December 1955.
142 NA, Cited in memo by B. Burrows, FO to UK Delegation in Geneva, 2 March 1949, FO371/75418.
143 NA, Kirkbride to Foreign Office, 4 March 1949, FO371/75420.
144 NA, quoted in Report of the Secretary General on UN Relief for Palestinian Refugees, 30 September 1949, FO371/75442.
145 R. Sayigh, *Palestinians: From Peasants to Revolutionaries* (London: Zed Press, 1991), p. 129.
146 *Hansard*, Commons, v. 532, c. 318, 2 November 1954.
147 Quoted in I. Lustick, *Arabs in the Jewish State* (Austin: University of Texas Press, 1980), p. 37.
148 S. Jiryis, *The Arabs in Israel* (New York: Monthly Review Press, 1976), p. 77; B. Kimmerling, *Zionism and Economy* (Cambridge, MA: Schenkman Publishing Co. 1983), p. 24.
149 J. Cook, *Disappearing Palestine* (London: Zed Books, 2008), p. 28.
150 E. Zureik, *The Palestinians in Israel* (London: Routledge & Kegan Paul, 1979), p. 132.
151 D. Peretz, *Israel and the Palestine Arabs* (Washington: Middle East Institute, 1958), p. 126.
152 Quoted in Lustick, *Arabs in the Jewish State*, p. 175.
153 *Hansard*, Commons, v. 460, c. 995, 26 January 1949. The size of the Palestinian population in Israel was cited by Crossman, on the basis of a 1948 Israeli census, as 70,000. Lustick estimates 160,000 to be more accurate for 1949, around 12.5 per cent of the total population. I. Lustick, *Arabs in a Jewish State* (Austin: University of Texas Press, 1980), p. 49.
154 *New Statesman* (7 February 1951).
155 Lustick, *Arabs in the Jewish State*, p. 96.
156 D. Peretz , 'Problems of Arab Refugee Compensation', *Middle East Journal*, 8:4 (1954), 403.
157 E. Monroe, 'The Arab-Israel Frontier', *International Affairs*, 29:4 (1953), 442.
158 B. Morris, *Israel's Border Wars* (Oxford: Oxford University Press, 2005), p. 428.
159 Wyatt, *The Jews at Home*, p. 21.

160 A. Shlaim, *The Iron Wall* (London: Penguin Books, 2000), p. 91: Morris, *Israel's Border Wars*, p. 261.
161 *Hansard*, Commons, 26 October 1953.
162 *New Statesman* (24 October 1953).
163 Morris, *Israel's Border Wars*, pp. 338–339, 342; Shlaim, *The Iron Wall*, p. 124.
164 *Tribune* (8 April 1955).
165 Levenberg Papers, H. Pinner to Israeli Ambassador, Letter, 21 October 1955, File 1/3.
166 E. Summerskill, *A Woman's World* (London: Heinemann, 1967), p. 173.
167 Quoted in Poale Zion Press release, Levenberg Papers, 7 October 1955, File 1/3.
168 *LPACR*, 1955, p. 177.
169 *LPACR*, 1955, p. 184.
170 Levenberg Papers, H. Pinner to Israeli Ambassador in UK, 21 October 1955, File 1/3.
171 B. Brivati, *Hugh Gaitskell* (London: Richard Cohen Books, 1996), pp. 192, 220.
172 Pinner to Israeli Ambassador.
173 S. Howe, *Anticolonialism in British Politics* (Oxford: Clarendon Press) p. 249.
174 *Peace News* (9 December 1955).
175 Ibid. (19 October 1956).
176 Ibid. (9 November 1956).
177 M. Foot, *Aneurin Bevan, 1945–1960*, vol. 2 (London: Davis-Poynter, 1973) p. 517.
178 Childers, *Road to Suez*, pp. 158–165.
179 *Tribune* (10 August 1956). Three years earlier, at a time when the Conservative government was taking steps to denationalise the British steel industry, Bevan wrote: 'The case for public ownership of steel has never been more clearly stated. It has a case which has application not only here in Britain , but all over the world'. *Tribune* (30 October 1953).
180 L. Epstein, *British Politics in the Suez Crisis* (London: Pall Mall Press, 1964), pp. 82–83.
181 Shlaim, *The Iron Wall*, p. 184.
182 Morris, *Righteous Victims*, p. 301.
183 Foot, *Bevan*, p. 517.
184 *Hansard*, Commons, v. 566, c. 1334, 14 March 1957.
185 R. Crossman, *A Nation Reborn* (London: Hamish Hamilton, 1960), p. 104.
186 Ibid., p. 95.
187 A. Howard, *Crossman* (London: Jonathan Cape, 1990), p. 126.
188 Crossman, *A Nation Reborn*, p. 97.
189 *New Statesman* (31 July 1970).
190 *Sunday Independent* (24 November 2002).
191 *New Statesman* (14 August 1970).

5 The new left and the Palestinians

Israel's rapid and overwhelming victory over its Arab enemies in 1967 was welcomed by most of the British press and political class. Nasser's decision to have the UN peacekeeping force withdraw from the Sinai and to re-enter his troops was intended to demonstrate Egyptian leadership of the Arab world after Israel had carried out a military raid deep inside Syria. The Egyptian leader's next step, to close the Straits of Tiran to Israeli shipping, did not pose an existential threat to Israel but was a threat that the Eshkol government, having been assured of US backing, interpreted as *casus belli*. Under the Johnson presidency, America's weapon supply to Israel switched from defensive weapons to highly sophisticated offensive arms and the value of its military aid in 1966 increased seven fold. In the lead up to the war, 'the president gave a secret authorisation to ship by air to Israel a variety of weapons system'.[1] In six days, the Israel army captured the Sinai peninsular, Gaza, the West Bank and the Golan Heights and appeared to have inflicted a devastating blow to Nasser's standing in the Arab world. 'The West must be profoundly grateful to Israel,' the *Daily Telegraph* declared, 'for doing, against its earnest advice, what it shrank from doing itself.'[2] For many Conservatives, Britain's humiliation over the Suez war had been avenged by proxy.

The Labour government's official position in the build up to the war had been to urge restraint on both sides but to insist that the Straits of Tiran was an international waterway and that it was prepared to enforce this by participating in an international naval force if necessary. Israel's subsequent military offensive sidelined this initiative but its victory broadly conformed to Britain's strategic objectives in the Middle East: to counter radical Arab nationalism and Soviet influence and to ensure that Israel had the military capacity to defend itself. When the war was over Arab hostility was directed in large measure at Britain and the US. The Labour government responded by making diplomatic efforts at damage limitation. It was concerned not only over how this hostility might advantage the Soviet Union but also over the harm that it could cause to the British economy. The Arab countries had imposed a ban on oil exports to Britain and the US and there were fears of negative repercussions on British exports to the Middle East which had exceeded £300 million the previous year.[3] To bring reconciliation with the Arab world was therefore in Britain's self-interest and it was with this aim in mind that George Brown, the Labour government's foreign secretary, in a speech to the UN General Assembly, declared Britain's opposition to 'territorial aggrandisement' and to Israel unilaterally changing the status of Jerusalem.[4] The Labour government also took a leading part in the formulation of Resolution 242, which balanced the demand for an Israeli withdrawal 'from territories of recent conflict', with the demand for the Arab states that they recognise Israel. Behind the British government's public stance, its sympathy and that of most Labour backbenchers was on the side of Israel. Brown, who in the Labour Party spectrum was considered pro-Arab, reportedly told a meeting of the Parliamentary party: 'We are all pleased and relieved at the outcome of the war.'[5] At the time, nearly two-thirds of Labour MPs were members of the Labour Friends of Israel. When Christopher Mayhew, one of the pro-Arab Labour MPs, addressed the party's Foreign Affairs Group to argue the Arab case he received a hostile reception. 'The interruption began when he argued that it was wrong to talk in terms of racial extermination by the Arab forces in their war against Israel ... He was almost shouted down when he went on to claim that the existence of the Palestinian refugees was the root of the crisis.'[6]

Disquiet over Israel's triumph was however no longer confined to the handful of pro-Arab MPs on the party's right-wing. The war divided the party's left. The Tribune group of left-wing MPs that in the 1966–1970 Parliament had forty-one MPs, 11 per cent of Labour MPs,[7] had some of the most committed Zionists but also Stan Newens and Michael Foot, who were sympathetic to Nasser and left-wing Arab nationalism. Tribune published articles supportive of Israel from three prominent left-wing MPs, Sidney Silverman, Ian Mikardo and Eric Heffer but its editorial line expressed unease at indications by Israel's prime minister, Levi Eshkol, and defence minister, Moshe Dayan that they wanted to hold on to some of the newly occupied territory. It was reasonable, an editorial argued, that Israel should carry out some adjustments to its borders but warned that 'rationalisation is one thing, territorial expansion is another'.[8] After a visit to Israel, Heffer responded to such worries by predicting that Israel would return the West Bank to Jordan. An added concern, the Tribune editorial had noted, was that, in the aftermath of the June war, some Palestinians had been made into refugees for a second time as a result of Israel forcing 200,000 Palestinians out of the West Bank into Jordan.[9]

The war also deeply divided the Marxist left, which was passing through a period of growth and intellectual effervescence, particularly among students. Loosely connected to a broader movement of cultural contestation, this was an intellectual current composed of individuals and groups which to varying degrees dissented from the policies and forms of organisation of the 'old left' represented by the Labour Party and the CPGB. This 'new left' was, by the late

1960s, in its second or even third phase of development, out of which emerged a reappraisal of attitudes to Israel and Zionism. Its chief ideological inspiration can be traced back to the 1950s, to a small group of left-wing intellectuals, mostly dissidents from the CPGB and activists in the Campaign for Nuclear Disarmament (CND), who began exploring alternative theoretical and political approaches to both social democracy and the communist movement. The Soviet repression of the Hungarian uprising in October 1956 and the Suez crisis which followed a few weeks later hot-housed this group's political formation. Stuart Hall, who took part in the new left's emergence, recalls: '"Hungary" brought to an end a certain kind of socialist "innocence". On the other hand, "Suez" underlined the enormity of the error in believing that lowering the Union Jack in a few ex-colonies necessarily signalled the "end of imperialism" ... The New Left came into existence in the aftermath of these two events. It attempted to define a 'third' political space.'[10] Its principal figures identified themselves with various interpretations of socialist humanism. Alongside this group, there developed from the early 1960s a more radical internationalism. It was prompted by the anti-colonial and anti-racist struggles of the Communist Party, the Movement for Colonial Freedom, the US Civil Rights movement and the anti-apartheid campaign which inspired a younger generation of left-wing activists, some of whom joined feminist, anarchist, Trotskyist and Maoist groups. These groups were mostly critical of the Soviet-directed Marxist orthodoxy, from a variety of positions. Their ideological orientation was reflected in the *New Left Review* from the early 1960s, the *Socialist Register*, the US Marxist journal *Monthly Review* and in several other less prominent publications which drip-fed Marxist and anti-imperialist ideas into a political mobilisation that coalesced around the campaign against the US war in Vietnam. By 1967 this had turned into a movement that did much to set the ideological context in which the radical left began to view the Palestinians' conflict with Israel as an anti-imperialist struggle.

The Six Day War caught this new left 'by surprise and found it disoriented and divided'.[11] The differences ranged over Israel's regional role, Zionism and Arab nationalism. The ensuing debates were often more analytical than the mainstream political discussion and the ideas from them percolated into that mainstream. Among the more significant early contributions was an interview published in the *New Left Review*, with Isaac Deutscher, the Marxist intellectual and biographer of Leon Trotsky. He saw the Arab-Israel war as part of the conflict between imperialism and rising nationalist movements in the developing world, which was overlaid by the Cold War rivalry between Washington and Moscow. Comparing the resolute backing that Israel received from the US with the prevarication in the Soviet support for Nasser, Deutscher argued that the Soviet leaders were torn between preserving the international *status quo* and retaining some credibility with movements and countries that clashed with American interests. He did not regard the Israelis, however, as simple instruments of the US, insisting that at the core of the Arab-Israeli conflict was 'a clash of two nationalisms'. Arab nationalism was still fighting for independence and 'has its historic justification and progressive aspect'. But even in this progressive phase, every nationalism, observed Deutscher, had 'an inclination to exclusiveness, national egoism and racism'. He was critical of Nasser's demagogy and autocratic rule but pointed out that despite his military defeat, Israel had not achieved its objective to remove him from power. 'The Arab masses who came out in the streets and squares of Cairo, Damascus and Beirut to demand that Nasser should stay in office, prevented it happening ... There are only very few cases in history when a people stood in this way by a defeated leader.' But if the war had not turned out to be disastrous for the Egyptian leader, he believed that, paradoxically, it 'will be seen one day in the not very remote future, to have been a disaster in the first instance for Israel itself'. He warned that the Israelis were becoming the Prussians of the Middle East, imbued after a succession of military victories with 'an absolute confidence in their own efficiency, a blind reliance on the force of their arms, chauvinistic arrogance, and contempt for other peoples'.[12]

On the historic role of Zionism, Deutscher's attitude was ambivalent. In 1954, he had explained, that he was not a Zionist but he had abandoned his anti-Zionism. 'If instead of arguing against Zionism in the 1920s and 1930s I had urged European Jews to go to Palestine, I might have saved some of the lives that were later extinguished in Hitler's gas chambers.'[13] Israel had emerged out of desperation, it was he said 'a raft state'. He returned to this theme in his post-June war interview, likening European Jewry establishing a state in Palestine to a person jumping from the top floor of a burning house who lands on the person standing below, breaking that person's arms and legs. Nazism had been the degenerate offspring of Western bourgeois 'civilisation': 'Yet it was the Arabs who were made to pay the price for the crimes the West committed towards the Jews.' Israel could have, Deutscher argued, 'tried to make friends with the innocent victim', by recognising and assuaging its grievance, but instead from the outset 'Zionism worked towards the creation of a purely Jewish state and was glad to rid the country of its Arab inhabitants'.[14] His earlier enthusiasm for Israel's uniqueness[15] abated by 1967: 'It was only with disgust that I could watch on television the scenes from Israel in those days; the displays of the conquerors' pride and brutality; the outbursts of chauvinism; and the wild celebrations of the inglorious triumph, all contrasting sharply with the pictures of Arab suffering and desolation.'[16] He implicitly ruled out that Israeli society could initiate a change of attitudes towards the Arabs, suggesting that Arab policy had to appeal to Israeli workers over the heads of their political leaders. If the Arabs gave clear pledges that 'Israel's legitimate interests are respected and that Israel may be welcome as a member of a future Middle Eastern Federation', Israeli workers could be freed from their leaders' chauvinism.[17]

Deutscher's intervention on the Arab-Israeli conflict made a less lasting impression on the new left than the French Marxist and Middle East specialist, Maxime Rodinson. His essay on the subject was first published, in June 1967, in a special issue of *Les Temps Modernes*, the journal closely linked to its founders, Sartre and de Beauvoir. Its core argument resonated with the ideas that were animating the anti-imperialist mobilisation against the US war in Vietnam and was similar to the view expressed around this period by a small Israeli Trotskyist group, the Israeli Socialist Organisation, known by the name of its journal *Matzpen* (*Compass*).[18] Rodinson analysed the Arab-Israeli conflict not as Deutscher, through the prism of the US-Soviet rivalry, but as arising out of 'the great European-American movement of expansion in the nineteenth and twentieth centuries whose aim was to settle new inhabitants among other peoples or to dominate them economically and politically'.[19] And instead of interpreting Zionism primarily by relation to the Holocaust, Rodinson insisted on the continuing relevance of Zionism's pre-Second World War history in Palestine to demonstrate that it was not merely a variant of nationalism but also of colonialism. Jewish settlement in Palestine was not established on the basis of exploiting indigenous labour but this was not a necessary characteristic of colonialism. 'The English in the East Indies were not landowners who exploited peasants, any more than they were for example, in Australia or New Zealand. Moreover, in a certain number of cases, there either was for all practical purposes no native population or it was exterminated, as in Tasmania. Are there those who would, as a result, entertain the idea that British expansion into all these territories was not colonial in nature?' Under Ottoman and British rule, the Zionist movement had gained land by legal means but 'throughout the entire world, lands colonized were acquired much less through the use of direct force than through seemingly legal deals, with the privileged position of the colonizer allowing him to use ruses and legal detours to his own advantage'. The Zionists' land acquisition had, in any case, also involved force for, he argued, whatever the causes for the Arab flight in 1948 'no one can claim that they were freely given [the] said territory by the Arabs'.[20]

Rodinson dismissed the argument that Zionism's conflict with the British in the last phase of the Mandate was evidence of it being anti-imperialist. British rule had protected the growth of the *Yishuv*, in much the same way that the French had protected the *pieds noirs* in Algeria, but the 'classical pattern' in such situations is that tensions arise between the colonists and the mother country, which out of regard for its wider interests, has to take into account the aspirations of the native population.[21] The Zionist settlement's socialist character could not absolve it of colonialism. It had merely given 'the great majority of Israelis and their friends on the left the same kind of good conscience that, for example, the internal political democracy existing inside France gave to the French colonists in the colonies'.[22] Rodinson did not challenge the notion that the foundations of Israeli society were socialist, he characterised its colonial character as manifesting itself only in its external relations to the Palestinians. He made no attempt therefore to establish the connection between, on the one hand, Israeli society's labour movement institutions, the *kibbutzim* and the Histadrut, and, on the other, its colonial character vis-à-vis the indigenous population. It is not until the 1980s through the work of Baruch Kimmerling, Zachary Lockman, Gershon Shafir and Zeev Sternhell, that this apparent paradox is resolved by demonstrating that the Labour Zionist institutions' 'socialist' character was subordinated to ethnic separatism. Yet this does not greatly affect Rodinson's analysis for he places no great consequence on Israel's internal social organisation. His argument is that Israel was forcibly imposed on the Arab world and to prevail in that relation of antagonism it had to ally itself with an imperialist power. For a possible way forward he alludes to the situation in South Africa: 'no one speaks of chasing the whites out of South Africa because of their colonial origins. They are asked simply to coexist with the Blacks as equals.' But Rodinson qualifies this just enough to suggest that the coexistence will require a restructuring of the power relations between the two nationalities, for the settler group 'can only claim to have left the colonial process behind when the native group, as a result of negotiated concessions, comes to accept this autonomy'.[23]

Rodinson's work formed the main theoretical backdrop to two essays on the Arab-Israeli conflict in the 1970 issue of *Socialist Register*. The journal's long-standing editors were two Marxist academics, the political theorist Ralph Miliband and the labour historian John Saville. Miliband felt, in the lead up to the June war, that the revolutionary left's support for Nasser was a sign of it being swept away by radical nationalist rhetoric and a simplistic analysis of the situation. His close friend, the Belgian Marxist Marcel Liebman, took a contrary view. For both, the issues raised by the Arab-Israel conflict were entwined with their personal histories, in which they had much in common. Miliband had fled to Britain with his father, in 1940, when the German army invaded Belgium and he questioned himself on whether being Jewish affected his point of view. Liebman was also Jewish. His elder brother had been transported by the Nazis to Auschwitz, in 1943, and died there. As Michael Newman, Miliband's biographer suggests, what probably accounts for their disagreement over the Middle East was that in the late 1950s and early 1960s Liebman, more of a political activist than Miliband, had been deeply involved in the Belgian solidarity campaign for the Algerian independence struggle.[24] The two men were good friends and corresponded regularly but their letters debating the 1967 war reflected the whirlwind of emotions that this conflict aroused not only in them but, more widely, on the left and, in particular, among left-wing Jews. Their friendship survived and, in 1971, when Liebman initiated legal action against a scurrilous article in a Belgian Zionist newspaper accusing him of being an anti-semite and likening him to Jews who collaborated with the Nazis, Miliband wrote a testimonial on his behalf.[25]

In 1967 Miliband felt that Nasser's closure of the Tiran Straits was, at the very least, aimed at weakening Israel and could only be justified 'if one accepts the goal of wiping out the state of Israel'. This he argued could not be supported either on anti-imperialist or on humanitarian grounds. He dismissed the idea that

Israel was a serious obstacle to socialist revolution in the Arab world. Israel's policy towards its neighbours was wrong but it played a minimal role in the US's confrontation with radical Arab nationalism. But even if it were important, 'I exclude the elimination of all national entities wherever', adding: 'Here there is another factor. It is that Israel is the refuge of 2,500,000 Jews who carry with them the suffering of centuries, and that the disappearance of that state would have an exceptional human dimension.'[26]

Liebman, distinguishing between the Israeli nation and the state, argued that, 'the Palestinian solution', the replacement of the Jewish state by a Palestinian state, could accommodate both Israeli and Palestinian national aspirations. He conceded, however, that the Arabs had still to clarify what they understood by the destruction of the state of Israel and whether, therefore, in a future Palestinian state, Jews would have only citizenship rights or also national rights.[27] Miliband, while agreeing that nation states were not immutable and forming larger units was desirable, saw the options for the time being to be either that Israel survived or that it was liquidated, entailing 'the massacre of an indeterminate number of Jews and the expulsion of the rest'.[28] But Liebman would not let go of the idea of one state for two nationalities and returned to this subject in 1969: 'Its realisation is improbable. And not being impossible, though very improbable, being just, it must be supported.' Moreover, he believed there to be grounds for optimism. Palestinian resistance was growing stronger and the Palestine Liberation Organisation's (PLO) political leadership repudiated the political line, associated with Ahmed Shukeiri, its first president, who had suggested that Jews on Palestinian land would be eliminated. With Shukeiri's departure, Liebman saw improved prospects for a relatively significant number of Israelis to come to understand that the Palestinians' struggle was directed against the political basis of the state and not against the collective existence of its Jewish population. If the 'Palestinian solution' seemed improbable, 'the Israeli and Zionist solution is barmy (délirant) and criminal'.[29]

The two men's private discussion, between 1967 and 1969, continued in the *Socialist Register*, with an article by Mervyn Jones putting the point of view that was close to Miliband's and another, by Liebman.

To the Rodinson-Liebman thesis that Israel had been established as a late extension of European colonialism, Jones' response was that this did not affect the state's legitimacy. 'In the course of history quite a number of nations (including Arab nations) have carried through the process by settlement or invasion.' It was possible, he added, to see Israel's formation as the product of errors and even crimes 'and yet still uphold Israel's right to exist'.[30] There were now two nationalisms in collision, each denying the other the right of statehood. Socialists, Jones argued, could not subordinate their position to a purely nationalist perspective. They supported nationhood by virtue of its potential to lead beyond national self-determination to a stage of greater liberation and, in this respect, he saw no difference between the two sides. Israel's connection to US interests was, in his view, historically contingent. Israeli leaders faced with Arab hostility secured support from where they could, just as the Mufti turning to Hitler for help during the Second World War did not make Palestinian nationalism into 'merely an outpost of fascism'.[31] In Jones' conception, Israeli leaders, given the political will, could draw a line under the colonial phase of Zionism. The ingathering of Jews was part of the state's *raison d'être* but, he argued, it could be disconnected from territorial expansion. He conceded there was a theocratic aspect to the Israeli state, but he suggested that it played no larger part than in Italy, Spain or Ireland and could be left to be dealt with by the country's democrats and humanists. Only a few sentences later, however, Jones undermined this claim by pointing to the connection between the theocratic element and Zionism's colonising drive: 'Zionism gained much of its emotional force from the Biblical tradition, especially from the concept of Palestine as a land promised to the Jewish people ... The claim to the entire city of Jerusalem, of course, is backed by this appeal to ancient tradition.'[32]

Whereas Jones began from the premise that in deciding whether to support a movement for nationhood 'the desires of the people concerned are the deciding factor',[33] Liebman looked beyond this justification, which nationalism itself claims. He held the origin of the Israeli state to be central to the understanding of its conduct because it defined its relation to Western interests in the Middle East and was at the root of its expansionist dynamic. It was not a moral quest to trace 'the ultimate beginnings of an injustice' but 'to show the constancy of a policy, the permanence of a kind of logic, the continuity of a situation which are now manifesting more gravely than before'.[34] Israel was organically linked to the West: its juridical legitimacy came from the Balfour Declaration and then from the UN. The state had been established without consulting the indigenous population it affected, claiming moral legitimacy from an event in European history, with which the Arabs had nothing to do. Liebman did not accept the explanation that Israel consistently allied itself with the Western imperial powers in the Middle East because of the Arab hostility it faced. The provisional government of the Front de Libération Nationale (FLN) had made friendly overtures to Algerian Jews and to Israel but 'Tel Aviv chose to follow a pro-French policy which *nothing obliged it to follow*'.[35] It would have been more accurate for Liebman to say that 'nothing obliged it' if Israel could have treated Algeria's independence on its own merits, but as he went on to argue, the Israeli state, having been imposed by force, existed in defiance of Arab nationalism. The antagonism flowed not from misguided policies but from Israel's founding principle of being a Jewish state. The corollary of the Zionist objective 'to maintain the Jewish character of a Jewish state', was the rejection of the right of the people it had displaced 'to recover their lands and homes, in any circumstances and even after a possible re-establishment of peace'.[36] Liebman remarked that even the so-called 'doves' among Israeli political leaders, on whom many on the left pinned their hopes for bringing about peace with the Arab states, opposed Israel's expansionism out of fear of the country's 'Levantinization', 'although the Jewish state had deliberately chosen to establish itself in the Levant'.[37]

At the time of the June war, Liebman had conceded to Miliband that the Arab nationalists had not yet spelled out how they planned to replace the state of Israel. Nevertheless, by the time he came to draft his article for the *Socialist Register*, he felt the Palestinian nationalist movement offered a solution that socialists could support. In the reappraisal in the Arab world that followed the 1967 war, Shukeirism was discarded by Fatah (the dominant organisation within the national movement), as it 'began to formulate a new concept of "liberation"'.[38] It was 'essential to stress', wrote Liebman, 'that all the Palestinian organisations have turned their backs on that earlier nihilism which, basing itself on a single consideration, the unjust origin of Israel, formerly refused to contemplate the possibility of coexisting with the Jews now settled in Israel ... Now they call upon the Jews of Israel to co-operate in building a new state.'[39] Arafat had announced Fatah's new conception of Palestinian liberation to an international conference in Cairo in January 1969: 'We are fighting today to create the new Palestine of tomorrow; a progressive, democratic and non-sectarian Palestine in which Christian, Muslim and Jew will worship, work, live peacefully and enjoy equal rights.'[40] A proposal that Jews could 'develop their national culture' was put forward by a left-wing group, the Popular Democratic Front for the Liberation of Palestine (PDFLP), led by Nayef Hawatmeh.[41] The PLO, however, adopted the position of Fatah, which stopped short of recognising the national rights of Israeli Jews but, nevertheless, proposed a Palestinian state, 'all of whose citizens, regardless of their religion, will enjoy equal rights'.[42]

Jones outlined the apparently more modest hope that Israel could be persuaded to make provisions for sharing Jerusalem, to withdraw to the pre-1967 borders and to recognise a sovereign Palestinian state in the West Bank and Gaza. He argued that the demand for a single democratic state and for all Palestinians to have the right to return to their former homes implied Israel's liquidation and thereby the denial of self-determination to its Jewish population. Liebman, by contrast, embraced the call of the PDFLP for a bi-national state. He expected the international left to ally with the Arab left in encouraging Israelis 'to reject the delusive guarantees and false enticements of Zionism'.[43] This optimistic scenario required a leap of faith in Israeli civil society, despite Liebman himself characterising Israel as one of the 'few examples to be found in the world of today, of such complete identification between state and nation, between political authority and civil society'.[44]

The position on the Arab-Israel conflict of the various political parties and groups to the left of the Labour Party ranged mostly along a spectrum that stretched from Jones to Liebman, with the CPGB, the largest of these organisations with around 30,000 members, being the significant exception.[45] In this period, Bert Ramelson, in a pamphlet, gave the Communist Party's view on the Middle East.

Ramelson's normal run of duty was to be the CPGB's national industrial organiser but he had worked for a year on a kibbutz in Palestine before joining the International Brigade to fight in the Spanish Civil War and was later active in the party's work in the Anglo-Jewish community.[46] His pamphlet on the Arab-Israeli conflict briefly rehearsed the international communist movement's account of the 1948 war, according to which Israel had been established with Soviet support, in a struggle against British imperialism and its Arab allies. He omitted to mention that support for the Zionist movement since the Second World War had come principally from the US which would have cast a different light on Israel's anti-imperialism. He also elided that the Arab opposition to the 1947 UN partition plan had popular support which the ruling cliques, to retain some credibility, translated into a poorly resourced and half-hearted military attack against the newly established Israeli state.[47] Ramelson emphasised that Israel had to refrain 'from occupying more territory than was allocated to her by the United Nations'; criticised the discriminations suffered by 'Israeli Arabs' and called for the refugees to be allowed 'to return to their homes and enjoy the full rights of citizenship'.[48]

The position outlined by Ramelson followed the Soviet leadership's limited policy objectives. In line with the UN General Assembly's Resolution 242, he supported the Arab states' demand that Israel withdraw to the 1967 borders but, did not seek the creation of an independent Palestinian state. In September 1970, when King Hussein of Jordan turned his army against the PLO fighters, Idris Cox, one of the party's international experts, used a more ambiguous formulation in calling for 'the achievement of the just rights of the Palestine refugees' but still within the framework of 242 and, therefore, short of Palestinian self-determination.[49]

Among the new left the identification with Palestinian nationalism was free of such equivocation. It had progressively strengthened from the late 1960s as Fatah and, more explicitly, the radical Popular Front for the Liberation of Palestine (PFLP) and PDFLP (a Marxist faction which had split from the PLFP in February 1969) began to present the Palestinian case not merely as part of the Arab national struggle but as having a distinct national dimension and akin to other anti-colonial movements. 'The struggle of the Palestinian people,' Fatah's 1969 programme stated, 'like that of the Vietnamese people and other peoples of Asia, Africa and Latin America, is part of the historic process of the liberation of the oppressed peoples from colonialism and imperialism.'[50] But within this politically radical but diverse new left there were differences over what state form the self-determination should take. In early 1969, *Black Dwarf*, the newspaper closely identified with the student movement, reported on 'the first ever big demonstration in Britain in solidarity with Palestine': 'The organisers of the march expected 500: there were over 2,000 Arabs, Jews and British.' The report highlighted the presence of Israeli Jews on the march alongside Arab socialists, which 'no less than the active participation of Jews in the guerrilla movement, confirms the socialist solidarity of both in the face of their common enemy the Zionist state'.[51] The demonstration appears to have acted as a springboard for the launch of the Palestine Solidarity Campaign (PSC). Its first membership conference in November 1969 was reported to have been attended by over 300 people.[52] The organisation's main objective was to support 'the right of the Palestinians to self-determination and national liberation in a de-Zionised, democratic Palestine where Jews and Arabs enjoy equal rights'. The campaign endorsed the Palestinian armed struggle and emphasised the link between Israel and US imperialism.[53] The leading elements in this first wave of solidarity activism came from Palestinian and Arab students living in London, who identified either with the PFLP or the PDFLP; from *Matzpen*; and from the Young Liberals, a largely student-based organisation that, throughout the 1970s, repeatedly clashed with their party's leadership for its strong support for Israel.

In 1970, the national organiser of the Young Liberals, Louis Eakes, took over the editorship of *Free Palestine* which had been launched as a monthly publication after the June 1967 war by a small group of Arab students and intellectuals. Eakes retained its seriousness but with considerable journalistic flair gave it a lively, campaigning style that provided in-depth reports on the Occupied Territories, critical analysis of the Western press and barbed commentary on the activities of the pro-Israel lobby.

The common denominator of the various groups involved in the solidarity campaign was that the national rights of both Palestinians and Israelis could be recognised in a single state. It was the political orientation that *Black Dwarf* promoted, presenting an interview with a left-wing Lebanese intellectual and articles by *Matzpen* members, two of whose founders, Moshe Machover and Akiva Orr, had characterised the Israeli state as 'the outcome of the colonization of Palestine by the Zionist movement at the expense of the Arabs'. They affirmed the right of Palestinian refugees to return to their land and for the two nationalities to coexist in a de-Zionized state.[54] *Matzpen* subsequently underwent several splits over differences on the relative importance of the national and the working-class struggle and similar ideological conflicts also fragmented the PSC once several of the key Palestinian activists, on completing their studies, departed from Britain. It left the solidarity campaign to small left-wing groups fighting to impose their particular political line. Thereafter, for some years, various Marxist and anti-racist organisations intermittently voiced solidarity with the Palestinian armed struggle, mainly when some action it, or the Israelis, undertook prompted coverage by the mainstream media. In 1972, Ghada Karmi, who had been exiled as a nine-year-old child with her family and subsequently became a doctor in London, took the lead in forming Palestine Action. 'Outside of the small Palestinian students' union,' Karmi recalls of this period, 'there were no Palestinian societies, no cultural or lobbying groups and no organised communal activities. The contrast with Britain's highly efficient and organised pro-Israeli lobby could not have been greater.'[55] Karmi set out to appeal beyond the radical left. Palestine Action's political programme made no mention of imperialism or armed struggle, focusing instead on the rights of Palestinians to return to their homes and the 'creation of a secular and democratic Palestine in which all have equal rights, irrespective of race or creed'.[56] The group worked closely with the pro-Arab Labour MPs who had set up the Labour Middle East Council (LMEC) and with a wide range of other organisations including the Young Liberals and *Matzpen*. The appeal of the Palestinian cause on this basis might have remained largely confined in Britain to small groups on the left but for the plight of the refugees, which as a result of armed clashes on Israel's borders periodically drew the attention of a wider public and gnawed at the liberal conscience.

In the lead up to the 1967 war, Frank Edmead, a leader writer on the *Guardian*, a newspaper that had a long record of support for Zionism and Israel, took up the refugee issue in a signed article. Why, he asked, if the Jews had the right to return to Palestine after 2,000 years, it was legitimate to deny Palestinians that right after only twenty years? 'At the receiving end, Zionism looked like yet another European colonial movement; settlers flowed in, to acquire much of the land, and all of the political power.'[57] A fortnight later, with the war over, the *Guardian*'s editor, Alastair Hetherington, in a leader, reaffirmed the newspaper's traditional pro-Israel orientation by, as Baram remarks, 'conveying some careful sympathy for Israeli expansionism'.[58] 'Voices have been raised in Israel,' Hetherington wrote, 'to insist that the old city must be held, that most of the Jordan's west bank must become Israeli territory, and that an Israeli garrison must be stationed at the Tiran Straits. It will be neither surprising nor wholly wrong if these demands become government policy.'[59] Edmead resigned. For him the difference over Israel came on top of seeing the *Guardian*'s critical editorial position on US policy in Vietnam being reversed after Hetherington on a visit there 'had been given free and welcoming access to American generals'.[60] The dispute in the *Guardian* over Israel resurfaced, however, following Edmead's departure as a result of a series of first-hand reports from Gaza and the West Bank by Michael Adams, which described human rights violations by the Israeli army, the demolition of Palestinian houses and the flow of refugees into Jordan. From 'Israel's point of view,' Adams concluded, 'the ideal solution to the problem of the occupied territories would be their absorption by Israel but without their Arab population'.[61] Adams's final despatch, detailing the destruction and expulsion of the inhabitants of three villages west of Jerusalem, Hetherington refused to publish. He 'accused Adams of concealing from the reader important facts, including that the destroyed villages were used as bases for attacks on Israel', though Israeli officials had confirmed that the villages had not been involved in the war.[62] Adams later remarked that 'if the story had been the other way round, with the Arabs destroying three Israeli villages and driving their inhabitants into destitution, every newspaper in Britain would have carried the story on its front page'.[63]

Israel's occupation of the West Bank and Gaza also aroused disapproval in the

Parliamentary Labour Party. The LMEC was set up by twenty-one Labour MPs to 'promote inside the Labour movement a constructive and balanced view of the Middle East'. In a memorandum to the party executive, the group argued: 'The party's pro-Israel views inevitably lead it to apply "double standards" on questions such as colonialism, racial discrimination, territorial expansion and respect for UN resolutions.' It called on the party to support Israeli withdrawal from the territories it occupied in 1967; to declare the changes carried out by Israel in the occupied Arab territories to be "null and void"; and to reject the US leadership over 'the supply of offensive weapons to Israel, and the encouragement given to her to cling to her conquest'.[64] Among the twenty-one MPs backing LMEC were Michael Foot, Stan Newens and Stan Orme from the party's left-wing, but its leading figures, Andrew Faulds and Christopher Mayhew, hailed from the party's right. Faulds was prone to express antipathy to pro-Israeli Jewish MPs on the basis that they had 'dual loyalties', though he made no such charge against the equally pro-Israeli Harold Wilson or Richard Crossman.[65] Mayhew, who had been a junior minister at the Foreign Office under Ernest Bevin, had a record of campaigning against fascism and anti-semitism and was successful in a libel action against a fellow Labour MP, Maurice Edelman, who had accused him of anti-semitism.[66] Faulds's and Mayhew's sympathy for the Palestinians was linked to their assessment that the Arab states, radical or conservative, were important allies for Britain, an outlook informed perhaps, in part, by imperial nostalgia but more importantly by what they considered to be the national interest. 'Britain should clearly and calmly assess,' Faulds advised in a Parliamentary debate on the Middle East, 'where her real interests lie. I stress "British interests".'[67]

The LMEC application for affiliation to the Labour Party was rejected on the grounds that its aims 'differ only in emphasis from those of the party', although it would have been difficult by this criterion to justify Poale Zion's continued affiliation or indeed of many other affiliated bodies.[68] The group had further indication of what it was up against when the 1970 Labour Party annual conference approved a policy statement on the Arab-Israeli conflict that placed the emphasis on Israel's security needs and, as Mayhew pointed out, was 'less precise than the UN Security Council resolution about justice to the refugees and withdrawal'.[69]

Harold Wilson was influential in holding the party's policy on the Middle East to its traditional, pro-Israel stance. He later claimed that as prime minister he had been 'the best friend Israel had in the Western world'.[70] In 1973, on a visit to Israel as Opposition leader, he felt free to abandon all pretence at even-handedness. He described Arab insistence on an Israeli withdrawal to the 1967 borders as 'utterly unreal' and agreed with Israel's interpretation of UN Resolution 242, as requiring her to withdraw only from *some* of the territories it had occupied. 'If our government had meant "all",' Wilson explained, 'we would have said "all".'[71] The preamble to the resolution, however, as critics at the time and since have pointed out, had unambiguously affirmed 'the inadmissibility of the acquisition of territory by war'.[72]

Yet Wilson, too, recognised that the Israeli government would have to make some concession to Palestinian aspirations. On a visit to Israel in 1972, just a couple of months after the Black September group had kidnapped and killed eleven Israeli athletes at the Munich Olympics, Wilson argued that violence by young Palestinians would continue until the refugee problem was resolved, though to make clear that for him this did not mean according national rights and much less national self-determination to the Palestinians, he added that: 'Israel's reaction is natural and proper in refusing to accept the Palestinians as a nation'.[73] But in the light of the military occupation's failure to subdue Palestinian resistance, the argument for self-determination acquired political momentum in the international arena. Newspaper reports of Israeli violations of human rights were given authoritative confirmation, in 1970, by the International Committee of the Red Cross and the Investigation Committee of the UN General Assembly.[74]

The 1973 Yom Kippur War widened the circle of sceptics over Israel's policy towards the Arab world. From the ranks of the Labour Party, too, Israel's victory this time elicited nothing like the enthusiasm that had greeted it in 1967. 'In the past six years, since her spectacular victory,' wrote *Labour Weekly*, the party's official newspaper, 'Israel has been warned time and again that if she held on to all the captured territories an Arab attack was inevitable.'[75] Eric Heffer, one of the standard-bearers of the *Tribune* group of MPs, maintained that Israel's political leaders did not want to expand the country's borders but a *Tribune* report contradicted him: 'The overwhelming feeling of the period immediately after the June war was that most of the newly occupied territories would be returned. The atmosphere now is such that parts of these territories are being settled by Israelis almost automatically.'[76] Israeli occupation and settlement policy in the Occupied Territories had eroded support for Israel in the PLP. In response to the Conservative government's announcement at the outbreak of the 1973 war that it was halting arms supply to both sides, the Shadow Cabinet led by Wilson wanted a three-line whip on backbenchers to vote down the government's policy and to vote for arms supply to Israel. David Watkins, a backbench MP and the treasurer of the LMEC, claims that after more than eighty MPs indicated that they would not obey the leadership, backbenchers were allowed a 'free' vote. 'In the event,' Watkins recounts, '15 of us voted in the government lobby and about 75 abstained ... In that historic vote on 18th October 1973, 50 years of Zionist domination of Labour attitudes were ended.'[77] The shift in perception of the Arab-Israeli conflict was neither as abrupt nor as radical as Watkins suggests but a change had taken place on the left of British politics and not merely in the PLP.

In 1967, when Liebman had characterised Israel as 'imperialist', Miliband had countered: 'There are no doubt Israelis, even in high places, who would like to annex a good chunk of Jordan, which is reprehensible. But are there serious

Israeli plans to conquer and subjugate Arab people outside of its territory? Nonsense.'[78] Soon after the June war, however, Israeli government leaders indicated their determination not to return to the previous borders. 'If no Jews settle in East Jerusalem,' the prime minister, Levi Eshkol declared, 'the world may one day ask what we fought for.'[79] Eshkol was generally considered to be on the moderate, pragmatic wing of Labour Zionism. The ideologically hard-line minister of labour and former military commander, Yigal Allon, had ambitions that went well beyond Jerusalem. He was reported as promising 'a new wave of pioneering and expansion': 'New settlements would establish an Israeli "presence" in areas selected by the Government and they would go up on a scale greater than anything seen during the thirty years of the British Mandate.'[80] The Allon Plan formulated in this period though not formally adopted was influential on official thinking. It viewed settlements as tools for annexing the Jordan valley and the area to the west of the Dead Sea, primarily as a land barrier against any ground attack from the east but also as a way to maximise Israeli control over the Palestinian population.

East Jerusalem, the commercial and political hub of the West Bank, was to be ringed by Jewish settlements to incorporate it into a Greater Jerusalem under Israeli control. The overall aim of the Allon Plan was to concentrate the Palestinians into two cantons, with Hebron the main town in one and Nablus in the other, but the spread of the settlements turned out to be even more far reaching. A group of religious zealots, the embryo of the settler movement, Gush Emunim, claiming to 'redeem Jewish land' by divine decree established settlements penetrating deep into areas of Palestinian concentration, one of the earliest in the heart of Hebron. It was convenient for the Israeli government, facing international criticism over these settlements, to be able to distance itself from the 'unofficial' land annexations while giving them covert backing. The settlements, illegal in international law, benefited from the full panoply of state power and resources. The state ensured the provision of roads, electricity, water supply and above all military protection. There was in any case no disguising the Israeli government's responsibility for the military rule over the Palestinians in the West Bank and Gaza and it was this which would prove most damaging to Israel's international standing. Attacks by Palestinian armed groups and unarmed youths on Israeli military patrols in the West Bank and Gaza led to the shooting of protestors, the bulldozing of houses belonging to the families of suspected militants and curfews often lasting several days.

The Yom Kippur War and the consequent Arab oil embargo and price increase brought home to European governments the need to address Israel's occupation of Arab land. Whereas the UN Resolution 242, passed in 1967, had not contained the word 'Palestinian' but only 'refugees', after the 1973 war the European Community slowly edged its way to joining the non-aligned movement and the Soviet Union in pressing for a solution to the Middle East conflict that looked to trading land for peace and, within that framework, respond to Palestinian demands.[81] And the General Assembly voted, in 1974, to reintroduce the 'Palestine Question' on its agenda, after twenty-two years during which it had figured only in the Annual Reports of the United Nations Relief and Works Agency. The debate was opened with an address by the PLO leader, Yasser Arafat, in which he signalled his 'dream' of a democratic state for Israelis and Palestinians but also his readiness to accept what was later termed the 'mini-state' option, of a Palestinian state based on the West Bank and Gaza. The Assembly voted overwhelmingly to affirm the Palestinian people's right not merely to self-determination but also to 'national independence'.[82]

Labour Party policy lagged behind the shift in favour of the Palestinians in the international arena. It also lagged behind the Conservative Party leadership which was more attuned to British commercial interests in the Arab world. Reginald Maudling, as shadow foreign secretary, told Parliament in 1975 that 'the time has come when it must be recognised that the PLO is, broadly speaking, the voice of the Palestinians' and suggested that, in the long run, the Palestinians would have to have 'a country of their own'.[83] The Labour Party's programme, the following year, by which time James Callaghan had taken over from Wilson as prime minister, merely asserted that 'the rights of the Palestinian people must be recognised'. The 'rights' were formulated in vague terms as 'the expression of its national identity'.[84] When Labour was again in opposition following its 1979 general election defeat, Callaghan criticised the prime minister, Margaret Thatcher, for agreeing to the European Council's Venice declaration, in which the leaders of the European Community's member states specified for the first time that the Palestinians had a right to pursue 'self-determination' within the framework of a peace settlement. The communiqué stopped short of recognising the PLO as the 'sole representative' of the Palestinian people but accepted that it 'will have to be associated with the negotiations'.[85] Callaghan, however, lined up behind the Israeli Labour Party's position that the Palestinians be placed under Jordanian jurisdiction. He suggested that Western diplomatic efforts should try to involve King Hussein of Jordan in resolving the Palestinian problem.[86]

By this time, Callaghan's effort to maintain the Labour Party's traditional tilt towards Israel was meeting opposition not only from the PLP, as in Wilson's period, but from the wider Labour movement. The opposition was fuelled by developments in Israel interacting with the Labour Party's internal politics. The election of a right-wing government in Israel in 1977 dampened its appeal in the ranks of the British labour movement. For the first time since the establishment of Israel, Labour Zionist parties did not form the government. Over the previous decade, successive Israeli Labour administrations led by Levi Eshkol, Golda Meir and Yitzhak Rabin had entrenched the military occupation and extended Jewish settlements in the West Bank, Gaza, Sinai and the Golan Heights. With varying caveats they reassured the international community that newly occupied land would be traded for peace in a future deal with the Arab countries. However, the Likud leader, Menachem Begin, one-time commander of the Irgun terrorist group, openly espousing Israel's right to *Eretz* Israel, ruled out territorial concessions over the West Bank and Gaza. In the tradition of Jabotinsky's Revisionist Zionism, he interpreted *Eretz* Israel to be the entire land of Palestine prior to the British lopping off Transjordan, in 1922, for their protégé, Emir Abdullah. The Likud government in alliance with the Gush Emunim national-religious movement, which had contributed to its electoral triumph, accelerated the spread of settlements in the Occupied Territories including, from December 1970, in Gaza, where they were launched with the establishment of a paramilitary *kibbutz*. The number of settlements registered with the Interior Ministry increased from 39 in 1978 to 67 in 1983, and the inhabitants, correspondingly, from 7,400 to 22,800.[87]

The settlement expansion was condemned by the Callaghan and Thatcher governments but without threatening sanctions if it continued. The Israeli Labour Party also distanced itself from Likud's policy by making a dubious distinction between settlements for Israel's security needs, which it supported, and the ideologically motivated ones, which it opposed. Poale Zion, in Britain, approved this position, as did the left-leaning Bermant, who raged in the *Jewish Chronicle*: 'the Prime Minister, Mr. Menachem Begin, must put an immediate halt to the efforts of his Agriculture Minister, Mr. Ariel Sharon, to pepper the West Bank with settlements which have no security aspect whatsoever.'[88] But by the early 1980s, left-Zionist dissent from Israeli policies was no longer effective in heading off the critics of Israel in the British labour movement, nor in blunting the appeal of the PLO's enhanced international standing.

An early Labour grassroots initiative to promote the Palestinian case came from the party's student organisation which, in 1978, affiliated to the LMEC. Two years later it mounted a campaign under the slogan 'Palestinians have rights too!'[89] By then, support was expressed for Palestinian self-determination also by some constituency activists. The party's traditional pro-Israel stance had cut across the left-right divide. Israel had been variously associated with the fight against fascism and anti-semitism; the struggle against communism and the introduction into the Arab world of a superior form of technical know-how and social organisation but these were less salient to the political activists who had joined the labour movement in the 1970s. The influx of these new members often with a background in campaigns or political groups associated with the new left formed part of a wider change in the social composition of the party membership. The demise of some traditional industries and inner-city communities had led to a decline in manual working-class members in local parties, which in many cases were run by small cliques that were active only at election times.[90] Into these parties came a new stratum which a study of the Labour Party characterises as 'relatively young, higher educated, public sector employees, often with working class parental backgrounds'.[91] The resultant shift to the left in the constituency parties followed the emergence between 1967 and 1969 of a more left-wing leadership among the larger trade unions.[92] Their combined forces put the left on the NEC in a position to commit the party to an economic programme that aimed to extend public ownership and state planning and, in 1980 and 1981, to secure changes in the party's constitution, which intended to make MPs and the party leader more accountable to the membership. But this leftward swing did not translate into a shift in the NEC's Middle East policy. The NEC 'left' was still the 'old left', defined by its attitude to greater state control over the economy, nuclear disarmament and détente in the Cold War. On the Middle East, however, its leading figures, Benn, Heffer and Mikardo were, until 1982, strong advocates for the Israeli point of view.

The vast majority of constituency Labour parties were untouched by the Palestine issue. They engaged mostly with local affairs and with the party's debates on economic strategy and constitutional changes. In the eight Labour Party annual conferences from 1974 to 1981 of the over 3,400 resolutions submitted only three were on the Middle East and two of those came from Poale Zion.[93] A relatively small number of left-wing activists were, however, raising the issue in the constituency parties and trade union branches and gaining support mainly from the left-wing. As a result, pressure was gradually building for a policy more supportive of the Palestinians.

The Militant Tendency, a Trotskyist organisation that had its own internal structures and publications and was most widely identified with the so-called 'hard left' in the party, did not play a role in this. From the perspective of its crude economism, the specific contradictions that generated the Palestine nationalist struggle were diversions from the logic of class struggle that alone was worthy of support. Echoing the international communist movement of the 1930s which it otherwise excoriated for Stalinism, Militant called for the unity of Arab and Jewish workers against the common class enemy. The solution to the conflict that the group's Middle East expert commended was 'the permanent revolution': the 'mighty class struggles' that will sweep across the Middle East and beyond. Allowing himself just a glimpse of the real world, he concluded: 'The programme of internationalism for the Democratic Socialist Middle East may not have a wide echo at the moment but there is no other way for the workers and peasants of the region.'[94] The Trotskyist influence that played a part in gaining support for the Palestinian struggle in the Labour Party came mainly via activists who had been in the International Marxist Group (IMG), an organisation that had been prominent in the Vietnam Solidarity Campaign and had enthusiastically embraced armed, nationalist struggles in Cuba, Southern Africa and elsewhere. Most of these activists on joining the Labour Party regrouped in Socialist Organiser, which allied itself with leading figures on the left of the Labour Party, particularly Tony Benn, who in 1981 narrowly lost to Denis Healey in the contest for the Labour Party's deputy leadership; Ken Livingstone, from May 1981, leader of the Greater London Council (GLC), and Ted Knight, leader of Lambeth Borough Council. The GLC, and to a lesser extent several other city councils, provided funding for a range of community projects, sustaining a thriving, left-oriented grassroots activism, in which anti-racist and feminist politics found an outlet. 'The Labour party in Brent', *London Briefing*, a newspaper linked to Socialist Organiser, reported in 1981, 'has undergone a significant transformation as a large number of black people – Asian and West Indians – have joined the Party.'[95] This new constituency, noted a LMEC discussion paper, brought into the party members with 'strong internationalist and anti-imperialist concerns'.[96] They formed part of a regrouping on the Labour Party's left-wing that developed a strong commitment to the recognition of the PLO and the establishment of a Palestinian state.

The Trade Union Friends of Palestine (TUFP), formed in the early 1980s by George Galloway, was successful in tabling pro-Palestinian resolutions at the Scottish Labour Party and TUC conferences.[97] There were also, on occasions, some highly publicised confrontations that helped to raise wider awareness of the Palestinian issue. In Hackney, a resolution passed by the local Labour Party, in July 1979, supporting 'the struggle of the Palestinian people for the liberation of their homeland and the establishment of a non-sectarian secular state in Palestine', led to a resignation from the local party's executive and to accusations of Trotskyist infiltration.[98] In November 1980, with the encouragement of TUFP, the Labour group on Dundee District Council voted to twin Dundee with Nablus, in the West Bank. There was extensive press coverage of the subsequent exchange of flags attended by the Provost in a ceremony outside Nablus and of a Scottish Conservative MP accusing the Council of 'anti-semitic ravings'.[99] In Brent East, there was an acrimonious campaign to deselect the sitting Labour MP, Reg Freeson, and nominate in his place Ken Livingstone, the GLC leader. Freeson's support for Israeli policies was one of the reasons for the campaign in support of Livingstone.[100]

Labour Party and trade union activists' pro-Palestinian campaigning met little resistance at the grassroots. Zionist activists had a presence in very few constituencies. Poale Zion's focus on lobbying Labour MPs and trade union leaders meant that it did not establish a network of supporters among Labour's rank and file. As Poale Zion membership declined after the war, the scope of its intervention in the labour movement narrowed still further to cultivating leading figures already committed to the Zionist cause. In the 1955 general election, Poale Zion activists were asked to assist the campaigns of candidates supportive of Israel. Canvassers, collections and cars were arranged to act as 'puller out' in the constituencies of Tony Greenwood, Ian Mikardo and Maurice Orbach and a further six candidates were sent donations to assist their campaigns.[101] By the 1970 general election, Poale Zion did not have sufficient constituency activists to call on. The parliamentary candidates it supported received a £10 donation through the post.[102] Much of its lobbying work in the labour movement had been taken over by the Labour Friends of Israel (LFI) but it too had a very limited reach.

The LFI had been launched after the Suez crisis, with the support of forty

MPs and on the initiative of Poale Zion leaders who had urged a new approach to rebuild the British labour movement's relations with the Israeli Labour Party.[103] Unlike Poale Zion, LFI did not restrict its membership to Jews. In the early 1970s, it reported seventeen branches mainly in London and 700 members, though they were essentially contacts with few demands made on them.[104] The executive, with one full-time official, sent out a bulletin three times a year, organised annual functions at the TUC and the Labour Party conferences and funded 'study tours' to Israel for MPs, party officials, and trade union leaders.[105] LFI's general secretary, Martin Cohen, reported in 1978 that its membership was in decline; it had only 250 paid-up members, with a further 450 in arrears. The organisation was also in financial difficulties. Its general secretary thought that 'some limited assistance could be available from the Israeli Embassy' but the underlying problem he diagnosed was that the LFI had been 'living off the past' through its close contact with leading Labour politicians.[106] The following year, the organisation claimed that of the 306 Labour MPs, 101 were LFI members, though the *Jewish Chronicle* estimated that 153 Labour MPs were pro-Israel.[107] The pro-Arab LMEC reported, in this period, the backing of 48 MPs.[108]

Despite the balance of forces in the PLP being weighted heavily in favour of Israel, Paul Rose, an MP until 1979, detected towards the end of his Parliamentary career the beginnings of a shift. Since 1964, when he had first entered Parliament, 'there had been,' he wrote, 'a slow but discernible erosion of sympathy with Israel in the Labour party'.[109] Yet, the 1979 intake appeared to refute him. With fewer Labour MPs than in the previous Parliament, 268 instead of 306, those who signed up to the LFI increased to 140.[110] The LMEC, however, also increased its membership to 55 MPs, suggesting that opinion in the PLP had become more polarised over the Israel/Palestine conflict. Rose correctly identified, nevertheless, the direction in which opinion was moving, if not in the PLP, certainly among the rank and file of the Labour Party and of the trade union movement. Cohen in his report on the LFI had also noted that although the organisation still had backing from some younger MPs, 'it has not had marked success in building support for Israel among trade unions, especially in relation to that group which will provide the next generation of trade union leadership'.[111] With the right-wing Menachem Begin and his party winning the 1977 Israeli general election and pursuing Jewish settlement expansion in the Occupied Territories, sympathy for Israel eroded across the political spectrum. A decisive change in Labour policy in favour of the Palestinians only came, however, in 1982 with Israel's invasion of Lebanon.

Lebanon was seen by successive Israeli governments as harbouring a military threat from both the Palestinians and the Syrians. The PLO had moved its headquarters to Beirut following King Hussein's Black September offensive in 1970, which ended with the expulsion of Palestinian fighters from Jordan. In Lebanon, Palestinian armed groups based in the refugee camp launched raids into Israel and became increasingly drawn into Lebanese politics. For the ruling

Maronite Christian clans, who dominated the Lebanese state, the Palestinian presence threatened to tip the country's delicate political balance decisively in favour of Muslim political forces. In 1975, the Lebanese army split along communal lines, as the country descended into civil war, in which Palestinians and Muslim leftists fought against Christian Maronite militias. The Syrian president, Hafez al-Assad, fearful that victory for the Palestinians and their allies would bring Israel into Lebanon, sent in the Syrian army in June 1976 to stabilise the situation by shoring up the positions of the Maronite forces. Five years after the start of the war, there was no Lebanese army or a central authority, only militias. 'In every sector of Beirut, militiamen crouched behind barricades built of broken, discarded furniture, ruined refrigerators, and the debris of bombed out buildings.'[112] Each armed group fought for its own ethnic enclave. In southern Lebanon, Israel set up a surrogate army, recruited from the local Christian villages, to create a buffer zone, in places sixteen miles deep, along its border with Lebanon but the PLO still fired from time to time Katyusha rockets into Israel's border regions. In March 1978, after PLO guerrillas had killed thirty-seven Israelis on the outskirts of Tel Aviv, 25,000 Israeli troops invaded southern Lebanon with the support of aerial bombardment to clear the PLO guerrillas south of the river Litani. 'Operation Litani', as the Israelis named it, caused the death of around 2,000 Lebanese and Palestinians and the flight northwards of around 285,000 people.[113] It set the pattern for subsequent Israeli invasions of Lebanon and, from 1981, Begin and his defence minister Ariel Sharon began preparing for one with wider ambitions. They planned to remake Lebanon into a Maronite state by destroying the PLO and forcing the withdrawal of the 30,000-strong Syrian army. Israel found a willing tool in Bashir Gemayel, the leader of the Phalange, the largest of the Christian militias whose ambition to become president and establish Maronite dominance depended on the Israeli army inflicting military defeat on the Palestinian-Muslim alliance. The Phalange was a sectarian force, inadequate as a fighting unit even with its Israeli-supplied military equipment, but needed by Begin and Sharon to furnish the Israeli invasion with the pretext that it was defending Lebanon's Christian community.

On 6 June 1982, with troop numbers reaching 100,000 and F-16 fighter bombers shelling Palestinian and Syrian positions throughout Lebanon, Israeli forces made rapid advance to encircle Beirut. At the end of the second week of the invasion 'up to 14,000 people – the vast majority civilians – had been killed and another 20,000 injured'.[114] For the next two-and-a-half months, the Israel military laid siege to west Beirut, cutting off food supplies, water and electricity and turning much of the city into rubble as it bombed apartment blocks and public buildings among which Palestinian fighters moved with their anti-aircraft guns and rocket launchers. Israeli air strikes and artillery fire were repeatedly aimed at Beirut's Palestinian refugee camps, Sabra, Shatila and Bourj al-Barajneh. The siege was brought to an end with a US-brokered agreement, under which the PLO agreed for its forces to be evacuated from west Beirut.

Two weeks after the PLO fighters boarded the ships that sailed them to Tunis, the TUC conference debated the Palestinians' plight. The conferences of 1967 and 1976 had expressed support for Israel, but on this occasion it passed an emergency resolution by the Fire Brigades' Union, deploring 'the death and destruction caused by the Israeli invasion' of Lebanon and calling for 'recognition of the national rights of the Palestinians to self-determination within an independent sovereign state'.[115] The General Council failed to dissuade delegates from the resolution. It was the first time that the TUC had adopted a policy despite being opposed by Labour Zionists. By the time the Labour Party conference met at the end of September, a turning point had been reached in the labour movement's attitude to the Israel/Palestine conflict. The *Jewish Chronicle* had noted in mid-August that only two resolutions out of the over 500 submitted to the Labour Party annual conference were concerned with the Middle East.[116] A month later, following the Israeli siege and bombardment of west Beirut, it reported that 'no fewer than 46 emergency resolutions have been sent to the Labour headquarters. Astonishingly, every one of them is very critical of Israel.'[117]

For the conference delegates gathering in Blackpool, the Labour leader, Michael Foot's proposal to rein in the Militant Tendency was the main debating point, but since the previous Monday, the events in the Middle East dominated international news as details of the massacres in the Sabra and Shatila refugee camps began to emerge. Phalangist militiamen with the permission of Israeli troops had entered the camps to perpetrate a massacre of around 3,000 defenceless people. 'What was happening in the camps could hardly escape the attention of the Israeli soldiers surrounding them. Their forward command post was a mere 200 metres from the main killing ground, and from the roof of this seven storey building they had a direct line of sight into the heart of the camps ... The soldiers blocked the entrances, several times turning back refugees frantic to get out.'[118] In *The Times*, Robert Fisk described entering Shatila: 'They were everywhere, in the roads, in laneways, in backyards and broken rooms, beneath crumpled masonry and across the top of garbage tips. The murderers – the Christian militiamen whom Israel had let into the camp to "flush out terrorists" 14 hours before had only just left. ... Down every alleyway there were corpses – women, young men, babies and grandparents – lying together in lazy and terrible profusion where they had been knifed or machine gunned to death.'[119]

Israel had succeeded, at a high price in Palestinian and Lebanese lives, to remove the Palestinian fighters from Lebanon but only by enhancing the PLO's political standing. As the *New Statesman* observed, the war had seriously weakened the Israeli case against the PLO, 'namely that the PLO indiscriminately murders civilians. In this war, 15,000 Palestinians and Lebanese were killed and 30,000 injured, according to preliminary Lebanese figures.'[120]

The shock and revulsion engendered by reports coming out of Beirut led to an emotionally charged debate on the Middle East at the Labour Party conference. In previous years, the carefully crafted NEC statement would have almost certainly sufficed. Its criticism of the Likud government was linked to a call for a judicial inquiry into the massacres demanded by the Israeli Labour Party and also by other Israeli and Jewish voices. It also placed equal weight on Israel's need for security and the establishment of a Palestinian state. It called for the PLO's participation in future negotiations but not for its recognition as the sole representative of the Palestinian people. For most delegates, however, these formulations tailored not to upset Labour Zionist sensibilities, did not adequately reflect either Israel's culpability for the deaths and destruction in Lebanon or give sufficient recognition to the fact that Israel was the more powerful side in its conflict with the Palestinians. The NEC statement was approved by the conference but two other resolutions put forward by Constituency Labour Parties (CLPs) were also debated. The first, from the Dundee East CLP, called for an independent sovereign Palestinian state but formulated as the 'inalienable rights' of its people, and, therefore, without making it conditional on guarantees for Israel's security.[121] The second resolution, from Norwood CLP, demanded recognition of the PLO as 'the sole legitimate representative of the Palestinian people'; an investigation into Israeli war crimes; Israel's immediate withdrawal from Lebanon; and for the Labour Party to support 'the establishment of a democratic secular state of Palestine as the long-term solution to the Palestine problem'. This resolution, like the one by Dundee East, was opposed by the NEC, as Denis Healey explained on its behalf, because 'they did not concede any justice to Israel's right to exist'.[122]

Behind the divergent positions that Healey highlighted, a significant shift of opinion in favour of the Palestinians had taken place. The left and, indeed, a significant section of the international community, had moved from considering the Palestinians as a refugee problem to recognising them as a nationality, with the right to establish a sovereign state. In subsequent years, on the basis of this new consensus, the struggle in the Labour movement over the Israel/Palestine conflict would often take the form of disputes over particular phrases or prescribed solutions but the crucial division hinged on whether Israel, on the basis of its security concerns or on any other grounds, should be allowed to determine whether the Palestinians can exercise their right to self-determination. Among left-wing pro-Palestinian supporters there were conflicting views on how self-determination should be realised. The Dundee resolution implied that it should be on the basis of a 'two-state solution', as it would be later termed, namely a Palestinian state alongside Israel within its pre-1967 borders, whereas the Norwood resolution envisaged the 'one-state solution', a single secular state for Jews and Arabs. This difference did not affect the conflict between pro-Palestinian and pro-Israel positions in which the main issues of contention were the recognition of the PLO and the Palestinians' right to self-determination. The latter was generally interpreted in the labour movement to be on basis of the two-state solution.

Despite the NEC's opposition, the conference passed Dundee's resolution overwhelmingly, and Norwood's by a narrow margin. The acceptance of these resolutions registered the changed perception of the Israeli-Palestinian conflict in wide sections of the labour movement. In the late 1960s, the new left had initiated support for Palestinian self-determination and this, in combination with developments on the international level, succeeded to move social democratic opinion in the same direction. Western European governments had come to accept a Palestinian state on the basis that Arab leaders and the PLO had scaled down their aims to a state existing alongside Israel. At the end of 1981, first Syria and then, in February 1982, Saudi Arabia called for the termination of the war between the Arab states and Israel. Syria's condition was that Israel agrees to 'an independent Palestinian state alongside of Israel', while the Saudis required that Israel recognises the PLO as a negotiating partner.[123] Pressure from non-aligned countries and Western European concerns over the Arab/Israeli conflict destabilising the Middle East had also created international pressure for addressing Palestinian nationalist demands. This had produced, by the early 1980s, a broad international consensus that any negotiated settlement of the conflict required the PLO's participation. Israel and the US were, as Chomsky has argued, the main 'rejectionists'.[124]

The Reagan administration's plan put forward in the midst of the Lebanon war mentioned neither self-determination for the Palestinians nor acceptance of the PLO as a negotiating partner. It proposed, as a confidence-building measure, an immediate halt to Jewish settlement building in the West Bank and Gaza, with a view towards negotiating an agreement that would secure autonomy for their inhabitants. This was to be preceded by a five-year transition period, 'to prove that the Palestinians can run their own affairs and that such Palestinian autonomy poses no threat to Israel'.[125] The US plan was predicated on the Palestinians developing a degree of self-government in association with Jordan. Despite the primacy that this accorded to Israeli security, the Likud government rejected the plan. It would not accept any restriction on Jewish settlement in the Occupied Territories. The Reagan plan was close to the Israeli Labour Party's proposal, which had similarly aimed at sidelining the PLO, by establishing some form of Palestinian local government under Jordanian control.

The British Labour Party aligned itself with the negotiating position of the Israeli Labour Party. Israel's Labour politicians knew how their policies towards the Arab world had to be translated for the British labour movement: they were couched in pacific sentiments, expressing concern for the Palestinians and professing pragmatism by finding a solution to the conflict through the exchange of land for peace. The Likud government of Begin and Shamir, however, spoke in a messianic and unyielding language. For Poale Zion and LFI this was a source of embarrassment. They continued to appeal for support by recalling Israel's social democratic heritage. During the Lebanon war, the issue of *Labour Weekly* reporting that Israeli troops were leaving in their wake 'thousands of dead and hundreds of thousands of displaced refugees' also contained a Poale Zion advertisement proclaiming: 'Israel is the only democracy in the Middle East ... Israel's Labour Party was the founder member of the Socialist International ... Israel together with only 2 of the 21 Arab states guarantees equal rights for women under the law.'[126]

The Lebanon war proved indefensible to many of Israel's staunchest friends. Harold Wilson described Begin, Sharon and Shamir as 'the evil three' and Sharon as 'the most evil man I have come across in Israeli politics'.[127] Mikardo similarly sought to narrow the target. He portrayed the true Israel as having been hijacked. In the debate on the Middle East at the 1982 Labour Party conference, he explained: 'The labour movement in Israel, the Labour alignment, the official opposition has totally opposed by solid votes in their parliament the extension of Begin's war aims and the march on Beirut. And the Israeli Peace Movement is much larger and much faster-growing even than our own happily large and fast-growing Campaign for Nuclear Disarmament'. But a delegate replying to Mikardo criticised the Israeli Labour Party and the record of the proceedings suggests that this met with considerable approval:

> 'There is no doubt that the Israeli Labour party is now calling for the withdrawal of Israeli troops from Beirut. But there is equally no doubt that the Israeli Labour party supported the invasion of the Lebanon. (*Applause*) The Israeli Labour party supported the earlier massacres in Tyre and Sidon. The Israeli Labour party have consistently supported the repression of the Palestinian people both within the state of Israel and in the occupied territories. (*Applause*)[128]

When Mikardo returned to the defence of the Israeli Labour Party in *Labour Weekly*, a reader's response was equally implacable: 'The Labour Front remained in power for another ten years after the Six Day War; during all that time it continued to occupy those areas, refused them any form of self-government and confiscated thousands of acres of the best land for Jewish colonisation'.[129] Eric Heffer resigned from the LFI. He had been effusive in his praise of Israel, in the past, describing it as 'in certain respects the most democratic State in the world' but he declared that the invasion had 'shaken him to the core': 'The Begin regime has made people suddenly realise that there is another side to the Israel story.'[130] The Lebanon war and, in particular, the massacre in Sabra and Shatila made a deep impression on the left. More than two years later, an attempt by the director of the LFI to get a pro-Israeli resolution passed at the Labour Party's women's conference by congratulating the Israeli government for 'saving thousands of Ethiopian Jews from death and starvation' met with hostility. 'Delegates responded,' the *Jewish Chronicle* reported, 'by criticising Israel for the "massacre" of Palestinian Arabs and overwhelmingly defeated the motion.'[131]

During the Lebanon war pressure from activists in the constituencies and in some of the trade unions supportive of pro-Palestinian demands found backing from the left of the trade union leadership and of the Labour Party's NEC. The left-wingers on the NEC were, by this time, mostly sympathetic to altering the party's policy in favour of Palestinian demands but they never quite commanded a majority and by the time the NEC discussed the Lebanese war,[132] some right-wing union leaders had successfully co-ordinated their voting to alter the composition of its membership to the detriment of the left. This shift to the right on the NEC enabled a pro-Israeli backlash to be launched in the Labour Party when, in 1983, Neil Kinnock took over the party's leadership, though in the trade union movement a pro-Israeli move was thwarted.

On the fringe of the 1983 TUC conference, two right-wing trade union leaders, Frank Chapple of the Electrical, Electronic Telecommunication and Plumbing Union (EETPU) and Gavin Laird of the Amalgamated Union of Engineering Workers (AUEW) took a leading role in the launch of the Trade Union Friends of Israel (TUFI).[133] In order to claw back some of the political ground gained by the pro-Palestinian campaigners at the previous years' TUC conference, they moved a resolution that spoke of the Palestinians' 'legitimate' not 'national' rights; called for 'defensible borders' for Israel, the formulation used by Israel for not returning to the pre-1967 borders; the withdrawal of all foreign forces from Lebanon, including the PLO, (though it had been evacuated to Tunis the previous year) and acclaimed 'the magnificent achievements of the Israeli trade union movement, the Histadrut, which is the only free trade union movement in the Middle East'.[134] Although the General Council, with some reservations, assented to this resolution, it was defeated on the floor of the conference.

The opposition to the pro-Israel resolution had come mainly from the more left-wing leaders of white-collar trade unions. A number of unions, among them NALGO, the local government workers' union; the Fire Brigades Union; the white-collar section of the engineering union, AUEW/TASS; and the print union, Sogat 82, had passed pro-Palestinian resolutions at their conferences.[135] The relationship with Palestinian labour organisations that the TUFP initiated, led to a British trade union delegation visiting Lebanon prior to the Israeli invasion and several more followed thereafter. NALGO was particularly active in sending delegations to the Occupied Territories. In 1986, it launched a fund with the National Union of Public Employees (NUPE), TGWU and the charities War on Want and Medical Aid for Palestine, to help run a clinic for workers in Gaza. In 1986, the National Union of Teachers invited a Palestinian academic from the West Bank to speak at its annual conference and when the Israeli authorities denied him an exit permit, 'over 1000 delegates signed a petition deploring the Israeli action'.[136] The Labour Zionist discourse that had, in the past, an uncritical reception in trade union circles was now regarded with scepticism and, sometimes, hostility. 'The TUC delegation to Israel in 1980 was told of the Histadrut's opposition to government policy,' a delegate from the National Graphical Association reported, adding, 'Yet the Histadrut owns the construction sites that are being illegally built on in the occupied part of the West Bank.'[137] A delegation led by the assistant general secretary of the TGWU that visited the Occupied Territories complained that a Palestinian electricity-generating plant lay idle because the Israeli military authorities insisted on the Palestinian sector importing most of its electricity from Israel. NALGO raised the Histadrut's involvement in the construction of settlements in the West Bank and its collaboration with apartheid South Africa through its partnership with the South African Steel Corporation and, Sentrachem, a chemical and fertiliser company.[138] A resolution by the Fire Brigade's Union at the 1987 TUC conference, reiterating support for Palestinian self-determination and statehood was endorsed after Ron Todd, the general secretary of the TGWU, on behalf of the General Council, opposed a wrecking amendment by the Northern Carpet Trade Union and the EETPU.[139] In the trade union movement taking sides in the Palestine conflict largely came to correspond to the left-right divide.

Mikardo had earlier claimed that the pro-Israel work in the unions was 'succeeding beyond every expectation'. He also felt that, 'LFI has done, and is doing, a considerable job at the leadership level in the Party' but added: 'The gap that remains to be filled is the vital area of the constituency Labour Parties'.[140] The Trade Union Friends of Israel was held up as a success by the LFI executive's report, in 1993, but there is no evidence that it won friends beyond a few right-wing trade union leaders. And the LFI's work on other fronts had still less success. A report by its executive conceded that all the organisation's work was carried out by the administrative centre consisting of a full-time director, secretary and assistant. 'From the late 1980s to date,' the report confirmed, 'there has been considerable contraction and decline of the LFI's work which has come to seem inexorable.'[141]

In the mid-1980s Mikardo hoped that the influx of some younger members from the university campuses would revive Poale Zion and particularly its youth wing but this did not materialise. The small number of young activists on whom he had pinned his hopes formed its own faction, the Jewish Labour Caucus, which had friendly relations with Socialist Organiser and became a source of dissent. It viewed the leadership as too right-wing and held it responsible for Poale Zion becoming 'a moribund organisation with little grassroots support'.[142] The political differences surfaced at the Poale Zion annual conference in 1986, at which the Caucus failed to get sufficient support for a resolution calling for the setting up of an independent Palestinian state but succeeded in blocking three resolutions which had sought approval for the Israeli Labour Party's policy of denying recognition to the PLO and negotiating over the future of the Occupied Territories with Jordan.[143] The conflict rumbled on leading to Mikardo's resignation as Poale Zion's chairperson, but the rest of the old guard managed to regain control.

Poale Zion's internal conflict did not directly impact on the Labour Party but it was symptomatic of a crisis in Labour Zionism, which in the past had set the guidelines for the British Labour Party's Palestine/Israel policy and had been the ideological basis of the close relationship between the two labour movements. In earlier periods, Labour Zionism had been tied to labour institutions and state-led industrialisation but the occupation of the West Bank and Gaza and the ensuing Palestinian resistance had pushed Israeli society to the right, ending the Labour Zionist parties' political dominance. After the 1982 Lebanon war, Israel's supporters in the British Labour Party had looked to the re-election of a Labour government under Shimon Peres to redeem Israel's 'socialist' reputation but, in the general elections of 1984 and 1988, the Israeli Labour Party failed to win an outright majority and ended up sharing power with Likud. The programme of privatisation and the opening of the Israeli economy to international investment that had been set in motion from the mid-1980s progressively weakened the state sector, the traditional basis of the Labour Zionist hegemony.[144] In relation to the Palestinians, there was little to distinguish between Labour and Likud. The Israeli Labour Party collaborated in the extension of Jewish settlements in the West Bank and Gaza and it was Labour's Yitzhak Rabin who, in August 1985, as defence minister, launched the policy of 'Iron Fist' aimed at crushing the Palestinian resistance. He was also at the forefront of Israel's military response to the Intifada, the civilian-based uprising that erupted in December 1987.[145]

The Intifada gradually forced the Palestinian issue back onto the British Labour Party's agenda. It had been allowed to fade into the background after Neil Kinnock became the leader in 1983, following the Labour Party's general election defeat. In the lead up to that election, Labour's campaign statement, *New Hope for Britain*, embraced 'the right of Israelis to live in peace and security in the State of Israel' and made no reference to the PLO, but asserted 'the right of the Palestinians to self-determination including the establishment of a Palestinian state'.[146] The 1988 party conference was asked to back, however, an NEC statement that affirmed Israel's right to secure borders yet spoke merely of 'a homeland for the Palestinians'. The phrase 'homeland', a delegate protested, evoked 'a Transkei West Bank'.[147]

The Intifada was in its tenth month when the 1988 Labour Party conference met. Over that period Israeli troops had killed around 400 Palestinians and the Palestinians had killed six Israelis. Alexander Cockburn, basing his figures on data collected by the Palestine Human Rights Information Centre, reported that between 9 December 1987 and 9 October 1988, 239 Palestinians homes had been destroyed, 33 people had been expelled and around 18,000 people had been imprisoned. 'Thousands have sustained crippling injuries from shootings, beatings, tear gas, injections, live burials and torture administered by soldiers and settlers.'[148] These developments found acknowledgement in a conference resolution calling for the PLO's recognition as 'the sole legitimate representative of the Palestinian people'; for Israeli withdrawal to the pre-1967 borders and for a Palestinian state. The delegates passed the resolution with an overwhelming majority despite the NEC's refusal to endorse it.

The leadership's attempt to reverse the pro-Palestinians policy statements made at the 1982 conference and in the 1983 campaign document formed part of Kinnock's renewed effort after the party's third electoral defeat in 1987 to make the policy changes that he believed would make the party more acceptable to the electorate. The ensuing struggle with the left-wing centred on his plan to jettison Labour's traditional social democratic commitment to state planning and public ownership in favour of allowing greater scope to the market, but the leadership also sought to redefine the party's position on the Middle East.

Soon after the 1987 general election defeat Kinnock appointed Gerald Kaufman to be Labour's spokesperson on foreign affairs, switching him from home affairs. Kinnock may have had a number of reasons for this but given his concern at the time over Jewish voters abandoning the Labour Party, he is likely to have seen Kaufman's longstanding association with the Labour Zionist movement as making him well suited to deal with the party's Middle East brief.[149] Kaufman had to reconcile rank-and-file pressure for recognition of the PLO and the demand for a Palestinian state, on the one hand, with the leadership's desire to improve the party's relationship with Britain's Jewish community, on the other. The compromise he tried to strike was to align the party's policy with that of the Israeli Labour Party. Kaufman was convinced that Israeli Labour leaders were prevented from reaching an agreement with the Palestinians only because the electoral arithmetic had forced them into coalitions with Likud. 'Actually, though,' as the Israeli sociologist Neve Gordon shows in a study of the Israeli occupation up to 2007, 'one-fourth of the settlements that currently exist were established within the first decade of occupation, and if one counts those that were being planned, almost one-third of the settlements existing today were initiated by Labour before it lost the 1977 election'.[150] What Kaufman and other British Labour Zionists appeared to find most objectionable about Likud was that it pursued settlement expansion without leaving the door ajar to an eventual exchange of land for peace. Kaufman described Begin as a 'fascist'; Shamir as 'the greatest enemy of Israel's security'; and the West Bank and Gaza as 'Israeli Sowetos'.[151] Under Likud, Israel had 'degenerated into an aggressive, expansionist, ruthless and repressive state'.[152] He also expressed sympathy for the *Intifada* and urged recognition of the PLO, yet his loyalty to Labour Zionism in this period led him to turn a blind eye not only to the Israeli Labour leadership's role in expanding the settlements but also in repressing the *Intifada* and seeking the destruction of the PLO.[153]

In February 1988, a few months into the *Intifada*, Kinnock on a visit to Israel expressed preference for the Jordanian option. 'He repeatedly floated the idea', the *Observer* reported, 'of a Jordanian-Palestinian confederation to achieve self-determination and warned Palestinian nationalists against holding out for full sovereignty. He spoke of a "homeland" rather than a state'.[154] The Labour leader further ingratiated himself to his hosts when he was taken on a tour of the Golan Heights, which Israel had seized from Syria in the 1967 war expelling 130,000 Syrian villagers and establishing its own settlements. With Balfour-like generosity, Kinnock declared: 'The idea that these Heights, which overlook so much of

Israel, would be given back to anyone but the Israelis is I think out of the question.'[155]

Despite such unrestrained declaration of friendship for Israel by the party leader, the overwhelmingly pro-Palestinian orientation in the labour movement set limits to how far the leadership could go in its pro-Israel orientation. After the 1988 resolution calling for a Palestinian state was passed by a two to one majority, the 'homeland' proposal made no further appearance in party documents. The struggle over policy continued, however, each side knowing how certain emphases and phrases could imply partisanship one way or the other. The Middle East section of a policy review drafted mainly by Kaufman and submitted to the 1989 party conference recognised a representative role for the PLO and 'self-determination for the Palestinians within a political and constitutional framework of their own choosing'. It indicated, however, that the party hoped to make this position acceptable to the Israeli Labour Party by stating that 'Jerusalem must never again be obscenely divided', a thinly veiled approval for Israel retaining control of the entire city.[156] On this occasion, a pro-Palestinian resolution was passed by an even larger majority than the previous year. It reiterated previous formulations calling for the PLO's recognition as 'the sole legitimate representative of the Palestinian people' and 'the right of the Israeli and Palestinian people to independent statehood and self-determination'.[157] The pro-Palestinian vote may have been boosted by the meeting of the Palestine National Council, the PLO's leading policy-making body, in November 1988. This meeting, widely seen at the time as a turning point in the history of the Palestinian nationalist struggle, voted to pursue the peaceful resolution of the conflict and expressed a willingness to negotiate with Israel, thereby according it tacit recognition.[158] However, once the New Labour project had gathered momentum, it was the pro-Israeli orientation that again gained the upper hand in defining the party's stance on the Middle East.

Soon after Tony Blair took over the party's leadership in 1994, he greeted the LFI, 'as one of the most important organisations within the Labour Movement'. His deputy, Gordon Brown, at the Balfour dinner held in Jerusalem the following November, declared that 'Labour Friends of Israel has today more support among our 270 MPs, than at any time in almost forty years since its foundation. Support for Israel is and remains firm right across the Labour Party.'[159] Only a few years earlier, LFI's director, the MP Reg Freeson, in a review of the organisation's recent history had reported that the autumn of 1992 'came near to seeing the end of LFI as an active body'.[160] The improved prospects for peace in Middle East was a factor in its sudden revival. The Madrid conference (1991), the Oslo Peace Accords (1993) and the Israel-Jordan peace treaty (1994) abated hostility to Israel among Labour's rank and file. But the main driving force behind LFI's change of fortune came from the new leadership of the party. The promoters of New Labour's electoral strategy saw its resurgence as playing an important role in restoring the party's relations with the Jewish community and with Jewish business leaders both to attract donations and as part of a concerted effort to improve Labour's standing in the wider business community.[161]

Notes

1. G. Lenczowski, *American Presidents and the Middle East* (Durham: Duke University Press, 1992), pp. 106 and 110.
2. *Daily Telegraph* (9 June 1967).
3. *Hansard*, Commons, v. 749, c. 2022, 6 July 1967.
4. *The Times* (22 June 1967).
5. *Jewish Chronicle* (14 July 1967).
6. *The Guardian* (7 June 1967) quoted in M. Adams and C. Mayhew, *Publish it Not ... The Middle East Cover-Up* (London: Longmans, 1975), p. 36.
7. P. Seyd, *The Rise and Fall of the Labour Left* (Basingstoke: Macmillan, 1987), p. 78.
8. *Tribune* (16 June 1967).
9. Seyd, *Rise and Fall*, p. 50.
10. R. Archer et al., *Out of Apathy* (London: Verso, 1989), p. 13.
11. I. Deutscher, 'On the Israeli-Arab War', *New Left Review*, 44 (July-August 1967) 42.
12. Ibid., pp. 38–39.
13. I. Deutscher, *The Non-Jewish Jew* (Oxford: Oxford University Press, 1968), p. 112.
14. Deutscher, 'On the Israeli-Arab War', p. 38.
15. N. Finkelstein, *Beyond Chutzpah* (London: Verso, 2005), p. 11.
16. Deutscher, *The Non-Jewish Jew*, p. 149.
17. Ibid., p. 147.
18. It was translated into English in 1973 as M. Rodinson, *Israel, a Colonial Settler State?* (New York: Pathfinder, 1973).
19. Rodinson, *Israel, a Colonial Settler State?*, p. 91.
20. Ibid., pp. 86–88.
21. Ibid., p. 65.
22. Ibid., p. 83.
23. Ibid., p. 90.
24. M. Newman, *Ralph Miliband and the Politics of the New Left* (London: The Merlin Press, 2002), pp. 128–134.
25. Leeds University, Miliband Papers, Liebman to Miliband, 5 January 1971 and Miliband's statement to the court, 13 November 1971, ML1.
26. Miliband to Liebman, 7 June 1967.
27. Liebman to Miliband, 30 May 1967.
28. Miliband to Liebman, 2 June 1967. This citation is taken from G. Achcar, *The Israeli Dilemma. A Debate Between Two Left-Wing Jews* (London: Merlin Press, 2006), p. 47.
29. Liebman to Miliband, 17 April 1969.
30. M. Jones, 'Israel, Palestine and Socialism', *Socialist Register*, 1970, 76.
31. Ibid., 71.
32. Ibid., 78.
33. Ibid., 68.
34. M. Liebman, 'Israel, Palestine and Zionism', *Socialist Register*, 1970, 90.
35. Jones, 'Israel, Palestine and Socialism', 94, emphasis in original.
36. Ibid., 97.
37. Ibid., 90.
38. D. Hirst, *The Gun and the Olive Branch* (London: Faber and Faber, 1977), p. 290.
39. Jones, 'Israel, Palestine and Socialism', 105.

40 Quoted in G. Achcar, *The Arabs and the Holocaust* (London: Saqibooks, 2010), p. 214.
41 In 1974, this group was renamed the Democratic Front for the Liberation of Palestine.
42 G. Achcar, *Eastern Cauldron* (London: Pluto Press, 2004), pp. 133–134.
43 Liebman, 'Israel, Palestine and Zionism', 108.
44 Ibid., 91.
45 H. Pelling, *The British Communist Party* (London: A. and C. Black, 1975), p. 193.
46 *Jewish Chronicle* (27 May 1994).
47 A class analysis the Arab nationalist response to the Palestine conflict was outlined by Fawwaz Trabulsi, 'The Palestine Problem: Zionism and Imperialism in the Middle East', *New Left Review*, 57, September–October 1969.
48 B. Ramelson, *The Middle East, Crisis: Causes, Solution* (London: Central Books, 1967), p. 40.
49 *Morning Star* (29 September 1970)
50 K. Kirisci, *The PLO and World Politics* (London: Frances Pinter, 1986), p. 45.
51 *Black Dwarf* (14 March 1969).
52 *Palestine News* (December 1969).
53 *Black Dwarf* (2 May 1969).
54 R. Greenstein, 'Class, Nation and Political Organisation: The Anti-Zionist Left in Israel/Palestine', *International Labour and Working-Class History*, 75 (Spring 2009), 96.
55 G. Karmi, *In Search of Fatima* (London: Verso, 2002), p. 394.
56 *Palestine News* (June 1972).
57 *The Guardian* (29 May 1967).
58 D. Baram, *Disenchantment, the Guardian and Israel* (London: Guardian Books, 2004), p. 108.
59 *The Guardian* (12 June 1967).
60 Obituary on Frank Edmead, *The Guardian* (7 March 2000).
61 *The Guardian* (19 February 1968).
62 Bahram, *Disenchantment*, p. 117.
63 Adams and Mayhew, *Publish it Not*, p. 80.
64 British Library of Economic and Social Science, Andrew Faulds Papers, Labour Middle East Council, File, 'The Labour Party and the Middle East', Memorandum submitted to the International Committee of the NEC, 18 April 1973.
65 *Hansard*, Commons, v. 848, c. 726, 14 December 1972.
66 Adams and Mayhew, *Publish it Not*, p. 57. Requests for affiliation by other groups, such as the Christian Socialist Movement and Labour Action for Peace, were also refused. See Seyd, *Rise and Fall*, p. 223 n.8.
67 *Hansard*, Commons, v. 861, c. 500, 18 October 1973.
68 Adams and Mayhew, *Publish it Not*, p. 43.
69 LPACR, 1970, p. 202.
70 *Jewish Chronicle* (8 October 1982).
71 Ibid. (5 January 1973).
72 Letter, *Tribune* (30 November 1973).
73 *Jewish Chronicle* (24 November 1972).
74 Ibid. (16 October 1970; 24 November 1970; 10 April 1972).
75 *Labour Weekly* (12 October 1973).
76 *Hansard*, Commons, v. 861, c. 521, 18 October 1973; *Tribune* (12 October 1973).
77 D. Watkins, *Seventy Years in Obscurity* (Sussex: The Book Guild, 1996), p. 119.
78 Miliband to Liebman, 2 June 1967, quoted in Achcar, *Israeli/ Dilemma*, p. 44.
79 *Jewish Chronicle* (29 September 1967).
80 Ibid. (29 September 1967).
81 A. Kapeliouk, *Israel: la fin des myths* (Paris: Albin Michel, 1975), p. 214.
82 F. Khoury, *The Arab Israeli Dilemma* (New York: Syracus University Press, 1976), p. 378.

83 *Hansard*, Commons, v. 899, c. 961–962, 10 November 1975. On this occasion, the Conservative MP, Jonathan Aitken, whose business dealings with the Arab world were to play a part in his political downfall and imprisonment, referred to Wilson's hug and kiss of Israeli Prime Minister, Golda Meir, on her reception at Downing Street, the previous December, as the 'kiss that nearly lost 1,000 ships full of British exports', c. 1030.
84 Labour Party, *Labour's Programme, 1976* (London: Labour Party, 1976), p. 136.
85 In response to the chairperson of the Zionist Federation requesting clarification on the how the EEC states understood their call for Israel's withdrawal from the territories it occupied, Lord Carrington, the foreign secretary, distanced the Conservative government from Harold Wilson's interpretation. 'I wish to leave you in no doubt of the Government's view that the provisions for Israeli withdrawal apply to East Jerusalem just as to the other territories …', *Jewish Chronicle* (22 July 1979).
86 *Hansard*, Commons, v. 986, c. 1126–1146, 16 June 1980. It was not until 1988, during the first *Intifada*, that the King renounced the right to negotiate on behalf of the Palestinians and thereby closed off the 'Jordanian option'. See A. Shlaim, *The Iron Wall* (London: Penguin Books, 2000), pp. 457–458.
87 I. Zertal and A. Eldar, *Lords of the Land* (New York: Nation Books, 2007), p. 99.
88 *Jewish Chronicle* (30 January 1981).
89 Ibid. (17 March 1978); Council for Arab British Understanding, J. Ward to J. Reddaway, 13 December 1980, Labour Middle East Council file.
90 Quoted in E. Shaw, *Discipline and Discord in the Labour Party* (Manchester: Manchester University Press, 1988), p. 219.
91 Seyd, *Rise and Fall*, p. 46.
92 L. Minkin, *The Contentious Alliance* (Edinburgh: Edinburgh University Press, 1991), p. 115.
93 LPA, *Labour Party Conference Resolutions* (annual publication) published by Transport House.
94 J. Pickard, 'Middle East Crisis', *Militant International Review*, 17 (Winter 1979).
95 London Briefing, No. 11, (June 1981); Hilary Wainwright, *Labour: A Tale of Two Parties* (London: Hogarth Press, 1987), pp. 188–205.
96 Andrew Faulds Papers, Labour Middle East Council, 3/2/50 Discussion paper for 3rd Working Party Meeting, 14 July (no year indicated but probably 1982).
97 *Palestine News* (July 1981).
98 *Jewish Chronicle* (19 October 1979).
99 *Palestine News* (February 1981; May 1981).
100 *Jewish Chronicle* (2 July, 17 September 1982).
101 Levenberg Papers, Poale Zion, Report on Activities Since Annual Conference, circa June 1955, File 1/2, S. Goldberg, to Zionist Federation, 23 May 1955, File 1/3.
102 Sheffield Archives, John Mendelson Papers, S. Goldberg to J. Mendelson, 4 June 1970, SY/360/J2/27.
103 *Jewish Chronicle* (4 October 1957).
104 Levenberg Papers, Director's Report to LFI Executive, 16 February 1993, Box 'Zionism'. In 1969, the Labour MP, Paul Rose, claimed that LFI had 18 branches and 3,000 members. See *Jewish Chronicle* (15 August 1969).
105 *Jewish Chronicle* (15 August 1969).
106 Levenberg Papers, M. Cohen, General Secretary's, Confidential Report 1978, Labour Friends of Israel, Box 'Zionism'.
107 *Jewish Chronicle* (31 March 1978).
108 LPA, Labour Middle East Council, 3/2/50, Chairman's Address and Executive Report, 10 December 1980.

109 *Jewish Chronicle* (26 June 1979).
110 Ibid. (5 December 1980).
111 Cohen, 'Confidential Report'.
112 S. Mackey, *Mirror of the Arab World* (New York: W.W. Norton & Co., 2009), p. 113.
113 R. Fisk, *Pity the Nation* (Oxford: Oxford University Press, 1992), pp. 130–132.
114 Fisk, *Pity the Nation*, p. 255.
115 *Report of the Annual Trades Union Congress, 1982* (London: TUC 1982), p. 615.
116 *Jewish Chronicle* (20 August 1982).
117 Ibid. (17 September 1982).
118 D. Hirst, *Beware of Small States* (London: Faber and Faber, 2010), pp. 157–158.
119 *The Times* (20 September 1982).
120 *New Statesman* (20 September 1982).
121 LPACR, 1982, p. 131.
122 LPACR, 1982, p. 133.
123 N. Chomsky, *The Fateful Triangle* (London: Pluto Press, 1983), p. 76.
124 Ibid., p. 44.
125 Lenczowski, *American Presidents*, p. 264.
126 *Labour Weekly* (18 June 1982).
127 *Jewish Chronicle* (8 October 1982).
128 LPACR, 1982, p. 136.
129 *Labour Weekly* (27 August 1982).
130 Hansard, Commons, v. 861, c.5, 1918 October 1973; Minutes, Middle East Sub-Committee, Labour Party, 5 May 1982; *Jewish Chronicle* (12 March 1982).
131 *Jewish Chronicle* (21 June 1985).
132 In the run-up to the 1982 conference, the NEC had voted 14 votes to 11 to reject the resolution put by the Dundee East CLP. LPACR 1982, p. 131.
133 *Jewish Chronicle* (26 August 1983).
134 *Report of the Annual Trades Union Congress, 1983* (London: TUC 1983), pp. 555–556.
135 *Jewish Chronicle* (26 August 1983; 9 September 1983); J. Edmunds, 'The Evolution of British Labour Party Policy on Israel from 1967 to the Intifada', *Twentieth Century British History*, 11:1 (2000), 34.
136 *Palestinian Trade Unions Rights* (London: Trade Union Friends of Palestine, n.d.)
137 *Report of the Annual Trades Union Congress, 1983* (London: TUC 1983), p. 557.
138 Trade Union Friends of Palestine, Bulletin, April 1986.
139 *Report of the Annual Trades Union Congress, 1987* (London: TUC 1987), pp. 592–594.
140 Levenberg Papers, Mikardo to Levenberg, 29 September 1986, Box 'Correspondence'.
141 Levenberg Papers, Directors Report for the Executive Committee, Labour Friends of Israel, 16 February 1993, Box 'Zionism'.
142 *Jewish Chronicle* (5 July 1985; 4 April 1986).
143 Ibid. (18 April 1986; 27 February 1987).
144 A. Hanieh, 'From State-Led Growth to Globalization: The Evolution of Israeli Capitalism', *Journal of Palestine Studies*, 32:4 (2003), 5–21.
145 A. Rigby, *Living the Intifada* (London: Zed Books, 1991).
146 Labour Party, *New Hope for Britain* (London: Labour Party, 1983), p. 30.
147 LPACR, 1988, p. 132.
148 A. Cockburn, 'Protofascism', *New Statesman* (9 December 1988).
149 *Jewish Chronicle* (9 September 1988).
150 N. Gordon, *Israel's Occupation* (Berkeley: University of California Press, 2008), p. 125.
151 *Jewish Chronicle* (2 April 1982); Hansard, Commons, v. 136, c. 561, 30 June 1988; 9 October 1987.
152 *Jewish Chronicle* (2 April 1982; 15 June 1984).

153 16 September 1988. In 1996, Kaufman endorsed Ma'aleh Adumim, a large Jewish settlement bloc built by confiscating Arab properties on the outskirts of East Jerusalem, that in accordance with the Allon plan aimed at altering the demographic composition of East Jerusalem in favour of its Jewish population and cut the West Bank into two. See *Jewish Chronicle* (9 June 1996). He became, however, increasingly critical of Israeli government policies towards the Palestinians and expressed his disillusionment with what Zionism had come to represent in a BBC2 documentary, 'End of the Affair', shown on 7 September 2002 and reported in *Jewish Chronicle* (13 September 2002).
154 *The Observer* (21 February 1988).
155 *Sunday Telegraph* (21 February 1988).
156 Labour Party, *Meet the Challenge, Make the Change* (London: Labour Party, 1988), p. 81.
157 *LPACR*, 1989, p. 156.
158 E. Said 'Arafat's Agenda', *New Statesman* (2 November 1988).
159 Levenberg Papers, quoted in letter from Labour Friends of Israel to members, 21 March 1996, Box 'Correspondence'.
160 Levenberg Papers, Director's Report, Labour Friends of Israel, 16 February 1993, Box 'Zionism'.
161 *Jewish Chronicle* (22 November 1996), reported: 'Leading Jewish businessmen have emerged as the key backers of a £500,000 fund in support of the Labour leader Tony Blair. Known as a 'blind fund,' it is one in which the recipient does not know the identity of the donors. But it was revealed this week in the Sunday Times that among the donors were Sir Trevor Chinn, president of the Joint Israel Appeal; the former Granada TV chairman, Alex Bernstein; the publishing millionaire, Bob Gavron; as well as former founder chairman of the forklift truck firm Lansing Bagnall, Sir Emmanuel Kaye'. See also Lord Michael Levy, *A Question of Honour* (London: Simon and Schuster, 2008), p. 138.

6 A new anti-semitism?

The research underpinning the historical account in the previous chapter turned up no evidence to suggest that anti-semitism has played a part in the British left's change of perception of the Israel-Palestine conflict. Yet, there have been persistent allegations that pro-Palestinian sympathy on the left is motivated by anti-semitism. At the 1982 Labour Party conference, Denis Healey, the party's deputy leader, chided delegates for the prominence they gave in the debate on foreign affairs to Israel's bombardment of West Beirut and its complicity in the massacre of Palestinians in the Sabra and Shatila refugee camps: 'I can only say that I wish people had shown equal concern at the massacre of 20,000 men, women and children in Hama Northern Syria last year by the troops of the Syrian government ... I wish, too, that our movement showed the same concern at the slaughter of hundreds of thousands of men in the war between Iraq and Iran.'[1] Criticism along these lines has continued to be made and with increasing stridency. The journalist Nick Cohen in a polemic that indicts the left for being indulgent of political Islam and of dictatorships that are in conflict with the US, asks: 'Why is Palestine a cause for the liberal-left, but not China, Sudan, Zimbabwe, the Congo or North Korea?'[2]

It is implied in such arguments that a left-wing internationalism, true to its principles, would not pick and choose among the world's most blatant injustices. However, not all such cases implicate Western policy to the same degree. Israeli repression of the Palestinians stands in a different relation to the Western left than, for example, China's repression of Tibetan national rights, because of Israel's intimate military, economic, political and cultural connections to the US-European Union power bloc.

What has turned the Palestinian resistance to Israeli occupation into an anti-imperialist rallying point in much the same way that the black struggle against the South African apartheid state was earlier is the privileged status that Western governments accord to Israel. 'Western support for Israel,' notes a former foreign editor of the *Guardian*, 'is part of the post-war moral and political settlement that was and is as important to us as Nato or the European community.'[3] But awkwardly for the left, Israel's conflict with the Arab world invokes conflicting historical loyalties. Israel's establishment emerged out of the triumph over fascism and as a restitution to the Jewish people for the Nazi Holocaust yet it was also the product of imperial expansion and has continued to be closely tied to protecting Western economic and strategic interests in the Middle East. The response from supporters of Israel has been to accuse the left in Britain, and elsewhere in Western Europe, of sliding back from its anti-fascism and along with much of the Islamic world promoting a new form of anti-semitism. Its 'newness' allegedly resides in disguising hostility to Jews behind the pretence of siding with the Palestinians in their conflict with Israel. Among the proponents of this interpretation is a group of MPs chaired by the Labour MP, Denis MacShane, that produced, in 2006, the Report of the *All-Party Parliamentary Inquiry Into Anti-Semitism*.

The 'new anti-semitism' thesis is invariably presented with the caveat that not all criticism of Israel is anti-semitic. Walter Laqueur writes:

> The fact that criticism of Israel is not *per se* antisemitism is so obvious that it hardly needs repeating once again. If Israel does not treat its non-Jewish citizens equally and humanely, if it persists in holding on to territories occupied in 1967 against the will of the local population, if it illegally seizes land elsewhere, if a racialist-chauvinist fringe inside Israel defies the law and elementary human rights ... if some people in Israel are unwilling to accept the rights of others, such behaviour invites condemnation.[4]

Anthony Julius details several more criticisms levied against Israel which, he contends, overlook both mitigating circumstances and faults on the Palestinian side, but are not anti-semitic. Among these are criticisms alleging that:

> Targeted assassinations have killed bystanders. The shootings (live rounds and rubber bullets), beatings, and tear gas, have injured many thousands of Palestinians; the punitive destruction of private property has made many hundreds of Palestinians homeless; the uprooting of orchards and fields, the destruction of factories, workshops, and hot-houses, has robbed many thousands of Palestinians of their means of livelihood ... The 'Security fence' (or 'Wall'), however much intended as a non-violent response to Palestinian violence, has generated it own oppressions – 'land grabs'[5]

On examining the left's record on Israel he finds, however, like Laqueur, that its criticisms are infected by the virus of anti-semitism. Their assessment is that the left's anti-Zionism continues in the tradition of the European right's anti-semitism. And what makes this latest manifestation still more dangerous is that the left has allied itself with Muslims, whose ideology is also a carrier of the virus. The principle that criticism of Israel is not *per se* anti-semitic attests in the literature on the 'new anti-semitism' to the open mindedness of Israel's defenders but rarely exonerates its critics.

MacShane explains the rationale for considering any and every criticism of Israel as covert anti-semitism. 'Today, Jew-haters try to avoid using the term "Jew" or "Jewish" and instead reach for the word "Zionist" or "Zionism" as a substitute that does not carry the obvious negativity of "Jew".'[6] The Parliamentary inquiry into anti-semitism, which he chaired, appears to propose, at first sight, a more evidence-based approach. It was guided in its definition of anti-semitism by the Macpherson report that arose out of an inquiry into the seriously flawed police investigation of a black teenager's murder in London, in 1993. The report recommended that the police and other state agencies for the purpose of recording and investigating alleged racist incidents, define these as 'any incident which is perceived to be racist by the victim or any other person'. Thus, similarly, the All-Party Inquiry's report states: 'We conclude that it is the Jewish community itself that is best qualified to determine what does and does not constitute anti-semitism.'[7] There is, in this formulation, a significant slippage from the usage proposed by Macpherson. He had recommended that allegations of racism, 'understood to include crimes and non-crimes in policing terms', be treated by the police and other state agencies as constituting a *prima facia* case for being racist and that, therefore they should 'be reported, recorded and investigated with equal commitment'. A complaint of racial harassment or racial discrimination does not circumvent the need to prove the allegation.

The Parliamentary inquiry by way of settling what should be considered anti-semitic, argues that the 'Jewish community' (in practice, those considered to be its spokespersons) should be the sole arbiter. This does not, however, render what constitutes anti-semitism uncontentious. A broad definition cited by the European Union Monitoring Centre on Racism and Xenophobia (EUMC) that is likely to command broad agreement, states that anti-semitism is 'a persisting latent hostile belief towards Jews as a collectivity'[8] but, as Brian Klug argues, this can still be interpreted in a variety of ways. He gives the following elaboration of anti-semitism, pointing out that whether one or other theme receives emphasis varies according to historical context:

> The Jews are the enemy of humanity. Wherever they go, they form a state within a state. Acting in secret, they work together to promote their own advantage at the expense of the nations in whose midst they dwell and on whom they prey. Collectively, they conspire to dominate the world. Across the globe, their hidden hand controls the banks, the markets and the media. Even governments are under their sway. And when revolutions occur or when nations go to war, it is the Jews – cohesive, powerful, clever, ruthless and vengeful – who invariably pull the strings, and reap the rewards.[9]

In all these themes, forms of real or imagined behaviour are depicted as qualities inherent to Jews. The Parliamentary inquiry favoured, however, the interpretation of anti-semitism put forward by the EUMC. This relied on a more capacious definition, which includes: 'Denying the Jewish people their right to self-determination, e.g., by claiming that the existence of a State of Israel is a racist endeavour', and 'Drawing comparisons of contemporary Israeli policy to that of the Nazis'.[10] Both these characterisations, irrespective of whether they are justified or not, refer to Israeli policies or to the Israeli polity, not to Jews.

The conflicting definitions of anti-semitism indicate the difficulty of determining whether it is on the rise. The Parliamentary Inquiry, in line with the proponents of the 'new anti-semitism' thesis, considered this to be the case and attribute its cause mainly to anti-Zionist campaigning by the left and Muslim groups. Its report states:

> Many of those who gave evidence recognised that with the outbreak of the second Palestinian *Intifada* in September 2000, most agencies monitoring anti-semitism throughout Europe and beyond, including the EUMC, have acknowledged a rise in anti-semitic incidents. Often these peak at times when there is a particular outbreak of violence in the Israeli-Palestinian conflict or somewhere else in the Middle East ... This trend is reflected in Britain. In 2005 the CST [Community Security Trust], a charitable organisation which provides security and defence services and advice to the Jewish community, recorded 455 anti-Semitic incidents, a 14% fall from 2004, but the second highest annual total since the Trust began recording incidents in 1984.[11]

A wider set of available data gathered by the Metropolitan Police Service (MPS) does not, however, bear out this portrayal. Significantly, the Parliamentarians' assessment makes only passing references to the MPS data on recorded incidents of anti-semitism in London and to the secondary analysis of that data carried out by Iganski *et al.* for the Institute for Jewish Policy Research. These two sources do not show an increase in anti-semitic incidents nor do they suggest that the incidents stemmed from pro-Palestinian political campaigning.[12]

Iganski and his co-researchers analysed the MPS data for the four calendar years, 2001–2004, when as a result of the second *Intifada* there was an upsurge of violence in the Israel-Palestine conflict. The MPS, responsible for policing London, records incidents of anti-semitism as a distinct category of race crime. Although this data is limited to Greater London, according to the 2001 Census, the 149,789 Londoners of Jewish religion represented 58 per cent of the Jewish population of England and Wales. In the January 2001 to December 2004 period, there were some fluctuations in the number of reported incidents of anti-semitism but the overall trend was downwards. In line with other crimes, there is under reporting of anti-semitic incidents but a countervailing factor is apparent from Iganski *et al.*'s analysis. In a sample of Metropolitan Police data, they categorised just under one-fifth of the cases, as 'interpreted incidents'. These are cases where either the police or the complainant interpreted the incident as anti-semitic, 'where there does not appear to be any direct or objective evidence of anti-semitism being involved'. Among such cases the researchers found that there were incidents where the 'the animus expressed was anti-Israeli and not specifically anti-Jewish'.[13] The number of incidents erroneously assumed to be anti-semitic when, in fact, they were more likely to have been anti-Israel, is likely to be higher in the CST data, which had informed the MPs' assessment. The CST is an organisation whose funding depends on providing security training and services to Jewish communal institutions and events, from which stem its 'considerable ability to sell the need for self-defence of various kinds to the people whom it serves'.[14]

To scrutinise the fluctuations in the overall downward trend in the MPS data, Iganski et al. grouped the incident rate into 'low', 'medium' and 'high' months to determine whether the different rates correlated with the intensity of media reporting on the Israel-Palestine conflict. In the two months that they rated as 'high intensity' media coverage, in a sample of 156 cases, they found that anti-Israel sentiment in the discourse of offenders was present in about 20 per cent of anti-semitic incidents, compared with just less than 5 per cent in the months of 'low intensity' media coverage.[15] They add two important observations. First, 'the detailed qualitative analysis of the sub-sample of incidents discussed above does not suggest that organised "extremists", of whatever political shade, are responsible for a significant number of anti-semitic incidents in London'.[16] Second:

> the discourse used by the perpetrators appears to shift in months of high political tension in the Middle East. Rather than using symbolism or discourse referring to Nazism or anti-semitism in general, more specific commentary is made about events occurring in the Middle East. It is important to note that this occurs in the context where the nature of the incidents and the profile of the perpetrators have not perceptibly changed. This indicates that these incidents do not involve new types of perpetrators with extremist views committing new crimes during these times. What we are seeing instead is similar types of perpetrators using the current political climate as a way of having a greater impact on the perceived vulnerability of their targets.[17]

In only a small minority of incidents was Middle East politics a motivating factor in the anti-semitic incidents recorded by the police. Not everyone holding anti-semitic prejudice goes on to commit a crime and an increase in anti-semitic attitudes would still be of concern, but pro-Palestinian politics does not inevitably slide into anti-semitism any more than exposing corruption in African states necessarily turns into the racist stereotyping of Africans as incapable of ruling themselves. One or other outcome hinges on how such issues are addressed. The only other alternative is to turn a blind eye to events for fear of them being exploited by racists, which however is likely to leave both the injustice and the prejudices intact. In both Britain and France, left-wing pro-Palestinian campaigning and Jewish groups acting in solidarity with the Palestinians have been emphatic on the distinction between condemning Israel and condemning Jews.

The Palestine Solidarity Campaign, the main pro-Palestinian organisation in

England and Wales (there is also a Scottish PSC) is characterised by Julius as one of the carriers of the 'new anti-semitism'. 'There is implicit in its politics,' he claims, 'a desire to see the end of Israel, if not Israelis.'[18] This single sentence is meant to capture the logic of anti-Zionism: it leads inexorably to ethnocide, perhaps even to genocide. PSC's alleged noxious aspiration is sustained by a campaigning organisation that is 'especially prominent' among what Julius calls 'boutique movements', implying that it is a pastime activity under consumer capitalism, which enables *politicos* to indulge themselves in 'causes' that take their fancy. Their ideologies, argues Julius in terms derived from critiques of the left by the right-wing, French *nouveaux philosophes*, reflect 'post-leftist accommodations with conventionally reactionary positions ... the products of a certain scaling back of political ambitions, a championing of more limited local causes', which lacking 'a unified vision or a coherent ideology have instead cohered into what might be termed "semi-ideologies"'. Symptomatic of this lack of coherence, according to Julius, is that anti-Zionism combines two, apparently incompatible, ideological strands. One is appropriated from liberalism, in the form of 'anti-national cosmopolitanism': 'It esteems post-national identities, multiple, pluralized forms of citizenship identities.' The other, appropriates 'the language of nationalism and of Islamic radicalism, it accommodates itself to reactionary positions among which is Jew-hatred'.[19] Julius turns to untangling the two strands to demonstrate that the first is merely the fluffy outer covering for the weight-bearing anti-semitism.

He cites the PSC's 'core values' to be: 'supporting the Palestinians right of return as stipulated in UN Resolution 194; organizing campaigns, demonstrations and public meetings; working to highlight the human rights abuses committed by the Israelis and raise awareness of the issue of Palestine to the general public'. Julius may have found a document which identifies these as 'core values' but as he rightly points out they hardly qualify as 'values' and therefore a more accurate representation of the PSC's political stand would have been to cite its five principal aims reproduced in every single issue of the organisation's quarterly publication, *Palestine News*, and in countless pamphlets and leaflets that the organisation has issued. These aims include, in addition to the ones listed by Julius: 'Campaigning against oppression and dispossession suffered by the Palestinian people' and 'Opposing anti-semitism and racism, including the apartheid and Zionist nature of the Israeli state'.

A declaration of aims is just that, a declaration; the PSC could still foster or collude in anti-semitism by insinuation though it is unlikely that this would have escaped the notice of its Jewish members or of such organisations as Jews for Justice for Palestinians, Independent Jewish Voices and the International Jewish Anti-Zionist Network with which the PSC has had mutually supportive working relations. From the voluminous PSC literature generated over nearly three decades, Julius gives just two examples. 'The PSC is remarkable,' he states, 'for being a campaigning organization that has no declared final position. It is not working towards a defined solution to the Israel-Palestine conflict. It appears to have no position on the one-state versus two-state solution, though the implication of its "right of return" position is that there would be two Palestinian states and no state at all for the Jewish people.'[20] But if anything is remarkable in this regard it is surely that the Israeli state has never placed a limit on its territorial ambition within the area of Mandatory Palestine (which initially had included Transjordan, now Jordan) by specifying where its borders lie. What is remarkable is Israel's deliberate ambiguity on whether it is pursuing an acceptance of a two-state solution or further settlement expansion in the Occupied Territories in order to achieve a one-state solution, with no state at all for the Palestinians. It is, pace Julius, completely unremarkable that a solidarity campaign in support of a movement for self-determination does not seek to prescribe to that movement what should be either its negotiating position or its final constitution.

Julius's other instance of PSC anti-semitism reveals, in his view, the organisation's predilection for the Jewish conspiracy trope:

> At the 2007 AGM of the PSC, for example, a resolution was tabled that contained – after much throat-clearing on the differences between anti-Zionism and anti-Semitism, and the wickedness of those who say otherwise – a paragraph rejecting talk of the "Jewish lobby" and "Jewish power". That objections to imperialism have often been deformed by anti-Semitic sentiment is a commonplace among historians and political scientists; the deformations are also acknowledged from time to time by activists too. But not on this occasion, and specifically not in relation to objections to Zionism. The resolution was rejected.

Julius, convinced that he has the clinching evidence to prove the PCS's equivocal position on anti-semitism, adds: 'In the debate on this resolution lies the irresolution of the new anti-Zionists before the Jewish conspiracy trope.'[21] This allegation rests on Julius's account of a PSC annual general meeting for which his source is a highly tendentious report by Engage, a pro-Israeli group set up to oppose the academic boycott of Israeli universities.

There were two quite lengthy resolutions submitted to the 2007 AGM, similar in their arguments, provoked, on the one hand, by the *Report of the All-Party Parliamentary Inquiry Into Anti-Semitism*, and on the other, by a US-based organisation, Deir Yassin Remembered, offering speakers to some PSC branches. The American organisation is believed to have leading members sympathetic to Holocaust denial. Both resolutions to the AGM called for a condemnation of Zionism and anti-semitism as forms of racism. One stated: 'Unlike anti-racist movements, Zionism has accepted the anti-semitic argument that Jews have no place in non-Jewish societies.' The other resolution said similarly: 'Conference agrees with the Zionist novelist A.B. Yehoshua, that, "Even today, in a perverse way, a real anti-Semite must be a Zionist"'. The two resolutions also condemned notions of 'the Jewish lobby' and 'Jewish power' or 'other sinister cabals and conspiracies' dictating US policy. The response to these resolutions showed not the slightest reluctance to condemn anti-semitism. They were rejected on the recommendation of the Executive Committee, who argued that it would be unproductive for the solidarity campaign to be drawn into the argument over Zionism being a form of racism. The Executive proposed instead that 'Conference reaffirms its opposition to all forms of racism, including anti-Jewish prejudice and that the expression of or support for anti-semitic viewpoints are incompatible with membership of the Palestine Solidarity Campaign', and called for PSC to resist, 'all attempts to deflect attention from the plight of the Palestinians'.[22] This resolution, which was passed, is not mentioned by Julius.

In the growing literature on the 'new anti-semitism', misrepresentation and exaggeration are the norm not the exception. Walter Laqueur, the doyen of Zionist historians, illustrates the pervasiveness of anti-semitism on the European left with the following example from British politics:

> When the British Labour party launched anti-Semitic attacks against two Conservative leaders (Michael Howard and Oliver Letwin) who were of Jewish extraction, this had nothing to do with Zionism and Israel since these political figures were in no way involved in pro-Israel (or indeed in Jewish life), but simply with the fact that as Jews they were vulnerable. (About half of the British electorate indicated that it would not want a Jew as prime minister.) It could well be that those who launched these attacks were motivated merely by 'practical' considerations. The influence of Muslim communities in western Europe is growing and they might well be decisive in dozens of electoral constituencies.[23]

The 'attacks' Laqueur refers to took place in the 2005 general election campaign when Labour Party officials circulated an e-mail to some party supporters with a range of election posters under consideration. One of these depicted Howard and Letwin as flying pigs and another caricatured Howard as a Fagin-like figure. Whatever message was intended by the posters their subtext could be read as attributing Conservative Party polices to the two politicians' Jewish origin and was, therefore, rightly condemned for being anti-semitic. But Laqueur exaggerates the significance of this incident by making out that anti-semitism formed part of the Labour Party's electoral strategy. His claim has even less credibility in light of the Labour leadership contest that followed the party's defeat in the 2010 general election. The leading candidates in that contest were Ed and David Miliband, who are of Jewish origin. Laqueur indicates no source for his figure that about half the electorate would not want a Jewish prime minister but the only poll of this nature was conducted by ICM, in January 2004, when Howard was the leader of the Conservative Party. It found that 18 per cent of the respondents disagreed with the proposition that 'a British Jew would make an equally acceptable Prime Minister as a member of any other faith', a further 28 per cent said they did not know or were neutral on the issue, while 53 per cent said that a Jewish prime minister would be as acceptable as any other.[24] These figures do not come anywhere near to showing that half the population is anti-semitic and do not lend any credibility to Laqueur's far-fetched idea that anti-semitism could be a useful electoral card for the Labour Party – nor could it be for any other mainstream party.

The ICM poll is, nevertheless, revealing of a stubbornly persistent, residual anti-semitism that is largely censored from the public sphere, but at a low intensity, is still widespread. This should not be allowed to obscure the fact that the dominant trend in British society and in Western Europe generally is towards the acceptance and assimilation of Jews. In 2009, the Israeli government launched a campaign urging Israelis to discourage their friends and relatives abroad from marrying non-Jews after surveys carried out by the Jewish People Policy Institute showed 'that Israel is the only country in the world with a significant Jewish population not decreasing in size. The decline elsewhere is ascribed both to low birth rates and to widespread intermarriage.'[25]

Antisemitism has declined, Bunzl notes, as a result of the capitalist integration of Europe. Antisemites, the guardians of the ethnically pure nation-state have become redundant in the 'supra-national context' of the European Union: 'while anti-Semitism was designed to protect the purity of the ethnic nation, Islamophobia is marshalled to safeguard the future of European civilisation'.[26] There is, he argues, 'no European party of any significance, and this includes the continent's various extreme right-wing movements, that currently champions a specifically anti-Semitic agenda'.[27] Bunzl overstates Europe's internal integration and the decline in the right's nostalgia for the ethnically pure state. In Eastern Europe, mainstream political parties still flirt with anti-semitic as well as anti-Roma racism, but even here where ethno-nationalism is deeply ingrained, the political and cultural hegemony of the West European states, exerted largely through the institutions of the European Union, is restricting the public space for anti-semitism.

In the post-Cold War era, the Muslim Other has come to be projected as Europe's external and internal threat. On the external front, this has turned Israel, once the frontline state in the battle against radical Arab nationalism, into a key ally in the battle against Islam. On the internal front, the immigrant population from Europe's former colonies has transformed the politics of race and nationalist discourse. As the left-liberal commitment to a multi-ethnic civil society has deepened, the right has sought to redraw the boundaries of national belonging. The 'new racism' by attributing the danger of the Other to cultural rather than biological difference has shifted its main target of attack from Jews to immigrants from the former colonies and their descendants.[28] They are the new aliens, and none more so than Muslims depicted as undermining the shared tastes, traditions and values which bind communities and the nation in the liberal democracies.

The political context of the invention of a 'new anti-semitism' is the decline of anti-semitism and the rise of Islamophobia. It is a rallying cry in defence of Israel, exploiting both the historically rooted insecurity of Jewish communities and the post-9/11 mistrust and enmity towards Muslims, who along with the left are arraigned as the new anti-semites. Antisemitism in Muslim communities, unlike on the left (which, of course, also includes Muslims) is widespread, but the self-serving explanation of the alarmists merely fans the flames of Islamophobia.

Laqueur writes:

> As Yehoshafat Harkabi pointed out many years ago, Arab and Muslim anti-semitism was the result of, not the reason for, the hostile Arab attitude towards Israel; it gradually became a 'means of deepening, justifying and institutionalizing this hostility among Arabs' and subsequently also among fellow Muslims. But it was not the only reason ... Because Islam had been traditionally a warring, expansionist religion, the defeats of 1948 and 1967 by an enemy whom no one had ever taken seriously represented a great trauma for Islam's adherents.[29]

Thus, while conceding that the European 'theological and later racialist' hostility to Jews did not exist in the Arab world, Laqueur is anxious to show that nevertheless Palestinian and Arab opposition derives not from Israel's dispossession of the Palestinians and its consequent military conflicts with the neighbouring Arab states but is inherent to Islamic doctrine, which he evokes as a monolithic aggressive ideology. Julius similarly wants to over-ride the connection between the impact on the Arab world of Israel's establishment and expansionism by backdating the Arab and Muslim opposition to Israel. He refers to 'horrible pogroms in Iraq and elsewhere in the Arab world' to draw the lesson that: 'The Holocaust was not solely a European story, then.'[30] This is not only meant to demonstrate that the Arabs have been hostile to Jews long before Israel was established, but also to dispose of the argument that the Arab world is paying recompense for a crime that they had no part in.

The Mufti of Jerusalem, Hajj Amin Al-Husseini, has long served the purpose in Zionist historiography of demonstrating that Palestinian nationalism ultimately stems from anti-semitism. The Mufti, the symbolic leader of Palestinian resistance to Zionism in the 1920s and 1930s, turned to Hitler for support, spending the wartime years in Berlin assisting with Nazi propaganda. Throughout the pre-state period Zionist propaganda maintained, with some justification, that the Mufti did not represent the masses in whose name he claimed to speak but pursued the narrow interest of the *effendi* class. Since then, however, the Mufti has had a makeover to be presented as the essence of Palestinian nationalism. Thus Julius's argument is drawn from a well-rehearsed repertoire but it is undermined by the evidence marshalled in several recent studies. Wildangel shows that the attempt to depict the Mufti as representative of Palestinian public opinion has been dictated by political considerations. There has been, he points out, a 'Mufti-isation' ('*Muftisierung*') of Palestinian nationalism, which exaggerates his importance and occludes the political views in Palestinian society which were hostile to fascism. 'Hajj Amin al-Husayni, in exile from 1937 was undoubtedly the most colourful and popular Palestinian figure in this period – he was, however, also a divisive character within Arab society and after his flight from the Mandated territory could have only a very limited influence on political developments in Palestine.'[31] It is not unproblematic to identify what constituted Palestinian public opinion at the time but in relation to matters unfolding mainly abroad it is likely to have been largely the views of the elite and of the urban classes and, among these strata, there were a range of views hostile to the fascism of both Mussolini and Hitler. The political party led by the Nashashibi family, old rivals of the Mufti, and the leaders of the National Defense Party looked to the British not to the Germans to advance Palestinian demands and denounced his alliance with the Axis powers. Wildangel points out that although the Palestinian Arab press was subject to censorship by the British authorities, and one newspaper used as an outlet for German propaganda was banned, it was never the simple mouthpiece for the British. From 1933 *Filastin*, and several other newspapers, published numerous articles critical of Nazism and of the persecution of Jews. Palestinian condemnation of Nazism stemmed from moral as well as pragmatic considerations. It was only too evident that the Nazi persecution of Jews was strengthening Zionism.[32]

In a study of Egyptian society's reaction to fascism, Gershoni and Janowski similarly contribute to undermine the notion that the Arab world generally viewed it favourably. On the basis of a detailed examination of the Egyptian press and of the views expressed by religious and secular intellectuals, they conclude that while some were initially drawn to aspects of fascism: 'By the eve of World War II, the bulk of informed Egyptian opinion had come to the consensus that fascist totalitarianism, racism and imperialism represented a manifest threat to Egypt, the Middle East, and the rest of the world.'[33] A similar conclusion emerges from a wider survey of Arab intellectual circles. Achcar, without glossing over anti-semitic views, reveals that, among the diverse intellectual currents in the Arab world, there existed both secular and religious opposition to anti-semitism. In relation to the 1941 Baghdad pogrom, alluded to by Julius, which claimed between 160 to 180 lives, he cites the account of the Israeli historian, Nissim Rejwan, an Iraqi Jew who was forced to leave Baghdad in 1947. 'Throughout the disturbances, with a few exceptions, Jewish homes in mixed neighbourhoods were defended and hundreds of Jews were saved by the willingness of their Muslim neighbours to protect them, in some cases at the cost of their own lives and limbs'.[34] The attackers were not a social movement but a rioting mob that was relatively easily dispersed by the Iraqi army. On the allegation of an all-pervasive anti-semitism across the Arab world, Achcar quotes from Robert Satloff's *Among the Righteous*: 'At every stage of the Nazi, Vichy, and Fascist persecution of Jews in Arab lands, and in every place that it occurred, Arabs helped Jews. Some Arabs spoke out against the persecution of Jews and took public stands of unity with them ... And there were occasions when certain Arabs chose to do more than just offer moral support to Jews. They bravely saved Jewish lives, at times risking their own in the process.'[35]

The advocates of the 'new anti-semitism' thesis, in seeking to delegitimise Israel's Muslim critics, not only want to characterise the Palestinians and the Arabs as the aggressors and Israel as the victim but also to present the Muslim world and its diaspora in Britain and elsewhere in Europe as part of a wider threat. 'The anti-semitism of old,' according to MacShane, 'has morphed into something new, one might call it "Endarkenment", which is seeking to de-Occidentalise the world.'[36] Anything that risks detracting from the image of a strong, determined foe may weaken the resolve to defend Israel and the Enlightenment values it claims to represent. Julius's thoughts on the subject of Islamophobia is that it has been exaggerated if not altogether invented in order to silence justified criticism of the Muslim community for its anti-semitic or other bigoted views. Citing the headline in *The Times*, 'Muslims are the new Jews', he comments: 'These claims were, and remain, somewhat overstated. Further, allegations of Islamophobia have had several unhappy consequences: the violent intimidation of people perceived to be "Islamophobes", and a consequent chilling effect on free speech; the suppression of any consideration of Islamic anti-semitism on the basis that the topic is itself in some sense "racist"; and a victim mentality among British Muslims.'[37] MacShane similarly belittles racism against Muslims. 'Neo-antisemitism and Islamophobia are,' he declares, 'if not quite twin sides of the same coin, certainly produced at the same mint.'[38] But the two coins turn out to be of very different magnitude, since he believes that there is 'no greater intolerance today than neo-antisemitism'.[39] This might be deemed a harmless misjudgement were it not for the fact that in the light of 'neo-antisemitism' even the blindingly obvious gets overlooked.

MacShane is the MP for Rotherham, a town with a significant Muslim minority where, over several years, the British National Party's (BNP) candidates have contested elections, relatively successfully, on a platform of incitement against Muslims. In the 2010 general election, the BNP candidate in MacShane's constituency gained 10.4 per cent of the votes, a 4.5 per cent increase by relation to its share of the votes in the 2005 election. In the neighbouring constituency of Rotherham West, the BNP candidate came second in the 2006 by-election, taking 26.2 per cent of the votes. What lends Islamophobia political momentum in contemporary Britain is, however, not the BNP or the English Defence League, two organisations whose support comes predominantly from the most impoverished and despairing sections of the working class, but the demonisation of Muslims from sections of the mainstream press and politicians, often coded in the language of 'the war on terror'. A study by researchers at the Cardiff School of Journalism on the print media's reporting on British Muslims from 2000 to 2008, classifying around 23,000 stories, found that 'four of the five most common discourses about Muslims in Britain in the British press associate Islam/Muslims with threats, problems or in opposition to dominant British values'.[40] According to a 2009 YouGov poll 44 per cent of voters agreed with the viewpoint that 'even in its milder forms Islam poses a danger to western civilisation'.[41]

The discovery of Muslims as the new internal and external threat to the West has inspired the invention of the new anti-semitism, as MacShane's reasoning illustrates:

> In 2005, a team of sociologists headed by France's foremost researcher into racism, Michel Wieviorka, investigated the depth and range of antisemitic thinking amongst Muslims in France. In the socially deprived suburbs where French urban planners dumped the massive north African population hoovered into France to do all the dirty, low-paid, boring and dangerous jobs that white French citizens did not want to do, the extent of antisemitic feeling is depressing and disturbing. Swastikas were found on the lifts serving the tall apartment blocks where poor Muslim families live. Walls were sprayed with anti-Jewish insults and in every interview the team of researchers carried out they recorded vile antisemitic epithets and abuse. All independent research studies show an alarming degree of anti-Jewish feeling amongst France's five million Muslims.[42]

MacShane's interpretation is the polar opposite of Wieviorka's, whose authority he claims in support. The difference between them is instructive for understanding this issue in the British context. Although Wieviorka acknowledges that anti-semitic ideas have common currency in France's Muslim community, he concludes: 'But it would be an error to think that immigrants from the Muslim-Arab world, and above all the youth, are hugely swayed by anti-semitic rantings. On the contrary, many talk in private, too, in nuanced or reasonable terms. The overwhelming majority of such populations have a strong sympathy for the Palestinians but this does not mean an automatic support for anti-semitic ideas, far from it.'[43] Wieviorka's assessment draws on his research into the views of Muslim youths in Roubaix, an industrial town in France a few kilometres from Lille. The town, once based on a thriving textile industry, has a large north African community that, reflecting the crisis of 'les banlieues', is confronted by chronic unemployment and urban decay. The youths, through the internet and the media, are also attuned to international developments and have heard the arguments of radical Muslim thinkers and groups in the Middle East and elsewhere.

Observing their interaction, Wieviorka witnessed Jews being commonly invoked as the source of all the wrong from which Muslims suffer in France and the world over. Many of the youth saw Jews as having acquired, in France, a privileged status and internationally to be wielding control over US foreign policy in the interest of Israel and to the detriment of the Palestinians and other Muslim peoples. 'The amalgam of Jews and Israeli policy leads on to a dislike of Jews.'[44] However, the few Jews who live in their midst are not assimilated into this hostile image and, according to the local police, there is no more vandalism directed at synagogues than at mosques or churches. When young Muslims are invited to address the specific problems that they want resolved in Roubaix, they make no attempt to link these to the stereotype of Jewish power or influence. The discrimination young Muslims face in the labour market and at the hands of police and criminal justice system are at the source of their anger: 'antisemitism is far from being the only or the principal problem of racism in the region'.[45] In the period 2002 to 2003, when antisetimic acts were the majority of hate crimes in France, 'other forms of racism and xenophobia increased by 150 per cent, and most of these were directed at the Muslim population'.[46] The young Muslims of Roubaix reflect on their own experience of exclusion and humiliation through the experience of the Palestinians. 'To identify oneself pro-Palestinian can be a way to say that one feels oneself Arab, Muslim, and at the same time dominated, excluded, abused. The far off and the nearby merge, the brutality for which the Israeli state is reproached has its counterpart in the failures for which the institutions here are accused of, and the logic of discrimination are seen as basically equivalent in the two cases.'[47] This picture bears little resemblance to MacShane's attempt to characterise instances of hostility in Muslim communities to Israel spilling over into anti-semitism as generated by the influence of a particular strand of Islam (Saudi Wahhabism). It suggests instead that, in such cases, anti-semitism is better understood as reactive to these communities' exclusion.[48]

The 'new anti-semitism' thesis echoes the narrative that Muslim and Palestinian opposition to Israel has evolved in a straight line from the right-wing nationalism of Hajj Amin Al-Husseini. Once Arafat became the leader of the Palestinian national movement he, too, was widely portrayed as a Hitler-like figure. Unsurprisingly, when Israel began negotiating with him during the Oslo Peace process, there was some puzzlement among Jewish communities around the world. A study carried out for the Institute for Jewish Policy Research on British Jews' attitude to Israel remarked: 'The opening of negotiations with the Palestinians and the other results of the peace process were widely welcomed in Britain but they also caused confusion. Yasser Arafat, implicitly and sometimes explicitly likened to Hitler in Israel fundraising material, suddenly became a partner for peace. The JIA [Joint Israel Appeal] and many other organisations had spent years using a demonized image of Arafat to galvanise support for Israel.'[49]

For MacShane, the Hamas Charter's claim that the Protocols of the Elders of Zion is an authoritative confirmation of a worldwide Zionist conspiracy amounts to 'one of the most virulent expressions of Jew-hatred ever written', while in Lebanon, Hezbollah's 'desire to kill Jews is overwhelming'.[50] By disconnecting these movements from the political context from which they emerged and currently operate, MacShane is able to paint them as irrational, demonic forces, living testimonies to anti-semitism being the source of Palestinian and Muslim hostility to Israel. With the Hitlerite character of Palestinian and Lebanese Muslim leaders established, Israel requires no further justification to assassinate them and lay siege to and bomb the civilians who elected them. The Hitlerite analogy is used by both sides and has become part of the propaganda battle. Zionist writers point to its ominous implications only when it is applied to Israel. Thus Robert Wistrich, one of the exponents of the 'new-anti-semitism' thesis, argues that: '"anti-Zionists" who insist on comparing Zionism and the Jews with Hitler and the Third Reich appear unmistakably to be *de facto* anti-semites, even if they vehemently deny the fact! This is largely because they knowingly exploit the reality that Nazism in the post-war world has become the defining metaphor of absolute evil.'[51] This is also the view of the EUMC which cites one of the ways in which anti-semitism manifests itself to be: 'Drawing comparisons of contemporary Israeli policies to that of the Nazis'.[52] At the heart of such arguments lies the fear that the Holocaust is in danger of losing its significance as Judeocide and that by consequence anti-semitism will cease to be regarded as a uniquely dangerous, genocidal force, distinct from other forms of racism. The uniqueness of the Holocaust is now routinely affirmed not to combat racism or, even more specifically, anti-semitism but to justify Israel's privileged connections to the West and its insistence on being a Jewish state, rather than a state for all its citizens, irrespective of religion and ethnicity. It is this particularistic and partisan appropriation of the Holocaust that the supporters of the Palestinian cause contest when they liken Israel's military assaults against Palestinians and its policies of ethnic cleansing to Nazism. It reflects in large measure the desire to translate the Palestinians' suffering into a language that might awaken the Western world's conscience. Far from representing a nostalgia for Judeocide it is an implicit acknowledgement that the Western world's moral universe is informed by a revulsion at Nazism.

There is a distinction to be made between the elimination of the biological existence of an ethnic group, attempted by the Nazis, and the elimination of a culture or political identity, which is what Israel is attempting. The policy of ethnocide or what Kimmerling has called 'politicide'[53] has different consequences from genocide not least in terms of the number of lives lost but rather than use the distinction to defend Israel's Palestine policy by insisting on its distance from the worst that humanity has yet invented, as the proponents of the new anti-semitism thesis would have it, it is infinitely preferable to be on the look out for the parallels. As Chaumont remarks, 'the use of comparisons to render a less extreme reality less banal rather than for the purpose of making the extreme reality seem banal can constitute the guiding principle for constructing an alternative discourse of remembering, one with which other victims of history can identify without having to minimise Auschwitz or exaggerate their own sufferings'.[54] The alternative discourse on the Israel-Palestine conflict that would accomplish this and begin the process of finding a solution to it requires an acknowledgement that the establishment of the Israeli state, supported by Western economic and military power, has led to the Palestinians' dispossession and continuing oppression.

Notes

1. LPACR, 1982, p. 136.
2. N. Cohen, *What's Left?* (London: Harper Perennial, 2007), p. 10; See also J. Freedland, 'Where is the Goldstone Report into Sri Lanka, Cogo, Darfur – or Britain?', *The Guardian* (6 April 2011).
3. M. Woolacott, 'Nightmare Looming Over a Post-War Dream', *The Guardian* (25 January 1995).
4. W. Laqueur, *The Changing Face of Antisemitism* (Oxford: Oxford University Press, 2006), p. 6.
5. A. Julius, *Trials of the Diaspora* (Oxford: Oxford University Press, 2010), p. 501.
6. D. MacShane, *Globalising Hatred, the New Antisemtism* (London: Phoenix, 2009), p. 82.
7. *Report of the All-Party Parliamentary Inquiry Into Antisemitism* (London: Stationary Office, 2006), p. 1.
8. Quoted in *All-Party Parliamentary Inquiry*, p. 6.
9. B. Klug, 'Is Europe a Lost Cause? The European Debate on Antisemitism and the Middle East Conflict', *Patterns of Prejudice*, 39:1 (2005), 51.
10. *All-Party Parliamentary Inquiry*, p. 6.
11. Ibid., p. 7.
12. Ibid., p. 47.
13. Ibid., p. 55–56.
14. R. Belcher, 'A Commentary on the All-Party Parliamentary Inquiry into Antisemitism' (March 2007), www.ffipp-uk.org/AS_rpt_070371.doc (accessed 10 January 2011).
15. P. Iganski, V. Kielinger and S. Paterson, *Hate Crimes Against London's Jews* (London: Institute for Jewish Policy Research, 2005), p. 52.
16. Ibid., p. 49.
17. Ibid., pp. 69–70.
18. Julius, *Trials*, p. 460.
19. Ibid., pp. 453, 455.
20. Ibid., p. 462.
21. Ibid., pp. 484–485.
22. Minutes of the PSC AGM and EC Resolution, available from PSC, info@palestinecampaign.org. The author received additional information from two PSC members who attended the 2007 AGM.
23. Laqueur, *Changing Face*, p. 149.
24. *Jewish Chronicle* (23 January 2005).
25. J. Cook, 'Israeli Ads Warn Against Marrying Non-Jews', www.countercurrents.org/cook080909.htm (accessed 4 August 2011).
26. M. Bunzl, *Anti-Semitism and Islamophobia: Hatreds Old and New in Europe* (Chicago: Prickly Paradigm Press, 2007), p. 45. In the April 2010 Hungarian general election, Jobbik, the far-right, openly anti-semitic party gained 16.7 per cent of the popular vote.
27. Ibid., p. 15.
28. M. Barker, *The New Racism: Conservatives and the Ideology of the Tribe* (London: Aletheia Books, 1982).
29. Laqueur, *Changing Face*, p. 197.
30. Julius, *Trials*, p. 506.
31. R. Wildangel, '"Der größte Feind der Menscheit". Der National sozialismus in der arabischen öffentlichen Meinung in Pälestina während des Zweiten Weltkrieges', in G. Höpp, P. Wien and R. Wildangel (eds), *Blind für Geschichte?* (Berlin: Klaus Schwarz Verlag, 2004), p. 119.
32. Ibid., p. 144.

33 I. Gershoni and J. Jankowski, *Confronting Fascism in Egypt* (Stanford: Stanford University Press, 2010), p. 268.
34 Achcar, *Arabs and the Holocaust*, p. 101.
35 Ibid., p. 102.
36 MacShane, *Globalising Hatred*, p. 159.
37 Julius, *Trials*, p. 518. It is worth noting, by contrast, the tone struck by Julius in his letter of 3 June 2008, to the General Secretary of the University and College Union (UCU) over union members voting in favour of boycotting Israeli universities for their role in the occupation of the West Bank and Gaza. As part of a letter threatening legal action if the union's executive did not rescind or ignore the membership's majority vote, the letter stated: 'The possible causes of action against the UCU and its trustees have been set out in detail in the unchallenged legal opinion obtained by Stop the Boycott (STB), and there is no need to repeat its content here. It is, however, worth elaborating the ambit of the likely claim against the UCU for harassment under s.3A(1) of the Race Relations Act, that is, the creating of an intimidating , hostile, degrading, humiliating and/or offensive environment for Jewish members of the union and/or violating their dignity'. http://spme.net/cgi-bin/articles.cgi?ID=4119 (accessed 14 February 2011). For the position in support of the boycott see, H. Rose and S. Rose, 'Israel, Europe and the Academic Boycott', *Race & Class*, 50:1 (2008), pp. 1–20; www.bricup.org.uk.
38 MacShane, *Globalising Hatred*, p. 164.
39 Ibid., p. ix. MacShane, outrageously distorting the reasons for the UCU boycott motion, writes: 'In May 2008, a tiny handful of union delegates obsessed with their search for an end to contact with Jews in Israeli universities successfully passed a resolution smearing Jewish professors and lecturers by accusing them of being "complicit" in the conflict' (ibid., p. 68). And no doubt, through MacShane's vision of the world, Jewish academics who voted for this resolution are self-hating Jews, as are the Israeli academics who supported the boycott call.
40 K. Moore, P. Mason, and J. Lewis, *Images of Islam in the UK* (Cardiff: Cardiff School of Journalism, Media and Cultural Studies, 2008), p. 15.
41 *Prospect Magazine* (22 June 2010), www.prospectmagazine.co.uk (accessed 21 November 2010).
42 MacShane, *Globalising Hatred*, p. 46.
43 'Mais ce serait une erreur de croire que les immigrés issus du monde arabo-musulman, et surtout les jeunes, sont massivement emportés dans des délires antisémites. Beaucoup, au contraire, y compris en privé, tiennes des propos nuancés, our rausinables. Une forte sensibilité propalestinian, très majoritiare dans ces populations, ne signifie pas une adhérence automatique à des idées antisémites, loin de la là.' M. Wieviorka, *L'Antisémitisme est-il de retour?* (Paris: Larousse, 2008), pp. 88-9.
44 'L'amalgame entre le peuple juif and la politique israélienne débouche sur l'aversion des Juifs.' M. Wieviorka, *La Tentation Antisémite* (Paris: Robert Laffont, 2005), p. 149.
45 'l'antisémitisme est loin d'être le seul ou le principal problème de racisme dans la région'. Wieviorka, *Ibid.*, p. 147.
46 P. Silverstein, 'The Context of Antisemitism and Islamophobia in France', *Patterns of Prejudice*, 41:1 (2008), 22.
47 'S'afficher propalestinian peut vouloir dire que l'on se sent arabe, musulman, en même temps que dominé, exclue, maltraité. Le lointain et le proche se confondent, la brutalité reprochée à l'État israélien, là-bas, trouve alors sa contrepartie dans la carences don't sont accusées les institutions, ici, et les loqiques de discrimination sont perçues comme étant finalement équivalentes dans les deux cas.' Wieviorka, *La Tentation*, p. 159.

48 O. Roy, *Globalised Islam* (London: Hurst & Company, 2002), p. 45.
49 B. Kosmin, A. Lerman and J. Goldberg, *The Attachment of British Jews to Israel* (London: Institute for Jewish Policy Research, 1997), p. 4.
50 MacShane, *Globalising Hatred*, p. 132.
51 R. Wistrich, 'Anti-Zionism and Anti-Semitism', *Jewish Political Studies Review*, 16:3–4 (2004), 29.
52 Quoted in *All-Party Parliamentary Inquiry*, p. 6.
53 Baruch Kimmerling defines the mixture of techniques deployed by Israel in the Occupied Territories as 'politicide': it involves the 'expropriation of lands and their colonization; restrictions on spatial mobility (curfews, closures, roadblocks); murder, localized massacres; mass detentions; divisions, or elimination, of leaders and elite groups; hindrance of regular education and schooling; physical destruction of public institutions and infrastructure, private homes and property; starvation; social and political isolation; re-education; and partial or, if feasible, complete ethnic cleansing, although this may not occur as a single dramatic action.' B. Kimmerling, 'From Barak to Road Map', *New Left Review*, 23, 2nd Series (September-October 2003), 141.
54 'l'utilisation des comparaisons pour débanaliser une réalité moins extrême plutôt que pour bananliser une réalité extrême peut constituer le principe d'une construction d'un discours alternatif de la mémoire auquel les autres victimes de l'histoire pourraient se raccrocher sans devoir du tout minimiser Auschwitz ou exagérer leurs tourments'. J-M.Chaumont, *La concurrence des victimes* (Paris: Editions la Découverte, 1997), p. 318.

Conclusion

The British left's realignment from support to an increasingly critical stance towards Israel and Zionism has developed primarily in response to Israel's occupation of the West Bank and Gaza and to the related implosion of Labour Zionism. But other factors have played their part, too. As anti-racism and human rights have assumed greater prominence in the left's political outlook, its opposition to Zionism's 'blood and soil' nationalism and to the expansion of Israeli settlements in the Occupied Territories has intensified.

Much of the energy for the Palestinian cause has continued to emanate from the radical left but support for it has also rallied more mainstream opinion. The politics of leftwing solidarity characterised by the iconography of Palestinian fighters wearing *kafiyas* and brandishing Kalashnikovs, which in the 1960s had symbolised national liberation struggle as much as the portraits of Che Guevara and Ho Chi-Minh, has been eclipsed by non-governmental organisations and activists monitoring Israeli violations of international law and interceding on behalf of Palestinians living under Israeli rule. The shift of emphasis in pro-Palestinian discourse from the armed struggle and anti-imperialism to human rights was made propitious by the 1967 war. The Palestinian population that had slipped out of Western consciousness after the 1948 war, once more commanded its attention by directly confronting Israeli military force in the West Bank and Gaza. But the radical left's ideological retreat after the mid-1970s was a factor, too, in a broader realignment on the left over the Israel-Palestine conflict that drew its ideological ballast from the human rights agenda.

There were indications soon after Israel had seized the West Bank and Gaza that liberal-minded observers and human rights agencies were going to play a prominent role in shaping the international perception of its occupation. Michael Adams' reports in the *Guardian* and the *Sunday Times*, in 1968, on Israel's punitive curfews and demolition of Palestinian houses were followed by similar newspaper reports and given authoritative confirmation, at the end of 1970, by two international agencies. The International Committee of the Red Cross accused

Israel of having violated the Geneva conventions by blowing up villages and houses as reprisal for Palestinian armed attacks on Israel. Later the same year, a UN Investigation Committee, composed of representatives from three non-aligned countries, Ceylon, Somalia and Yugoslavia, reported after visiting the West Bank: 'The occupying power is pursuing a conscious and deliberate policy calculated to depopulate the occupied territories of their Arab inhabitants'.[1] In 1972, the executive of the Liberal Party's student organisation decided to run a campaign on Palestinian political prisoners and, shortly after, Amnesty International published a report on Arab detainees held without trial in Israeli captivity for over a year.[2] Around this time, the Israeli League for Human and Civil Rights similarly protested over the Israeli army's treatment of Palestinians. The organisation's chairperson, Israel Shahak, a professor of chemistry at the Hebrew University in Jerusalem, with very limited resources and largely dependent on Israeli press reports, used his academic status to try to draw international attention to violations of international law.

In Britain, Palestine Action, an organisation launched in 1972, on the fifth anniversary of the Six Day War, with the support of two Labour MPs and the South African anti-apartheid activist, Ruth First, also indicated a more human rights-centred approach. Invoking the Universal Declaration of Human Rights, its emphasis was on the demand for 'a secular and democratic Palestine in which all have equal rights, irrespective of race or creed and equal protection from discrimination', rather than on the collective, national goal of self-determination for the Palestinians.[3] This early initiative to develop a broad-front, solidarity campaign for Palestine was influenced by the Anti-Apartheid Movement's success. The AAM launched in 1960, had secured within a few years an impressive level of political support that included liberals, churches, peace groups, Labour parties, trade unions, communists and radicals of various sorts on a platform that all citizens of South Africa should have equal rights. Its campaign became an anti-racist rallying point.

The language of human rights had existed earlier and was deployed in such landmark statements as the Atlantic Charter of 1941, the UN Charter signed in 1945 and the UN's 1948 Universal Declaration of Human Rights, but whereas in the post-war period individual rights were conceived as flowing from the sovereignty of the state, in the human rights discourse that came to prominence in the 1970s individual rights were prioritised: 'within one decade human rights would be invoked across the developed world and by many more ordinary people than ever before. Instead of implying colonial liberation and the creation of emancipated nations, human rights most often now meant individual protection against the state.'[4] The new conceptualisation of human rights was popularised by a section of the political class in the US to pressure the Soviet authorities to allow Jewish emigration to Israel and to loosen up the statism in the newly decolonised countries. The Carter presidency made it a central plank of its foreign policy in 1977 and thereby gave a powerful boost to the proliferation of non-governmental humanitarian organisations. Funded mainly by the US and west European states, such NGOs were largely oriented to promote civil society, seen as conducive to the individual citizen who would be governed by the inducements of the free market rather than the injunctions of the state.[5] In this assertion of individual rights the defence of property from the state was always implied. It was a programme aimed at shunting aside the nationalist and radical left agenda that had sought to challenge the post-colonial imperial order on the basis of mass mobilisation and collective forms of political action aimed at transforming the economic structures of capitalism. The internationalisation of human rights standards promoted through the proliferation of single-issue advocacy groups, while helping to stifle class politics, has enabled some of these groups to demand that the US and its allies should also abide by the standards they professed to uphold. They salvaged thereby a defensive weapon in a period when leftwing movements were in retreat from bringing about fundamental social and political changes. In the Occupied Territories, a number of human rights groups, at times joined by solidarity activists, provide the international network of human rights organisations a constant flow of documentation on Israel's repression and flouting of international law. The use of collective punishment; expansion of Jewish settlements; confiscation of Palestinian land on pretexts ranging from security needs to development priorities, and so on, have all been extensively reported on by Palestinian, Israeli and international NGOs, validating Palestinian grievances and putting Israel at odds with international standards on human rights.

With little prospect of the Israeli state abiding by those standards, its rift with the left, in Britain and elsewhere, is set to widen. Its efforts to overcome Palestinian and, regionally, Arab nationalism are taking it down the path of intransigence and militarism. The dynamics of this process is highlighted by Gabi Taub even as he tries to demonstrate the contrary. In what amounts to a plea for Western left-wing and liberal forces to support Israel, Taub claims that mainstream Zionism remains committed to Jewish self-determination on the basis of a democratic, national state and that this position, as the only realistic one, will prevail over the messianic settler movement that is seeking to absorb the Occupied Territories into Israel. Secular Zionism viewed the settlement of land, he states, as a means to establishing a sovereign democratic state for Jews, while for the religious settler movement, 'political sovereignty was always a springboard, an instrument for settlement, which would advance the higher metaphysical purpose of redemption'.[6] The two positions turn out, however, not to be as distinct from one another as Taub implies. Zionism had to construct a collective identity for an immigrant society that had little shared past. The Jewish religious narrative provided the myth of a common heritage centred on the biblical land of Israel, without which Zionism could not claim that its connection to the land was morally superior to that of Palestinians.[7] But Taub sees the settlers' aim of forming *Eretz* Israel in the name of Judaism to be in contradiction with secular Zionism's commitment to Jewish national sovereignty based on democracy.

> The so-called demographic problem – the fear that if Israel stays in the territories Jews will become a minority in Israel too, as they are everywhere else – is also the democratic problem; those who worry about demography worry about it only because they do not dream of changing Israel's democratic character. In the long run, they reason, annexing the territories would force Israel to make a choice between two options, both of which will be an end to Zionism: a Jewish apartheid, where the Arab majority is barred from voting, and a democracy where the Jewish character of the state would be voted down by that Arab majority (it is far from clear that this alternative would remain a democracy).[8]

Taub rejects the view that Israel functions as an ethnic democracy and argues that it will recoil from instituting a system of apartheid in the Occupied Territories because it would represent a radical departure from the principles that the state has hitherto upheld. In Israel, he insists, 'all citizens together constitute "the sovereign," and each have the right to vote and to run for political office, regardless of race, religion, gender, or – strikingly – national identity'.[9] These political entitlements only serve to underline that Taub's citizens have to be restricted to very few rights to sustain his case. Measures which discriminate against the Palestinian minority in Israel range from ones enshrined in laws to those embedded in the regulations and development programmes of government agencies. Some operate indirectly, by restricting certain benefits to military veterans which disqualifies Palestinians because they are not permitted to serve in the armed forces. Others operate through the state's allocation of funds for infrastructure. Palestinian communities 'are almost always excluded from national priority areas and development zones, making it difficult to attract businesses and industry. And, in addition, the state has refused to establish a single new Palestinian community since Israel's founding six decades ago.'[10] The Planning and Building Law of 1965 has been used to depopulate forty Palestinian villages by cutting them off from electricity and other services.[11] The Jewish National Fund, which own 13 per cent of Israeli territory and also supervises the Israel Lands Authority responsible for a further 80 per cent that is owned by the state has been the main instrument for expropriating Palestinian-owned land and restricting the leasing of land to Jews only. In the Negev, which is mainly desert and forms nearly half of Israel's territory, successive governments have sought to move the region's inhabitants, Palestinian Bedouins, who are traditionally pastoralists, into a few restricted areas and to the neighbouring Arab states. Israel has demolished and expropriated Bedouin villages and land on a variety of grounds, such as state security, development purposes and for forestation promoted by the Jewish National Fund.[12]

There is internal consistency and historical continuity in Israel's overall strategy towards the Palestinians, the policies adopted in the Occupied Territories extend those pursued in Israel.[13] Their objective is to concentrate the Palestinians into small enclaves to prevent the emergence of a national entity or, if political circumstances make that impossible, to allow it in a feeble and impoverished form. The charge of ethnic democracy is not misplaced, there are some ominous parallels in Israel's rule over the Palestinians with the South African system of apartheid.[14]

In 2011, Ron Prosor, the Israeli Ambassador to the UK in an interview shortly before leaving to take up a posting at the UN, reflected on Israel's support in Britain: 'In the penthouse – that is to say, on a government level – things are good. There is co-operation, understanding, on issues such as Iran and counter-terrorism. But unfortunately, lower down, there is serious damage and leaking in the basement.'[15] More importantly, most of the basement's inhabitants have moved on.

Notes

1 *Palestine News* (November 1970).
2 Ibid. (October 1972).
3 Ibid. (June 1972).
4 S. Moyne, *The Last Utopia* (Cambridge, MA: The Belknap Press of Harvard University Press, 2010), p. 4.
5 O. Roy, *The Politics of Chaos in the Middle East* (New York: Columbia University Press, 2008), pp. 32–33.
6 G. Taub, *The Settlers, And the Struggle Over the Meaning of Zionism* (London: Yale University Press, 2010), p. 67.
7 On the fictive construction of ancient Israel by the biblical narrative and biblical studies, see K. Whitelam, *The Invention of Ancient Israel* (London: Routledge, 1996); N. Masalha, *The Bible: Invented Traditions, Archaeology and Post-Colonialism in Palestine-Israel* (London: Zed Press, 2007) and S. Sand, *The Invention of the Jewish People* (London: Verso, 2009).
8 Taub, *The Settlers*, p. 13.
9 Ibid., p. 174.
10 J. Cook, *Disappearing Palestine: Israel's Experiments in Human Despair* (London: Zed Books, 2008), p. 38.
11 D. Kirshbaum, 'Israeli Apartheid – A Basic Legal Perspective', Israel Law Resource Centre, 2007, www.geocities.com/savepalestinenow/israellaws/essays/israellaw sessay.htm (accessed 7 January 2011).
12 I. Abu-Sa'ad, 'Forced Sedentarisation, Land Rights and Indigenous Resistance: The Palestinian Bedouin in the Negev', in N. Masalha (ed.), *Catastrophe Remembered* (London: Zed Press, 2005).
13 Z. Sabbagh, 'Palestinian Workers in Israel: labour in a colonial context?' (PhD thesis, Manchester, 1996)
14 See O. Yiftachel, *Ethnocracy* (Philadelphia: University of Pennsylvania Press, 2006).
15 *Jewish Chronicle* (26 May 2011).

Bibliography

Abu-Lughod, I. (ed.), *The Transformation of Palestine* (Evanston: Northwestern University Press, 1971).
Abu-Lughod, L. and A. Sa'di (eds), *Nakba, 1948 and the Claims of Memory* (New York: Columbia University Press, 2007).
Abu-Sa'ad, I., 'Forced Sedentarisation, Land Rights and Indigenous Resistance: The Palestinian Bedouin in the Negev', in N. Masalha (ed.), *Catastrophe Remembered* (London: Zed Press, 2005).
Achcar, G., *Eastern Cauldron* (London: Pluto Press, 2004).
Achcar, G., *The Israeli Dilemma. A Debate Between Two Left-Wing Jews* (London: Merlin Press, 2006).
Achcar, G., *The Arabs and the Holocaust* (London: Saqibooks, 2010).
Adams, M. and C. Mayhew, *Publish It Not ... The Middle East Cover-Up* (London: Longmans, 1975).
Addison, P., *The Road to 1945* (London: Pimlico, 1994).
Alderman, G., *London Jewry and London Politics 1889–1986* (London: Routledge, 1989).
Alderman, G., *Modern British Jewry* (Oxford: Clarendon Press, 1998).
Angell, N. and D. Buxton, *You and the Refugee* (Middlesex: Penguin Books, 1939).
Archer, R. et al., *Out of Apathy* (London: Verso, 1989).
Arendt, H., *Eichmann in Jerusalem* (London: Faber & Faber, 1963).
Arendt, H., *The Jewish Writings* (New York: Shocken Books, 2007).
Aridan, N., *Britain, Israel and Anglo-Jewry 1949–1957* (London: Routledge, 2007).
Aris, A., *The Jews in Business* (London: Jonathan Cape, 1970).
Baram, D., *Disenchantment, the Guardian and Israel* (London: Guardian Books, 2004).
Barker, B. (ed.), *Ramsay MacDonald's Political Writings* (London: Allen Lane, 1972).
Barker, M., *The New Racism: Conservatives and the Ideology of the Tribe* (London: Aletheia Books, 1982).
Barker, R., *Education and Politics 1900–1951* (Oxford: Clarendon Press, 1972).
Barou, N., *The Jews in Work and Trade* (London: Trades Advisory Council, 1948).
Belcher, R. 'A Commentary on the All-Party Parliamentary Inquiry into Antisemitism', March 2007, www.ffipp-uk.org/AS_rpt_070371.doc.
Bellamy, J. and J. Saville (eds), *Dictionary of Labour Biography*, vol .2 (Basingstoke: Macmillan, 1974).
Ben-Gurion, D., *Letters to Paula* (London: Valentine, Mitchell, 1971).
Benin, J., 'The United States-Israel Alliance', in T. Kushner and A. Solomon (eds), *Wrestling With Zion* (New York: Grove Press, 2003).
Bennett, E., 'Lausanne – and After', *Foreign Affairs* (December 1922).

Ben-Porat, A., *Between Class and Nation* (New York: Greenwod Press, 1986).
Bentwich, N., *They Found Refuge* (London: The Cresset Press, 1956).
Berkowitz, M., *Western Jewry and the Zionist Project, 1914–1933* (Cambridge: Cambridge University Press, 1997).
Bermant, C., *Troubled Eden, An Anatomy of British Jewry* (London: Valentine, Mitchell, 1969).
Bernstein, D., 'From Split Labour Market Strategy to Political Co-optation: The Palestine Labour League', *Middle Eastern Studies*, 31:4 (1995), 775–771.
Billig, M., *Banal Nationalism* (London: Sage, 1997).
Black, G., *J.F.S.: A History of the Jewish Free School, London since 1732* (London: Tymseder Publishing, 1998).
Bober, A. (ed.), *The Other Israel: The Radical Case Against Zionism* (New York: Anchor Books, 1972).
Bolchover, R. *British Jewry and the Holocaust* (Cambridge: Cambridge University Press, 1993).
Brand, C.F., *British Labour's Rise to Power* (Stanford: Stanford University Press, 1941).
Brailsford, H.N., *Subject India* (London: Gollancz, 1943).
Brailsford, N.A., *A League of Nations* (London: Headley Brothers, 1917).
Braude, J., 'Jewish Education in Britain Today', in S. Lipman and V. Lipman (eds) *Jewish Life in Britain, 1962–1977* (New York: K.G. Saur, 1981).
Brivati, B., *Hugh Gaitskell* (London: Richard Cohen Books, 1996).
Brook, S., *The Club: the Jews of Modern Britain* (London: Constable, 1989).
Budeiri, M., *The Palestine Communist Party* (London: Ithaca Press, 1979).
Bullock, A., *Life and Times of Ernest Bevin*, vol. 1 (London: Heinemann, 1960).
Bunt, S., *Jewish Youth Work in Britain* (London: Bedford Press Square of the National Council of Social Services, 1975).
Bunzl, M., *Anti-Semitism and Islamophobia: Hatreds Old and New in Europe* (Chicago: Prickly Paradigm Press, 2007).
Carruthers, S., *Winning Hearts and Minds* (London: Leicester University Press, 1995).
Chaumont, J-M., *La concurrence des victimes* (Paris: Editions la Decouverte, 1997).
Childers, E. 'The Worldless Wish: From Citizens to Refugees', in I. Abu-Lughod (ed.), *The Transformation of Palestine* (Evanston: Northwestern University Press, 1971).
Childers, E., *The Road to Suez* (London: MacGibbon and Kee, 1962).
Chomsky, N., *The Fateful Triangle* (London: Pluto Press, 1983).
Cohen, E.H., *Youth Tourism to Israel* (Clevendon: Channel View Publications, 2008).
Cohen, G., 'From "Insuffrable Petty Bourgeois" to Trusted Communist: Jack Gaster, the Revolutionary Policy Committee and the Communist Party', in J. McIlroy, K. Morgan and A. Campbell (eds), *Party People Communist Lives* (London: Lawrence & Wishart, 2001).
Cohen, N., *What's Left?* (London: Harper Perennial, 2007).
Cohen, M.J., *Retreat from the Mandate* (London: Elek, 1978).
Cohen, S.A., *English Zionists and British Jews* (New Jersey: Princeton University Press, 1982).
Conway, E., 'The Future of Jewish Schools', in P. Bander (ed.), *Looking Forward to the Seventies* (Buckinghamshire: Colin Smythie, 1968).
Cook, J. 'Israeli Ads Warn Against Marrying Non-Jews', www.countercurrents.org/cook 080909.htm.
Cook, J., *Disappearing Palestine: Israel's Experiments in Human Despair* (London: Zed Books, 2008).
Crewe, I., 'Is there a "Jewish vote" in Britain', *Patterns of Prejudice*, 18:1 (1984).
Crossman, R., *Palestine Mission* (London: Hamish Hamilton, 1947).
Crossman, R., *A Nation Reborn* (London: Hamish Hamilton, 1960).
Curtis, M., *Unpeople* (London: Vintage, 2004).
Defries, H., *Conservative Party and Attitudes to Jews, 1900–1950* (London: Frank Cass, 2001).
Deutscher, I., 'On the Israeli-Arab War', *New Left Review*, 44 (July-August 1967).

Deutscher, I., *The Non-Jewish Jew* (Oxford: Oxford University Press, 1968).
Dockrill, M. and J. Douglas Gould, *Peace Without Promise, Britain and the Peace Conferences, 1919–1923* (London: Batsford Academic and Educational, 1981).
Donoughue, B. and G.W. Jones, *Herbert Morrison: Portrait of a Politician* (London: Weidenfeld & Nicolson, 1973).
Eaden, J. and D. Renton, *The Communist Party of Great Britain since 1920* (Basington: Palgrave, 2002).
Edmunds, J., 'The Evolution of British Labour Party Policy on Israel from 1967 to the Intifada', *Twentieth Century British History*, 11:1 (2000).
Epstein, L., *British Politics in the Suez Crisis* (London: Pall Mall Press, 1964).
Fejtő, F., *Les Juifs et L'Antisemitisme dans les Pays Communistes* (Paris: Librairie Plon, 1960).
Finkelstein, N., *Beyond Chutzpah* (London: Verso, 2005).
Fischbach, M., *Records of Dispossession* (New York: Columbia University Press, 2003).
Fishman, I. and H. Levy, 'Jewish Education in Great Britain', in J. Gould and S. Esh (eds), *Jewish Life in Modern Britain* (London: Routledge & Kegan Paul, 1964).
Fishman, N. and K. Morgan (eds), *Opening the Books* (London: Pluto, 1995).
Fisk, R., *Pity the Nation* (Oxford: Oxford University Press, 1992).
Flanders, A., 'Rita Hinden', in J. Bellamy and J. Saville (eds), *Dictionary of Labour Biography*, vol. 2 (Basingstoke: Macmillan, 1974).
Foot, M., *Aneurin Bevan, 1945–1960*, vol. 2 (London: Davis-Poynter, 1973).
Franzen, J., 'Communism versus Zionism: The Comintern, Yishuvism, and the Palestine Communist Party', *Journal of Palestine Studies*, 34:2 (2007).
Freedland, J., *Jacob's Gift* (London: Penguin Books, 2006).
Freedman, M. (ed.), *A Minority in Britain* (London: Vallentine, Mitchell and Co., 1955).
General Federation of Jewish Labour, *Documents and Essays, On Jewish Labour Policy in Palestine* (Greenport: Greenwood Press, 1975).
Gershoni, I. and Jankowski, J., *Confronting Fascism in Egypt* (Stanford: Stanford University Press, 2010),
Gewirtz, S., 'Anti-Fascist Activity in Manchester's Jewish Community in the 1930s'. *Manchester Region History Review*, 4:1 (1990).
Ginzberg, J., 'Sympathy and Resentment, Jew and Coloureds in London's East End', *Patterns of Prejudice*, 13:2–3 (1979).
Glasneck, J., 'Die Internazionale Sozialdemokratie und die Zionistische Palastina-Kolonisation in den Jahren 1929/30', *Wissenschaftliche Zeitschrift der Martin Luther Universitat*, 26:4 (1977).
Glazer, S., 'Picketing for Hebrew Labour: A Window on Histadrut Tactics and Strategy', *Journal of Palestine Studies*, 30:4 (2001).
Gollancz, V., *Let My People Go* (London: Gollancz, 1942).
Gordon, N., *Israel's Occupation* (Berkeley: University of California Press, 2008).
Gorny, Y., *The British Labour Movement and Zionism* (London: Frank Cass, 1983).
Goodman, P., *Zionism in England, 1899–1929* (London: English Zionist Federation, 1929).
Graves, P., *Labour Women: Women in British Working-Class Politics 1918–1939* (Cambridge: Cambridge University Press, 1994).
Greenstein, R., 'Class, Nation and Political Organisation: The Anti-Zionist Left in Israel/Palestine', *International Labour and Working-Class History*, 75 (Spring 2009).
Grizzard, N. and P. Raisman, 'Inner City Jews in Leeds', *Journal of Jewish Sociology*, 22:1 (1980).
Grodzinsky, Y., *In the Shadow of the Holocaust* (Monroe: Common Courage Press, 2004).
Győri Szabó, R., *A kommunizmus és a zsidóság az 1945 utáni Magyarországon* [Communism and Jews in post-1945 Hungary] (Budapest: Gondolat, 2009).
Hanieh, A., 'From State-Led Growth to Globalization: the Evolution of Israeli Capitalism',

Journal of Palestine Studies, 32:4 (2003).
Harrison, E., 'The Treatment of Displaced Jews in the United States Zone of Occupation in Germany, 1945', www.ess.uwe.ac.uk/documents/harrison_report.htm.
Hass, A., *Drinking the Sea at Gaza* (New York: Metropolitan Books, 1999).
Haseler, S., *The Gateskelites: Revisionism in the British Labour Party, 1951–1964* (London: Macmillan, 1969).
Healey, D., *Cards on the Table, An Interpretation of Labour's Foreign Policy* (London: Labour Party, 1948).
Henriques, R., *Survey of Jewish Interests* (Bedford: Rush and Warwick, 1949).
Heppell, J., 'A Question of "Jewish Politics"? The Jewish Section of the Communist Party of Great Britain 1936-1945', in C. Collette and S. Bird (eds), *Jews, Labour and the Left* (Aldershot: Ashgate, 2000).
Herschon, C., *To Make Them English* (Bristol: Palavas Press, 1983).
Hirst, D., *The Gun and the Olive Branch* (London: Faber and Faber, 1977).
Hirst, D., *Beware of Small States* (London: Faber and Faber, 2010).
Hobson, J.A., *Imperialism, A Study* (London: Allen & Unwin, 1961).
Hodgkin, T., *Letters from Palestine 1932–1936* (London: Quartet, 1986).
Hope Simpson, Sir J., *The Refugee Problem, Report of a Survey* (London: Oxford University Press, 1939).
Hourani, A., 'The Case Against A Jewish State in Palestine: Albert Hourani's Statement to the Anglo-American Committee of Inquiry of 1946', *Journal of Palestine Studies*, 35:1 (August 2005).
Howard, A., *Crossman* (London: Jonathan Cape, 1990).
Howe, S., *Anticolonialism in British Politics* (Oxford: Clarendon Press, 1993).
Hyamson, A., 'A Letter from London', *Contemporary Jewish Record*, 6:5 (October 1943).
Iganski, P., V. Kielinger, S. Paterson, *Hate Crimes Against London's Jews* (London: Institute for Jewish Policy Research, 2005).
J.B. 'The Class Character of the Palestine Rising' Pts.1 and 2, *Labour Monthly*, 12:3 and 4 (1930).
Jacobs, J., *Out of the Ghetto* (London: Calverts North Star Press, 1978).
James, L., *The Making and Unmaking of British India* (London: Abacus, 1998)
Jiryis, S., *The Arabs in Israel* (New York: Monthly Review Press, 1976).
Jones, M., 'Israel, Palestine and Socialism', *Socialist Register* 1970.
Judt, T., *Postwar: A History of Europe Since 1945* (London: Pimlico, 2007)
Julius, A., *Trials of the Diaspora* (Oxford: Oxford University Press, 2010).
Kapeliouk, A., *Israel: la fin des myths* (Paris: Albin Michel, 1975).
Kaplansky, S., *The Jews and the War* (The Hague: Poale Zion, 1916).
Kaplansky, S., 'Jews and Arabs in Palestine', *Socialist Review* (March 1922).
Karmi, G., *In Search of Fatima* (London: Verso, 2002).
Kaufman, G., *To Build the Promised Land* (London: Weidenfeld and Nicholson, 1973).
Khalidi, W., *Palestine Reborn* (London: I.B. Tauris, 1992).
Khoury, F., *The Arab Israeli Dilemma* (New York: Syracuse University Press, 1976).
Kimmerling, B., *Zionism and Territory: the Socio-Territorial Dimensions of Zionist Politics* (Berkeley: University of California Press, 1983).
Kimmerling, B., *Zionism and Economy* (Cambridge: MA: Schenkman Publishing Company, 1983).
Kimmerling, B., 'From Barak to Road Map', *New Left Review*, 23, 2nd Series (September-October 2003).
Kingston, P.W.T., *Britain and the Politics of Modernization on the Middle East 1945–1958* (Cambridge: Cambridge University Press, 2002).
Kirisci, K., *The PLO and World Politics* (London: Frances Pinter, 1986).

Kirshbaum, D., 'Israeli Apartheid – A Basic Legal Perspective', Israel Law Resource Centre (2007), www.geocities.com/savepalestinenow/israellaws/ essays/israellawsessay.htm.

Kishtainy, K. *The New Statesman and the Middle East* (Beirut: Palestine Research Centre, 1972).

Klug, B., 'Is Europe a Lost Cause? The European debate on antisemitism and the Middle East conflict', *Patterns of Prejudice*, 39:1 (2005).

Kochavi, A., *Post-Holocaust Politics: Britain, the United States and Jewish Refugees* (Chapel Hill: University of North Carolina Press, 2001).

Kosmin, B., A. Lerman and J. Goldberg, *The Attachment of British Jews to Israel* (Institute for Jewish Policy Research, 1997).

Krausz, E., 'The Economic and Social Structure of Anglo-Jewry', in J. Gould and S. Esh (eds), *Jewish Life in Modern Britain* (London: Routledge and Kegan Paul, 1964)

Krausz, E., *Leeds Jewry* (Cambridge: The Jewish Historical Society of England, 1964).

Krausz, E., 'The Edgware Survey: Occupation and Social Class', *The Jewish Journal of Sociology*, 11:1 (1969).

Krausz, E., 'The Edgware Survey: Factors in Jewish Identification', *The Jewish Journal of Sociology*, 11:2 (1969).

Kushner T. and K. Lunn (eds), *Traditions of Intolerance, Historical Perspectives on Fascism and Race Discourse in Britain* (Manchester: Manchester University Press, 1989).

Kushner, T., *The Holocaust and the Liberal Imagination* (Oxford: Blackwell, 1994).

Kushner T. and A. Solomon (eds), *Wrestling With Zion* (New York: Grove Press, 2003).

Labour Party, *War Aims Memorandum* (London: Labour Party, 1917).

Labour Party, *Handbook for Speakers 1948–49* (London: Labour Party, 1948)

Labour Party, *Labour's Foreign Policy* (London: Labour Party Publications, 1952).

Labour Party, *Labour's Programme, 1976* (London: Labour Party, 1976)

Labour Party, *New Hope for Britain* (London: Labour Party, 1983).

Labour Party, *Meet the Challenge, Make the Change* (London: Labour Party, 1988).

Laqueur, W., *The Changing Face of Antisemitism* (Oxford: Oxford University Press, 2006).

Leach, D., 'Explosion at the King David Hotel', in M. Sissons and P. French (eds), *Age of Austerity* (Harmondsworth: Penguin Books, 1964).

Lenczowski, G., *American Presidents and the Middle East* (Durham: Duke University Press, 1992).

Levenberg, S., 'Zionism in British Politics' in P. Goodman (ed.), *The Jewish National Home* (London: J. Dent and Sons, 1943)

Levenberg, S., *The Jews and Palestine: A Study in Labour Zionism* (London: Poale Zion, 1945).

Levy, M.A., *Question of Honour* (London: Simon and Schuster, 2008).

Liebman, M., 'Israel, Palestine and Zionism', *Socialist Register*, 1970.

Lipman, V., *A Century of Social Service, 1859–1959* (London: RKP, 1959).

Lockman, Z., *Comrades and Enemies, Arabs and Jewish Workers in Palestine, 1906–1948* (Berkeley: University of California Press, 1996).

Lorwin, L., *Labour and Internationalism* (London: Allen and Unwin, 1929).

London, L., *Whitehall and the Jews, 1933–1948* (Cambridge: Cambridge University Press, 2003).

Louis, Wm. R., *The British Empire in the Middle East 1945–1951* (Oxford: Clarendon Press, 1984).

Lucas, N., *Modern History of Israel* (London: Weidenfeld and Nicholson, 1974).

Lustick, I., *Arabs in a Jewish State* (Austin: University of Texas Press, 1980).

MacDonald, J.R., *A Socialist in Palestine* (London: Poale Zion, 1922).

MacDonald, J.R., 'Labour and International Relations' Address delivered on 24 November 1917 at the Annual Conference of the Derby and District ILP Federation (Derby and District Federation, 1917).

MacKenzie, J. and N. (eds), *The Diary of Beatrice Webb*, vol. 4 (London: Virago, 1985).

MacKenzie, N., *The Letters of Sidney and Beatrice Webb*, vol. 3 (Cambridge: Cambridge University Press, 1978).
Mackey, S., *Mirror of the Arab World* (New York: W.W. Norton & Co., 2009).
MacShane, D., *Globalising Hatred, the New Antisemtism* (London: Phoenix, 2009).
MacIntyre, S., *Imperialism and the British Labour Movement in the 1920s*, Pamphlet No. 64, Our History (London: CPGB, Autumn 1975).
MacIntyre, S., 'Socialism, the Unions and the Labour Party', *Bulletin of the Society for the Study of Labour History*, 31 (Autumn 1975).
Manela, E., *The Wilsonian Moment* (Oxford: Oxford University Press, 2007).
Masalha, N., *Expulsion of the Palestinians: The Concept of 'Transfer' in Zionist Political Thought, 1882–1948* (London: I.B. Tauris, 1992).
Masalha, N., *A Land Without a People* (London: Faber & Faber, 1997).
Masalha, N., *The Bible: Invented Traditions, Archaeology and Post-Colonialism in Palestine-Israel* (London: Zed Press, 2007).
Mayer, A., *Wilson vs. Lenin, Political Origins of the New Diplomacy 1917–1918* (New York: Vinatge Books, 1970).
McCarthy, J., *The Population of Palestine* (New York: Columbia University Press, 1988).
McCurdy, C., *A Clean Peace* (London: W.H. Smith & Son, 1918).
McDermott, K. and J. Agnew, *Comintern: A History of International Communism from Lenin to Stalin* (Basingstoke: Macmillan, 1996).
Miller, R., *Divided Against Zion* (London: Frank Cass, 2000).
Miller, R., 'The Other Side of the Coin: Arab Propaganda and the Battle Against Zionism in London, 1937–48', in E. Karsh (ed.), *Israel's Transition from Community to State* (London: Frank Cass, 1999).
Minkin, L., *The Contentious Alliance* (Edinburgh: Edinburgh University Press, 1991).
Monroe, E., 'The Arab-Israel Frontier', *International Affairs*, 29:4.
Moore, K., P. Mason, and J. Lewis, *Images of Islam in the UK* (Cardiff: Cardiff School of Journalism, Media and Cultural Studies, 2008).
Morgan, K. 'The Communist Party and the Daily Worker 1930–1956' in G. Andrews, K. Morgan, G. Cohen and A. Flinn, *Communists and British Society 1920–1921* (London: Rivers Oran Press, 2007).
Morgan, K. and A. Campbell (eds), *Party People Communist Lives* (London: Lawrence & Wishart, 2001).
Morris, B., 'The Crystallization of Israeli Policy Against a Return of the Arab Refugees: April–December, 1948', *Studies in Zionism*, 6:1 (1985).
Morris, B., *Righteous Victims* (New York: Vintage Books, 2001).
Morris, B., *The Birth of the Palestinian Refugee Problem Revisited* (Cambridge: Cambridge University Press, 2004).
Morris, B., *Israel's Border Wars* (Oxford: Oxford University Press, 2005).
Moyne, S., *The Last Utopia* (Cambridge, MA: The Belknap Press of Harvard University Press, 2010).
Nachmani, A., *Great Powers Discord in Palestine* (London: Frank Cass, 1987).
Neustatter, H. 'Demographic and Other Statistical Aspects of Anglo-Jewry', in M. Freedman (ed.), *A Minority in Britain* (London: Vallentine, Mitchell & Co., 1955).
Newman, M., *Ralph Miliband and the Politics of the New Left* (London: The Merlin Press, 2002).
Norris, J., 'Repression and Rebellion: Britain's Response to the Arab Revolt in Palestine of 1936–39', *Journal of Imperial and Commonwealth History*, 36:1 (2008).
Northedge, F.S., 'Britain and the Middle East', in R. Ovendale (ed.) *The Foreign Policy of the British Labour Government* (Leicester: Leicester University Press, 1984).
Orwell, G., 'Antisemitism in Britain', *Contemporary Jewish Record*, 8:2 (April 1945).

Owen, N., *The British Left and India, Metropolitan Anti-Imperialism* (Oxford: Oxford University Press, 2007).
Pappe, I., *Britain and the Israeli Conflict* (Basingstoke: Macmillan, 1988).
Pappe, I., *The Ethnic Cleansing Of Palestine* (Oxford: Oneworld, 2006).
Pattison, W. K., 'The Delayed British Recognition of Israel', *Middle East Journal*, 37:3 (1983).
Paul, K., *Whitewashing Britain, Race and Citizenship in the Postwar Era* (Ithaca: Cornell University Press, 1997).
Peace, T., 'Un antisemtisme nouveau? The debate about a "new anti-Semitism" in France', *Patterns of Prejudice*, 43:2 (May 2009).
Pedersen, S., *Eleanor Rathbone and the Politics of Conscience* (New Haven: Yale University Press, 2004).
Pelling, H., *The British Communist Party* (London: A. and C. Black, 1975).
Peretz, D., 'Problems of Arab Refugee Compensation', *Middle East Journal*, 8:4 (1954).
Peretz, D., *Israel and the Palestine Arabs* (Washington: The Middle East Institute, 1958).
Pickard, J., 'Middle East Crisis', *Militant International Review*, 17 (Winter 1979).
Piratin, P., *For Peace in Palestine* (London: CPGB, 1946).
Porter, B., *Critics of Empire* (London: Macmillan, 1968).
Ramelson, B., *The Middle East, Crisis: Causes, Solution* (London: Central Books, 1967).
Rathbone, E., *Rescue the Perishing* (London: National Committee for the Rescue of Jews from Nazi Terror, June 1943).
Reberioux M. and G. Haupt, 'L'attitude de l'Internationale', *Le Movement Sociale*, 45 (October 1963).
Reid, A. and H. Pelling, *A Short History of the Labour Party* (Basingstoke: Palgrave, 2005)
Rennap, I., *Anti-Semitism and the Jewish Question* (London: Lawrence & Wishart, 1942).
Report of the All-Party Parliamentary Inquiry Into Antisemitism (London: Stationary Office, 2006).
Reynolds, R., *Beware of Africans* (London: Jarrolds 1955).
Royal Commission Report, *Palestine*, Cmd. 5479, (London: HMS, 1937).
Rigby, A., *Living the Intifada* (London: Zed Books, 1991).
Rose, E., *Colour and Citizenship, A Report on British Race Relations* (London: Oxford University Press, 1969).
Rose, H. and S. Rose, 'Israel, Europe and the academic boycott', *Race & Class*, 50:1 (2008).
Rose, N. (ed.), *Baffy, the Diaries of Blanche Dugdale, 1936–1947* (London: Valentine, Mitchell, 1973).
Rosen, H., *Are You Still Circumcised? East End Memories* (Nottingham: Five Leaves Publication, 1999).
Roth, C., 'Postscript from London', *Contemporary Jewish Record*, 8:1 (1945).
Roy, O., *Globalised Islam* (London: Hurst & Company, 2002).
Roy, O., *The Politics of Chaos in the Middle East* (New York: Columbia University Press, 2008).
Rubinstein, W.D., 'Zionism and the Jewish People, 1918–1960: From Minority to Hegemony', *The Jewish Journal of Sociology*, 43:1&2 (2001).
Royal Commission, *Immigration, Land Settlement and Development in Palestine (Hope Simpson) Report*, Cmd. 3686 (London: HMSO, 1930).
Sa'di, A., 'Modernization as an Explanatory Discourse of Zionist-Palestinian Relations', *British Journal of Middle East Studies*, 24:1 (1997).
Samuel, R., 'Staying Power: the Lost World of British Communism', *New Left Review*, 156, (March/April 1986).
Samidei, M. 'Les Socialistes francais et le probleme colonial entre les deux guerres, 1919–1939', *Revue francaise du science politique*.
Said, E., *The Question of Palestine* (London: Vintage, 1982).
Sand, S., *The Invention of the Jewish People* (London: Verso, 2009).
Sayigh, R., *Palestinians: From Peasants to Revolutionaries* (London: Zed Press, 1991).

Schor, R., L'opinion francaise et les étrangers en France, 1919–1939 (Paris: Publication de la Sorbonne, 1985).

Segev, T., The Seventh Million (New York: Hill and Wang, 1993).

Seyd, P., The Rise and Fall of the Labour Left (Basingstoke: Macmillan, 1987).

Shafir, G., Land, Labour and the Origins of the Israeli-Palestinian Conflict 1882–1914 (Berkeley: University of California Press, 1996).

Shalev, M., Labour and the Political Economy of Israel (Oxford: OUP, 1992).

Shalev, M., 'Time for Theory: Critical Notes on Lissak and Sternhell', Israeli Studies, 1:2 (1996).

Shalev, M., 'Jewish Organised Labour and the Palestinians: A Study of State/Society Relations in Israel', in B. Kimmerling (ed.), The Israeli State and Society, Boundaries and Frontiers (New York: State University of New York, 1989).

Shapiro, Y., The Formative Years of the Israel Labour Party (London: Sage, 1976).

Shaw, E., Discipline and Discord in the Labour Party (Manchester: Manchester University Press, 1988).

Sheffer, G., 'Intentions and Results of British Policy in Palestine: Passfield's White Paper', Middle Eastern Studies, 9:1 (1973).

Shepherd, N., Ploughing the Sand: British Rule in Palestine 1917–1948 (London: John Murray, 1999).

Sherman, A.J., Island Refuge (London: Paul Elek, 1973).

Shimoni, G., 'Poale-Zion: A Zionist Transplant in Britain', in P. Medding (ed.), Studies in Contemporary Jewry, vol. 2 (London: Bloomington University Press, 1986).

Shlaim, A., Collusion Across the Jordan (Oxford: Clarendon Press, 1988).

Shlaim, A., The Iron Wall (London: Penguin Books, 2000).

Silberklang, D., 'Jewish Politics and Rescue: The Founding of the Council for German Jewry', Holocaust and Genocide Studies, 7:3 (1993).

Silverstein, P., 'The context of antisemitism and Islamophobia in France', Patterns of Prejudice, 41:1 (2008).

Simons, C., International Proposals to Transfer Arabs from Palestine, 1895–1947 (New Jersey: Tavistock Publishing House, 1988).

Smith, B., The Roots of Separatism (London: I.B. Tauris, 1993).

Srebrnik, H., London Jews and British Communism 1935–1945 (Ilford: Valentine Mitchell, 1995).

Srebrnik, H. 'Sidestepping the Contradictions: the Communist Party, Jewish Communists and Zionism 1935–48', in G. Andrews, N. Fishman and K. Morgan (eds) Opening the Books: Essays on the Cultural and Social History of British Communism (London: Pluto, 1995).

Sternhell, Z., The Founding Myths of Israel (Princeton: Princeton University Press, 1997).

Stevens, R., American Zionism and U.S. Foreign Policy (New York: Pageant Press, 1962).

Strizhov, I. 'The Soviet Position on the Establishment of the State Of Israel', in Y. Ro'i (ed.) Jews and Jewish Life in Russia and the Soviet Union (Essex: Frank Cass, 1995).

Summerskill, E., A Woman's World (London: Heinemann, 1967).

Taub, G., The Settlers, And the Struggle Over the Meaning of Zionism (London: Yale University Press, 2010).

Taylor, A.J.P., The Trouble Makers (London: Hamilton, 1957).

Thorpe, A., 'The Membership of the Communist Party of Great Britain, 1920–1945', The Historical Journal, 43:3 (2000).

Townshend, J., 'J. A. Hobson: Anti-Imperialist?', International Review of History and Political Science, 19:2 (1982).

Trabulsi, F., 'The Palestine Problem: Zionism and Imperialism in the Middle East', New Left Review, 57 (1969).

Truman, H., Memoirs of Harry S. Truman, vol. 2, (New York: Da Capo Press, 1956).

Visram, R., Asians in Britain, 400 Years of History (London: Pluto Press, 2002).

Vandervelde, E., *Le pays d'Israel* (Paris: Rider, 1929).
Valins, O., B. Kosmin and J. Goldberg, *The Future of Jewish Schooling in the United Kingdom* (Institute of Jewish Policy Research (2002), www.jpr.org.uk.
Wainwright, H., *A Tale of Two Parties* (London: Hogarth Press, 1987).
Wasserstein, B., *The British in Palestine* (London: Royal Historical Society, 1978).
Wasserstein, B., *Britain and the Jews of Europe, 1939–1945* (Oxford: Oxford University Press, 1979).
Wasserstein, B., *Vanishing Diaspora* (Cambridge: Harvard University Press, 1996).
Watkins, D., *Seventeen Years in Obscurity: Memoirs of a Backbencher* (Sussex: The Book Guild, 1996).
Wedgwood, J.C., *The Seventh Dominion* (London: The Labour Publishing Company, 1928).
Weizmann, C. 'Palestine's Role in the Solution of the Jewish Problem', *Foreign Affairs*, 20:2 (January 1942).
Weizmann, C., *Trial and Error* (London: Hamish Hamilton, 1949).
Weizmann, C., *Letters and Papers*, Series A, vols 5 and 7 (Oxford: Oxford University Press, 1975).
Weizmann, C., *Letters and Papers*, Series A, vols 8, 12, 14, 17 (New Brunswick: Transaction Books, 1977).
Whitelam, K., *The Invention of Ancient Israel* (London: Routledge, 1996).
Wieviorka, M., *La Tentation Antisémite* (Paris: Robert Laffont, 2005).
Wieviorka, M., *L'Antisémitisme est-il de retour?* (Paris: Larousse, 2008).
Wildangel, R. '"Der größte Feind der Menscheit". Der National sozialismus in der arabischen öffentlichen Meinung in Pälestina während des Zweiten Weltkrieges', in G. Höpp, P. Wien and R. Wildangel (eds), *Blind für Geschichte?* (Berlin: Klaus Schwarz Verlag, 2004).
Williams, B., *Manchester Jewry* (Manchester: Archives Publications, 1988).
Williams, B., '"East and West": Class and Community in Manchester Jewry, 1850–1914', in D. Cesarani (ed.), *The Making of Modern Anglo-Jewry* (London: Blackwell, 1990).
Williams, B., *Michael Fidler (1916–1989), A Study in Leadership* (Stockport: R. & D. Graphics, 1997).
Williams, B., *Sir Sidney Hamburger and Manchester Jewry* (London: Valentine Mitchell, 1999).
Winter, J.M., 'The Webbs and the Non-White World: A Case of Socialist Racialism', *Journal of Contemporary History*, 9:1 (1974).
Wistrich, R., 'Anti-Zionism and anti-Semitism', *Jewish Political Studies Review*, 16:3–4 (2004).
Wolf, L., *Essays in Jewish History* (London: The Jewish Historical Society of England, 1934).
Wyatt, W., *The Jews at Home* (London: A Tribune Pamphlet, 1950).
Zertal, I., *Israel's Holocaust and the Politics of Nationhood* (Cambridge: Cambridge University Press, 2005).
Zertal, I. and A. Eldar, *Lords of the Land* (New York: Nation Books, 2007).
Zureik, E., *The Palestinians in Israel* (London: Routledge & Kegan Paul, 1979).

Newspapers

Black Dwarf
Bulletin of the Labour and Socialist International
Bulletin, Comité Socialist pour la Palestine Ouvrière
The Call
Communist Review
Contemporary Jewish Record
The Daily Herald
The Daily Telegraph

Daily Worker
East London Advertiser
The Economist
The Guardian
The Herald
Inprecor
Jerusalem Post
Jewish Chronicle
The Jewish Clarion
Jewish Labour
Jewish Observer and Middle East Review
Jewish Vanguard
Labour Leader
The Manchester Guardian
The Morning Star
Labour Weekly
London Briefing
New Leader
New Left Review
New Statesman
The New York Review of Books
The Observer
Palestine News
Prospect Magazine
The Spectator
Socialist Worker
Socialist Commentary
South Africa Jewish Frontier,
Sozialistische Monatshefte
Sunday Independent
Sunday Telegraph
The Times
Tribune
World News and Views
The Zionist Review

Archives

Charles Ashbee Memoirs, National Art Library, Victoria and Albert Museum
Braunthal Papers. Institute of Social History, Amsterdam
Reginald Bridgeman Papers, Hull University Library
Council for Arab British Understanding, Labour Middle East Council
CPGB Papers, Manchester People's History Museum
CO 733 and CO 935 Colonial Office, National Archives
A. Creech Jones Papers, Rhodes House, Oxford University
Andrew Faulds Papers, British Library of Political and Economic Science, London School of Economics
Victor Gollancz Papers, Modern Records Centre, University of Warwick Library
FO371 Foreign Office, National Archives
India Office Collections, Public and Judicial Department, British Library

Labour Party Archive (LPA), Manchester People's History Museum
Schneier Levenberg Papers, British Library of Political and Economic Science,
    John Mendelson Papers, Sheffield Archives
J. Ramsay MacDonald Papers, National Archives
J. Ramsay MacDonald Papers, John Rylands Library, Deansgate, Manchester University.
Mass Observation, University of Sussex
V. K. Krishna Menon Papers, Nehru Memorial Museum and Library, Delhi
Ralph Miliband Papers, Leeds University
Palestine Protest Committee, Central Zionist Archives, Jerusalem
Papers of the Federation of Women Zionists, London Metropolitan Archives
Papers of the TUC, Modern Records Centre, University of Warwick Library
Papers of the Transport and General Workers' Union, Modern Records Centre, University of Warwick Library
Passfield Papers, British Library of Political and Economic Science
Beatrice Webb Diaries, British Library of Political and Economic Science
Zaidman Papers, Sheffield University

Theses

Cesarani, D., 'Zionism in England, 1917–1939', DPhil dissertation, University of Oxford, 1986.
Colbenson, P., 'British Socialism and anti-semitism, 1884–1914', PhD thesis, Georgia State University, 1979.
Farrow, R., 'An Examination and Analysis of the Operations of the Jordanian Branch of the United Nations Relief and Works Agency for Palestinian Refugees in the Near East', PhD thesis, University of Manchester, 2002.
Sabbagh, Z., 'Palestinian Workers in Israel: labour in a colonial context?', PhD thesis, University of Manchester, 1996.
Sargent, A., 'The British Labour Party and Palestine 1917–1949', PhD thesis, Nottingham University, 1980.

Index

Achcar, Gilbert 195
Adams, Michael 161
Alexander, Sam 97
Allon Plan 164
American Friends' Service Committee 135
Angell, Norman 16, 62
Anglo-American Committee of Inquiry 100, 114, 118–119, 136
    report of 117, 120
Anti-Apartheid Movement (AAM) 152, 204
anti-semitism 5, 11, 33, 49, 54, 57–58, 67, 71, 75, 97, 106, 111, 142–143, 186–188, 191, 193–194, 199
anti-Zionism 2, 35, 94, 100, 190–191, 199
Anti-Zionist Network 190
Arab
    general strike 30–31, 90
    Higher Committee 30, 32, 90, 92
    Liberation Army 105
    nationalism 152, 157–158, 205
    Rebellion (1936–1939) 30, 32, 91–94
Arafat, Yasser 158, 165, 198
Arendt, Hannah 1, 113
Arnot, Page 60
Ashbee, Charles 20
Atiyah, Edward 126
Attlee, Clement 24, 114, 121, 134
Avineri, Shlomo 41n100

Bakstansky, Lavy 74

Balfour Declaration 5, 11–12, 20–21, 33, 35, 116, 157
Baram, Daphna 161
Bedouins 18, 85n214, 89, 206
Begin, Menachem 165–166, 169–170, 174, 178
Ben-Gurion, David 1, 24, 28, 31, 34, 55, 58, 69, 96, 103, 106, 125, 141
Benn, Tony 167
Bentwich, Norman 30, 35
Bermant, Chaim 45, 53, 66, 74, 77, 166
Bernstein, Eduard 25
Bevan, Aneurin 139, 141–142, 149n179
Bevanites 140
Bevin, Ernest 100, 111, 114, 119, 122–126, 128–129, 131, 133–134, 140
Black Dwarf 159
Black September 169
Blair, Tony 2, 179, 184n161
Blum, Leon 30, 58
Board of Jewish Deputies 29, 44, 47, 53–54, 63, 72–73
Bolchover, Richard 61
Bourj al-Barajneh 170
Brailsford, Henry Noel 13–14, 16, 37
Bramley, Ted 93
British Communist Party *see* Communist Party of Great Britain
British National Party (BNP) 196
British Red Cross 127
British Socialist Party 12
British Union of Fascists (BUF) 29, 50, 54, 61, 88
Brit Shalom 30

Brodetsky, Selig 29, 53–54, 64
Brown, George 140, 151
Brown, Gordon 179
Bund, the 49, 120
Bunzl, Matt 193
Burrows, Herbert 17
Buxton, Charles 14, 16
Buxton, Dorothy 62

Callaghan, James 165
Campaign for Nuclear Disarmament (CND) 152, 174
Cardiff School of Journalism 196
Carrington, Lord 182n85
Carter, President Jimmy 204
Central British Fund for German Jewry (CBF) 55–56
Chancellor, Sir John 19
Chapple, Frank 175
Chaumont, Jean-Michel 199
Chomsky, Noam 173
Churchill, Winston 35, 126
Cilento, Sir Raphael 104, 126
Citrine, Walter 130
Cliff, Tony 29
Cockburn, Alexander 177
Cohen, Nick 185
Cohen, Stuart 46
Comintern 86, 89, 90, 93
Communist Party of Great Britain (CPGB) 2, 13, 29, 33, 60–61, 68, 70, 86, 88, 93–95, 102, 105–106, 111, 126, 151–152, 158–159
  Central Committee 91, 93–94, 102–103
  Jewish membership of 98
  National Jewish Committee 64, 70, 87, 92, 97, 99, 101
Community Security Trust (CST) 188–189
Confederation Generale du Travail (CGT) 57
Conservative Friends of Israel 47
Conservative Party 5, 45, 47, 59, 134, 165, 192
Co-operative movement 60
Cox, Idris 159
Creech Jones, Arthur 5, 31, 95, 123
Cripps, Sir Stafford 32
Crossman, Richard 5, 113, 115, 117–119, 121, 124–126, 132, 137–138, 142–144, 148n153, 162

Daily Herald 31–2, 91, 125, 133
Daily Worker 33, 60, 90, 92, 95, 103, 105
Dalton, Hugh 36–38, 133, 135
Dayan, Moshe 51
Deakin, Arthur 129
Deir Yassin 125
Deutscher, Isaac 152–154
Displaced Persons (DPs) 67, 71, 99–100, 111, 113–116, 119–120
Dublansky, Israel 49
Dundee District Council 168
Dutt, Palme 95, 99, 100

Eakes, Louis 160
East End 22, 44–45, 50, 52–53, 68, 70, 87–88, 95, 97
Easterman, A.L. 31
Eban, Abba 143
Edelman, Maurice 162
Eden, Anthony 63, 134–135, 140
Edmead, Frank 161
Electronic, Telecommunication and Plumbing Union (EETPU) 176
Engage 191
English Defence League (EDL) 196
English Zionist Federation (EZF) 4, 6, 23, 30, 46–48, 52–54, 59, 65–66, 69, 71–72, 74, 76–77, 97, 182
Eretz Israel 166
Eshkol, Levi 150–151, 164–165
European Union Monitoring Centre on Racism and Xenophobia (EUMC) 187, 199

Fabian Colonial Bureau 123
Fabians 12
Fatah 158
Faulds, Andrew 162
Federation of Jewish Youth Societies 47
Federation of Women Zionists (FWZ) 48, 65–67, 74–75
Fidler, Michael 46–47
Fire Brigades Union (FBU) 171, 175–176
First, Ruth 204
Fischbach, Michael 147n126
Fisk, Robert 171

Foot, Michael 6, 32, 119, 121, 141–142, 151, 162, 171
Freedman, Maurice 69
Free Palestine 160
Freeson, Reg 168, 179

Gaitskell, Hugh 134, 139, 141
Gallacher, William 98
Galloway, George 168
Gallup Poll 63
Gaster, Jack 98, 100–102
Gaza 127, 138–139, 143, 150, 158, 161, 164–166, 173, 175, 177–178, 203
Gemayel, Bashir 170
Gillies, William 58
Golan Heights 150, 165, 178
Gollancz, Victor 132
Gorny, Joseph 7
Greater London Council (GLC) 167
Greenwood, Arthur 115, 139
Greenwood, Tony 168
Gromyko, Andrei 100–101
Guardian, the 11, 125, 127, 161, 185
Gush Emunim 164, 166
Gyori Szabo, Robert 110n110

Hacohen, David 29
Haganah 26, 102, 104, 106, 125
Hamas 198
Hamburger, Sidney 46
Harrison, Earl 114
Hashomer Hatzair 29, 106, 115
Hawatmeh, Nayef 158
Healey, Denis 122, 167, 172, 185
Hebrew labour campaign *see* boycott of Arab labour; Histadrut
Heffer, Eric 151, 163, 167, 174
Henderson, Arthur 13, 23
Henriquez, Basil 50, 79n41
Herald, the 12
Herzl, Theodor 8, 36, 51
Hetherington, Alastair 161
Hezbollah 198
Hinden, Rita 123
Histadrut 7, 18, 22–24, 28–30, 36–37, 89–90, 95–96, 102, 125, 133, 137–139, 154, 175–176
and boycott of Arab labour 19, 22, 24, 28–31, 35–36, 92–93, 95, 102
Hobson, J.A. 14

Hodgkin, Thomas 91–93
Holocaust 1, 36–37, 154, 194, 199
Hope Simpson, Sir John 19–20, 22, 59, 121
report of 19, 21, 28
Hourani, Albert 118, 126, 136
Howard, Michael 192
Hoz, Dov 25, 27
Hussein, King of Jordan 159, 165, 169, 182
Hyamson, Alfred 65

ICM poll 192–193
Igansky, Paul 188
Independent Labour Party (ILP) 12–13, 18, 27, 130
India League 5–6
International Committee of the Red Cross 163, 203
International Marxist Group (IMG) 167
Intifada 177–178, 188
Irgun 69, 111, 121, 125, 165
Islamophobia 193, 196
Israel 2, 9, 69, 71–75, 77–78, 103
Israeli
 army 105, 138, 170, 204
 government 164–165, 193
 Labour Party 69, 143, 165–166, 169, 172–174, 176–179
 League of Human Rights 204
 military administration 136
 occupation 163, 186
 policy 2, 105, 163, 197
Israeli Socialist Organisation (ISO) *see* Matzpen

Jacobs, Joe 95
Janner, Barnet 138
Jewish Chronicle 17, 28, 30, 50–51, 55, 64, 72–73, 75–76, 111, 133, 166, 169, 171, 174
Jewish Clarion 97
Jewish
 Agency 23, 114
 attitude to black community 73–74
 charity organisations 44
 community in Britain 44, 54, 64–65, 69–71, 73–74, 76, 86–87, 94, 99, 106, 113, 132, 178–179
 communists 54, 98
 DPs *see* Displaced Persons

Lads' Brigade 50
embourgeoisement 8
immigrants 44, 55–56, 66, 100, 136
immigration 30, 33, 38, 56, 60, 70, 90–91, 100, 102, 111, 123
middle class 45, 47–48, 67–69, 71, 73–75, 77–78, 87
National Fund (JNF) 8, 19, 22, 30, 53, 58, 66, 72–73, 206
nouveaux riches 75
population in Britain 44, 97
refugees 53, 55–59, 63–64, 118
schools 44, 75–77
settlement in Palestine 21, 26, 67, 91, 131, 137, 143–144, 164, 169, 173, 204
vote 8, 22–23, 70–71
working class 49–50, 52–53, 65, 70, 72, 74, 87, 93–94, 98
youth clubs 50
Jewish Society for Human Suffering (JSHS) 132–133
Jewish Vanguard 70, 139
Jews for Justice for Palestinians 190
Johnson, President Lyndon 150
Joint Israel Appeal 184
Joint Palestine Appeal (JPA) 72–74, 78, 198
Jones, Mervyn, 156–158
Jordan Valley 127–128
Julius, Anthony 186, 190–192, 194

Kaplansky, Shlomo 15
Karmi, Ghada 160
Kartun, Derek 103–104
Katznelson, Berl 18
Kaufman, Gerald 178–179, 184n153
Kautsky, Karl 25
Keep Left 119
Keren Hayesod 8, 56, 72–73
kibbutzim 7, 27–30, 96, 143, 154, 159, 166
Kimche, Jon 125–126, 131
Kimmerling, Baruch 155, 199, 202n53
Kinnock, Neil 175, 178
Kirkbride, Sir Alec 127
Klug, Brian 187
Knight, Ted 167
Krausz, Ernest 68, 72–73
Kristallnacht 58–62
Kushner, Tony 62

Labour and Socialist International 7
Labour Friends of Israel (LFI) 151, 168–169, 173–174, 176, 179
Labour Middle East Council (LMEC) 161–163, 166, 168–169
Labour Forward 12
Labour Leader 12
Labour Monthly 89, 91, 100, 105
Labour Party
  Annual Conference (1921) 15; (1929) 26; (1930) 18–19; (1936) 95; (1939) 35, 95; (1940) 35, 95; (1944) 36, 114, 138; (1945) 38; (1948) 119; (1949) 133; (1952) 134; (1955) 139; (1970) 162; (1982) 171, 174, 177, 185; (1988) 177; (1989) 179
  Advisory Committee on Imperial Questions 14, 16, 21, 29, 35
  attitude to Labour Zionism 2, 7, 18, 25–28, 30–32
  government 112, 122, 124, 134, 150
  International sub-committee 37
  membership 12, 166
  National Executive Committee (NEC) 16, 26, 133, 139, 167, 171–177, 179, 177
  policy on Palestine/Israel 9, 11, 13, 34–35, 38, 60, 91, 134, 162, 165, 167, 176
  on colonial affairs 16, 86
  in parliament 140, 151, 163, 165, 169
  statement on Palestine/Israel 13, 36–37, 171, 177
  War Aims Memorandum 11, 13, 20
Labour Weekly 163, 173
Labour Zionism 4, 7, 18, 25–26, 28, 30–31, 52, 55, 58, 69, 72, 86, 96, 112, 118, 121–122, 142, 164, 176
Laird, Gavin 175
Lansbury, George 58
Laqueur, Walter 186, 192, 194
Laski, Neville 54, 72
Laski, Harold 31, 69
Lawther, William 129
Lebanon 170
  Israeli invasion of 169–170, 177
Lee, Jennie 121
Lenin, V.I. 13
Letwin, Oliver 192

Levenberg, Schneier 10n25, 44, 49, 51–52, 54–55, 66, 69, 71, 74, 131
Lever, Leslie 46, 54
Levy, Hyman 102
Leys, Norman 16
Liberal Party 5, 26, 59–60, 63, 130, 204
Liebman, Marcel 155–158, 163
Likud, 165–166, 172–173, 177–178
Livingstone, Ken 167–168
Locker, Berl 37, 42n133
Lockman, Zachary 155
London Briefing 168
London, Louise 61
Louis, Wm. Roger 115
Lustick, Ian 41n100, 137, 148n153

Maccabi Association 47
MacDonald, J.Ramsay 5, 15–16, 19, 22–23, 25–26
Machover, Moshe 160
MacShane, Denis 186–187, 196–198, 201n39
MacIntyre, Stuart 17
Manchester Guardian see Guardian
Mansur, George 39n44
Mapai 24, 41n100, 69, 90, 139
 see also Israeli Labour Party
Marks, Simon 45
Marks and Spencer 45, 74
Marxism 51, 87
Matzpen 154, 160–161
Maudling, Reginald 165
Mayer, Arno 13
Mayhew, Christopher 140, 151, 162
Medical Aid for Palestine (MAP) 175
Meir, Goda 165, 182
Menon, V.K.Krishna 5–6, 130
Metropolitan Police Service (MPS) 188
Middleton, James 17
Mikardo, Ian 119, 124, 167–168, 174, 176
Miliband, David 192
Miliband, Ed 192
Miliband, Ralph 155–156, 158, 163
Militant Tendency 167, 171
Mindle, Mick 95
Monroe, Elizabeth 123, 137
Montagu, Ivor 93
Monthly Review 152
Morris, Ben 125, 137–138, 141
Morrison, Herbert 5, 26–27, 31, 34–35, 60, 71, 91, 115, 120–121, 135, 139, 142
Morrison Grady Plan 120–121
Mosley, Oswald 50, 52
Movement for Colonial Freedom (MCF) 122, 140, 152
Mufti of Jerusalem (Hajj Amin Al-Husseini) 18, 21, 30–31, 93, 96, 131, 157, 194
Murphy, J.T. 89
Muslim 14, 170, 186, 193–198

Nasser, Gamal Abdel 141, 150–153, 155
National Association of Local Government Officers (NALGO) 175–176
National Jewish Committee *see* Communist Party of Great Britain
National Union of Public Employees (NUPE) 175
National Union of Mineworkers (NUM) 133
National Union of Teachers (NUT) 175
Newens, Stan 151, 162
New Labour 2, 179
New Leader 18
New Left Review 152
Newman, Michael 155
New Statesman 17, 126, 138, 143, 171
Noel-Baker, Philip 35, 37, 60
Northern Carpet Trades Union 176

Observer 178
Occupied Territories 143, 160, 163, 166, 169, 175–176, 191, 205–206
Orbach, Maurice 54, 168
Orme, Stan 162
Ormsby-Gore, David 34
Orr, Akiva 160
Orwell, George 67, 122
Oslo Peace Accords 179

Palestine Action 160–161, 204
Palestine Arab Workers' Society (PAWS) 25
Palestine Communist Party (PCP) 89–90, 93, 96, 102
Palestine Labour League (PLL) 24
Palestine Liberation Organisation (PLO) 156, 158–159, 165, 169–170, 172–173, 175–179

Palestine News 190
Palestinian
 expulsion of 111, 125–126, 130, 138
 fedayeen 138
 land expropriated 136
 nationalism 34, 157, 194
 refugees 105, 111, 123, 126–135, 137, 139–140, 151, 159–161, 164
 self-determination 2, 133, 159, 163, 165–166, 171–173, 176–177, 179
Palestine Solidarity Campaign (PSC) 160, 189–192
Pappe, Ilan 125
Passfield White Paper 19, 21–23, 31
Peres, Shimon 177
Peace News 140–142
Peel Commission's Report 32–34, 87
philanthropic activity 8, 45, 53, 55, 74
Phillips, Morgan 71
Pinner, Hayim 139–140
Piratin, Phil 87, 100, 120
Poale Zion 2–4, 6, 8, 15, 23, 35, 44, 50–54, 66, 69–72, 78, 90, 94–95, 139, 162, 166–169, 173, 176
Pollitt, Harry 105
Popular Front for the Liberation of Palestine (PFLP) 159
Popular Democratic Front for the Liberation of Palestine (PDFLP) 158–160
Porter, Bernard 16
Prosor, Ron 207

Rabin, Yitzhak 165, 177
Ramelson, Bert 158–159
Rathbone, Eleanor 61, 63
Regan plan 173
Reid, Tom 29, 35
Rejwan, Nissim 195
Rennap, Issie 96, 98
Reynolds, Reginald 40n45
Roosevelt, President Theodore 58, 113
Rose, Paul
Rosen, Harold 49
Rosenberg, Chanie 29
Royal Commission Report on Palestine (1937) *see* Peel Commission

Sabra and Shatila 170–171, 185
Sacher, Harry 46, 50
Sa'di, Ahmad 39n38
Safad 33, 91, 104
Sargent, Andrew 38n3
Satloff, Robert 195
Sayigh, Rosemary 135
Seifert, Connie 29
self-determination 13, 16
settlement colonies 14
Schonfeld, Rabbi Solomon 63
Scottish Labour Party 168
Shafir, Gershon 155
Shahak, Israel 204
Shamir, Yitzhak 173–174, 178
Sharret, Moshe 32
Sharon, Ariel 138, 166, 170, 174
Shaw, Sir Walter 18
Shaw report 19, 31
Sherman, Alf 98, 108n71
Shields, Jim 91
Shukeiri, Ahmed 156, 158
Sief, Israel 45, 74–75
Silverman, Sidney 121, 128, 138, 151
Sinai 150, 165
Six Day War (1967) 78, 150, 152, 155, 161–162, 165, 174, 178, 204
Snell, Harry 18
Social Democratic Federation 27
Socialist Commentary 122–123
Socialist Committee for Workers' Palestine 25, 30
Socialist Register 152, 155–156, 158
Socialist Organiser 167–168, 176
Socialist Workers' Party 29
Sogat '82 175
Soviet Union 9, 16, 64, 96, 99, 101, 103, 105–106, 111, 122, 150, 204
Spears, Sir Edward 129
Srebrnik, Henry 87–88
Stanley, Oliver 119
Sternhell, Zeev 7, 155
Suez War 9, 141, 150, 152
Summerskill, Edith 139–140

Taub, Gabi 205–206
Taylor, A.J.P. 12
Thatcher, Margaret 165
Todd, Ron 176
Touma, Emile 105
Trade Advisory Council (TAC) 54, 68
Trades Union Congress (TUC) 26, 57, 129–130, 168–170, 171, 175

Trade Union Friends of Palestine (TUFP) 168, 175
Trade Union Friends of Israel 175–176
transfer proposal 37, 42n133
Transport and General Workers' Union (TGWU) 23, 129
Tribune 12–16, 122, 131–132, 137–138, 151, 163
Troutbeck, Sir John 128
Truman, President Harry 113–114, 119, 121

United States 3, 8, 44–45, 89, 64, 113, 120, 122, 128, 130, 133, 139, 152, 162, 173, 185, 204–205
University and College Union (UCU) 201n37 and n39
Universal Declaration of Human Rights 204
United Nations 105, 121, 124, 126, 129, 137–138, 141, 150, 157
  and partition 104, 123–126, 128, 134–135, 159
  and resolutions (194) 190, (242) 159, 162, 164
United Synagogue 76
Union of Democratic Control (UDC) 12
United Nations Relief and Works Agency 142, 165, 185

Vandervelde, Emile 25–26, 30, 117
Vietnam Solidarity Campaign 167
Vilner, Meyer 102

War Aims Memorandum *see* Labour Party
War on Want 175
Watkins, David 163
Watson, Sam 71, 133, 137
Webb, Beatrice 13, 20, 22
Webb, Sidney (Lord Passfield) 17, 19–21, 24, 38
Wedgwood, Josiah 16, 59
Weizmann, Chaim 3–4, 33–34, 45–46, 56–57, 59, 61, 96, 127, 142–143
West Bank 143–144, 150–151, 158, 161, 164–166, 173, 176–178, 203
Whitechapel 22, 44
White Paper (1939) 34–35, 96, 100, 102, 112
Wieviorka, Michel 197
Wildangel, Rene 194–195

Williams, Bill 78
Williams, Tom 31, 34
Wilson, Harold 115, 162–163, 174, 182n83 and n85
Wilson, President Woodrow 13, 16, 121, 134, 137
Wistrich, Robert 199
Wolfson, Issac 73–75
Women's Zionist Society 65
Woodhouse Commission 35
Woolf, Leonard 16
World Zionist Congress 48, 68, 71, 76
World Zionist Organisation (WZO) 2–4, 7–8, 22, 24, 65, 78, 90
Workers' Circle 51, 95, 97
Wyatt, Woodrow 13, 16, 121, 134, 137

Yishuv 4, 19, 22–24, 26, 28, 32–33, 48, 52, 56, 96, 98, 102–103, 120, 154
Yishuvism 99–100, 102
Young Communist League 49
Young Liberals 160
Yom Kippur War (1973) 163–164

Zionist Review 48, 54, 59, 63–64, 67, 13
Zionism
  support for 17, 49, 64–65, 67, 70–71, 78, 94, 106, 113
Zionist
  armed forces 101–102, 111, 119, 121, 124–125, 132
  Federation *see* English Zionist Federation (EZF)
  land acquisition 18, 117, 154
  movement 3, 7, 11, 18, 22, 52, 58, 69, 72, 86, 96, 112, 121, 154, 159–160
  settlement 18, 22, 27, 34, 89, 93, 115, 154
  societies 48